# LEE KUAN YEW
## THE MAN AND HIS IDEAS

# LEE KUAN YEW
## THE MAN AND HIS IDEAS

**Han Fook Kwang**

**Warren Fernandez**

**Sumiko Tan**

 *Singapore Press Holdings*

TIMES EDITIONS

**Sources accompany all extracts in the book with the exception of the authors' interviews with Lee Kuan Yew.**

© 1998 Times Editions Pte Ltd,
The Straits Times Press

Published by

Times Editions Pte Ltd
a member of the Times Publishing Group
Times Centre, 1 New Industrial Road
Singapore 536196
Tel: (65) 2848844 Fax: (65) 2854871
e-mail: te@corp.tpl.com.sg

and

The Straits Times Press
a member of Singapore Press Holdings
Times House
390 Kim Seng Road
Singapore 239495

Printed in Singapore

ISBN 981 204 049 8

# Acknowledgements

We are grateful to Mr Lee Kuan Yew for his support of the project and the many hours he spent with us in interviews for the book, and for his advice and encouragement throughout. Our thanks, too, to Mrs Lee for the use of photographs from the family album.

We would like to thank the Executive Chairman of Singapore Press Holdings, Mr Lim Kim San, and the Editor-in-chief of its English and Malay newspapers division, Mr Cheong Yip Seng, for their support of the project.

Several people helped in the research and in reading the drafts, especially Straits Times journalist Pang Gek Choo, who was invaluable in both.

Our thanks are due also to The Straits Times, the National Archives of Singapore, Lianhe Zaobao and the Ministry of Information and the Arts for the use of their resources.

# Contents

# Introduction

When Lee Kuan Yew wanted Singapore to become a garden city, to soften the harshness of life in one of the world's most densely populated countries, he did not write a memorandum to the environment minister or to the head of the agency responsible for parks and trees. He did not form a committee nor seek outside help to hire the best landscapists money could buy. For one thing, in the 1960s, when he was thinking of these matters, money was in short supply. In fact, having been unceremoniously booted out of Malaysia, the country's economic survival was hanging in the balance. For another, there was no environment minister to speak of then, so low down in the list of priorities were these matters. When jobs had to be created and communists fought in the streets, only the birds were interested in flowers and trees.

But Lee was interested. And he became personally involved in the project of transforming Singapore from just concrete and steel to concrete, steel, trees, shrubs, flowers and parks. He would become personally knowledgeable about soil and vegetation, trees and drainage, climate and fertilisers. And he surveyed the world for ideas, taking advantage of his travels abroad to look out for them. In France, for example, he discovered that the broad tree-lined boulevards were possible because a drainage system had been built below the pavements. Around each tree was a metal grating through which surface water flowed into the underground system.

The problem of the grass in Singapore, which everyone could see in the bald, yellow football fields, needed a nationwide solution. When he saw beautiful rolling meadows in New Zealand he was moved to ask for the services of two experts from the country under the Colombo Plan technical assistance scheme. Lee was told that Singapore did not have a grassland climate in which rain fell gently from the skies. Instead, being part of an equatorial region, it experienced torrential rainfall that would wash off the topsoil and with it the vital nutrients necessary for strong plant growth. In an equatorial forest, with tall big trees forming a canopy, the rain water drips down. But in Singapore, where the trees had been chopped down, it would all come down in a big wash.

But Lee was not one to let climate get in the way. Fertilisers would replenish the soil, and so began the task of making compost from rubbish dumps, adding calcium, and lime where the ground was too acidic.

Years later, when economic survival was no longer an issue and Singapore's success was acknowledged worldwide, he was still working at it to make the garden city possible. When expressways and flyovers sprouted all over the island, he had officials look for plants which could survive below the flyovers where the sun seldom shone. And instead of having to water these plants regularly, which was costly, he got them to devise a way to channel water from the roads, after filtering it to get rid of the oil and grime from the traffic above.

The constant search for solutions would not end. When development intensified even further and the roads and flyovers became broader still, shutting out the light completely from the plants below, he did not give up. The road was split into two so there would be a gap in the middle with enough space for sunshine and rain to seep through and greenery and vegetation to thrive below. "I sent them on missions all along the Equator and the tropical, subtropical zones, looking for new types of trees, plants, creepers and so on. From Africa, the Caribbean, Latin, Middle, Central America, we've come back with new plants. It's a very small sum. But if you get the place greened up, if you get all those creepers up, you take away the heat, you'll have a different city," he said.

Making Singapore a different city! That has been Lee's constant obsession. Even when the difference had to do with trees and flowers, subjects which one would not normally associate with the man who has been at Singapore's helm for 38 years, 31 of which he served as prime minister, his approach to the problem has been typical – hardheaded and pragmatic. For him, the object of the exercise was not all about smelling roses. In the end it was about keeping Singapore ahead of the competition. A well kept garden, he would say, is a daily effort, and would demonstrate to outsiders the people's ability to organise and to be systematic. "The grass has got to be mown every other day, the trees have to be tended, the flowers in the gardens have to be looked after so they know this place gives attention to detail."


The story of how Lee transformed Singapore is a fascinating one because no other leader in the modern world has had such a hand in influencing and directing his country's progress from independence to developed nation status the way he has. None has straddled the two worlds with as much success: the revolutionary world in the first half of this century for independence from empire, and the development world in the second half for wealth and progress.

The great Asian revolutionaries – Mao Zedong, Pandit Nehru, Sukarno and Ho Chi Minh – earned their rightful place in history but failed to build on their revolutionary zeal. Lee's place is, of course, smaller. But he has been able to achieve what they could not, which was not only to destroy the old system but also to create a new and more successful one. That Singapore is a success today and the success is largely attributable to Lee, there can be few doubts, even among his most severe critics.

What were those ideas of his which made the critical difference in Singapore? How did he come round to those views? How were they made to work in Singapore?

This book has been written for those interested in the answers to these questions. It is a book about Lee Kuan Yew and his ideas and how those ideas have shaped modern Singapore and made it what it is today. For the story of Singapore's transformation from a British colonial outpost with an uncertain future into the ninth richest country in per capita terms is a story of how Lee's ideas have been put into practice on an island of 600 square kilometres, on which three million people today enjoy a standard of living higher than their former colonial masters.

Lee's views are thus significant for two reasons. First, they enable us to understand the man himself: what he stands for, how he approaches problems, what he believes in. Second, they help us understand Singapore: what key ideas have been put to the test here, how they have worked or not worked in practice, what have been tried, discarded or modified.

The first task of the authors was to survey Lee's entire range of ideas and views over almost a half century of his political life, beginning with the first political speech he made in Britain as a student in 1950. In all, we read more than 2,000 speeches. Then came the job of identifying those we believed to be crucial to Singapore, which had made a difference to life here. We narrowed the field to seven key areas: the secret of good government, economic development, politics and democracy, law and order, the importance of culture, the nature of human society, and media.

The most interesting part of the assignment was a series of interviews with Lee on these subjects – 13 in all over about 30 hours in 1994 and 1995, the most extensive he has given to anyone so far.

In these interviews, he talked about how he came round to those key ideas, the circumstances surrounding their genesis, and whether experience later led him to modify them or strengthened his belief even more. Some of the most revealing interviews were about his early days and the three events that shaped his outlook on life: the Japanese Occupation from 1942 to 1945, the battles with the communists in the 1950s and 1960s, and the trauma of merger with Malaysia in 1963 and separation two years later. Not surprisingly, these were the events which in the authors' view had the greatest impact on modern Singapore.

The Japanese Occupation made Lee decide to become a politician, the communist battles turned him into a hardened politician, and separation from Malaysia provided the final drama which led to Singapore's independence, and made Lee govern it the way he has. How Lee went through those tumultuous events, his views about them today and how they affected him: the answers to these questions are essential for anyone who wants to understand the man that Lee is today and the Singapore that he has shaped.

The first three chapters cover these areas, and set the stage for the rest of the book, which is organised thematically according to those key ideas of his that have been applied to Singapore.

His revelations of his early life in Chapter 1 might surprise some. He remembers carefree days at Telok Kurau Primary School, catching fish in drains, flying kites and challenging friends to duels with spinning tops. The pace quickened at Raffles Institution, and then at Raffles College, where his education was interrupted by the war.

Lee's accounts of life in Japanese-occupied Singapore are especially interesting. Not only was there high drama, as when he was under suspicion by the dreaded secret police, the Kempeitai, there was also political education in the raw when he saw, at first hand, how power poured out from the barrel of a gun.

Political soul-searching continued when the war ended and he left for England to study law. His account of life there is revealing. How many people know that in Britain Lee had campaigned for the Labour Party, driving his friend, David Widdicombe, the Labour candidate for Totnes, Devon in a lorry and making campaign speeches for him? The text of one of those speeches, possibly Lee's earliest political speech, is reproduced in this book. In another landmark speech, made in London at the Malayan Forum, he spoke about the political situation in Malaya and all but declared his intention to do something about it when he returned.

And what a battle it turned out to be when he did return! For those interested in how Lee fought, first the communists, and then the leadership in Malaysia, Chapters 2 and 3 should prove enlightening. They tell the story of the making of a politician, and of a fledgling nation.

Chapters 4–10 discuss Lee's views on key issues which he strongly believes in, and which when applied in the governance of Singapore has made it what it is today. Some of the big questions they answer are:

- How did he see the economic situation facing Singapore in 1965 when it was booted out of Malaysia, and what did he set out to do?
- What does he consider the most important ingredient for any government, and how did he go about making sure it was present in Singapore?
- What are his views on leadership, and on democracy?
- How did Lee maintain law and order in the gangster-ridden Singapore of the 1960s?
- What are his views on the nature of human society and how best to organise people so that they can make the maximum effort to improve their lives?
- How did Lee form his ideas about which societies are more likely to succeed than others? Where do the differences lie?
- Why has he taken such a robust stand against the foreign press?

The last chapter is devoted to his personal life, how he would describe himself, what he holds most dear as well as his thoughts on subjects such as religion, his family and personal wealth.

An important part of the book are the 46 speeches we have selected out of the more than 2,000 speeches Lee has made throughout his political life. Taken together, this selection should give readers a comprehensive picture of Lee's outlook and thoughts on the essential issues of the day. The speeches are in the last section of the book.

One question should be answered here at the outset: is there one golden thread running through Lee's views? Does he believe in one central theme which has guided him through the years?

The answer is yes, and no.

No, because Lee is not an ideological or dogmatic person. In fact, he eschews theory and fine argument. What matters to him is whether a thing works or not, with practice providing the best test. If it has been tried out elsewhere, he would want to know what the experience has been. If it has not, he would be willing to try it out if it was worthwhile doing so. This has been a constant refrain in his speeches and interviews. There is no grand theory to explain the world according to Lee.

And yet we could not help noticing throughout the 2,000 speeches we read, and in the interviews, that there are several constants in his approach to problem-solving, which when taken together, provide as good a composite picture of the man as you can ever get.

First is his capacity to learn from experience, and, if necessary, to change his beliefs, even radically, when they do not conform to reality. One radical change happened very early in his political career when he parted company with the socialism of the British Labour Party because he could see that it was not working in Britain, and would not work in Singapore. He had started off as a student in England believing that wealth generation was a natural product of labour, and that the difference between a good society and a bad one was in how the fruits of that labour were distributed. But when he saw how costly such a system was to maintain, and the practical consequences of subsidising a man for the rest of his life, whether for health care or public housing, he made the switch in Singapore. If a man did not own his home but rented it from the state, why would he look after it properly? If medical service were free, would it not lead to an unsustainable system and a bottomless pit? Soon after assuming office, he made Singaporeans pay for medical prescriptions, even if it was a very small sum to begin with, and the government sold public flats to the people.

Whenever he was confronted with theory which did not work in practice, he chose the latter. "Practice decided for me, in the final implementation of policies. It was not the theory of capitalism, not Milton Friedman, that decided my policies. But in each instance, we calculated – if that doesn't work, this wouldn't work."

If there is one golden thread in Lee's approach, it is his constant striving to seek results, not in proving a theory right.

Second is his doggedness to achieve those results, never losing sight of his objectives, and relentlessly clearing all obstacles in the way. His determination to make Singapore a garden city, the personal effort and interest he put into the project, is typical of the man. More than any other trait of his, his determination is one which Singaporeans know only too well. He put it this way in an interview with the authors:

> "I would say that I'm very determined when I set out to do something. First, I've got to decide whether something is worth doing. If it's not worth doing, well, I'm not prepared to spend the time over it, to make the effort. Then I just coast along, it doesn't matter whether it succeeds or doesn't succeed, it's of no consequence.
>
> "But if I decide that something is worth doing, then I'll put my heart and soul into it. I'll give everything I've got to make it succeed. So I would put my strength, determination and willingness to see my objective to its conclusion. Whether I can succeed or not, that's another matter – but I will give everything I've got to make sure it succeeds. If I've got to get good people, I get good people. If I've got to change tack, I will change tack. If you have decided something is worth doing, you've got to remove all obstacles to get there."

Third is the fact that Lee formed many of his political beliefs very early in his political life, and he has been consistent about them once he has accepted their validity. For example, his misgivings about the workings of democracy in Asian societies which have just become independent date back to the early 1960s, when he himself had just attained political power through the ballot box. His scepticism is hence not of a man who wants to hang on to power and to change the rules midstream but of one who has himself seen, in the early years, how one after another of the newly independent countries had been ruined by the system of one-man-one-vote.

His tough-minded approach to the media also goes back to the 1960s, when he first had problems with the local press. It is consistent with his recent observations of how the American media had debased public respect for their leaders and had played a key part in changing social customs and mores, not necessarily for the better.

His conversion from socialism to capitalism, perhaps his most radical U-turn, was complete in the early 1960s, so too his belief in the importance of culture in determining the dynamism of any society. Meritocracy, the belief that genes played a major role in deciding a man's ability, the high standards he set for political leaders in their public conduct – these are all issues he had made up his mind about early on.

Lee has had the advantage of very many years of testing the validity of these views and of working them within the Singapore system. Is he always right? Of course not. But he has one not insignificant argument going for him with which to rebut his critics: Singapore. Whether an idea was worth pursuing must ultimately rest on whether it worked in real life, and Singapore has worked for 38 years.

This book is not entirely about serious ideas and life-and-death issues. An important aim of the authors was to try to understand the man himself, his personal beliefs and philosophy. Some of the revelations might surprise readers. As often happens with public figures, a stereotype of Lee has formed over the last 30-odd years: the Western media especially see him as ruthless, autocratic, power-hungry. But he is a much more complex person, and there are interesting insights of him throughout the book which, when taken together, should give a better picture of the man. In interviews with the authors, for example, he talked about God and religion, why he chose to become a lawyer, where he gets his ideas, and how he regards money and wealth.

One final point: this book is not a critique of his views and there has been no attempt to be so, or to provide contrary arguments to many of Lee's controversial ideas. The aim of the authors is much more modest: to present his views in a systematic and organised way for those who want to understand him and the Singapore he transformed – never mind if they agree or disagree with him.

We believe that our approach in distilling the essence of his views – from the more than 2,000 speeches and the 30-odd hours of interviews with him – has not been attempted by anyone before. We leave the critique to others better qualified to do the job. More than anyone else, Lee has made Singapore what it is today. For anyone interested in how his ideas have transformed Singapore, this book should be a useful starting point.

# THE MAKING OF
# A POLITICIAN

# 1

# It Began When My World Collapsed

**This extract is from an interview with the authors. All extracts will carry the source at the end of the extract, except for interviews with the authors.**

The world as Lee Kuan Yew knew it came to an end on the morning of December 8, 1941. Another brave new world was about to begin. But at that very moment when the old one crumbled and its replacement burst from the sky bearing the emblem of the Japanese air force, there was only terror and destruction. Japanese war planes struck with impunity on an unsuspecting city that quiet morning to shatter 123 years of unchallenged British rule.

"On December 8, early in the morning, when the bombs dropped, I was in Raffles College in the hostel and we were in the middle of it. Then a few days later, the two battleships, *Prince of Wales* and *Repulse*, were sunk. That was a disaster. That jolted us.

"Then they kept on advancing and advancing. And we were recruited into the MAS, Medical Auxiliary Services, the students in Raffles College, and we volunteered. We ran around with an ambulance, collected injured people after air raids; towards the end we collected injured people after shelling. And they were, I think from the beginning of February or late January, filing into Singapore. Next thing, they were in Singapore."

That air attack on Singapore, which was launched simultaneously with the main Japanese landings at Singora and Patani in southern Thailand, and at Kota Bharu on the east coast of Malaya, was the first of the Pacific War. One hour and ten minutes later, on the other side of the ocean, Japanese forces in the Pacific would devastate the American fleet at Pearl Harbor. It was followed by the Japanese invasion of Hongkong, and attacks on Clark airbase in the Philippines, Guam and Wake Island. Within 12 hours the might of Japan would be felt all over the Pacific Ocean.

By February 1942 the triumphant Imperial Army was in Singapore. Lee ran into his first Japanese soldier at his maternal grandfather's home in Telok Kurau. "I looked at this strange person with flaps on his cap. It took me a moment to realise he was a Japanese. That's that." For the first year undergraduate from Raffles College, it was the biggest shock of his life. His world had turned upside down and from this unexpected perspective he would receive what he now regards as the political education of his life.

"The dark ages had descended on us. It was brutal, cruel. In looking back, I think it was the biggest single political education of my life because, for three and a half years, I saw the meaning of power and how power and politics and government went together, and I also understood how people trapped in a power situation responded because they had to live. One day, the British were there, immovable, complete masters; next day, the Japanese, whom we derided, mocked as short, stunted people with shortsighted squint eyes."

The Japanese were especially brutal towards the Chinese population. In one particularly infamous incident, known as Sook Ching, every male Chinese between the ages of 18 and 50 was rounded up for registration and identification. Aimed at flushing out anti-Japanese elements among the Chinese volunteers who had fought so tenaciously against the invading Japanese army, it resulted in 6,000 Chinese being massacred, according to estimates from the Japanese secret police, the Kempeitai. Other estimates put the figure at five times as high.

Tumultuous changes were taking place everywhere as the old order on which the British Empire was firmly rooted collapsed. The German and Japanese armies were on the move throughout Europe and Asia.

For the people of Singapore, as it was for those of Malaya, Indo-China and Indonesia, the unthinkable had happened. The great white colonial masters of Great Britain, France and the Netherlands were being overrun by the bow-legged, squat and squint-eyed yellow terror from the Land of the Rising Sun. English would be replaced by Nippon-go, *God Save the King* by *Kimigayo* and the civil orderly ways of the Anglo-Saxon world by the raw brutality and stoicism of the samurai.

Lee Kuan Yew saw all this close up. But he was no mere spectator. It was raw politics itself, and he was right in the middle of it. To understand Lee today, what he is, what he believes in, why he does certain things and what he stands for, it is necessary to understand the temper of those tumultuous years and how they seized and shaped him. Those earthshaking events would also mould Lee's generation and the generation before them in Singapore and all over Asia.

If there is one point in Lee's life when his political education began, when the idea that things could change and would be changed for better or for worse – which is the very essence of politics – this was it. For the story of Lee Kuan Yew and modern Singapore, this beginning was as brutal as it was unexpected. But it did not take place in a vacuum. It burst out of the old world with an impatience that Lee would epitomise later. To understand why it happened, it is necessary, too, to understand the old world, a world which Lee inhabited for 18 years before those Japanese fighter planes put an end to it.

# Beginnings

*Above: Lee's roots can be traced to his great-grandfather Lee Bok Boon, who left Guangdong, China, at 16 to eke out a living in Singapore. This watercolour painting was commissioned after he returned, a much wealthier man, to his ancestral village in Taipu. A similar painting can be found at the manor house he built there.*

*Right: Lee's grandfather, Lee Hoon Leong, rose to riches but saw his fortunes decline with the Great Depression in the 1930s. He died during the Japanese Occupation. "My grandfather was very fond of me and I used to visit him and live with him on weekends and school holidays," Lee recalled in an interview with the authors.*

When Lee's great grandfather Lee Bok Boon left Guangdong province for Singapore in 1863 at the age of 16, he was following the footsteps of thousands of Chinese emigrants who had left their ancestral villages, many with just the shirts on their backs, to seek a new life in Southeast Asia. Their numbers fluctuated depending on the state of the economy in the receiving countries and whether it had been a good or bad harvest in their own villages. In 1907, 227,000 Chinese immigrants landed in Singapore. The number dropped to 152,000 in 1909, but rose dramatically to 270,000 in 1911, which was a year of flood and famine in southern China.

Bok Boon married a Chinese shopkeeper's daughter, Seow Huan Nio, in Singapore. Like many of his contemporaries his heart was still in the Middle Kingdom, and so, after making some money here, he decided to go back in 1882. But Huan Nio, who was born in Singapore and had never been to China, and was by then a mother of three children, refused to go along. Bok Boon returned to his home village to start a new life there. He died just two years later. But he could not have done too badly as the family in Singapore received a picture of a little manor house he had built and news that he had become, or rather bought for himself, a mandarinate of sorts.

The family that Bok Boon left behind in Singapore did not need a mandarin to do well. They did what most people who wanted to get ahead in life here did; they made sure their children received an English education.

Lee's grandfather, Hoon Leong, went to an English school and began a career as a pharmacist. His fortunes improved markedly when he joined a Chinese shipping company, Heap Eng Mo Shipping Company, as a purser, making regular trips between Singapore and Indonesia. On one of these voyages he met Ko Liem Nio in Semarang. They married and he brought her to Singapore. He moved up the company and eventually possessed power of attorney over the concerns of Sugar King Oei Tiong Ham. His fortunes rose with Oei's. By the time Kuan Yew was born on September 16, 1923, Hoon Leong was head of a wealthy family, though its fortunes suffered somewhat during the Depression of 1929–32.

As was the practice in those days, the marriage between Lee's parents, Lee Chin Koon and Chua Jim Neo, was an arranged one. Both came from successful middle-class families and were educated in English schools. Lee's maternal grandfather owned

*Opposite: Lee as a baby with his father, Lee Chin Koon.*

*Right: A capable woman – tremendously resourceful, possessing great energy and drive, said Lee of his mother, Chua Jim Neo. She was the one who effectively ran the household, managed the finances and even had small businesses to keep the family going. "Without her, the family would have failed," Lee told the authors.*

*Far right: 147 Neil Road. Lee lived in his paternal grandfather's two-storey terrace house as a boy. Bought in 1920 for $25,000, the building stands restored today in the colourful and bustling business district of Tanjong Pagar, where Lee has served as Member of Parliament since 1955.*

*Right, bottom: Lee (standing centre) was the eldest child in his family. "I would not classify myself as wealthy, but we were not in want of food or clothes or other things in life," he said of his family.*

# Catching fish, flying kites and spinning tops

*Lee with his younger brothers Kim Yew (Dennis) and Thiam Yew (Freddy), seated. As a boy, he caught fighting fish in the drains along Changi Road, flew kites and spun tops. "It was a more do-it-yourself, amuse-yourself childhood than what the children now have, where toys are just given to them to be amused," he told the authors.*

"I didn't do any work. I was too keen on running around, catching fighting fish in the drains along Changi Road, Joo Chiat Road. They were all rubber estates and they had these open drains. At the open drains … you can catch good fighting fish and you keep them in bottles and you bury them in the earth and then you feed them with worms and you put a bit of green plants to oxygenate the water. There was great fun also flying kites and putting the thread on two poles, pounding the glue and the glass, fixing the line so you can cut the other fellow's line. And then playing tops: you armour your top, you get a top and you put thumbtacks, polish it up and then you hit the other fellow's and make a scar on his. It was a more do-it-yourself, amuse-yourself childhood than what children now have, where toys are just given to them to be amused. But here, you've got to amuse yourself, which I think in retrospect was a better way.

"In primary school, I had no trouble doing well. Probably because my fellow students were poor and they were not very bright and advantaged … I had no trouble staying ahead of the class, so I did not try at all. I had to try later on in RI because then I met the top 150 from all over Singapore. When I got to RI, the first year, we were divided into five classes – A, B, C, D, E … We came from different schools. The segregation, the streaming, started in standard seven. So I had to make an effort in standard six to make sure that I got to the top class in standard seven and got the better teachers and was with the faster students. So when I got to standard six in 1936, I began to make some effort.

"It was a leisurely life. They were the best and the brightest; I had to work harder than in Telok Kurau, but there was a lot of time. I played cricket. Later, in the Junior Cambridge class, I played tennis. I also took up chess, swimming. I joined the Scouts for two or three years. I don't think I liked football. I don't know why I preferred cricket. I do not remember it as an intense period. I made some effort in standard six, then I got into 7A. I think I came second in the school, and the chap who came first was a fellow called Teo Kah Leong, who later got into the admin service.

"Then in Junior Cambridge, there was a scholarship going – awarded on standard seven results, about two or three hundred dollars a year for the first student and the second student. … So I put in an effort and I got the scholarship and I bought myself a Meister bicycle – German bicycle, sold by a shop in Victoria Street … So that was my first purchase in life. I earned it. I bought it.

"Then the next year, based on Junior Cambridge results, I came first, so I got another big scholarship, the Tan Jiak Kim scholarship. This time, $350, vast sum at that time, and I bought myself a Raleigh bicycle. I upgraded from a Meister to a Raleigh. By that time, I was hoping to go up to the special class and sit for the Queen's scholarship. Because I came top in the School Certificate … the John Anderson scholarship was open that year, tenable in Raffles College, so I got this scholarship to Raffles College. It was the best-going scholarship then, roughly $900 a year, which paid for all my fees and my stay at the hostel too and left me with a bit extra."

the former Katong market, rubber estates at Chai Chee and a row of houses next to the present Thai embassy at Orchard Road. Those were the days when successful Chinese businessmen working within the colonial system in Singapore were able to make vast fortunes mainly in trading and property development.

The Depression took its toll and both Lee's grandfathers' wealth declined considerably. Lee's father worked first as a storekeeper at Shell, the Anglo-Dutch oil giant, and was later put in charge of various depots in Johor Bahru, Stulang and Batu Pahat. But it was his mother Jim Neo to whom Lee attributes much of the family's success in overcoming the financial difficulties. By then the family had a house in Telok Kurau. For Lee and his three brothers and a sister, these were carefree days. But even though, by his own admission, he did not work very hard in school, he was always there at the top of the class.

The pace quickened somewhat after he enrolled at Raffles Institution; Lee emerged top Malayan boy in the Senior Cambridge examinations. His decision to become a lawyer, which would have a profound effect on his political activities later, came about from purely pragmatic considerations.

> "My father and mother had friends from their wealthier days who after the slump were still wealthy because they had professions, either doctors or lawyers. The doctors were people like Dr Loh Poon Lip, the father of Robert Loh. The lawyer was Richard Lim Chuan Ho, who was the father of Arthur Lim, the eye surgeon. And then there was a chap called Philip Hoalim Senior. They did not become poor because they had professions. My father didn't have a profession, so he became poor and he became a storekeeper. Their message, or their moral for me, was, I'd better take a profession or I'd run the risk of a very precarious life.
>
> "There were three choices for a profession – medicine, law, engineering. We had a medical school; we had no law school or engineering. I didn't like medicine. Engineering, if you take, you've got to work for a company. Law, you can be on your own, you're self-employed. So I decided, all right, in that case, I would be a lawyer."

# Raw power

Those plans were shattered when Japanese forces landed at Kota Bharu on the northeast coast of Malaya in the early hours of December 8, 1941. But the political education which followed would leave a lasting impression and change Lee's life forever.

> "They [the Japanese] were the masters. They swaggered around with big swords, they occupied all the big offices and the houses and the big cars and they gave the orders. So that determines who is the authority. Then because they had the authority, they printed the money, they controlled the wealth of the country, the banks, they made the Chinese pay a $50 million tribute. You need a job, you need a permit, you need to import and distribute rice – they controlled everything.
>
> "So people adjusted and they bowed, they ingratiated themselves, they had to live. Quietly, they cursed away behind the backs of the Japanese. But in the face of the Japanese,

# I thought the Kempeitai was on to me

"I was well informed about the progress of the war because for a year and a half, from … I think from the beginning, either the end of 1943 to the beginning of 1945 or late '44, I was working in the propaganda department at Cathay Building, on the top floor.

*Cathay Building, which used to house the British Malaya Broadcasting Corporation before the Japanese converted it during the war into their propaganda headquarters, where Lee worked during the Japanese Occupation.*

"I was a cable editor in English. What the job was – it was just like a crossword puzzle. They had radio reception, Morse code, so they hired; for one session, there would be about eight or ten radio operators. And they intercepted allied news agencies – Reuters, UP, AP, Tass, Central News Agency. But except for the very middle of the night, one, two, three o'clock in the morning, reception was always bad, interference, so missing words and it was like filling up a crossword puzzle, so I filled it up. And then from my floor, 12th floor, it will go down to the 11th floor where they cooked it, they turned the news around for propaganda. So I knew, I read, I can check the date, because I had endless reports from Tass and Reuters and AP on the battle of Stalingrad, I think Stalingrad was '43. Then D-Day in Europe, June '44.

"And at the same time, the British were mounting an offensive in Burma, Arakan Coast, and they were going into Mandalay. So I told my family, I said, 'Better get out of Singapore! Those Japanese are going to fight every inch of the way and they will come down to the Peninsula and this will be a final sort of showdown. We'll all be dead.' So I resigned from the Hodobu. I had done a recce and looked at a possible farm, a piece of land to hire and grow vegetables and tapioca, sweet potatoes in Cameron Highlands.

"But when I resigned, the liftboy at the Cathay Building told me, 'Your file has been taken out.' You see, everybody who works at Hodobu is security checked. And they've got a Kempeitai office there. Because you are leaking news, you see. So when they took out my file, this liftboy – I didn't know how he knew it but he was friendly to me – he said, 'Your file has been taken. Please be careful.' I felt a cold chill. I think I made the right decision not to go. I told my mother and father, 'Cannot go. I'll be in trouble. They will think that I'm running away, I've got something to hide. Better stay here.'

"So I was followed around for about three months, everywhere I went. They found nothing wrong so they left me alone. I knew that they had no chance. By the time I resigned, I already knew that they had lost and that they were going to get it in the neck and we would also die with them."

you submit, you appear docile, you're obedient and you try to be ingratiating. I understood how power operated on people.

"As time went on, food became short and medicine became short. Whisky, brandy, all the luxuries which could be kept in either bottles or tins – cigarettes, 555s in tins – became valuables. The people who traded with the Japanese, who pandered to their wishes, provided them with supplies, clothes, uniforms, whatever, bought these things and gave them to the officers. And some ran gambling farms in the New World and Great World. And millions of Japanese dollars were won and lost each night. They collected the money, shared it with, I suppose, whoever were in charge: the Japanese Kempeitai and the government or generals or whatever. Then they bought properties. In that way they became very wealthy at the end of the war because the property transactions were recognised. But the notes were not.

"Because people had to live, you've got to submit. I started off hating them and not wanting to learn Japanese. I spent my time learning Chinese to read their notices. After six months, I learnt how to read Chinese, but I couldn't read Japanese. I couldn't read the Katakana and the Hiragana. Finally, I registered at a Japanese school in Queen Street. Three months passed. I got a job with my grandfather's old friend … a textile importer and exporter called Shimoda. He came, opened his office … Before that, it was in Middle Road. Now it's a big office in Raffles Place. I worked there as a clerk, copy typist, copied the Japanese Kanji and so on, it's clerical work.

"But you saw how people had to live, they had to get rice, food, they had to feed their children, therefore they had to submit. So it was my first lesson on power and government and system and how human beings reacted.

"Some were heroic, maybe misguided. They listened to the radio, against the Japanese, they spread news, got captured by the Kempeitai, tortured. Some were just collaborators, did everything the Japanese wanted. And it was an education on human beings, human nature and human systems of government."

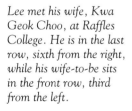

*Lee met his wife, Kwa Geok Choo, at Raffles College. He is in the last row, sixth from the right, while his wife-to-be sits in the front row, third from the left.*

Top: Thanks to a sympathetic censor of Fitzwilliam House, W.S. Thatcher (middle), Lee got himself out of the London School of Economics and moved to Cambridge University. Kwa Geok Choo is on the right.

Bottom: Student life at Cambridge became more pleasant and orderly as Lee settled in, going from lecture halls to the hostel to the dining hall on his bicycle. "Suddenly, life became more in proportion," he recalled later, of his move to Cambridge.

# The scales fell

When the war ended Lee had to decide between returning to Raffles College to work for the scholarship which would fund his law studies in England or going there on his own steam. Britain, land of his colonial masters and the epicentre of the vast if fast declining Empire, might have elicited from a subservient subject of a distant outpost, 11,000 kilometres away, the reverence it once undoubtedly deserved. But war-torn England of 1946 was a different proposition altogether. For Lee, the first few months were disorienting, hectic and miserable. Arriving in October, he was already late for college admission. But being first boy in the Senior Cambridge examinations for all Malaya helped. The dean of the law faculty at the London School of Economics was suitably impressed and Lee found himself thrown into the rough and tumble of undergraduate life in the imperial capital, an experience he found thoroughly unpleasant. With the help of some friends in Cambridge and a sympathetic censor of Fitzwilliam House, he got himself admitted and moved to the university town.

Lee went on to distinguish himself in Cambridge, obtaining a rare double first. But though his top priority was his studies, something else much more intense was stirring in him. It was in England that he began to seriously question the continued right of the British to govern Singapore. The Japanese Occupation had demonstrated in a way nothing else could have done that the English were not a superior people with a God-given right to govern. What he saw of them during those four years in England convinced him even more of this. They were in it for their own benefit, and he read all about this in their own newspapers.

"Why should they run this place for your benefit? And when it comes tumbling down, I'm the chap who suffers. That, I think, was the start of it all. At that time, it was also the year following my stay in England and insurgency had started (in Malaya) and I had also seen the communist Malayan People's Anti-Japanese Army (MPAJA) marching on the streets.

"I would say Japanese Occupation, one year here seeing MPAJA and seeing the British trying to re-establish their administration, not very adept … I mean the old mechanisms had gone and the old habits of obedience and respect had also gone because people had seen them run away. They packed up. Women and children, those who could get away. We were supposed, the local population was supposed to panic when the bombs fell, but we found they panicked more than we did. So it was no longer the old relationship.

"I saw Britain and I saw the British people as they were. And whilst I met nothing but consideration and a certain benevolence from people at the top, at the bottom, when I had to deal with landladies and the shopkeepers and so on, it was pretty rough. They treated you as colonials and I resented that. Here in Singapore, you didn't come across the white man so much. He was in a superior position. But there you are in a superior position meeting white men and white women in an inferior position, socially, I mean. They have to serve you and so on in the shops. And I saw no reason why they should be governing me; they're not superior. I decided, when I got back, I was going to put an end to this."

# Lee the Chinaman campaigns for Labour in Devon

"If I were an Englishman, I would not have to explain my presence on this platform for it is the right and indeed the duty of every Englishman to take sides in a general election. You may well wonder what a Chinaman should be doing here. You have important domestic issues to discuss that should not concern any foreigner. Let me say at once that I am not a foreigner. I am a British subject from British Malaya. And I am here because your vote on February 23 will affect me and 7 million other Malayans some 8,000 miles away. It is your Colonial Office here which decides our fate. It may be that some of you could not care less what happens to a lot of ignorant and illiterate natives. But, unfortunately, what happens to my ignorant fellow countrymen, and what they do, is going to affect you in England."

So began Lee Kuan Yew in a campaign speech on behalf of his Labour Party friend, David Widdicombe, during the British general election of 1950. Lee had moved to Cornwall because he disliked living in London. When he heard that Widdicombe was contesting a seat at Totnes in Devon, he wrote to wish him luck. Back came the reply: "Come and help me." In no time, Lee was driving Widdicombe in a lorry, making the rounds in the constituency, stopping by the gates of factories and delivering speeches from the back of the vehicle.

This speech focused on the difference between a Tory and a Labour government regarding their policies on the colonies. Lee argued that the Conservatives were only interested in extracting the utmost out of the colonies without any regard for the welfare of the people there. He argued that, in the case of Malaya, a Tory government would drive more people into the communist camp which, if it came to power, would mean the end of Britain's links with Malaya. That would be a severe setback for the British economy which, at that time, benefited more from Malaya in dollar terms than it did from the American Marshall Aid.

How was Lee's speech received by the English working class? He recalled, in an interview with the authors, "I suppose it created interest because here is a Chinaman and he speaks English and he speaks educated English and he's able to make an intelligent coherent presentation. So it did attract some attention, caused some amusement, I suppose. I'm not sure I convinced anybody.

"But the communist candidate came up to me at the counting station. There was a communist campaign in Totnes. And he came up with his election agent, and he said, 'Well, you should not be talking for this Labour Party man. You should be talking for us. We are the chaps who would give you freedom.'

"So I looked at him and I said, 'I don't think you will. You will never get into power. They may. They are in power, they may do it. But you will never get into power.'"

*(Text of campaign speech at Totnes on page 253)*

His own political inclinations then were naturally left-wing and sympathetic to the British Labour Party, mainly because of its position on the future of the Empire. The Conservatives, as Lee saw it, were mainly interested in retaining power and furthering British interests in their colonies. He even campaigned for a Labour Party friend, David Widdicombe, in Totnes, Devon, driving him in a lorry and making a dozen campaign speeches on his behalf.

"One particular Union Society debate I remember, one young Tory student standing up for King and the Empire and so on – it was still King George VI, I think, before he died. And I said, 'Oh, we'll have trouble with this chap, we're going to have a tough time.' So when I went to the toilet, I was standing up against the wall. Two Africans were also standing up against the wall, peeing. And one African said to the other, he said, 'When we get back, we'll show them what we mean by Empire, the Imperial Raj and so on, we'll show them.' So I thought to myself, 'Well, this is big trouble for the whites.'"

Trouble for the British was also brewing in Malaya, which had its own particular set of problems because of the special position of the main Malay population *vis-à-vis* the Chinese. After the war ended, in 1946, the Colonial Office announced a plan to create, under the Malayan Union scheme, a unitary state consisting of the Federated Malay States, the Unfederated Malay States and the Straits Settlements excluding Singapore. The plan would confer fairly liberal citizenship based on the principle of *jus soli* (by birth) and equal rights for all citizens. This broke with the past practice of preserving Malay political rights and provoked a spontaneous and widespread protest by the Malay community, which resulted in a Malay nationalist movement under the auspices of the United Malays National Organisation (UMNO).

In an effort to appease the Malay ground, secret talks between the British and Malay leaders were held, which resulted in the Malayan Union scheme being revoked and replaced by the Federation of Malaya Agreement in 1948. Sovereignty of the sultans and the special position of the Malays were preserved, and citizenship criteria were tightened.

As news of the secret talks leaked that Malay objections would prevail, a hastily convened coalition of non-Malay interests was galvanised into action, a coalition of the Malayan Democratic Union (MDU), the first political party formed in Singapore by English-educated intellectuals fighting for an independent Malaya, and the Communist Party of Malaya (CPM), which had its roots in the anti-Japanese struggle. This front, calling itself the Pan-Malayan Council for Joint Action (PMCJA), produced a People's Constitution which represented the first attempt to create a Malayan nationality beyond the traditional Malay/non-Malay divide. The effort collapsed for lack of support and interest within the Chinese community, especially from businessmen and traders who feared that agitation would jeopardise their interests. More importantly, the British refused to negotiate with an organisation so obviously anti-colonial and supported by the CPM. In 1948, the CPM gave up the constitutional struggle and took up armed insurrection against the British. The MDU was voluntarily dissolved soon after.

# I shall return – Lee's first political speech

*Every drop counts. If not for the efforts of nationalistic Indians, the vast subcontinent would not be ready for Mahatma Gandhi and his fight for Indian independence, said Lee in his first political speech.*

"What actual steps we take when we get back will depend on the political temper at that time. Whether we can openly advocate and propagate our views or whether we should be more discreet and less vociferous is something that can be answered only when the time comes. … We must break the soporific Malayan atmosphere and bring home the urgency of the problems facing us. We must break down the belief that we are inferior and will always remain inferior to the Europeans. If every returned student makes known his convictions to his own immediate circle, the cumulative effect will be tremendous. A small pebble dropped in a pond can cause extensive ripples. Without the countless unnamed Indian patriots who did their share in awakening a sense of national pride and dignity and independence, there could have been no Congress Party, no Gandhi, no Nehru and no Indian Republic."

Lee's speech in January 1950 at the Malayan Forum in London is remarkable in several respects. It was the first political speech he made of which the full text is still available. It is hence of some historical significance. More important, it sets out for the first time the thoughts of a 26-year-old man, studying in one of his colonial master's best universities, about what his and his contemporaries' role should be in shaping their country's future when they returned. There can be no doubt that as much as Lee was calling on the audience to take destiny into their hands, he was also making known his personal stand that that was what he intended to do back in Singapore.

Lee's message was a simple one: English-educated Malayan students were in the best position to take over from the British administration in a smooth transfer of power. If they did not, independence would still come to the people of Malaya and Singapore but the changeover was likely to be violent, precipitated by the communists who were the most tightly organised political force in the country. As he saw it, the problem was complicated by the division among the races. Indeed, while it was only a matter of time before independence was obtained, it would have come sooner if there had been a more homogeneous population.

How to obtain independence and maintain the delicate harmony between the races? Segments of the Chinese population were already drawn into the communist movement which was almost entirely Chinese-dominated. But the reality for this group was that the British would never allow it to capture power in Singapore as that would mean the unacceptable loss of a strategic outpost of vital importance to the Empire. Under the circumstances, Lee argued that the English-educated, especially those who had studied in British universities and would assume leadership positions when they returned to Singapore, were best placed to manage the transfer of power.

Seven months after making the speech, in August 1950, he returned to Singapore. And true to those words, he would, in the nine years up to 1959 when he became Singapore's first prime minister, pull it off.

*(Text of speech "The returned student" on page 256)*

Against this backdrop, a discussion group called the Malayan Forum was formed in 1949 in London. Its members, students in British universities, included Lee, Tun Abdul Razak (who would succeed Tunku Abdul Rahman as prime minister of Malaysia), Goh Keng Swee (founder and first chairman of the Malayan Forum) and Toh Chin Chye. They believed the time had come to organise a broad-based pan-Malayan movement, led by English-educated intellectuals fired by a desire to end British rule and to further the socialist ideals of achieving a more equal society. Lee argued in a speech, his first political speech for which a written text is available, that if they did not take action, the changeover would be a violent one involving the CPM.

# Back home

Lee returned to Singapore in August 1950, joined the law firm Laycock & Ong at a salary of $500 a month, and quickly established himself as a formidable lawyer. But it was his legal work with various trade unions that thrust him in the public eye. These were busy years for unionists as they fought for better pay and rights against policies that discriminated against locals. As legal adviser to several unions, Lee cut his political teeth.

"At the beginning of January or February '52, A.P. Rajah sent the postmen over. They were politicians, Progressive Party. The postmen had a grievance against the government and had been to see them. They didn't have the time or they couldn't do it so they sent him [a representative] over to Laycock & Ong. I asked Laycock whether I should take it on; he said, go ahead. I took it on. And they went on strike. I handled the strike, that was how it began.

"And from then, I went from one union to another because I received considerable publicity out of it. I handled all the press statements, I handled the negotiations. It came to a successful conclusion, so I established my competence.

"Then there were a series of other unions, Singapore Harbour Board, Naval Base, and so it went on. Of course, I suppose Laycock must have believed that all this was capital for the Progressive Party, but actually, it was capital for the PAP, although it wasn't formed yet.

"In all this work, we were meeting regularly – Goh Keng Swee, K.M. Byrne, myself, Rajaratnam. So we took on all this other union work. I alone couldn't do all the salary scales, so I had K.M. Byrne, an establishment officer who knows all about salary scales; he helped me so I had the end product just to present.

"They also started the Council of Joint Action, government unions, because the expats gave themselves a big salary. And in order to fight expat pay, just with the local officers, there was no weight. So we built it into a big issue, pay for everybody, including the lowest paid, so that organised the whole government service, from daily-rated upwards. That became another powerful mass base, workers in government service. So in that way, we built up."

By the time of the first general election, which the People's Action Party contested in 1955, its mass appeal was such that it was able to win three of the four seats it contested. Lee won his seat at Tanjong Pagar. The years 1955 to 1959 were eventful ones for the

# I chose Tanjong Pagar because …

*Lee waving to residents and passers-by while going on his rounds of Tanjong Pagar constituency during the 1968 hustings.*

Lee has held the Tanjong Pagar seat for 42 years and 11 elections. In one of his earliest campaign speeches, in 1955, he tells the voters why he chose their constituency.

"I had 25 divisions to choose from when the PAP nominated me to stand for elections. I chose Tanjong Pagar. The people of Tanjong Pagar have a right to know why.

"Tanjong Pagar is a working class area. No other division has such a high proportion of workers – wage earners, small traders – and such a low proportion of wealthy merchants and landlords living in it. I wanted to represent workers, wage earners and small traders, not wealthy merchants or landlords. So I chose Tanjong Pagar, not Tanglin.

"Mr Peter Lim Seck Tiong and Mr Lam Thian have also chosen Tanjong Pagar. But up till now they have done nothing for the people. Both of them say they have lived in Tanjong Pagar for nearly 30 years. Why then have they done nothing for the people all these years? It is only now, before the elections, that they say they want to serve you.

"I have not lived in Tanjong Pagar. But I do not have to live here to know the hardships and problems of the people. When the printing workers of *The Straits Times* who live in Anson Road in the Tanjong Pagar division were on strike two years ago, I fought for them. When the postmen who live in Maxwell Road in the Tanjong Pagar division were on strike three years ago, I fought with them.

"No one heard of Mr Peter Lim Seck Tiong or Mr Lam Thian coming out from their homes nearby to help these people. I can predict that no one will hear of Mr Lim or Mr Lam fighting for the people after these elections, especially if Mr Lim or Mr Lam are not elected. But win or lose, I shall fight on for what is right, for a better life for the people in an independent democratic Malaya."

From those modest claims to fight for the right of the people in Tanjong Pagar for a better life, made during his first general election rally on March 17, 1955 at the East Reclamation Road ground, Lee has gone on to fight for a better life for Singaporeans.

He is still the Member for Tanjong Pagar today, 42 years and 11 general elections on. As for that 1955 election, the PAP had three other candidates in the 25-seat contest, the first to be held under the Rendell Constitution which gave limited powers to the legislative assembly: Lim Chin Siong, Goh Chew Chua and Devan Nair. Of the four, only Nair failed to win a seat. The Labour Front polled the most number of seats, 10 out of the 17 it contested, and its leader David Marshall became Singapore's first chief minister.

PAP and Singapore. For the party, they were years when its mass base, especially with the Chinese-educated ground, expanded considerably. In opposition in the Assembly, the PAP was able to exploit the weakness of the Labour Front government, led first by David Marshall and later by Lim Yew Hock.

The PAP was not alone in courting the hearts and minds of Singaporeans. The Malayan Communist Party had infiltrated the trade unions and had set out to capture the PAP itself. A dramatic battle to control the party began in earnest during the PAP's third annual conference in August 1957, when left-wing elements succeeded in winning half the seats in the central executive committee. Their success was short-lived. In a security sweep, the Lim Yew Hock government detained 35 communists including five members of the newly elected PAP central executive committee and 11 PAP branch officials. Lee and his colleagues took the opportunity to consolidate their strength by creating a cadre system within the party. Only cadres were allowed to vote for the CEC. In turn, only the CEC could approve cadre membership. Thus Lee and his largely English-educated colleagues were able to retain leadership of the party even though most of its ordinary members were Chinese-educated.

By the time of the 1959 election, the PAP was the strongest party around. This time there was no question of it being prepared to govern Singapore.

"We campaigned to win. We had a great deal of anxiety about what would happen after we won because we knew the problems were there. Winning was not the problem. The other side had been destroyed. Labour Front had been destroyed. Progressive Party and the Democratic Party had joined up and joined the Labour Front. You know, all the various groups had been destroyed. It was as we analysed it, our perception of them was right, that they were not serious players. So it was really the communists versus us."

*Right: The first PAP team to lead Singapore, in 1959.*

In the event, the PAP won a landslide victory, capturing 43 of the 51 seats. But for Lee personally, there was no exhilaration on becoming Singapore's first prime minister.

"We knew this wasn't going up for first prize, we're going to be hammered, we are in the firing zone. I believe that very few colonial territories' leaders ever took power with greater forebodings of problems to come. Because we had seen them [the communists] and we knew their strength and we knew their intensity and we knew their capabilities."

# The first victory speech at the Padang

Lee Kuan Yew became Singapore's first prime minister when the People's Action Party swept into power in the 1959 general election, winning 43 of the 51 seats. In this victory speech, he spoke about the challenges ahead.

"Once in a long while in the history of a people there comes a moment of great change. Tonight is such a moment in our lives. Last Saturday saw the end of an era. This morning the new constitution was promulgated. We begin a new chapter in the history of Singapore.

"The power of the people through their elected government is limited to our internal affairs. This is not what we really want. But it is a step forward towards merger and *merdeka*. But even so, tonight marks a significant break with the past. For 14 years since British colonial rule was restored after the Second World War, a series of colonial administrators have ruled and ordered our lives. True, in the last four years some of the trappings of power were transferred to local ministers. But the reality of power was never in their hands, and anyway they were weak and feeble hands, incapable of wielding power effectively on our behalf.

"This rally tonight is symbolic of the nature of your government, a people's government. Unlike the previous rulers, we have no compensation or abolition terms. Unlike the previous local ministers, we have no iron mines in Ipoh to provide for a rainy day. We have no personal future apart from your future. Your joys and your sorrows are ours. We share the same future, be it good, indifferent or bad. And so it is our duty to see that it is a bright and cheerful future. We held no private celebrations to rejoice in victory. Instead, we come tonight to rejoice with you. We, the people of Singapore, have decided to run the affairs of Singapore. We have come here to celebrate on this Padang and to use the steps of this building as our stage....

"There are many more easy changes like this which we can effect. But there are other changes which are not so quick and easy to effect. All of us want a better and a fuller life, but a rise in the standard of living of our people cannot be created overnight. The good things of life … can only come by hard work over a long time.

"… all the planning and effort on the part of your government will not produce the desired results unless you, the people, will support and sustain the work of your government. We shall do our duty to our people but our people must do their duty to themselves and their fellow citizens.

"Lastly, let it not be forgotten that we have been elected to govern on behalf of all the people of Singapore. The paramount interest is that of the people as a whole. There may be times when in the interest of the whole community we may have to take steps which are unpopular with a section of the community. On such occasions, remember, the principle which guides our actions is that the paramount interest of the whole community must prevail.

"Let us work together as a more united people towards a brighter and a better future. May the next five years be happy, peaceful and prosperous years for all of us."

*(Victory rally at the Padang, June 3, 1959)*

The battle lines were thus drawn. As Lee had predicted in his speech at the Malayan Forum nine years before, the returned students from Britain stood the best chance of achieving a smooth transfer of power from the British. But as he had also outlined in that speech, their most formidable rival for power was the communist united front, and they had not thrown their hat in the ring yet, having stayed away from the elections.

The forthcoming battles with the communists would shape Lee the politician in a way nothing else could have done. They would be the defining political battles of his life, and Singapore's, in its struggle towards nationhood.

# Taking on the Communists

*Opposite: A contingent of the communist-controlled Malayan People's Anti-Japanese Army (MPAJA) going out on a victory march in Johor Bahru after the Japanese surrender in August 1945. Its killing of local people who had collaborated with the Japanese left a deep impression on Lee.*

Fleeting figures hurtling through the night, followed by muffled shouts and groans – then a deadly silence. Peering out of the window from his flat above a petrol station at Victoria Street, the 21-year-old Lee Kuan Yew saw how communist elements exacted revenge on locals who had aided the enemy during the war.

It was August 1945, and the Japanese had surrendered on the 15th of the month. In the weeks before the return of the British administration, the communists, who had aligned themselves to the British-trained Malayan People's Anti-Japanese Army (MPAJA) during the war, slipped out of the jungles to embark on a "dog extermination campaign". Collaborators were hunted down, some were tied to lampposts and had their ears and noses snipped off, while others were killed summarily. Hardened as Lee was by the brutality of the Japanese during the Occupation, he found this other brand of violence and terror no less disturbing.

> "I could hear chaps being chased and being killed. The communists had come out and were killing whoever they thought was a collaborator or an informer. It was summary justice. There was a certain streak of cruelty … Maybe they deserved to die but that's not the way to do it. I mean, are you sure this is the chap? And you just catch hold of him, get him in a corner and bom! bom! bom! and he's dead. So that left a deep impression on me, that these are ruthless, brutal … There was no sense of fairness in retribution."

The atomic bomb cut short the Occupation, and in the days before the British returned to Singapore in September, the communist-controlled MPAJA was feted as heroes by the local population. Lee saw the communists again in January 1946, marching at a victory parade outside City Hall, where Admiral Lord Louis Mountbatten (the Supreme Allied Commander for Southeast Asia in World War II) and other guests had gathered.

"Strange caps they wore. I did not take to them. They had their headquarters in Queen Street, near where Selegie House now is. They took over one compound house there. It had about it that same sort of atmosphere as the Kempeitai. The Kempeitai had knocked us around … I got the feeling that the communists intimidate people … I was instinctively driven away from them. I did not accept what they did as reasonable or proper.

"There was a certain ruthlessness about the way they manipulated people and got friends to fix other friends and control them. And if you break away from the organisation, then they'll fix you and destroy you. There was a … lack of humanity about it."

Lee would get to see a great deal more of them in the years to come. His encounters with the communists, his close association with some of them, their working together to boot out the British, and his later battles with them for the hearts and minds of Singaporeans are now part of Singapore's political history. If the Japanese Occupation provided him with his first political education in how power poured out from the barrel of a gun, his dealings with the communists in the '50s and '60s showed him a more subtle approach to gaining political power.

Of course the communists, as they revealed immediately after the Japanese surrender, were as adept in the use of gunpowder to get their way. But that was a short-term measure. In the longer drawn-out battle to win over Singaporeans, they would demonstrate to Lee and his colleagues that they had already mastered the tricks of the trade. For Lee, it was an unforgettable lesson in how a tightly organised group of committed men and women, fired by the heady idealism of the Left and the exploits of Mao and Stalin, could mobilise the ground, wreak havoc in the streets at the drop of a hat, and capture the popular imagination of youths and workers in Singapore.

And they almost pulled it off. That they did not, and were eventually outmanoeuvred by the PAP, is a testimony to Lee's own political skills and some good fortune. If it had turned out differently, it would have changed completely the course of Singapore's history, and perhaps the region's too. Of this there can be no doubt.

But there is more to it than this seemingly obvious fact. Singapore's history was altered not just as a result of the PAP's victory against the communists. Lee believes that the battles themselves were the defining moments, that they provided the necessary plots and subplots in the story of Singapore's survival as a nation. And – more importantly – that without the struggle against the communists, Singapore would not, could not, have survived the subsequent tests of nationhood. The story of Lee's encounters with the communists is hence as much a story of his making as a politician as it is of Singapore's struggle for survival.

"When you come out alive out of such an encounter, you are no longer a political innocent, you're a veteran of a real battle. Very few things will be new. You have gone through fear, near-defeats, terror, you have had tricks played on you and you somehow scramble out of them, many skirmishes. And at the end of it all you are battle-scarred and pretty resolute yourself inside because that was the only way we could have survived."

# Seeds of communism

*In 1949, the first Chinese communist flag to make its appearance in Singapore flew alongside the Union Jack, at the premises of the Mayfair Dramatic and Musical Association in Robinson Road.*

In 1922, a year before Lee was born, the Chinese Communist Party set up an office in Singapore under the banner of the Nanyang Communist Party. Its aim was to establish a Communist People's Republic in Singapore and Malaya, and to do this it planned to infiltrate trade unions and other mass-based bodies. In 1930, a separate Malayan Communist Party, the MCP, was founded to take its place. The MCP cultivated all races into its fold. Feeding on the Depression of the 1930s, it fomented labour unrest that culminated in a strike of 6,000 workers in Selangor in 1935. From the 1930s, the party was involved in clandestine politics with the communist operators hiding behind innocent fronts such as trade unions, coffeeshop associations, restaurateurs' associations, musical groups and old boys' associations.

The fall of Singapore to the Japanese in February 1942 forced the communists to retreat into the jungle. There, they became members of MPAJA, which received military aid and training from the British. By the time the Japanese surrendered, MPAJA was an intimidating force said to be 10,000-strong. The British Military Administration decided to disband MPAJA but the jungle fighters gave up only their heavier weapons. The communist leadership decided that the day to rise in revolt had not yet come.

At the start of 1946, the MCP issued a modest programme in which they spoke only of self-rule and the creation of a fully-elected Malayan national assembly. For the first time, the party emerged as a legally recognised political force. It was not for long.

Some factions called for more radical action against the British, and industrial strife was orchestrated. When the police arrested the ringleaders and raided their headquarters, the communists struck back with fire and bombs. In 1948, the Malayan government issued an ordinance stipulating that membership of a federation of labour must be limited to trade unions of workers in similar crafts. This frustrated the communist method of slipping their men into these bodies and creating unrest.

The communists retreated to the jungle and started an armed insurrection. When, in mid-June, they shot dead three British estate managers and two Chinese in cold blood, the British declared an Emergency. The police were given special powers to arrest and detain suspects without trial, to search houses and seize documents without a warrant, and to impose curfews and close roads. The communists were now branded "terrorists".

"That was a fierce and grim revolt. The angry young men from the Chinese middle schools, who hated colonialism and the British, joined the communists to rid the country of British imperialism.

"In those tough years, 1949 and 1950, we got our first taste of the practical realities of politics. We had learned the theories of socialism, communism and capitalism in books, and read the histories of revolutions. But we now began to understand the meaning of revolution in terms of life and blood, liberty and incarceration, hate and fear, love and comradeship."

*(Speech broadcast on September 15, 1961; text on page 266)*

*Uniformed policemen assemble for a raid on a communist hideout in Changi in 1947.*

# Embracing the communists

Back in Singapore in August 1950, with a double first degree in law from Cambridge, the 27-year-old Lee Kuan Yew joined the firm of Laycock & Ong in Malacca Street. Confident, energetic and with a tongue as sharp as his gaze, he quickly gained fame as a lawyer championing the rights of workers.

"At that time every genuine nationalist who hated the British colonial system wanted freedom and independence. That was a time when only weak men and stooges came out and performed on the local political stage. Fierce men were silent or had gone underground to join the communists.

"There were the Progressive Party and their feeble leaders. There were the clowns of the Labour Party [Labour Front] of Singapore. When I met acquaintances like Lim Kean Chye and John Eber and asked them what they were doing, why they were allowing these things to go on, they smiled and said, 'Ah well! What can be done in such a situation?'

"One morning in January 1951, I woke up and read in the newspapers that John Eber had been arrested, that Lim Kean Chye had disappeared and escaped arrest. Shortly afterwards a reward was offered for his arrest. Politics in Malaya was a deadly serious business. These are not clowns or jokers. They had decided to go with the communists.

"So my colleagues and I pressed on, working with the unions. The only unions able to take fierce and militant action were those with no communist affiliations whatsoever. The postmen went on strike. I acted for them. We extracted every ounce of political and material advantage out of the dispute with the colonial government and got them maximum benefits.

**Lim Kean Chye and John Eber— Leaders of the Malayan Democratic Union (MDU), formed in 1945, a party conceived by the Malayan Communist Party as its front organisation.**

Dr Goh Keng Swee and K.M. Byrne— Civil servants who united the civil service unions and associations behind a Council of Joint Action, to fight for improved conditions and terms of service for local officers.

Lim Chin Siong and Fong Swee Suan — Prominent communist united front cadres, they began their careers as Chinese middle school student leaders who organised boycotts of classes and other militant pro-communist activities.

"The Post and Telegraph workers wanted their salaries to be revised and backdated. The dispute went to arbitration. We helped them and exposed the stupidities and inadequacies of the colonial administration. The whole of the government civil service was organised to revolt against non-pensionable expatriation pay for the benefit of a few white men. … my colleagues, Dr Goh Keng Swee and K.M. Byrne, organised a fight against the European half of the civil service. So we went on organising the workers in their unions, rallying them to fight the British colonial system for freedom, for a more just and equal society.

"Meanwhile, I had got in touch with the people who were detained in the same batch as John Eber. They were the English-educated group of the Anti-British League, a communist organisation. The ABL relation to the MCP is like that of the volunteer force to the regular professional army.

"… Then one day in 1954 we came into contact with the Chinese-educated world. The Chinese middle school students were in revolt against national service and they were beaten down. Riots took place, charges were preferred in court.

"Through devious ways they came into contact with us. We bridged the gap to the Chinese-educated world – a world teeming with vitality, dynamism and revolution, a world in which the communists had been working for over the last 30 years with considerable success. We, the English-educated revolutionaries, went in trying to tap this oil field of political resources, and soon found our pipelines crossing those of the Communist Party. We were latecomers trying to tap the same oil fields. We were considered by the communists as poaching in their exclusive territory.

"In this world we came to know Lim Chin Siong and Fong Swee Suan. They joined us in the PAP. In 1955 we contested the elections. Our initiation into the intricacies and ramifications of the communist underground organisation in the trade unions and cultural associations had begun.

"It is a strange business, working in this world. When you meet a union leader you will quickly have to decide which side he is on and whether or not he is a communist. You can find out by the language he uses, and his behaviour, whether or not he is in the inner circle which makes the decisions. These are things from which you determine whether he is an outsider or an insider in the communist underworld.

"I came to know dozens of them. They are not crooks or opportunists. These are men with great resolve, dedicated to the communist revolution and to the establishment of the communist state, believing that it is the best thing in the world for mankind. Many of them are prepared to pay the price for the communist cause in terms of personal freedom and sacrifice. They know they run the risk of detention if they are found out and caught. Often my colleagues and I disagreed with them, and intense fights took place, all concealed from the outside world because they were communists working in one united anti-colonial front with us against the common enemy, and it would not do to betray them.

"Eventually many of them landed in jail, in the purges in 1956 and 1957. I used to see them there, arguing their appeals, reading their captured documents and the Special Branch precis of the cases against them."

*(Speech broadcast on September 18, 1961; text on page 269)*

# What Lim Chin Siong told Lee about communism

Right: Lim Chin Siong (seated) and his leftist colleagues taught Lee the meaning of dedication to a cause. "I liked and respected him for his simple lifestyle and his selflessness. He did not seek financial gain or political glory. He was totally committed to the advancement of his cause," Lee wrote in his obituary of this former PAP cadre, who died in February 1996.

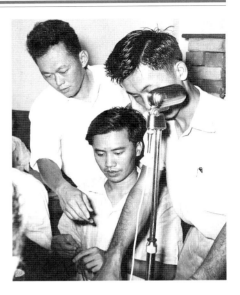

Lee is one of the few leaders in the free world to have worked so closely with the communists, first as comrade-in-arms, and later as mortal enemy. He told the authors what drew some of those he knew into the communist world.

"First, they believed that they had seen the light. It's like blinding faith, that this is the way to bring about a happy, fair society. It's a very, very simple, a simplistic assessment, of the world. I don't want to belittle the impact of how they became communists ... But I will explain how they became what they did.

"Lim Chin Siong comes from a poor family, from Kulai, Pontian, some place in Johor. And I think the father must have made great efforts, sacrifices, to send him down to Chinese High School here. And from there, he got involved with communist activities, so he became a cadre and got sent to the Bus Workers' Union.

"At our first constitutional conference in London in 1956, he went to Colletts bookshop, a left-wing bookshop in London; they sell communist books – Karl Marx, Lenin and all the rest of it. And he bought a book and gave it to me. *The Story of Zoya and Shura* (by L. Kosmodemyanskaya) – I've still got the book. It's a book about a young boy and a girl, a Russian book translated into English, but he must have read it in Chinese, you see. He said, 'Lee, read this, this is a good book. I read it when I was in school. It will tell you why you must do these things.'

"It's an idealistic sort of ... the Dutch boy with his finger in the dike, you know what I mean? It's an appeal to youthful idealism. But I was past that stage! I'm questioning fundamentals. So really, there was no meeting of minds. ...

"It is not possible to have lengthy discussions with them because to them, you read this book and everything is in this book. They were not profound thinkers ... You cannot carry on a philosophical discussion with an active communist cadre. He thinks you're a buffoon, you're wasting time."

**David Marshall—**
**Founder of the Labour Front. In 1955, his party won 10 of the 25 elected Legislative Assembly seats and he became the chief minister.**

**Lim Yew Hock—Labour Front leader who advocated removing communist influence from the trade unions.**

**C.C. Tan—In 1947, he formed the Singapore Progressive Party and was its first chairman.**

**A.P. Rajah—A member of the Progressive Party in the late 1940s and early 1950s.**

On November 21, 1954, the People's Action Party was formally inaugurated at the Victoria Memorial Hall to fight colonialism. The list of conveners was a mix of non-communist English-educated socialists like Lee and English and Chinese-educated political activists with communist leanings. Besides Lee, the others were Samad Ismail, the chief sub-editor of *Utusan Melayu*, and Devan Nair, a teacher. Both men were known to the British Special Branch to be pro-communist. Then there was S. Rajaratnam, a journalist, Tan Wee Tiong, a lawyer, Tan Wee Keng, Wee Tiong's brother and a unionist, Dr Toh Chin Chye, a lecturer, Chan Chiaw Thor, a Chinese schoolteacher, and Fong Swee Suan, a former Chinese High School student who headed the Singapore Bus Workers' Union. To many outsiders, there seemed little doubt that, with such a line-up, a radical, left-wing party had been born.

At the time, the major political players in Singapore included the Progressive Party, led by lawyer C.C. Tan and comprising mostly English-educated Straits Chinese who were successful in working within the colonial system and so had a vested interest in preserving as much of the status quo as possible. The Labour Front, headed first by David Marshall then Lim Yew Hock, was a collection of mostly English-educated individuals with leftist views. The Democratic Party was supported by the Chinese Chamber of Commerce and had a marked communal thrust, addressing mainly citizenship and Chinese language issues.

Lee thought poorly of these politicians, dismissing them as dilettantes playing at politics. It was clear to him that if the newly formed PAP were to achieve its goal of getting rid of the British, it had to rally the people. For that, it needed a bridge to the Chinese-educated world, which was "teeming with vitality, dynamism and revolution". Among the political players, only the outlawed communists had a line to that world.

"David Marshall, Lim Yew Hock, C.C. Tan and A.P. Rajah – theirs was part-time politics, a diversion … They were not men of substance, they had no political convictions, no political ideas. They were not going to be a permanent political force. We knew the serious people in the ring were the communists and us and the British. That was the position and it stayed that way for a long time, and it's that way today …

"There was no choice. You have to enter the Chinese-educated world because that's the mass of the votes, I would say about 70 per cent maybe, maybe slightly more. The English-educated, the Malays, the Indians were, I think, at the most 30 per cent. The rest were dialect-speaking and Mandarin-speaking.

"If you do not want to associate with anybody who has left-wing ideas, you're left with crooks and opportunists. Theirs was such an overwhelming embrace. They had captured all the idealistic and active young; and the others were neutrals, and those against them were gangster-types or very right-wing, and not effective. So there was no option.

"We had to look for activists, cadres if you like to call them. Supposing you go around to evangelise and convert people, how do you go? The priest has got to find supporters, isn't it? You've got to find activists to sell; one to one, finally, is how you convince people. So you must have activists on your side. When you say 'let's organise', you're not just saying, 'sign up here and please vote for me'. Somebody has got to go out and say, 'please sign up, vote for me, you know, I represent so-and-so'."

# An uneasy alliance

The Labour Front had a landslide victory in the 1955 general election, and David Marshall became Singapore's first chief minister. The PAP put up four candidates, two of whom were pro-communists. Lee won comfortably in Tanjong Pagar, while Goh Chew Chua, a non-communist, took Punggol-Tampines. Bukit Timah went to Lim Chin Siong, a former Chinese High School student who headed the Singapore Bus Workers' Union and had communist links. Devan Nair, the other pro-communist, lost in Farrer Park.

The PAP's close association with pro-communist elements within the party was to set the stage for the latter's battle with the democratic socialist camp which Lee represented. Much of the struggle was carried out within the PAP itself as both sides tried to wrest control of the leadership. But there were also larger battles in the streets, in Parliament and, ultimately, in the ballot boxes of the '50s and '60s. Throughout these battles, Lee was to witness up close the workings of his pro-communist partners who were already masters at mobilising the ground and capturing control of the trade unions and student bodies in the Chinese language schools. In contrast, the PAP entered the fight largely as novices of the game.

"We were innocents. We were learning about how to form a political party. These people had been working since 1922 at methods, Leninist methods, highly organised, tightly controlled, secretive, with an armed force to create a chaotic situation in which they are the one organised group that can capture power. So they are formidable. So they had their acolytes and their supporters in the schools, in the old boys' associations, in their cultural groups. Oh, you name them, they've got them. And the success of China was, of course, a tremendous example."

For Lee, the lessons came thick and fast. They were years of learning very quickly the art of political street fighting without which he would not have survived. Many of those battles were within the very heart of the PAP leadership, and defeat would have been fatal. There was, for example, the time when Lee almost lost control of the central executive committee of the party.

"In 1954, when it [the PAP] was formed, we, the non-communists, were in complete control of the party. The only persons who would press the communist point of view were Fong Swee Suan, Chan Chiaw Thor and Devan Nair, three out of twelve members of the central executive committee. After the election of the new central executive committee in 1956, pro-communist strength in the party had increased to four out of the twelve members. They were Lim Chin Siong, Devan Nair, Chia Ek Tian and Goh Boon Toh.

"At that time there was a subcommittee to redraft the constitution of the party. The communists through James Puthucheary were pressing very hard for a constitution which would allow the branches complete control in the party and allow all branch committees to nominate members to the central executive committee. Such a constitution would in effect mean that the communists would be able to capture the party. Penetration of the branches of the party is a relatively easy matter because branches are open to everybody to join and participate in without serious checks. And from time to time these branches do come under communist control and manipulation. Unfortunately for them, while they were pressing to capture the party, they were also planning to capture the trade unions. In 1956 they were all detained in a purge which was accompanied by riots and arson. That was the end of their attempt to change the party constitution and capture the PAP.

"But again in 1957, the pro-communists tried to capture the party. To do this they made use of membership admission cards to the annual party conference, which had been posted to members who had given trade union premises as their addresses. They used these cards and brought in non-members and finally succeeded in voting in six out of the twelve members of the central executive.

"… in August 1957 there was a minor crisis in the PAP when my colleagues – Toh Chin Chye and myself and four others – refused to take office in the PAP, for to have done so would have been to lend cover to the six who were pro-communists. For we would not have been able to get a decisive vote to carry through our non-communist policies. For a short while, Tan Chong Kin became the chairman of the party and T.T. Rajah the secretary-general. Again unfortunately for them, they were planning also to capture the TUC [Trade Union Congress]. They got involved in a purge in which five out of the six pro-communist members in the central executive were arrested. Three of the five were banished to China.

*Above and opposite: The Chinese middle school students' riots of the 1950s. "These were the idealistic young men and women, largely from the Chinese middle schools … They were new men fighting under different conditions with different methods and tactics to create a communist Malaya," said Lee of these youngsters.*

**James Puthucheary — Former union leader with pro-communist sympathies, who later joined the left-wing group of the PAP.**

"After this experience we amended our party constitution to make sure that the party cannot be so easily captured. We instituted two classes of members – ordinary members and cadre members. Ordinary membership is open to all and secret penetration by communists into this group is easy if they send in their people who are not yet well known. But only those who have proved over a period of time that they are sincerely and honestly with the party can become cadre members. An election of the central executive committee is only by cadre members."

*(Speech broadcast on September 20, 1961)*

Lee also witnessed the ability of the communists to create unrest to undermine the government in power. One such incident took place in October 1956, when the Labour Front government told the Chinese High School and Chung Cheng High School to expel 142 students on grounds of subversion. Students staged a strike, supported by youths from other schools and even parents of these youngsters, and riots and panic spread to the city. The authorities, helped by army helicopters and armoured cars, contained the riots.

But although the Lim Yew Hock government restored order, it was, to ordinary people, seen as nothing more than a stooge of the British. And so the communists achieved exactly what they had set out to do.

# Tremendous munching at Happy World

Chief among the strengths of the communists was their ability to rally supporters, in particular the energetic Chinese middle school students of the 1950s. Lee recalled one incident in an interview with the authors:

*Gay World, once called Happy World, where mass communist activities were staged. It has since been demolished.*

"The dynamism, the drive, the idealism, the organisational capabilities – oh, it was tremendous! Most impressive. Their ability to move thousands of students to picnics, to meetings. It was a very impressive demonstration of mass organisation and mass discipline.

"I will give you some memorable vignettes. Once, we had a meeting at the Happy World; there was an old stadium there, probably it could have taken about five thousand or so. They must have packed it with about seven or eight thousand. It was in the middle '50s. This was soon after I met them in '54.

"And the emcee barked out orders like, you know, a sergeant major on parade. Everybody obeyed. Then they passed up peanuts and apples or whatever, little parcels up the aisle, and they were all distributed by hand, one to the other. Then they said, 'Rest, we'll eat now.' So there was tremendous munching going on. And they collected all the peel and put it back in the paperbags and collected it back and carried it away.

"I watched this with tremendous awe, that they brought about this discipline, grouped together. Buses came from all over the place, all over Singapore, met there. And then they disappeared after the meeting, back to the buses and back to their schools and home.

"Of course, at that time, I did not know, which I later knew, that the logistical organisation and so on were done by overaged students, those who had stayed on. Because of the war, there were many overaged students in the Japanese period with no schooling. So these overaged students stayed on.

"They were bright students ... [they stayed] not because they couldn't pass. But they stayed on in order to nurture younger generations of cadres to recruit into their ranks. And they used the young ones to be the emcees and to be in the public limelight. They were, in fact, planning the operations behind the scenes. But even so, they were not old people, they were probably in their late teens or early 20s. So it was very impressive."

# Watching the communist magician

Working so closely with the communists gave Lee an insight into the way they worked, methods he would use later to great effect himself. It was evident to him, for example, that chief among their strengths was how just one person could mobilise thousands through slowly and consistently winning over their confidence.

"How one person can manage 5,000. You only need to get one person. The key person must be on your side – he's the organiser. And you've got a whole group on your side …

"One key union was the bus workers. When they go on strike, the whole city is paralysed. All they had was nominally Fong Swee Suan. Lim Chin Siong was helping but Fong was there in the bus workers' union all the time. He's the key organiser, very quiet, humble man who worked hard, very dedicated. So the workers are totally committed to him, the active workers. Having won their confidence, he then brought in – I would say not communists, but activists, generally sympathetic to the communist cause … I think that when he started in '54, just a handful of them. And he was the key player, he'll call a strike and that's that.

"So similarly, having learnt from that, I put in Jamit Singh in Harbour Board, I put Woodhull in Naval Base. They were people willing to work for less than in the private sector. It was work you did for a cause. No office hours, you're running around all the time, it takes a lot of time, you must like it. You know, it builds a tremendous ego because you can make a speech and everybody cheers you. But you must have a political objective at the end.

*Fong Swee Suan (left) and Lim Chin Siong. "He is the key organiser, very quiet, humble man who worked hard, very dedicated. So the workers are totally committed to him … He'll call a strike and that's that." That was Lee's impression of Fong Swee Suan.*

# The Plen moves into action

*The Plen of the Malayan Communist Party, Fang Chuang Pi, in a picture taken in 1963.*

Lee was to meet many communists, and among them was Fang Chuang Pi, an envoy of the Communist Party of Malaya. Lee nicknamed him "the Plen", short for Plenipotentiary. He recounted in a radio speech on September 22, 1961, how he met the man.

"In March 1958, before I went with the All-Party Merdeka Mission to the London talks, someone whom I knew to be connected with the communist organisation approached me and arranged for me to see a man who he said would like to see me and discuss some matters.

"I met him in Singapore one afternoon on the road between Victoria Memorial Hall and the Legislative Assembly and took him to a room in the Legislative Assembly. He was a Chinese-educated young man several years younger than myself – an able and determined person.

"He told me that he was a representative of the Communist Party in Singapore. I told him that I did not know who he was and I had no way of knowing the truth of his claim. He explained that his purpose in seeing me was to establish cooperation between the communists and non-communists in the PAP ... We spoke in Chinese. Sometimes I used English words to clarify my meaning and I found that he understood English.

"I asked him for proof to show me that he was a genuine representative of the MCP. He smiled and said that I had to take his word for it. I then asked him whether he had authority over the open-front communist cadres in the unions and political parties, and I gave as an example Chang Yuen Tong. Chang was then a city councillor and executive committee member of the Workers' Party ... I knew he was one of the pro-communist trade union workers.

"I told the Plen that I thought the communists were trying to make use of David Marshall's Workers' Party to fight the PAP ... I said that as evidence of his credentials that he was a real representative of the Communist Command in Singapore and his good faith in not wishing to attack the PAP by using the Workers' Party as an instrument, he should give the word for the resignation of Chang Yuen Tong from the Workers' Party and the City Council and let the Workers' Party and David Marshall go on their own.

"He said, 'All right. Give us some time. We shall see that it is done.' Several weeks later, in April 1958, while I was in London for the constitutional talks, I read in the newspapers that Chang Yuen Tong had resigned from the Workers' Party and from the City Council. The MCP had given orders. The Plen had proved his credentials."

"So really, when you say you're fighting for the hearts of the people, you're fighting for the loyalties of key players."

They were lessons he would acknowledge later to be so invaluable that without them the PAP might not have survived its first term in office, and the story of Singapore might have taken a completely different turn.

"Throughout that period, what I learnt was, God, these communists really know how to fix you … I think without those learning years, four years, it's like being on stage with the magician and watching all his tricks and knowing how some of his tricks were done, not all, because you couldn't see all the movements. But you say, ah, that's how he puts the rabbit in there, I see. And so he tapped it here and he changed this. So we learnt how they operated. When it came, we knew that if ever we took over, that they were going to mount it on us in a very big way. So we made a quiet note of all these dangerous things they could do to us or to anyone in power and thought of how if we were in charge, we could escape such a fate.

"I have no doubts in my mind that without '55 to '59, learning the job, learning about Singapore, but most of all learning how communists fixed the colonial government and fixed the Singapore government run by the chief minister and his colleagues, we would never have survived. Supposing there had been no experience of that, we had just been separate, we had just been divorced from that and run a completely non-communist group, and that we had won in '59, we would have been destroyed. I have no doubts about it."

## The communists duped

For Lee and his colleagues, no battle was larger than that over merger with Malaysia; it was the cornerstone of the PAP's policy on independence. It was the conventional wisdom of the day that Singapore could not survive politically and economically without being part of the larger hinterland.

On this, the PAP would clash head-on with pro-communist elements within the party who believed that merger would endanger the communist cause by increasing the likelihood of the central government in Kuala Lumpur cracking down on them. It would also dilute the Chinese majority in Singapore from which the communists drew almost all of their support. Quite naturally, they preferred the status quo, with internal security still under British control, which they could then resist under the cover of anti-colonialism.

Throughout this battle, Lee was not afraid to counter the communists by bringing the debate out into the open so Singaporeans could decide which side they wanted to support. In September and October 1961, he gave a series of 12 radio broadcasts entitled "Battle for Merger". It was vintage Lee, in which he captured the attention of the population with his stories about how the communists operated, his first encounters with them and how they were trying to subvert the country. He explained why he took this approach to the Legislative Assembly.

"Our battle with the communists must be won by argument. We will prove that the democratic socialist forces in Singapore are honest and sincere to the people and have not and will not sell out their rights to anybody. It will also be shown that the communists have not only been duped by the British but duped to the extent that they betrayed their PAP comrades in the nationalists-left united front.

"The battle for men's minds cannot be won by the simple smearing of a man being either anti-communist and reactionary or a wavering bourgeoisie, social democrat or communist. Not all those who oppose the British are nationalists. Some anti-colonialists are nationalists and some are communists.

"We must also see this distinction that not all who oppose the PAP are communists; some are communists, some reactionaries, some opportunists and some merely confused. Therefore, in this battle of ideas it is necessary that we should call a spade a spade and put across truthfully and honestly the respective position of everyone."

*(Speech to the Legislative Assembly on July 20, 1961)*

The approach proved effective for Lee. In the merger referendum of September 1962, 71 per cent of the people in Singapore voted for merger in the form that he had campaigned for. This was a clear signal that, in the minds of the people, he and not the communists had won the day.

The duping of the communists by the British which Lee had referred to in his speech to the Legislative Assembly was one of the major turning points of the struggle. At social events over several months in 1961, British officials met Lim Chin Siong and his friends and gave them the impression that the British would be quite happy to let them run the island so long as the British military bases were left untouched. At the same time, the British pressed Lee and the non-communists in the PAP to curb the subversive activities of Lim and company. It became apparent to Lee that the aim of the British was to get the communists to create trouble for the Singapore government, thereby forcing it to embark on a purge.

"I assumed, and I think I assumed rightly, that the Special Branch knew there was this tussle going on inside. And the reason why they allowed us to carry on instead of locking us up and saying, 'Look, you're infiltrated, you're under the control of the communists and you're a Trojan horse to the communists' was that they, the Special Branch, thought it was worthwhile giving us a chance to fight the communists our way and see whether we cannot capture part of the communist base. It was for the Special Branch a calculated risk and for the British government too, the colonial government.

"On the one side, you have the outright anti-communists in there – Progressive Party, C.C. Tan or David Marshall and Lim Yew Hock. But as against their anti-communism was also their inability to get any support. They could not reach out to the Chinese-educated world. We could. Not as strong as the communists, but we could … They were hoping that we would increase our strength as time went on, so they allowed us this grey area …

"The Special Branch reported to the Governor and the Chief Secretary. And they had to make up their minds whether they thought we're a hopeless cause and will be captured and used by the communists, or whether we would stay our ground and in the end hold our position against the communists. And as it turned out, we were able to do that."

Emboldened by the British overtures, the communists made plans to overrun the party. They saw an opportunity in the Anson by-election of July 1961. Two days before the poll, eight PAP members of the Legislative Assembly declared their support for pro-communist trade union leaders. The PAP, not surprisingly, lost the by-election.

On July 20, 1961, 13 other PAP assemblymen defected to the opposition. One group of eight was led by Dr Lee Siew Choh, and another group of five was headed by Dr Sheng Nam Chin. They were not themselves communists, Lee said then, but Dr Lee thought there was no harm espousing the communist cause, while Dr Sheng felt the communists would win in the long run and he was not prepared to resist them. The 13 defectors, having decided to join hands with the pro-communist trade unions, were expelled on July 26 from the PAP. They formed a new political party, the Barisan Sosialis, which four years later, in December 1965, boycotted Parliament.

In the meantime, however, the pro-communist trade union leaders were applying pressure on the industrial sector to cause the maximum economic disruption. By then, it was clear to Special Branch that the communists were linked up with the Indonesians, who were embarking on Confrontation with Singapore and Malaya.

On February 3, 1963, the Internal Security Council sanctioned Operation Cold Store. All in, 113 communists, including Lim Chin Siong, were detained. A document entitled "The Communist Conspiracy" was released by Special Branch, detailing the methods employed by the communists to secure a mass base for the establishment of a "workers-peasant alliance".

"The Tunku and the British decided that we should move now, not wait for them to create more trouble. From our point of view, the easier thing would be to wait until merger, and then the Tunku would be in charge of security, he has to take action. We knew that he has to take action, so we could have waited until '63.

"But we decided, well, if we wait, the Tunku will really be angry with us, saddling him with a bigger burden. And we had also already established in the minds of the people that we were not doing this for the sake of the British, we are doing this for nationalist Malaya and we had to take action. And we did and we succeeded without losing the government. But don't forget that in the elections, the communists still got 33 or 34 per cent of the votes, you know. That was considerable in September '63."

Lee has no doubt to this day that it was necessary to use extra legal means to neutralise the communist threat, that while he was prepared to counter them with the open argument and to put the matter before the people in a referendum and through the ballot box, force had to be met by force in the end.

# *Piong!* And a man was killed.

A guerilla of the Malayan Communist Party, a group "out to seize power by force," said Lee.

Lee had no illusions about the communists using violence to achieve their aim. He himself had a close shave once. As he told the authors:

"They (the communists) had been working since 1923; they sent a group from Shanghai. The Comintern sent them here, I suppose, financed by the Soviet Union. Then their chance came during the war, when the British were desperate, just before the surrender. They armed this group that were in prison, communists, a few hundreds, probably about 600, and a few others outside also joined them, to fight the Japanese.

"It was a last-minute, last-ditch effort. They were ferocious fighters because of their firm belief. They gave the Japanese a hard time, and inflicted casualties in a desperate, no-win position, and a few escaped into Malaya. And then, of course, they grew as a guerilla force. The British supplied them with arms, Force 136, Spencer Chapman and so on came in, and they grew into the communist movement with an armed wing.

"We were innocents, we were learning about how to form a political party. These people had been working since 1923 at methods, Leninist methods, highly organised, tightly controlled, secretive, with an armed force to create a chaotic situation in which they were the one organised group that could capture power. So they were formidable, they had their acolytes and their supporters in the schools, in the old boys' associations, in their cultural groups. You name them, they'd got them. And the success of China was, of course, a tremendous example. So do you want to be on the winning side or the losing side? That is really how they won those cadres.

"In 1959, just after I'd won my seat, the Char Yong Huay Kuan, which is a Hakka association, gave me a tea party, at Cairnhill Road. And next door was an old boys', some musical association. And *piong!* A rifle shot and this chap was killed. Police never found the killer. They had an elimination squad here, they had bombs, they had arson. Oh, this is a group organised to seize power by force, to create turmoil ...

"You know the Leninist theory of how you seize power? As society becomes unjust and unequal, there's chaos and confusion. And you are a well-organised group responding to secret signals which nobody else understands and knows about. Then you seize, put yourself in the key position, and at the right moment, in the midst of total confusion, you seize power. And to seize power, you must have also armed strength to eliminate people.

"Their job was to seize power, and if the PAP is in power they must knock out the PAP. It must be, it is inevitable. If you are too strong, like UMNO was, because they could not penetrate the Malay race, then their approach would be, first, united front until they are strong enough to push you over. Part of the plan was to capture the PAP, capture power."

"If you just take Singapore alone and you had no extra legal powers to deal with them and you allowed them to use the combination of persuasion and force, they would have won. I would go one step further and say that if the population of Malaya were the same as the population of Singapore, 70, 80 per cent dialect-speaking and/or Mandarin-speaking, enthralled by what is happening in China, and they had the same freedom to organise, to persuade and use force, surreptitious force if necessary, by assassination, fear and terror – I think they would also have won.

"You had to use extra legal means to cripple the organisation because behind it all is terror. Anybody who opposes them in the Chinese schools is eliminated. So you are either with them or neutral. You cannot compete with them on a purely canvassing or open debate position. That is an organisation that has been accustomed to … using force when it is prevented from achieving its aims. It is ingrained in the methods of the organisation."

Lee would be the first to acknowledge that beneath the terror and violence he knew the communists were capable of inflicting – all of Singapore knew it – were commitment and dedication to a higher cause. Though he disagreed profoundly with the ideology, he had nothing but admiration for the courage with which the believers pursued their objectives.

"For years since the beginning of the Emergency in 1948, communism has been painted in terms of violence, terror, brutality and evil. There was violence, there was terror, there was brutality, and there were evil men. But that is not the whole story. For if it was as simple as that, the communists would have died and perished with the collapse of their armed revolt. It is because, together with these weaknesses, they have some strong qualities that they have been able to survive in spite of the collapse of their armed revolt … they have been able to continue the struggle for the communist cause through new methods.

"Many of their old supporters in the jungle have died or been banished. Some have drifted back anonymously into the towns. Only a hard core remains on the Malayan-Thai border. But new recruits have been found. These are the idealistic young men and women, largely from the Chinese middle schools of Malaya, both the Federation and Singapore. These are new men fighting under different conditions, with different methods and tactics to create a communist Malaya. Partly by persuasion, mainly by fanaticism and faith that the future belongs to the communists, these new recruits are continuing the struggle. They press on, capturing the leadership of trade unions, cultural organisations and old boys' associations. Most important of all, they try to capture the power to manipulate the lawful political parties."

(*Speech broadcast on September 15, 1961; text on page 266*)

These students were energised by the communist victory in China, believing that the revolutionary fervour sweeping that country then could be transplanted in Singapore and Malaya.

"China had been transformed since 1949 into a great power. The Chinese communist army fought the US army to a standstill in Korea. That was not a laughing matter. With relatively poor equipment or low-tech equipment, they fought the American army to a standstill until there was a ceasefire in the 38th parallel. China was supposed to be a leader in vast, major industries – this, that and the other. The inevitability of it all, the surge of optimism that theirs was the future, that history was on their side."

At the intellectual level, what he could not subscribe to was their belief that it was possible to construct a perfect society from a set of arguments derived from first principles. He explained this to the authors:

"I wasn't at all sure that you could analyse life and society in a scientific way. I mean, everything was about scientific socialism ... The word itself, the phrase itself, repels me because there's no scientific possibilities in managing people's lives. I did not believe that. But they believed it, they thought that all this would work out like a mathematical formula. Whereas we believed that so long as we had equal opportunities, each must be given a free play of his own life. You don't want to order people's lives around. If you want to be an artist, well, go ahead and be an artist. And if you want to be a Muslim, so be it. But they will not allow that. They say, 'Belief in God is nonsense, we must destroy it, we must debunk this superstition.' That is a certain thoroughness because they believed they had the answer to everything – which makes it suspect to me.

"I'm not sure whether there's a God or there's no God, I'm not sure whether the world was created by God or by an accident. But don't go around knocking other people's gods and other people's culture. Even if there is no God, this group of people have been held together and sustained through all their tragedies and all their sorrows by a belief, by a certain belief that they are all together under one God ... therefore they share certain things in common. Why should you go and demolish that? I disagreed with that profoundly."

The PAP's defeat of the communists by a combination of force and the use of the open argument ranks as one of Lee's finest political achievements. After the Barisan Sosialis' ill-conceived boycott of Parliament in 1965, it faded away from the scene and no longer posed a serious threat. There were occasional incidents such as the arrest of a group of English-educated Marxist Catholics in 1987, but they were novices compared to the communists of the 1950s and 1960s.

What were the reasons behind a PAP victory in the end? Lee put it down to the communists' Chinese chauvinism, their lack of understanding of the non-Chinese world, and an unfamiliarity with the constitution.

"I would say the fundamental factor was their appeal was really based on Chinese chauvinism, pride in the Chinese Communist Party's success, and in the China the Chinese Communist Party had created. So that narrowed them down to only Chinese chauvinists and a few idealists and ideologues like Devan Nair, Woodhull, James Puthucheary, that sprinkling of them, right? That's limitation number one. They were not geared for a Malayan revolution, they were geared for Chinese revolution.

"Second, their leaders lacked an understanding of the non-Chinese world. They saw the world through Chinese eyes and with communist spectacles. They could not see the wider world and that led them to make many serious mistakes.

"And one serious mistake was that they believed – and this is how they lost the referendum and they lost the elections – they believed that they could break away from the PAP and capture enough votes either in the Assembly or later on in the elections to form the government and use limited, not full power of an independent state, but self-governing power of a Singapore still under British military forces, with British troops on the island, to help the communists in Malaya. They were one party. They were not two parties. So the communists here were part of the communists in Malaya. And the communists here, when they fled to Malaya, they took positions there and they fought. So there was no distinction for them between Singapore and Malaya. I think that was the second mistake.

"And the third weakness was complete ignorance of constitutional practices. They did not understand the rules of the game, so to speak, which we did. We played the game according to British rules, so we played within those rules and the British understood us. But they didn't understand those rules at all, so they got tripped up by the rules."

With the demise of the communist organisation in Singapore, Lee's political strength grew manifold. He and his colleagues could claim the moral and political authority to govern independent Singapore, not unlike Mao's long marchers claiming their right to rule China after defeating the Kuomintang, but with an important difference: the PAP's mandate would be reconfirmed many more times through the ballot box. How Lee and the PAP defeated the communists and became political giants in the eyes of Singaporeans is hence of immense importance in understanding the history of modern Singapore and how it was able to make the transition from a political hot spot to one of the world's most peaceful and stable countries.

"I believe they underestimated our determination. They believed we were English-educated, bourgeois and very soft, not prepared to die. And therefore, in a real showdown, we may panic and beat a retreat. I think they were unprepared for our resolution and our determination to lose and lose everything but continue to fight them. That must have been a surprise to them.

"They thought we would be so intimidated by this that we would not dare take them on. I mean, everywhere they had cadres. The overwhelming strength they had was the sense of inevitability that they would win because of China. They had won in China, this was part of a whole revolution.

"And the Chinese-educated were completely enthralled. And those who were against them were scared. If you are against, do you really want to take them on? You know, the KMT had already lost, finished. So why not be neutral? And then they will leave you alone, maybe you can join the united front and so on.

# The hardcore supporters never switched sides

*Hundreds of people, including Lim Chin Siong's former comrades, turned up at Mount Vernon Crematorium in February 1996.*

When Lim Chin Siong suffered a heart attack on February 5, 1996, his death attracted considerable interest from his former comrades-in-arms. Several hundred attended the wake and the funeral service, and there were emotional speeches by former detainees Said Zahari and Lim Hock Siew about Lim's contributions to the country. During a memorial service in Kuala Lumpur a few days later, attended by about 500 people, eulogies were read by some of his closest colleagues in the political battles of the '50s and '60s, including Samad Ismail, Dominic Puthucheary and Fong Swee Suan.

Lee Kuan Yew believes that they came not so much to honour Lim as to honour themselves, to show the world that they had not weakened, that they were still strong at heart, and in a fighting mood – that they were, in fact, brandishing their clenched fists. It was the latest example, to Lee, that while the communist threat might have disappeared, the hardcore left-wingers are still around, ever ready to strike if they had a chance.

"They fought back in many ways and they kept on fighting … With diminishing resources, the old chaps continued to put up a tremendous fight to find some way, to find some new recruits to carry on the battle. They never gave up. The hard core was on the border. Then there were pockets in Pahang. There was total cooperation between Malaysian Special Branch and our Internal Security Department. So we knew, for instance, which groups had moved where and so on, as information arrived. The border plus pockets in Pahang, in Perak and so on and there was another pocket in Changsha. We did not know it was Changsha, we thought it was Yunnan where they were broadcasting things down south.

"And even when we dried up their recruiting ground, as the schools became more and more English-educated or as the students went to English schools and Chinese became a second language, they still did not give up; they were trying to win them over … It becomes a way of life. They know no other battle, no other issue. That is what they will do and they will continue to do. And given a chance, they will start again.

"… The adults of the '50s and '60s had no doubts that it was a battle of life and death. And those who were on their side will remain on their side. Very few switched sides. I could follow the voting pattern for years afterwards. Even as we resettled them from Nee Soon or from Bukit Timah or from Jurong, there were pockets of opposition in the old estate, in the new estates that we moved them to. Although their lives had improved, their sympathies stayed with them. Their hardcore supporters never switched.

"Of course, now it's weakened by time and they have seen China fail. I think the biggest shock and disillusionment to them was to see that China was after all not a success, that it was a mirage. That was the biggest shock because these people were trading on that belief, that if you help them win here, they would produce the same China miracle. But then there was no China miracle, which was the biggest shock of all."

"We were frightened, but not so frightened as to give up. I did not believe that their system was right, that it would win. I believed it was basically flawed, it was evil. They had personal attractive qualities, they wanted to do good to the people. But the system was such that in the end it would do harm to people, completely ruthless. I don't know, maybe it's just a visceral reaction; you see, it is not something you argue intellectually.

"Even for people like us, we had our moments of doubt whether we were wise in taking them on, so I used to discuss it with Goh Keng Swee. One book we discussed was Hugh Seton Watson on Russia and how the communists took over, on Lenin's methods and so on. And at that time, we thought that the Soviet Union had become transformed as a powerful industrial state. We didn't know that it was all just a Potemkin village, just a façade."

# Can they ever give up?

In May 1987, the Internal Security Department uncovered a Marxist plot involving people in the Catholic Church and opposition parties, mainly English-educated people. Lee was not surprised that the communists had now turned to the English-educated for converts. As he pointed out in a speech to Parliament on May 27, 1988,

"Can they give up? A whole lifetime of tens of thousands of people, determined, dedicated, zealous. They don't give up. They must dive into the English-educated world and capture new recruits, however difficult. If reading Mao in the translation is difficult and doesn't enthuse and fire them, well maybe they can read whatever literature French or Italian communists read. Or maybe nearer home, what Filipinos are putting out in English …"

Lee told the authors,

"They need not start as a communist party. You know, just like in Europe they become social democrats and so on. But the method of organisation to capture power has nothing to do with the ideology. It is a technique of acquiring power. There are two different things. One is the ideology, your beliefs, which helps to generate the sense of inevitability and therefore making the recruitment easier. Inevitability of victory. The other is the method of organising secretly, using persuasion and force when necessary and capturing power, creating disorder. And that is independent of ideology. And that, I think, we must prevent them from ever bringing back to Singapore."

# The Union Divided

One sultry July afternoon in 1964, the streets of Singapore exploded with such violence that it not only left 21 persons dead and 460 injured, but also marked the beginning of the end of Singapore's place in Malaysia. The expulsion would take place 13 months later, but there is no doubt now that the fuse was lighted that riotous afternoon. Exactly who was responsible has never been brought out into the open and there is reluctance even now to reopen old wounds. But many suspect there were larger forces at work than just the random explosion of anger and hatred between Chinese and Malays in Singapore.

The day itself had begun peacefully enough when 25,000 Muslims gathered on the Padang to celebrate Prophet Mohammed's birthday and began to move towards the largely Malay district of Geylang. Fighting first erupted shortly after 5 pm as the main body moved along Kallang Road. Police and riot squads were called in and a curfew was imposed until the following morning, then reimposed and progressively lifted over the next 11 days. According to Lee Kuan Yew, then the prime minister, who went on the air that night to appeal for calm, the first spark was ignited when a member of the Federal Reserve Unit asked a group which was straggling away from the procession to rejoin the main body. Instead of being obeyed, he was set upon. This differed from the version offered by the Federation's Acting Prime Minister Tun Razak the next day. He traced the origin to a mischief-maker who had flung a bottle at the procession as it passed through the Kallang area. The conflicting reports underscored the suspicion and tension between the two sides, and did not help calm the already nervous and agitated population.

To understand why it happened and, more important, why when it did happen it would lead eventually to the end of Singapore's 23-month merger in Malaysia, it is necessary to delve into the history of the union. How Singapore became a part of Malaysia, why so many men believed it was inevitable, the subsequent problems with merger when perhaps even more people wanted Singapore out, and the final act of expulsion – these

are now indelibly etched in the nation's history. But they have a significance beyond being just a part of history.

More than anything else, these events defined the birth of modern, independent Singapore. Lee was at the forefront of it all, first leading the campaign for merger, and then at the centre of the conflict which led to expulsion. His role in this tumultuous period and his views about the union and the subsequent problems are hence of immense importance in understanding the nature of Singapore's creation.

# The biggest regret

To this day, Lee counts the failure of merger with Malaysia as his biggest political regret. But he also believes that without the experience of merger and the subsequent expulsion, Singapore would not have survived the early test of nationhood. The experience, he has no doubt, made Singaporeans acutely conscious of the difficulties ahead, of the unique circumstances surrounding the unplanned birth of independent Singapore, and made them want to put in the extra effort to make it alone.

It was a costly experience, of this there can be no doubt. It not only brought the two major races in Singapore into conflict, it pitted the political leadership of Singapore against that of the federal government in Kuala Lumpur. And it made Indonesia embark on an open confrontation with Malaysia. Despite all these, Lee was at the time convinced that merger was absolutely vital.

"Had the British heeded the history of the peoples of Malaya and geography and economic realities, they would have put Singapore into the Malayan Union, just like Penang and Malacca. But they had other considerations in mind. A military base, the fact that an island of 224 square miles would be easily controlled militarily, and that although it may be difficult to deny independence to 7 millions in 50,000 square miles of the Federation up in revolt, it may well be possible to maintain power for quite some time in an island of 224 square miles. And so by the fancy of planners and map-makers in London, we are today out on a limb, the victim of a freak man-made frontier. For the time being, the aims of these London map-makers look like being successful, at least in the immediate short term. For now the British are in the happy position of saying that it is the Federation government that does not want Singapore and that is the reason why there is no merger. I would hazard a guess that if tomorrow a Federation government said it wanted Singapore, the British would be the most unhappy and unwilling people in the world.

"But whatever the twists and turns of events in the immediate present, the relentless logic of geography and the force of historical, ethnic and economic forces must prevail. Throughout history, Singapore, or Temasek as it was called, was part of the Johor mainland. Raffles contrived to separate Singapore from the mainland politically by settling with the Temenggong of Johor. And to this day, as part of this settlement, the Singapore government has to pay the descendants of Sultan Husain a yearly pension, now about $50,000 per annum. Never in recorded history has Temasek existed otherwise than as a part and parcel of the mainland in Johor. And in fact, in more recent history Singapore was the capital of the Straits Settlements from 1867, and the capital of the High Commissioner of the Federated Malay States and the Unfederated Malay States. And to formalise the link the causeway was built and completed in 1923."

*(Speech to the Guild of Nanyang University Graduates, November 6, 1960)*

The problem with the idea, so eminently sensible from an economic perspective, arose out of the racial composition of Malaya, which was predominantly Malay, and Singapore, which was mainly Chinese. This ethnic imbalance was complicated by the historical role of the Malay rulers, which had been protected under British colonial administration. Malay rights were entrenched in the Malay states, and there were job quotas for Malays in the civil service and in enrolment in schools and the university. This was radically different from the way in which the Straits Settlements of Penang, Malacca and Singapore operated, with open competition among the races in the economy.

Malay leaders in the peninsula were anxious to ensure that their privileged position was not eroded by any other political arrangement. Indeed, when the colonial office in London announced, in 1946, a plan to create a unitary state consisting of the Federated Malay States, the Unfederated Malay States and the Straits Settlements under the Malayan Union scheme, the reaction from the Malay leadership was so adverse, the plan had to be scuttled. In its place came the Federation of Malaya Agreement in 1948, in which the sovereignty of the sultans and the special position of the Malays were preserved.

Under the circumstances, it was hardly surprising that the idea of Singapore merging with Malaya, no matter how mutually advantageous for the two countries, would be resisted by the Malay ground. Merger would dilute their numerical strength. In 1960, they numbered 3.1 million compared to 2.3 million Chinese and 700,000 Indians. With Singapore included in the equation, the Malay majority would end, with their population at 3.4 million (42 per cent), less than the combined Chinese population of 3.6 million (45 per cent).

It was not, however, just the numerical issue which worried the Malays but the qualitative nature of those numbers. The Chinese leadership in Singapore, with Lee and his largely English-educated colleagues pitted against their mainly Chinese-educated opponents both within the PAP and in various communist united front organisations, could not but be viewed with some apprehension in Kuala Lumpur. Here was a group of men impatient to change their country's destiny, to kick the British out but who no one doubted would then turn to the larger battle to decide who had the right to govern Singapore. And so the merger idea, while it might have had the weight of history behind it, was never embraced by the Malay leadership with much enthusiasm.

But, as Lee explained in a speech in 1962, the reluctance to embrace Singapore was gradually being overtaken by the realisation that it could become a very serious political and security risk for Malaya if left to its own devices. The possibility of Singapore turning communist, which might then begin to create problems for the peninsula, was very real.

*A relaxed meeting between Singapore government ministers and leaders from Sarawak and North Borneo in 1961, to discuss the Malaysia Plan, which spelt out terms for the merger with the Peninsula.*

"Officially, Malaysia began when the Tunku, the prime minister of the Federation of Malaya, came down to Singapore to make a speech to some foreign correspondents in May of last year, and he said he was all in favour of closer economic and political association between Malaya, Singapore and the Borneo territories; a fateful pronouncement, because for the first time he acknowledged that he had to have economic and political association with Singapore. Since 1955, when he was somewhat aghast at the boisterousness of the people in Singapore, his policy has been one of systematic isolation and the cutting of all ties between Singapore and the Federation in the fond belief that the British could look after Singapore.

"I spent a great deal of time and effort between 1955 and 1959, when I assumed office, trying to convince him that in the long run he had to reckon with Singapore, and that it was easier if he included us in his overall calculations and started on the basis of Singapore as part of his overall problems than if he tried to pass the problem-child over to the British. I will tell you that I was amazed and astonished at the turn of events which, between 1959 and 1961, helped me to bring home to him the realities of the position. Of course, the British, in their own pragmatic way, also helped, but I would say that nobody, however well-informed, could have foreseen the rapidity with which events developed in and around Malaysia. I certainly did not, because I had envisaged an unpleasant time trying to contain an almost uncontainable situation in isolation from Malaya. But, fortunately, our enemies made a number of mistakes which helped us: first in convincing the Tunku that Singapore mattered to him, that the British could not look after Singapore for him indefinitely, that he had to come to terms with Singapore, and that the best way of coming to terms with Singapore was to come to terms with Malaysia in the context of Southeast Asia. That is really the heart of the matter with regard to Malaysia. The Tunku never thought about the Borneo

# The battle for merger

*A joyous celebration marked symbolically by the release of pigeons as eight PAP leaders walked out of Changi Prison in June 1959, days after the new PAP government came into power. Lee had secured from them an undertaking that they would support a non-communist Malaya.*

Singapore's place in Malaysia was sealed when the people voted overwhelmingly to support the government's proposals in a 1962 referendum. The result: 71 per cent voted in favour of merger under the terms proposed by the government, with only 25 per cent heeding the Barisan Sosialis' call to return blank votes. The defeat of the Barisan marked the turning point for the party and for the fortunes of the communist united front in Singapore.

In September 1963, a year after the referendum, Lee called a snap election in which the PAP won a landslide victory, capturing 37 of the 51 seats. Lee related to the authors how the PAP gained the upper hand in this battle for the hearts and minds of Singaporeans.

"The basic programme was no independence until merger because we knew independence before merger would lead to a real danger of a communist government. So after merger, if a communist government emerged, it's only a communist state government, not an international government, a sovereign government.

"In 1957, when I came back from the constitutional talks in London, I defended my position that we should accept this constitution as the first step and we cannot have independence until we get merger and we will then fight and work for merger.

"So before we fought to win the elections in '59, I got an undertaking from the key players – Lim Chin Siong, Fong Swee Suan, James Puthucheary, Woodhull and Devan Nair (four PAP members imprisoned by the Lim Yew Hock government in a security swoop in 1956) – a statement on the principles of democratic socialism which stated quite clearly that we are working for a non-communist Malaya and merger as the way to independence. And they signed it. The draft was done by them and approved by me before they signed it. When merger came, they could not back out because that was the agreed programme on which the PAP fought and won the elections.

"So it was a matter of being committed to a policy which they could not back out from. I took the precaution of having everything spelt out in a document. Partly my legal training. I wasn't going to accept their verbal protestations of loyalty. I said, 'Do you agree with it? Yes? Sign it.' So they could not go back. And they did go back, but they could not credibly say, 'No, we want 95 per cent independence but still under the British, not under Malaysia.' That really was their position. It was an untenable position which they had committed themselves to before we fought and won the elections."

territories. He never imagined that he would be a sponsor of a plan that would form a viable broadly-based nation in Southeast Asia comprising these five British possessions. His attitude between 1955 and 1959 was one which is not unnatural in people who have just inherited tremendous problems of their own, of just minding their own business, and he had a lot of business to mind in Malaya. He was doing well, and he saw no reason why he should undertake problems, the nature of which he did not like and the prospects of providing solutions to which he was uncertain of.

"… But in the course of the first 18 months we were able to convince him and his colleagues that if he allowed the Singapore situation to continue in isolation to Malaya he would create a position where it was worthwhile to make a political appeal based on the Chinese alone. Because if 70 per cent of the people in Singapore are Chinese, and you can win the majority of the 70, you can win political power on the basis of one-man-one-vote, and whatever he tried to do with his 2.5 million Chinese in the Federation, as long as a contrary cause was going on in Singapore, he would fail to win over these 2.5 million Chinese in the Federation, because they are one people and one political situation; what happened in the Federation had its effect on Singapore and vice versa. The argument convinced him, and he was coming round to the view that it was better to move ahead of events, hence that momentous speech when he casually mentioned closer political and economic association. We responded, we welcomed it, and we said that if Malaysia helped merger we were all in favour of it, and that led off a chain of events which has completely altered the outlook in Malaysia for the next decade."

*(Speech at the Royal Society of International Affairs in London, May 1962; text of speech on page 279)*

## Communists and communalists

*Ong Eng Guan, who rode to victory at the Hong Lim by-election on the crest of Chinese chauvinism.*

The one critical event which was the turning point for the Tunku and made him agree, reluctantly, to an idea he had long tried to avoid was the PAP's defeat at the Hong Lim by-election in April 1961. The victor, Ong Eng Guan, was a former PAP maverick sacked from the party and disrobed of his National Development Ministry post after he criticised government policies and party structure. During the one-and-a-half-month campaign to win back his seat, he was attacked incessantly by the party for his character flaws but emerged unscathed to win a landslide victory against the PAP candidate. What had swayed the Hong Lim voters was his appeal to Chinese chauvinism and anti-colonialism and his demand for immediate and unconditional independence from Britain.

"We had just lost the Hong Lim by-election so he (Tunku) knew that Chinese chauvinism, which Ong Eng Guan represented, was going to be a major force, and Chinese chauvinism would move in the same direction as communism. At the same time, I believe the British must have been presenting him with the arguments why, in the long run, he had to absorb Singapore in the Federation. In fact, we now know that they had a meeting in London."

*A victory for the PAP government that marked a milestone in the run-up to merger with Malaysia. "The verdict of the people is a terrifying thing for the politically dishonest. The verdict is decisive. It is the seal of public and popular approval for merger and Malaysia. We are off to a good start."*

With the Tunku finally in favour of merger, the one remaining opposition to it would come from the communist united front led by the Barisan Sosialis, the breakaway left-wing faction of the PAP. The Barisan Sosialis opposed the merger for obvious reasons: a Singapore subsumed under an anti-communist government in Kuala Lumpur would mean the end of its bid to create a communist state in Singapore.

Its battle against the PAP for the hearts and minds of Singaporeans would end with its defeat at a referendum in September 1962, when 71 per cent of Singaporeans voted for merger under the terms proposed by the government. But even as the PAP appeared to be winning its battles with the communists, its problems with the Malay leadership in Malaysia were growing by the day. The warning signs were already there, at the outset, during the protracted negotiations between the two governments on the terms for merger. The critical discussions were of course those between Lee and the Tunku.

"The hours I spent, you know, negotiating and playing golf and eating meals with the Tunku. He is not a man who will sit down and negotiate seriously and finish in two hours all the difficult issues and say, 'All right, we can't finish it – tomorrow, we'll meet again.' He works at his own pace. And when he comes to a tricky problem, he will take weeks to think about it. Meanwhile, you play golf with him, you play poker with him, you go to weddings with him. And slowly, he begins to reshape his thinking and test out his new ideas. Then finally, when he's cleared it up in his own mind, he agrees to something which may be what we had wanted or modified what we wanted."

*Right: Lee enjoying a light moment with the Tunku during a meet-the-press session on October 1, 1962. "Today we are dealing with a reasonable man in the Tunku. And he is a reasonable man, otherwise he wouldn't have given this agreement."*

But the Tunku was not, as far as Lee was concerned, the problem. Indeed, in several speeches he made at the time, Lee said that Singapore was fortunate in having to deal with a man as reasonable as the Tunku and so had to take advantage of this opportune moment for merger.

"You know, if we are farsighted we should move ahead of history and in keeping with our history. If we are foolish, obstinate or selfish and want to thwart history, then remember this: today we are dealing with a reasonable man in the Tunku. And he is a reasonable man, otherwise he wouldn't have given this agreement which has been put in the White Paper on merger. There is no selling out Singapore to him because he does not want to buy out Singapore …

"So, I say to the people of Singapore, my duty to them is to do my best for them. And my best, in fact, best in the circumstances, is to reach reasonable agreement with a reasonable prime minister in charge of the Federation of Malaya. Nobody doubts, particularly the Chinese, that the Tunku is not anti-Chinese.

"If you don't want to reach agreement with the Tunku – let us assume one day – supposing you get a Pan-Malayan Islamic Party prime minister in the Federation, and the chap says why not close down Nanyang University – you've heard it in Parliament itself, they want to close down Nanyang University – Chinese middle schools would be wiped out, and a lot of other things besides. Bank of China will be closed, that is part of the Federation banking laws. We have looked after the entrepôt trade. We say Singapore depends for its survival on free trade with the whole world, including China. And the Tunku, you heard him … he is basically a reasonable man, and he says, 'Well all right, this is running well, leave it alone, carry on.'

"You wait – if one of these days, and God forbid, there is an unreasonable man, I am not saying all PMIP chaps are unreasonable but, you know, fanatical people, particularly religiously fanatical, are likely to be bigoted and bigotry leads to all kinds of harshness and uncompromising attitudes. So let us cement our relations in a mould which suits us while we have the opportunity to do so."

*(Speech broadcast on November 19, 1961)*

## Endless bargaining

The problem however was that it was not all up to the Tunku. His advisers and ministers made things difficult for Lee and the PAP. The signs, even then, did not portend well for the future.

## If I'm arrested …

*"One thing we cannot give away: a Malaysian Malaysia." It was on this principle that the Malaysian Solidarity Convention, drawing together parties from Singapore, Sarawak, Sabah and Malaya, was founded. It held its first rally at Singapore's National Theatre on June 6, 1965.*

At the height of Lee's problems with the Malay leadership in Kuala Lumpur in 1965, rumour was rife that he would be detained and put out of action. At the time, when Lee was asked whether he knew how close he was to being incarcerated, he spoke about what the reaction in Singapore might be to such a move.

"Do you believe that you can just arrest a few PAP leaders and then life in Singapore will go on with these leaders quietly stashed away, being fed, I hope, kindly and adequately, and all the other leaders will carry on and govern Singapore quietly and keep the workers happy, and factories will go up and all will be nice and happy? Or do you think, step after step, it goes on until finally, again you have no democratic or representative government and it is ruled by extra-constitutional methods? It must lead to that, isn't it? And when it leads to that, I say, what is the way out? Can they sustain that kind of a Malaysia? Can Australia, New Zealand afford to be associated in defence of that sort of Malaysia? Can Britain? Has she got the capacity of the Americans in Vietnam to sustain that sort of Malaysia? Because that is required once you move into that situation. A thousand miles of frontier on the Borneo border, 600 to 700 miles from Singapore to Perlis, a guerilla civil war restarts, the British can support that? First of all, will they want to support it? Secondly, assuming that they have to because they are committed, have they got the capacity to do that for one, two, three, or ten years?

"… Once you have a revulsion of feeling, an antipathy against a regime, where, do you think, the communists will come up? You mean they will just cheer and say, 'Well, three cheers now the PAP is out of the way'; they will take over the constitutional stage and they will win the next elections and govern Singapore and keep Singapore happy? Or do you think they will mount, together as others mount, mount a campaign which must lead in the end to the complete dissolution of Malaysia? … Therefore, we try very hard to be as patient and as forbearing as we can.

"But on one thing we cannot give way: a Malaysian Malaysia. Otherwise, it means nothing to us. It means nothing to me and to the other Malaysians who are here with me. Any other kind of Malaysia, I have no place. I have therefore no stake in that kind of Malaysia, and I am not going to help defend, protect or advance its cause. Why should I?"

*(Press conference May 22, 1965; extracts on page 290)*

"On his (the Tunku's) side, he was quite happy to have us run everything, except police and army. But in the negotiations, his finance minister wanted our money, his post and telecoms minister wanted this. So at the departmental ministerial level, they wanted to take over everything. Whereas the bargain between him and me was: You be the New York, you do exactly what you like; don't give me trouble in internal security and foreign affairs and defence, you be New York, don't worry. But his ministers or their civil servants and particularly Tan Siew Sin, the finance minister, wanted to put his finger into every single pie in Singapore. So there was endless argument and bargaining."

Those arguments would continue even after Singapore became a part of Malaysia on August 31, 1963, and would intensify in degree and vitriol over the next two years. There were disputes over how much of its revenue Singapore should contribute towards the entity, and heated exchanges ensued when the Federation asked for 60 per cent and not 40 per cent, as originally agreed. Singapore also opposed Kuala Lumpur's plan to raise taxes and was particularly shocked by a new turnover tax and payroll tax which it felt would hurt the country's labour-intensive industries already suffering from the trade embargo with Indonesia. On top of that, Singapore businessmen complained that they were treated unfairly in the granting of tax concessions and apportioning of textile export quotas.

On the political front, one particularly contentious issue was the extent in which the ruling parties in Singapore and peninsular Malaysia could participate in the domestic politics of each other's territory. Should the PAP campaign in Malaya? Likewise, should the Alliance party be allowed to take on the PAP in Singapore? Whatever the unspoken agreement on either side before merger, punches were not pulled soon after. Alliance leaders came to Singapore, evidently to give support to the Malayan Chinese Association branch there. Responding, the PAP fielded 11 parliamentary and 15 state candidates for the 1964 general election, sparking off some of the most heated exchanges between the two sides. Tan Siew Sin saw this as "nothing less than a challenge to the MCA as to whether it is the PAP or the MCA that should represent the Chinese in Malaysia."

Alliance leaders were also uneasy about the PAP's intentions in the Federation following its hints of changing deeply entrenched social and economic policies there if it could supplant the MCA as UMNO's biggest partner. The PAP was questioned on its definition of social revolution, and asked if this meant the disappearance of the Sultans in Malaysia or the nationalisation of rubber estates and tin mines. Deputy Prime Minister Tun Razak also said he doubted the sincerity of the party towards the Malays and their welfare. Lee is adamant that what the PAP sought to do was no more than what any legitimate political party was expected to do in a parliamentary democracy. But he believed too that the Kuala Lumpur leadership had a

*Right: The Federation's finance minister was Tan Siew Sin, whom Lee described to the authors as wanting "to put his finger into every single pie in Singapore". Constant bickering over money matters marked the brief period of union.*

# Was he against Malay rights?

*"How does our talking Malay here or writing … in Malay increase the production of the Malay farmers?" The Malays, Lee contended, would be helped not by special rights, but by concrete policies that would uplift their lives.*

Lee's most provocative speech throughout the 23-month merger with Malaysia was made in the heart of the Malay leadership in Kuala Lumpur when he spoke in the Federal Parliament. It was all the more remarkable because he delivered parts of it in fluent Malay. Neither the language he used nor the message he conveyed would have endeared him to his increasingly vexed audience, for the thrust of his argument was that their policies would do nothing to uplift the Malays. The issue was not Malay rights, but whether those rights by themselves would bring progress and development to the country.

"This is a very dangerous thing, leading people to believe that if we just switch in 1967 from talking English in the courts, and in business, to speaking Malay, therefore the imbalance in social and economic development will disappear. It will not disappear. How does our talking Malay here or writing to the ministers of the federal government, both Malays and non-Malays, in Malay, how does that increase the production of the Malay farmers? The price he gets for his products, the facilities he gets from the government, fertilisation, research into better seeds, marketing boards. How does that raise him? In fact our worry is not with Article 153, which gives special reservations to Malays for jobs and licences. I am saying it is inimical to the country. What I am saying is that it has been in force now for 10 years with the imbalance between the rural and the urban areas widening.

"… Of course, there are Chinese millionaires in big cars and big houses. Is it the answer to make a few Malay millionaires with big cars and big houses? That is what Alliance means. Mr Speaker, Sir, I am sorry to say it, but that is how it works. How does that solve the ground problem? How does telling the Malay bus driver that he should support the party of his Malay director and the Chinese conductor to join another party of his Chinese director – how does that improve the living standards of the Malay bus driver and the Chinese bus conductor who are both workers of the same company? It is just splitting the workers up. We have taken some time before, we have come down to the bone and it cannot go on like this.

"If we delude people into believing that they are poor because there are not Malay rights or because opposition members oppose Malay rights – where are we going to end up? You let people in the kampongs believe that they are poor because we don't speak Malay, because the government does not write in Malay, so he expects a miracle to take place in 1967. The moment we all start speaking Malay, he is going to have an uplift in the standard of living, and if it doesn't happen, what happens then?"

*(Debate in the Federal Parliament, May 27, 1965; extracts on page 296)*

completely different view about the sanctity of its rule and the limits to which it would allow the PAP to alter that status quo.

> "We were limited in franchise in the centre, in the sense that our voting strength was not reflected in the Federal Parliament. But we were not limited in our political influence to persuade the other voters in Malaya and Sabah and Sarawak to follow and support our policies. That was open to us and that was what the Tunku got very vexed about. … It was very clear from the beginning that what the Tunku would like and what we hoped to achieve in the end were not identical. But we were convinced that once Malaysia came about, change was inevitable and that the Tunku would change in accordance with the new situation. But we also knew we would take a very long time to be able to persuade the people outside of Singapore to a policy and a programme which would benefit them as much as Singapore. It's not easy, because their interest meant that they would want investments all over, development, education, to be spread out. So it would be a gradual process which may take 20, 30 or more years. And we were prepared for that.
>
> "… In retrospect – this is with six-by-six vision hindsight – what the Tunku never made explicit, but which his aides made explicit after Malaysia: you can persuade the non-Malays inside Malaya, but you are forbidden to touch the Malays, that is against the rule.
>
> "Indeed, they went one step further: even the Malays in Singapore, we cannot persuade. We must lay off the Malays. That was never made explicit. But it became explicit once we started campaigning … it was their way of ensuring Malay supremacy. Make the Malays feel different. They will vote differently. They are a different bloc. Nobody should interfere. Non-Malays cannot interfere in this bloc. And until we came along, there were no effective parties making an appeal to the Malays. And we presented an alternative."

## Not accustomed to Malay rule

If there was one speech that captured the essence of the fundamental conflict between the PAP and the Malay leadership, it was made by Lee at his last appearance in the Dewan Rakyat (the Federal Parliament in Kuala Lumpur) on May 27, 1965. He gave a brutally frank assessment of what he thought were the inadequacies of the Alliance's policies, delivered in Malay with a directness the people in Kuala Lumpur were unaccustomed to.

Lee would refer to the speech a few months later, back in Singapore, when he would be as frank to his own people about what he thought was the problem with the Kuala Lumpur leadership.

> "Not so long ago, in June, they tested our mettle – openly, in Parliament in Kuala Lumpur. They got a prominent backbencher to move the Address of Thanks to the King's speech. He said, 'The trouble with Singapore is that it is not accustomed to Malay rule' – very fierce words to tell us, face to face, in Parliament!

"And that was a moment of truth for us. They stared us in the eye and said, 'You are not accustomed to Malay rule, and you are going to get it!'

"Had we melted, I say it would have been lost. We stood up on our hind legs and we said, 'You show me where we agreed to Malay rule. We have never been accustomed to it and do not intend to become accustomed. We will fight.'

"We did not actually say it in words so crude as that. At that time, if we had said that in that crude way, it would have led to a fight. But we said it politely, leaving them to the clear conclusion that if we have to die, so be it. They said, 'Right, in that case, get out.'"

*(Speech given at the Convent of the Holy Infant Jesus on December 11, 1965)*

He explained later to the authors why his speech in Kuala Lumpur caused such a stir there.

"Their leaders reacted with horror and alarm because it was so radical, it was so disturbing. It broke all the taboos, you know, that you should not make an appeal to the Malays and so on, making a direct appeal to help … For instance, in my last speech in Parliament, I spoke in Malay. And my Malay was very fluent then because I had been campaigning in Malay. I had made a very simple point. I am speaking to you in Malay. In 20 years, all the non-Malays would be able to speak in Malay to you. How does that change the price of your rubber or your palm oil?

"The taxes you pay, turnover tax, which Tan Siew Sin [the finance minister] had implemented, you pay as much as the others. Surely what is more important to you is what policies are being implemented, whether they would help you and your children to progress or they will not help you to progress. I think it had an electric effect because it was a demonstration of what was going to come. But of course, having seen that, they had established very clear rules in Malaya. You can't make that appeal to the Malays. It's off-limits. Every time you do that, there's a riot."

For Lee, the need to improve the living standards of all in Malaysia meant taking hardheaded decisions which – and this was perhaps at the heart of the problem – meant changing the old way of doing things. The PAP was a revolutionary party, determined to alter the existing social and political structure of Singapore and to create a democratic socialist state. Having merged to form Malaysia, it saw its mission encompassing the wider hinterland. That inevitably brought it into open conflict with the Kuala Lumpur government, which he saw as being much too conservative and protective of the existing vested interests.

"It was unenlightened. It does not build for the future. For a country which wants to go far, which wants to remove poverty, ignorance, you have to invest heavily in education, in health, increase your infrastructure, get investments, get growth.

"And if I could choose one example, it would sort of encapsulate the problem. Everywhere I went with the Tunku, I was seeing new mosques being put up to consolidate Malayism.

One day, I said to him, we were quite friendly so I said, 'Tunku, why not build polyclinics? There are enough mosques, but they need doctors for little ailments, coughs, whooping coughs, inoculation and so on.' He told me, 'Kuan Yew, you don't understand. The Malays are a very different people, they are a very simple people. Their demands are very small. Just give them what they want and they'll be happy. Don't disturb their way of life.'

"So he saw the future as a continuation of what he knew in his youth: the Malays as rice farmers, the Chinese as traders and the Sultans as rulers and the Indians as rubber tappers. That was not possible."

# Malaysian Malaysia

The PAP thought it possible to mobilise a coalition of like-minded parties which could in time become an alternative political force to the Alliance. The Malaysian Solidarity Convention (MSC) provided the ideal political vehicle to launch that process. Convened in May 1965, it drew together five opposition parties: Singapore's PAP, the People's Progressive Party and the United Democratic Party from Malaya, the Sarawak United People's Party and Machinda, also from Sarawak. Eschewing communal politics, it aimed instead to work towards a "democratic Malaysian Malaysia" by making common political ideologies and common social and economic aspirations, rather than race, the basis for political affiliations. Rallies would be held throughout Malaysia to propagate the idea.

"Over time, our ideas would prevail. We may or may not be able to expand as the PAP in Malaya. We may have to join forces with the PPP in Perak, with SUPP in Sarawak and the United Democratic Party in Penang, because they were already formed. They had groups in various states. The leaders were Lim Chong Eu in Penang, Seenivasagam in Perak, Ong Kee Hui in Kuching. So we will have to join up with them and find a common ground, we'll all start recruiting afresh, which should take a very long time. So the Malaysian Solidarity Convention came about in response to the very strong Malay policies which upset everybody.

"Supposing we had been allowed to continue constitutionally. I think, within two to three years, there would have been a very solid bloc. The PAP would have to modify its programme. It would not be the PAP programme as it was in Singapore, because we had to adjust to the needs of rural constituents, particularly in the Borneo states."

But it was not to be.

The MSC held only two meetings before Singapore was expelled from Malaysia. Already in June, following Lee's speech in the Malaysian Parliament, the Tunku had been urged by UMNO extremists to take constitutional measures to evict Singapore or "put Lee Kuan Yew away to sober him up". But the Tunku held his hand, partly to avoid incurring the displeasure of British Prime Minister Harold Wilson, who had warned him that if his government arrested or detained Lee, he would not be welcome at the Commonwealth Prime Ministers' Conference in London the following month. Talk of plans to arrest Lee surfaced again during the Tunku's absence when he was away in London, and the war of words between the two sides intensified, with Alliance leaders accusing Singapore leaders of challenging the position of Malays and the rulers.

To add to the animosity, the two sides engaged in a fresh round of disputes over Singapore's contribution to the central coffers and quarrelled over its financial commitment towards Sabah and Sarawak. And in an extremely unpopular move, the central government also ordered the closure of the Bank of China in Singapore, which hurt the island's small businessmen.

In July, Tun Razak met Lee and held discussions with Singapore's ministers, in particular Finance Minister Goh Keng Swee, to resolve their differences, but no compromise was reached. Later that month, Tun Razak wrote to the Tunku, who was then recovering from a bout of shingles in London, to say that senior cabinet members in the central government were all agreed that Singapore should go its own way. The Tunku's reply, which came a few days later, gave them the go-ahead to prepare the necessary constitutional and legal documents. Singapore was out on August 9, 1965.

Lee tried up to the bitter end to avoid separation.

"I met the Tunku on Saturday the 7th at half past 12. I remember it distinctly. The appointment was supposed to be at 12 o'clock. I arrived. I waited for him for half an hour. Some of his ministers were there. We talked little nothings. He came and we went to a separate room. I said, 'Tunku, is there no other way? Why not loosen it into a confederation? Give me common market. We will run all our activities ourselves. We will go slow in the rest of Malaysia. Give me common market; give me the right to take initiative in security matters so that the communalists cannot start riots in Singapore, and we carry on in Malaysia slowly: take it in 20, 30 years. And he said, 'No.' I said, 'My colleagues will not believe this.' I said, 'Will you see my colleagues … Dr Toh?' Dr Toh was born and bred in Taiping; his family is there. Every year, he does a biannual pilgrimage. You know, Chinese families have reunions: Chinese New Year and some other moon festival. Dr Toh is not going to say 'Yes'.

"For two million people moving forward faster and quicker, we abandoned eight million; abandoned them and left them in a slow and sluggish situation. And the Tunku did not want to see Dr Toh."

(Extracts of interview with the press on page 305)

He would recall to the authors the moment of anguish.

"Having spent so much time bringing about Malaysia, I felt very strongly that we should not leave Malaysia under the pressures of strong emotions on both sides. That the rational thing was to disengage, get a looser federation, then we leave them alone for the time being, they leave us alone. We carry on as a kind of confederation. But don't leave it. Don't leave, don't break it up. Then when things have cooled down, we can re-engage. I put that to the Tunku. He didn't want it. He knew what he wanted. And what he wanted was quiet and peace and none of this multiracialism running around disturbing his peace of mind."

# The waste of it

For Lee, the failure of merger was not just a personal and political setback. There was for him a profound sense of having let down those who had rallied behind the cause.

"My thoughts were, the waste of it, the waste of all the effort put in. And secondly, letting down so many people in that Malaysian Solidarity Convention, so many parties, so many groups. Because without us, they may not have had the cutting edge, the willingness to define the issues and to expound effectively, not just within the country but internationally. And it was very painful to do. Because by ourselves, we could be no threat. But with them, we became a Pan-Malaysian problem – and the sense of betrayal of fellow warriors for a common destiny. You abandon them, it's very bad. I felt very bad about it.

"In fact, Rajaratnam and Dr Toh Chin Chye felt so strongly about it that they almost did not sign that separation agreement because they had organised this Malaysian Solidarity Convention more than I did. They were Malaysians, you see. One came from Taiping, Perak, the other came from Seremban. They drew on all their friends and the people they knew and they had organised this. How could they just abandon them? They felt very strongly that we were just letting them down the drain."

The people of Singapore received the news about separation with mixed emotions. There was foreboding about what the future held, whether Singapore could really go it alone. But the acrimonious years in Malaysia, the bitter quarrels with their heavy communal overtones, the threat of radical action by the Kuala Lumpur government against the PAP leadership – all these had made the general population weary and uneasy about the relationship. Indeed there might even have been some relief over the clean break and the opportunity to start afresh. Whatever the individual sentiments over separation, there can be no doubts that the experience was a cathartic one for all.

It had one other side effect, perhaps not known to the anxious population at the time. According to Lee the separation had tremendous educational value as well.

"I think it is not possible for all of us, for any of us who have been through that period, not to have been tempered by bruising battles. We got to know people in the raw … what they were fighting over, why they wanted power, how they exercised power on behalf of ethnic groups. Race, language, religion became dominant themes in all these issues. So all our lives since then we have been extremely conscious that we've got to make sure that this does not take place in Singapore. We must never allow race, language, religion to dominate our politics because it will bring disaster upon us.

"So Chinese chauvinism was just not on. We made a decision to move away from any such tendency. Deciding on English as the working language was the first decision we had to make. We left Malay as the national language. We left the national anthem alone. We allowed the [military] commands to carry on in Malay, but we moved over to English as the working language. It was the first move, one of the first fundamental decisions we made

# This will be a metropolis. Never fear!

*From mud swamp to metropolis: Singapore's dramatic transformation can be seen in its changing skyline.*

It has been 32 years since separation, and the old angst has largely dissipated. But the years immediately following Singapore's expulsion from Malaysia were not problem-free: fresh wounds take time to heal. For Singapore, they would be years of a strong and overpowering determination to prove that it could go alone, and that its policies would triumph. Lee was most determined, for obvious reasons.

"I was sad not because Singapore was going to suffer: no. I was sad because by this separation, we could not help millions, several millions of our own people, our own countrymen – in Malaya, in Sabah and Sarawak – to progress with us. That was why I was sad. We could not help them any more. They have now got to help themselves. They have got to throw up their own leaders and they have got to take a stand. We cannot interfere.

"Here in Singapore, in ten years, Geylang Serai will be another and better Queenstown – all the shacks will be demolished. I say that for Singapore because I do not think Singapore is boasting when it says it can do it. It will do it. But do you think in ten years the kampongs in Malaya will have Queenstowns? I do not think so. If you want that, then you must have the thrust, the ideas, the dynamism, the push, the tolerance of each other. That is why I was sad for them who are our people.

Not just Chinese and Chinese, Indians and Indians. There are many Malays here.

"Half of our police force comes from Malaya. Their families are left behind there. They will be quartered; they will live in modern civilised conditions. Their families will come down here and they will want to stay with them, and we will have to say 'No' because there is a limit to what we can absorb. We have only got 224 square miles. It is a cruel thing to do this, but it has to be done. Some people wanted it this way. We could have helped them emerge, but it was not to be.

"But I say to you: here we make the model multiracial society. This is not a country that belongs to any single community: it belongs to all of us. You helped build it; your fathers, your grandfathers helped build this. There was no naval base here, and it is not the British who built it. It was your labour, your father's labour which built that. My great grandfather came here and built. Yes, he came here looking for his fortune, but he stayed – my grandfather was born here.

"Over 100 years ago, this was a mudflat, swamp. Today, this is a modern city. Ten years from now, this will be a metropolis. Never fear!"

*(Speech, September 12, 1965; text on page 310)*

within a few weeks of separation because we've got to have a working language. Before that, we were working on Malay as the national language. After that, we had to link up with the outside world and we decided on English.

"For that generation [of Singaporeans], they had no doubts at all that communalism is a dangerous business and will ruin the country. So when we took strong measures against Chinese-language chauvinists and arrested them, newspaper editors and so on, the people were solidly behind us. You would not have today's Singapore [if we had allowed Chinese chauvinism to grow unchecked]. I could not have got on with Indonesian President Suharto. … He understood me and he knew exactly what was at the back of all our plans, that we cannot give up Chinese as the second language. But we will not be a Chinese community, we will be a Southeast Asian community. We are ethnically Chinese, we cannot change nor can we give up our cultural habits which is our strength. But our thinking and our political objectives are different. And I think he understood that. And that's how we were able to build up the kind of relations with him.

"I am absolutely convinced that without the experience, the two years in Malaysia – first fighting the communists '61, '63 and then fighting the communalists '63, '65 – Singapore would not have made it. If you had given Singapore independence in '61, we would have been ruined, it could not have been done. That experience, it's like Moses going out in the wilderness before he went to Judea. You have to go through that. Then the people became realistic, a sober appraisal of a difficult future and they made the effort. And no more quarrels about foolish things like language, culture and so on. We just sat down and pushed the economy forward and live and let live. Without that, we would not have succeeded."

The history books would record that the story of modern, independent Singapore began on August 9, 1965 with Lee as its founding father. If those books could speak, the chapters preceding that date would shout with riotous voices, many angry and impatient but mostly earnest and impassioned. They would resonate with the tumultuous events of that era: the fall of Singapore to the Japanese, the subsequent surrender, the trials and tribulations of the PAP in its formative years when it was almost captured by the communists, the battle for the hearts and minds of the people over merger with Malaysia, the querulous years inside it, the racial riots and the eventual separation. These events made Singapore, they caused it to come into being. They were years of intense politics and of political ideas. After August 9, 1965, the chapters would become considerably quieter. But the pace of development would quicken, so fast in fact that within 30 years the country would make the leap from Third World to First.

One man dominated this period. Lee Kuan Yew was even more determined, after the experience in Malaysia, to make Singapore succeed. His ideas would prevail, and they would shape the country in a way which very few modern politicians have been able to do for their own countries. The story of modern, independent Singapore, of its transformation to the ninth richest country in the world in 1996 (in per capita terms) cannot be told without telling the story of Lee, and of his ideas and how those ideas changed the nation. It is to these ideas that we turn in the next eight chapters.

# IDEAS THAT
# MADE A NATION

# The Secret of Good Government

It was 1970 and the American spaceship Apollo 13 was in desperate trouble 328,000 kilometres out in space. A mysterious explosion had knocked out all the key controls on board, wrecking the lunar landing mission and threatening to maroon the three astronauts. The world held its breath as the three intrepid spacemen tried one manoeuvre after another to regain control. The do-or-die trick: to set the spaceship on a looping trajectory round the moon and back to earth. One error, one mistimed firing of a rocket engine, and Apollo 13 would be catapulted into unreachable space forever.

Lee Kuan Yew was fascinated too by the unfolding drama, but one aspect of it was of particular interest to him, and he would return to it several times later: how did NASA (National Aeronautics and Space Administration) select those three men out of so many aspiring candidates? How did it know they had the greatest probability of remaining calm and collected throughout the ordeal, and to make the critical manoeuvres that mattered? What in the selection process showed they would not buckle under the severest test? In other words, how do you find such good men?

"If we can test men, weed out the nervous and jittery, you can bank on your future in Singapore long after this government has stood down. We have got to find them. We have some of them. For any group of men, the final achievement is to see their creation bloom and flourish. They must be able to select, to judge, to impart what has been learned from experience and then say, 'Now, the rest is up to you.' There will be new problems but the basic factors are the same. The world is different, the economy is more complex and sophisticated, but what makes a society tick, what gives a people the flexibility, the cohesiveness, the thrust, the dynamism, always seeking new ways to overcome new problems or old problems – that's as old as the beginning of man and the first tribes. That, I hope, will be the story of Singapore."

*(National Day Rally speech, August 19, 1979)*

# A few good men

If there is one starting point in Lee's quest for good government it is that what is needed first and foremost are good men, with ability, integrity, commitment and that special quality which will make them keep their cool under fire. Nothing matters more than this seemingly self-evident truth which has received scant attention in the great tracts of political philosophy.

Getting the system or the institutions right, of course, helps. But even a bad system can be made to work by a group of capable leaders. Few countries, however well endowed with natural resources or with time-tested institutions, will be able to last under a corrupt and inept leadership.

"At the heart of the question is, what makes a good government? That is the core of the question. Can you have a good government without good men in charge of government? American liberals believe you can, that you can have a good system of government with proper separation of powers between the Executive, the Legislature and the Judiciary, plus checks and balances between them, regular tussles between Congress and the White House, and between the House of Representatives and the Senate in the US, and there will be good government, even if weak or not so good men win elections and take charge. That's their belief.

"My experience in Asia has led me to a different conclusion. To get good government, you must have good men in charge of government. I have observed in the last 40 years that even with a poor system of government, but with good strong men in charge, people get passable government with decent progress.

"On the other hand, I have seen many ideal systems of government fail. Britain and France between them wrote over 80 constitutions for their different colonies. Nothing wrong with the constitution, with the institutions and the checks and the balances. But the societies did not have the leaders who could work those institutions, nor the men who respected those institutions. Furthermore, the esteem, the habits of obedience to a person because of his office, not because of his person, is something that takes generations to build into a people. But the leaders who inherited these constitutions were not equal to the job and their countries failed and their system collapsed in riots, in coups and in revolution. …

"Singapore must get some of its best in each year's crop of graduates into government. When I say best, I don't mean just academic results. His 'O' levels, 'A' levels, university degree will only tell you his powers of analysis. That is only one-third of the helicopter quality. You've then got to assess him for his sense of reality, his imagination, his quality of leadership, his dynamism. But most of all, his character and his motivation, because the smarter a man is, the more harm he will do society."

*(Speech in Parliament on the White Paper on ministerial salaries, November 1, 1994;*

*text of speech on page 331)*

## Three Old Guards in hospital at the same time

*From left: Goh Keng Swee, Hon Sui Sen and S. Rajaratnam.*

"I do not know how much time the Old Guards have. My senior colleagues and I are in our early and late 60s. Last October, three senior ministers were in hospital at the same time, in different parts of the world – one in New York and two in Singapore. Rajaratnam had a heart attack when he was at the UN. Goh Keng Swee was in SGH for treatment. Hon Sui Sen joined him after a heart attack. Sui Sen was recovering and was talking to Keng Swee before lunch. They were in adjoining rooms. After lunch Hon Sui Sen had a massive infarct. He died that same afternoon.

"A skilful surgeon in London, through delicate additional plumbing to his heart, has given Rajaratnam a reprieve. Goh Keng Swee has got a remission. But he has given me notice that he is not standing for re-election. Rajaratnam too wants to stand down. Goh Keng Swee cannot be moved. I am trying to persuade Rajaratnam to go on for another term or at least half a term.

"The amber lights are flashing. The practice of big American corporations is for the chief executive officer to step down at 65. I believe this is based on sound medical grounds. The chief executive officer has to ensure a smooth succession to secure the continuing progress of the enterprise. I have a duty to do the same for Singapore."

*(National Day Rally speech, August 19, 1984)*

## Borrowing a brigadier for Singapore

*Lee meeting officers of the Singapore Armed Forces, which was built from scratch in 1967.*

When a country has to borrow a brigadier from its neighbour to lead its army, it is in a serious situation. So small was the leadership pool in Singapore in 1965, not only in government but also in the military, the private sector and the civic organisations, that Lee said they could all fit into a Jumbo jet. And if it crashed, Singapore would disintegrate overnight.

"We are now looking for a really good man to be general and commanding officer – and he is a very important person. He should be tough, he should be a man of integrity, he should be a man of action, and he should be a man of great intelligence and decisiveness. But at the time he was recruited, 20 years or 25 years ago, the British did not want such types.

"We were trained, if at all, just to be corporals and privates – not to be generals. But today we need a general, and it is a job now to produce a general within the next three to five years. And one must be found. At the moment, we have a brigadier borrowed from the Malaysian Armed Forces. However grateful we are for their consideration in lending us their brigadier, I think it is much better all round for our *amour propre* and our sense of patriotism if we have our own general in charge."

*(Speech at a seminar on communism and democracy, April 28, 1971; extracts on page 313)*

Stated so baldly, it seems obvious that it should be the first rule of any government. But why is there so little discussion either in the textbooks of political science or in the media about getting good men to serve in government? How does a country get its best and its brightest to govern? How does it ensure that only the most capable, the honest and the uncorrupt do so?

And what sort of men should be attracted to leadership? What qualities are needed to govern effectively? Under what circumstances will the most capable and the most upright be thrown up and offer themselves for government? What system, if any, needs to be put in place to make sure that they will come forward, and not the dishonest, the corrupt and the self-serving?

The conventional wisdom is that good men will come forward willy-nilly, that it is in the nature of human society that they will inevitably be found. History, after all, is awash with great leaders who rose out of the most desperate of times and the most corrupt of systems. Liberal thinkers will argue that they will come forward but only in a liberal democratic system which allows them to express their political ideas freely, to actively advocate them to the people who should be free to choose or reject them in a free and fair election.

In a free contest of ideas, and of their advocates, the best will, in time, prevail because the people will be able to distinguish the good from the rotten. All the important institutions, the legal system and the mass media should work to support the system. It is a powerful set of ideals that has inspired men through the years to live, to fight and certainly to die for them.

But in practice, it has not quite worked out. In fact, according to Lee, in many instances, the outcome has been nothing short of disastrous. What happened in the newly independent countries of the 1940s and 1950s as one after another plunged into strife and turmoil has had a tremendous impact on him.

> "Having watched how things turned out with Lim Yew Hock and Marshall, we knew that they would fail. They had nobody of any competence. Marshall could make a speech, yes. But he had no idea what the government was supposed to do, what he had to achieve. He's by training and by nature not a builder, he's a speech-maker. And even if he wanted to build, who was there that he could rely on?
>
> "So we could see that it was going to fail and I could see what was happening in Ceylon. The system was supposed to work. I could see, watching Ceylon, watching India, watching Pakistan (they had just got their independence), watching Burma with their constitutions and their peoples – could we work our constitution?"

As one of the first generation leaders who fought the colonial powers to gain independence for his country, Lee understood the forces and the motivation that had driven them to action. He knew only too well the force of circumstances and the uncertain temper of the times that had thrown up these men. What may surprise the modern reader is how early in Lee's political career he came to this conclusion. The problem did not

# Getting the civil service to shape up

*Lee addressing government servants at the opening of the Political Study Centre in August 1959.*

One of Lee's first tasks on becoming prime minister was to make sure the civil service would be an efficient and effective machine able to carry out the government's plans. But to do this he first had to get civil servants to understand Singapore's political goals, and more important, to understand that the game had changed considerably since the colonial days. Now the elected politicians and the civil servants were in it together and it would be their combined effort which would determine the quality of public service. And if the people were dissatisfied with it, they would boot out the government.

"There were two broad sectors. One was the political goals which we had to achieve, independence through merger. That was separate, in that the civil service cannot make a difference. The other was improving life for people, how the administration or the officials dealt with the public, the kind of service they rendered, the kind of treatment people got at all these counters when they had to apply for permits or pay their fees, etc.

"That's a public relations exercise; you have to educate them to understand that this is an elected government. If you offend and antagonise people then they vote against the government. Whereas, with the colonial government they don't care, you just please your boss and if the people don't like it, they just lump it. So that's the first change we required of them.

"So we started the Political Study Centre to re-orientate their thinking, so that they understood why we felt it was urgent, why we felt the civil service must be politically focused before they can become effective."

Lee set out his thoughts on these issues when he opened the Political Study Centre on August 15, 1959, in a speech which called on civil servants to work with the government, regardless of their political beliefs. At stake was nothing less than the survival of the democratic system, he said.

"… It is in our interest to show that under the system of 'one-man-one-vote' there can be an honest and efficient government which works through an efficient administration in the interests of the people. If we do not do our best, then we have only ourselves to blame when the people lose faith, not just in you, the public service, and in us, the democratic political leadership, but also in the democratic system of which you and I are working parts. And when they lose faith, then they will look for alternative forms of government. And let us never forget that the communists are only too ready to offer the people more drastic alternatives in social revolution than the democratic system of government. It is our duty to see that the people are never confronted with such an alternative of despair."

*(Text of speech on page 317)*

suddenly dawn on him in the twilight of his political career when succession became a pressing issue. When he spoke of it in 1966, barely one year into Singapore's independence, almost the entire Old Guard leadership were relatively young and intact.

Perhaps even more surprising is that in an interview made 30 years ago he had already identified one core aspect of the problem which in the 1990s received much attention – improving the incentives for young men and women to join the government.

"I would say the real problem now in Singapore politically – as different from the economics of it – is how do we, over the next ten years, allow a new generation to emerge to take over from us? This is important. We are not getting younger. We cannot go on forever. And you must allow sufficient free play on the ground for a new generation to emerge well in time to take over.

"My problem is there are so many career opportunities now that unless we do something to make politics more attractive incentive-wise, your best men are going into executive and managerial careers. This will leave your second-best careerist … Any party faces it. They faced it all along Eastern Europe. The second generation communist is more of a careerist than an idealist. The first generation [communists] who were captured by Hitler and put in concentration camps all along – I have met them – they are all the first generation. They emerged naturally just as we emerged, and the process of selection was natural.

"Either you felt strongly about the colonial system and you wanted a better society enough to take the risk of being locked up or being clobbered by the British and then of being shot and killed or murdered by the communists … Unless you feel strongly enough, you don't emerge; you just subside beneath the broad mass.

"It is not the same now. Everybody says, 'Well, the country is running all right; three cheers to them. And I am after a good job.' And there are many good jobs. This is the problem. And somehow, some device, some method, some system must be brought about to tap your best into political leadership. Otherwise, the country won't tick."

*(July 28, 1966 television interview with journalists)*

# Not leaving it to chance

How does a government get those bright young ones who will make the country tick and put in place a system to achieve this? This was a radical way of framing the problem for a newly emerging country but it would be typical of the Lee approach to governance. If there was a problem he thought would get in the way of the country's well-being, he was determined to find a solution to it, even if it meant going against conventional wisdom. And what could be more important than finding good men to serve in government?

He believed that the problem was especially acute for newly emerging countries; developed countries already had an established tradition for throwing up leaders. Yet it was the newly independent countries that cried out for capable leaders to solve their numerous and pressing problems.

# What happens when Lee presses a button and nothing happens?

Lee was nothing if not a hands-on leader, especially in the early years. This quality, combined with his thoroughness in attending to important details, has been instrumental in developing a civil service that has been an effective machine in carrying out the government's programmes, and is now acknowledged as one of the best in the world. But it was not always like that. In the early days the bureaucratic top-down culture of the service made it haughty at the top and lackadaisical and unresponsive at the bottom.

The PAP government sought to change all that. Lee's penchant for pulling up officers for sloppy work or publicly dressing down an entire organisation is legendary, its effect on the service immediate and sobering. For some it must have seemed like a cold water shower, as when he caught a works brigade napping and hauled up those responsible the next day. Even ministers were not spared if caught wanting.

Listening to this speech to senior civil servants at the Victoria Theatre on September 20, 1965, not a few ministers must have squirmed in their seats.

"You know, I will not tolerate this. I went to a government bungalow the other day and I pressed the button and nothing happened. And I went to the kitchen and I told my son, 'Press the button now' and he pressed and nothing happened. And I wondered how it was. Succeeding families had been living there – prominent government ministers and officers – without that being put right. I just don't understand. And the following day, all buttons worked.

"Now, if I may explain that to you in a graphic way. When you have a button, there must be a purpose. When you click it, the light goes off. So that is what it is for. When you want the light on, you make sure you click it and it is on.

"I have now, perforce – because I am travelling from place to place, looking after more than just my own ministry – to have a telephone in my car, which is something I dislike intensely. In my office, there is only one telephone, and I don't like three telephones to be buzzing around. And I don't allow them to buzz because it drives you crackers to have four, five telephones buzzing. And my telephone only shows one light and a dull thud, and at any one time, I talk to only one person, and I flick on and off at will, which chap is priority, which chap waits. But you know, every morning the driver has instructions to take that telephone and to test-dial it. I want to make sure that when I want it and I pick it up, it is working. And that is what I want this government to do."

(*Text of speech on page 321*)

"Any society needs leadership. The established ones have their system. I am most familiar with the British system because that is where I had most contacts. It had a ruling elite, with public schools, universities, designed to bring forth qualities of leadership.

"How do you create it, in this area, without tradition, without a past to fall back on? Can it be created? Can you talent-scout? Can you, in fact, prejudge 20 or 30 years before a man matures, that he is likely to make a more than above average contribution? The wastage rate is very high. No Rhodes' Scholar – and they assess these people extremely carefully – has ever become a national leader of any distinction. These scholars are chosen at university level, very carefully.

"What are the qualities of leadership? Integrity, drive, verve, intelligence, physical and mental discipline. And yet, no Rhodes' Scholar has ever become a prime minister or the president of any of the English-speaking countries of the world. But a good number of them have become very good second-rank leaders – permanent secretaries, under-secretaries and so on. No president of the Oxford and Cambridge Union – now the Oxford Union and Cambridge Union Debating Societies – has in the last 20 years since the war become the prime minister of Great Britain. They were not the qualities that were required: wit and witticism have their uses, but not in looking after the destiny of a people.

"What is it then? This is the problem with Asia. At least, these established societies, whatever their shortcomings, did contrive some system which, in a broad stream of talent, provided every now and again the more-than-average performer to give leadership.

"Being confronted with this problem myself, I have often asked, 'How do we ensure succession?' – not on the basis of 'I like A and therefore I groom A for leadership.' Unless you want long periods of anarchy and chaos, you have to create a self-continuing – not a self-perpetuating – but a self-continuing power structure.

"Human beings should be equal. But they never are. Some can do more; some can give more of themselves than others. How do we anticipate that? Why is it that often we can't? The problem of all countries in Asia is how to establish some system which will bring forth an unending stream of people with character.

"True, Khrushchev never went to a university; neither did Stalin. Mao, it seems, spent some time in the libraries of Peking University. But if you leave these things to chance, then surely you are taking chances with your own people's lives and destinies. So it is that in the established societies – in Britain, the United States, large parts of Western Europe, even in Australia – all their leadership comes from a broad stratum of people who have gone to universities.

"But there are large parts of Asia where this is not the case. The idealism that fired a leader in his early stages, instead of staying with him to the end and making him want to pass the torch on to a younger generation, is corrupted and debased in the process, and leaders lose interest in their future beyond their lifetimes.

"And so, automatically, you go on to military leaderships. When you pass from a leadership, endowed at least with some political motivations, on to one which is there as of might, then the future becomes extremely problematical, unless there are other leavening

# Cabinet decision-making, the Lee way

*Not just pure military sums – when it came to a toss between the superior American Hawk (below) and the less impressive British Bloodhound (above), Lee chose the latter, bearing in mind the long-term goodwill of the British.*

"In the Cabinet, I would say there were about five or six strong ministers with strong views. And you want to get a consensus if you can. If you can't, then you get a majority. And by that, I mean not just a majority in numbers: I would prefer the strong ministers to back the policy. If one or two strong ministers strongly felt, very fervently, against the policy, I would postpone it because I would take their objections very seriously.

"Supposing on an economic matter, if Dr Goh had very strong views to the contrary, I would postpone it. I would not overrule him lightly, because I know that he has a deep understanding of the subject. His opposition would not be based on personal considerations. But if I had personal knowledge, if I had the expertise on the subject and I felt confident of it, then I would be happy even with a weak majority. And even if some strong minister objected, I would feel confident that in this area I am more of a specialist than he is.

"In most cases, I would say in 80, or maybe even 85 per cent of the papers that come up, the answer is quite simple. Between A, B, C, D, it's quite obvious you've got to choose A. It's only that 10, 15 per cent where, you know, it could be A, it could be B and it's a toss-up; then you say, 'What's the price if it fails, if A fails; what if B fails? Supposing B costs less after failure, maybe we try B. And then if it fails, we go back to A.' But there are some decisions you make which do not allow that kind of simple cutting of losses, then you've got to be extremely careful.

"I'll give you an example. This is where militarily I was wrong, but politically I was right. We had to buy surface-to-air missiles. And the superior missile was the Hawk, American. This was in the 1960s as the British were withdrawing. And the British had installed Bloodhounds and they were prepared to let us have it at giveaway prices, but we had to refurbish them. Now, the Bloodhound is a high-level missile. It can reach up to 30, 40, 50 thousand feet up in the air, long range. So the professionals weighed the comparisons and said the Hawk was a better missile. It's mobile, it's not fixed on the ground, so is not easily targeted. And the aircraft coming in can come in lower and then this Bloodhound cannot reach them.

"But I decided that if we are going to get cooperation from the British and we want them to leave their air bases without denuding them, then we've got to try and go as much as we can with the British so that we do not make them feel they are being discarded for higher American technology, or that we do not take their interests into account. So despite the technical superiority arguments, I decided on the Bloodhounds. And I think, politically, it was the right decision and we had a very smooth transfer when the Royal Air Force withdrew in '71 and gave up all their bases. We had no trouble. They left most of the hangars and all fixtures. We took over all fixtures."

influences which can counteract the corrupting tendencies of power. These are problems which will beset us for a long time to come …

"You start off with idealism, you should end up in maturity with a great deal of sophistication giving a gloss to that idealism. But what usually happens is a great deal of erosion by the soft and baneful influences of power, leaving almost nothing of the idealism behind and only the professionalism of political leadership without its leavening values."

*(Speech at a conference on youth and leadership, April 10, 1967)*

# Wit and will

Having made getting good leaders the first prerequisite of good government, two practical problems arise: first, how to identify these people; second, having identified them, how to attract them into government.

There are two schools of thought on the first problem. Lee was naturally inclined to the one that held out the hope that a solution was possible.

"There are two schools of thought. Dr Goh Keng Swee once asked an Israeli general, 'How do you find out whether a commander will stand up under fire?' He wanted to find out, of the commanders he's got, who will stand up and who will wilt.

"The general said, 'There's no way of knowing. Wait till the fire comes, and you will know who are the ones who are cool and collected, and who are not. Sometimes the ones you thought would be the calmest, the coolest and the most calculating under fire, they have cracked, and the least promising have turned out to be the ones with the ballast, the calm, the detachment, the verve under pressure.'

"I do not accept that. That might have been true, but look at Apollo 13. The Americans had to choose astronauts. The three astronauts had only one chance: listen closely to ground control, preserve power, take one swing around the moon and come back. If they had missed it, they would have gone on forever and ever into outer space. If any one of the three had panicked, all three would have gone.

"The Americans must have found some way of testing men in pressure chambers, claustrophobic conditions, simulated real crisis conditions to cause fright, and eliminated those who panicked. Because not one of the three panicked, Apollo 13 came back."

*(National Day Rally speech, August 19, 1979)*

And then there was that indefinable quality called character, which is so essential for any leader. How to find out if someone has it or not?

"The problem is that the human being is unable yet to assess this thing called 'character'. You can assess a man's intelligence: set him tests, then rate his IQ; and you can say, 'Well, you are 141 as against norm 100.' Of course, if you have a leader with a good IQ, that helps – because you don't have to go through the memorandum or the minutes with him three

# Can the Singapore system be replicated elsewhere?

One perennial question which has been raised is whether Singapore's method of governance and especially its system of inducting the best and the brightest into government can be replicated elsewhere. What appeals to many about the Singapore system is its record of not only achieving rapid economic development but of doing so with a government acknowledged for its clean and open style.

*The small talent pool in Singapore, said Lee, makes it impossible to reject good leaders just because they had never been through tough battles.*

Can the Singapore way be transplanted elsewhere? Lee recognises the limitations of the model.

"I do not want to be dogmatic. If we were 30 million and not three million, I think the system would work differently because the number of people available to form a Cabinet would multiply by 10, right? Or if we were 300 million people, then it will multiply by 100. Then if you have so many people, although you may run a good system, it is still possible somebody outside there, some maverick, can get together a comparable group and can challenge you. And in a moment of unhappiness, the people will vote the other way.

"But when you're dealing with three million people and the talent pool is so small, I think really competent people to be in government, between the ages of 35 to 65, fit people I would entrust the government to, would not number more than 100. So where is the alternative?

"If we reject people who are natural activists with ideas, with ability, with dedication, then the PAP is inviting breakdown of the system. It cannot reject people who are committed with ideas and ability. It must absorb and allow change to take place from within because the party cannot have the foresight to incorporate in its programme and its policies all the changes that are going to happen in this world.

"But we devised this system because we were confronted with a problem of succession and we analysed our situation and said, 'Well, this is it.' No other way. And there were honest differences of opinion. In the end, Dr Toh Chin Chye and Ong Pang Boon, they were not very enthusiastic about this. They said, 'No, we're getting a lot of careerists, people who have not gone through battle.'

"But there are no battles. And if we don't do this, who takes our place? The branch activists? He may deserve it because he's run around for so long. But can you, in good conscience, hand over your authority, even for a few years or a few months, to people who you know do not have that helicopter quality?"

times over and explain what it means. You just have to go through three-quarters of the way and he has seen the last one-quarter that you want to lead him to.

"It is amazing the number of highly intelligent persons in the world who make no contribution at all to the well-being of their fellowmen.

"And it is this as yet unmeasurable quality called 'character' which, plus your mental capacity or knowledge or discipline, makes for leadership.

"I read recently the account of someone who spent some years in Buchenwald (a Nazi concentration camp). A French Roman Catholic, he survived it to write his diaries. And, reading parts of it, I thought they were most illuminating.

"He said: 'Some of the most intelligent, some of the most socially distinguished of people, in normal situations, if put under the pressure of those abnormal and, in fact, subhuman conditions, are soon exposed and often destroyed. And it has nothing to do with quality of the mind, the quickness of wit and intellect or even intellectual discipline. It has to do with something called the "will" which may or may not be related with one's beliefs, dedication, convictions, values.'

"He recounted two instances: one was a dietician, a distinguished dietician in ordinary civilian life. He knew just how much food he must consume – a certain number of calories per day – or he must die. But he loved cigarettes and he traded these precious calories for cigarettes. And he died.

"He recounted also how a famous surgeon – a man of great intellectual distinction, with skill and, obviously, with discipline to bring about such a sustained skill – could not contain his own physical weaknesses. There was a fire in this hut in Buchenwald, in the centre of a dormitory, to keep them warm at nights, the long winter nights. If you go and sleep very near the fire, you will be comfortable but when you are rudely awakened at five o'clock in the morning to take the roll-call outside in the cold, you will get pneumonia and die. This surgeon knew that. And so did the others, who were not surgeons. So an optimum point was worked out beyond which you could go closer to the fire only at your peril. But this surgeon could not contain himself. He lost that will to live. He went closer and closer as the weeks went by, and the winter became deeper and longer. And sure enough, one day at five, it was too cold: he had pneumonia and died.

"You see, this is the other quality that is required in leadership: character – whether your melting point is low or high; whether you believe enough and fervently in what you have to do, to go through a great deal of trial and tribulation."

*(Speech at a conference on youth and leadership, April 10, 1967)*

There were other qualities which he looked out for and considered important in the making of a leader.

"You need, besides determination, all the other attributes that will push a project along. You must have application, you must be prepared to work hard, you must be prepared to get people to work with you. Especially for political leaders, you've got to have people work for

# Don't impress me with big words

*"That which is written without much effort is seldom read with much pleasure," Lee would tell civil servants in February 1979. Seen here, reading with evident pleasure, is Lee as a law student in Cambridge.*

How hands-on was Lee as an administrator? On February 27, 1979, he gathered the top brass of the government and the civil service at the Regional Language Centre for a discussion on falling standards of written English. It was one long session on the simple rules of writing clearly and concisely, with Lee going through various examples of sloppy writing, culled from Cabinet papers. But more than just delivering an English lesson, he wanted to persuade the audience that the problem was a pressing one, that it was worth their while to master the art of writing clearly.

"The written English we want is clean, clear prose. I choose my words carefully – not elegant, not stylish, just clean, clear prose. It means simplifying, polishing and tightening. ... Remember: That which is written without much effort is seldom read with much pleasure. The more the pleasure, you can assume, as a rule of thumb, the greater the effort. ...

"So when you send me or send your minister a minute or a memo, or a draft that has to be published, like the President's Address, do not try to impress by big words – impress by the clarity of your ideas. Then I am impressed. I speak as a practitioner. If I had not been able to reduce complex ideas into simple words and project them vividly for mass understanding, I would not be here today. The communists simplified ideas into slogans to sway people's feelings, win people's hearts and settle people's minds, to get the people to move in directions which would have done us harm. I had to check and to counter them. I learned fast. The first thing I had to do was to express ideas in simple words....

"First item: 'With increasing urbanisation and industrialisation, we will require continued assistance particularly in the technological and managerial fields.' I asked myself, 'What have I missed in this? What has the first part about urbanisation and industrialisation to do with the second part about continued assistance? Why do we need more assistance particularly in technological and managerial skills because of increasing urbanisation and industrialisation?' It is a *non sequitur*. We need technological and managerial assistance anyway. The first part does not lead to the second part.

"Item from the Ministry of Education: '(It is necessary to study) the correlation between language aptitude, intelligence and values and attitudes to ensure that the various echelons of leaders are not only effectively bilingual but also of the desirable calibre.' I read it over and over again. It made no sense. This is gibberish. I inquired and I was told, well, they were trying to find out how language ability and intelligence should influence the methods for instilling good social values and attitudes. Well, then say so. But somebody wanted to impress me by dressing up his ideas in many important words. Next time impress me with the simple way you get your ideas across to me."

*(Extracts of the speech on page 324)*

you and work with you. You've got to enthuse them with the same fire and the same eagerness that pushes you along. I think that's a very big factor in leadership."

Intelligence, he says, is crucial, though not the be-all and end-all.

"That's the capacity to absorb information, organise it, then use it to deploy enough facts and argument to answer a specific point and, in the process, score marks. But after all these years choosing people for jobs, choosing ministers, I know that … your examination results are important, but it only shows one side of you. It shows IQ, application, systematic thinking and logic.

"That's why the Shell system impressed me. Its simplicity: reduced to its essentials, its 'helicopter quality'. You must have powers of analysis which are demonstrated by your examination results. You must have imagination and a sense of reality. You must have then the qualities of leadership and a natural ability to enthuse people.

"At the end of the day, you also must have idealism to succeed, to make people come with you. You must have that vision of what is at the bottom of the rainbow you want to reach. But you must have a sense of reality … to feel when this vision is not practical, that it will ruin us.

"A leader without the vision, to strive to improve things, is no good. Then you'll just stay put, you won't progress."

# Picking winners

How, then, to pick these men, whether to explore space or to run a country? It was a problem that exercised Lee's mind for some time. To a large extent Singapore's meritocratic system makes the process simpler and more straightforward than it otherwise might have been.

The first requirement is a successful career. This usually applies to those who had excelled academically – first class honours or a good second class degree, many with a doctorate or master's degree. Selection by PAP leaders is done through a systematic round of "tea sessions" and interviews, including psychological tests. In 1984, the party had a data bank of 2,000 candidates, compiled from the lists of local scholars, returned scholars and registers of professionals. The exercise has far more in common with the search for chief executive officers and executive chairmen of multi-million dollar enterprises than the rough and tumble tussle at the grassroots for political leadership common in other countries.

This uniquely Singapore system has been developed and refined over many years now and is a hallmark of the political process in which Lee has had a pivotal role. In part it stems from his belief that whatever the problem it was possible to find a solution.

"There is a process in anything, right. That Singapore Symphony Orchestra has now been about for 12, 15 years or so. It's still not a complete Singapore orchestra because

*Opposite: Lee would enthral audiences on many occasions with his passionate speeches during election rallies, which were once traditionally held at Fullerton Square, in the heart of Singapore's financial district. To build a country, Lee would say often, you need "passion" as well as good men at the helm.*

you don't have the people who want to be musicians. Whereas Israel, with a population of four million Jews, has six or seven world-class orchestras. You've got to select people, test them, train them. They must have the talent, the discipline.

"And nobody ever remains in power for long unless he's good at seeing through people and judging them. You must be able to know the real man regardless of what his words are telling you. Assess him. Can this chap do it? Is he just flannelling away or does he know his stuff? For instance, in the PSC [Public Service Commission] I would say the best chairman we had was Tan Teck Chwee. He's very good at choosing people, he's very sharp, he has a good mind, he goes very thoroughly into every single officer, grasp for detail, and he's able to see through an officer and he knows a good one from a not-good one. So if you put him on the selection board, he will come up with winners each time.

"If there isn't a system, you've got to set one up."

It is 30 years now since Lee spoke of the need to improve the incentives to draw the best and the brightest into government. Over the years the financial incentives have been increased. But 1995 saw the most radical move ever made by any government, indeed any organisation, to tackle the problem once and for all. Henceforth, ministers' salaries will be based on a formula pegging them to the six highest paid men in the private sector – in banking, manufacturing, accountancy, engineering, law and managing multinational corporations.

There can be no greater departure from the conventional wisdom that political leaders must be motivated differently from bankers and lawyers as far as rewards go. But having thought through this particular problem of getting good men into government for 30-odd years, Lee finally came to the conclusion that there is no need to re-invent the wheel, that the answer had already been found and tested over the decades, in the private sector.

His speech in Parliament in November 1994 advocating the use of such a formula to peg ministers' salaries leaves no doubts about his conviction, that after 35 years in government looking for good men, paying them top salaries was necessary in the changing times of the 1990s and beyond.

"I've spent 40 years trying to select men for big jobs – ministers, civil servants, statutory boards' chairmen. So I've gone through many systems, spoken to many CEOs, how did they select. Finally, I decided that Shell had the best system of them all, and the government switched from 40 attributes to three, which they called 'helicopter qualities', which they have implemented and they are able to judge their executives worldwide and grade them for helicopter qualities. What are they? Powers of analysis; logical grasp of the facts; concentration on the basic points, extracting the principles. You score high marks in mathematics, you've got it. But that's not enough. There are brilliant mathematicians but they make poor executives. They must have a sense of reality of what is possible. But if you are just realistic, you become pedestrian, plebeian, you will fail. Therefore you must be able to soar above the reality and say, 'This is also possible' – a sense of imagination. …

*Opposite: Lee recognised that the world, and Singapore, had changed dramatically from his early days, when young men like himself were drawn into the political arena by circumstances. Unlike in 1966, when he gamely braved the rains to go on a walkabout in the country's backward southern islands, the young these days were swept up by a powerful wave of prosperity, which had caused them to shun politics for more lucrative endeavours, Lee noted in 1995 "with almost a touch of nostalgia for older and better times".*

"But now, a powerful wave has swept up our young and some of our not-so-young. There is an eagerness, almost anxiety, that they miss the escalator that is moving up and that can carry them to golden opportunities. And in fairness to the young, I will add this, with almost a touch of nostalgia for older and better times – it has swept up part of the older generation too. Because the old guards, they don't just die away. In Hollywood movies, you walk into the sunset and music and clouds. But in real life you live on, you become a little bit more infirm, you need medical treatment, and you have needs to meet. For example, Dr Goh Keng Swee. Recently he resigned from the Board of the Government Investment Corporation in order to avoid conflict of interest situations with the GIC when he advises several financial institutions on investments in Singapore and abroad which may also be of interest to GIC fund managers. That's quite a shift in the world. It's as if I suddenly decided that I'll join Henry Kissinger Associates. And the rewards are in, for key personnel, it's six, seven figures. Or I don't even have to leave Singapore. I could go back to Lee & Lee. I started the firm. ...

"I'm prepared to put my experience and my judgement against all the arguments the doubters can muster. In five to 10 years, when it works and Singapore has got a good government, this formula will be accepted as conventional wisdom."

*(Speech in Parliament on the White Paper on ministerial salaries, November 1, 1994; text of speech on page 331)*

# From Third World to First

Lee Kuan Yew flew to London in 1968 to persuade the Labour government to postpone its military withdrawal from Singapore. The mission made major headline news that year. Success was critical because a sudden pullout would bring devastating consequences to the Singapore economy, with the loss of thousands of civilian jobs. The military bases in Singapore, Britain's largest east of Suez, meant a great deal to the Singapore economy, contributing 12.7 per cent to its Gross National Product. In the event, Britain's Labour Party Premier Harold Wilson relented and pushed the withdrawal date to the end of 1971, instead of the beginning, and so held out the hope that if the Conservatives triumphed in the general election due at the end of that year, it might decide to keep the bases in Singapore.

These were trying times for Singapore, and for Lee, who had to use all his persuasive powers to put forth his case. But for all the stresses and strains that he must have felt at the time, he has not forgotten one incident that had nothing to do with the talks and did not make any headlines. It stayed with him to this day because of what it said then about the state of the Singapore economy.

As news of the talks were publicised on British television and in the newspapers, Marcus Sieff of the retailing chain Marks & Spencer's asked to see Lee in his hotel in Hyde Park. Sieff wanted Lee, who was known to be a good friend of Gamal Abdel Nasser, to persuade the Egyptian leader to make peace with Israel. Lee listened to him and said that he would try. Sieff, who might have felt obligated to do something in return, then said to Lee, "Look, if you need to create jobs, why don't you make fishhooks? It takes a lot of labour and skill. And you've got to put feathers on the hook, you know, for trout fishing and so on, and it's high value-added." Nasser did not make peace with Israel, but a Norwegian company, Mustaad & Co, did set up shop in Singapore to make fishhooks, and employed a few hundred workers.

It might seem somewhat comical now, 29 years later, that a well meaning businessman in London saw the making of fishhooks as a lifeline for the struggling Singapore economy. But it was no laughing matter then. At stake was nothing less than the survival of a fledgling reluctant nation with no natural resources which had, three years before, been booted out of Malaysia. Fishhooks, motorcar tyres, cameras – what did it matter then, as long as it provided jobs?

How a country in such trying circumstances – dismissed by many commentators as another basket case of the Third World – managed to make the economic transition to First World status in 30 years is the success story of the region, if not the world. Of all Singapore's achievements, its economic transformation is the most remarkable, and one which even its most severe critics accept.

In 1965, Singapore's Gross Domestic Product stood at US$970 million, the same as Jamaica's. But by 1990, the figure had ballooned to US$34.5 billion, almost 10 times the Caribbean country's. Measured by income per head, it now ranks number nine in the world in purchasing power parity terms. As for social indicators such as school enrolment and infant mortality, measures that reflect how well economic growth has reached the masses, Singapore is also comparable to the developed world. Emerging economies like China, Vietnam and Myanmar have in recent years turned to Singapore for economic ideas and investment, and Singapore-modelled industrial parks are being built in as far-flung spots as Suzhou in China and Bangalore in India.

What lies behind the story?

Much has already been written about the subject and the classic explanations are well known. They include the development of an export-driven economy relying mainly on foreign direct investments for capital and technology, and trading openly with the rest of the world. Other important ingredients that have been identified by bodies such as the World Bank, and which have also been said to account for much of the East Asian economic miracle, are a high savings rate, a rigorous education system, a hardworking people and critical government intervention in key industries and sectors.

But much of this is *post facto* wisdom, with the benefit of perfect hindsight. Indeed the principles that have now been distilled from the Singapore experience – and those of Hongkong, Taiwan and South Korea – are now the accepted wisdom of the day.

What is not so well known, and perhaps more interesting, is how Lee and his colleagues saw the problem at the time when the economy was struggling and survival was at stake, the general principles which guided them then, and how these were tested in practice and modified along the way. It is a story of how a group of men led by Lee worked against the conventional wisdom of the day, which at the time eschewed foreign investments as being exploitative in nature.

The story of Singapore's economic transformation and Lee's role in it can be told in three parts: First, how Lee saw the problem in the early years. Second, his analysis of how it could be solved, in particular his explanations about how countries develop their economies and improve their living standards. And finally his assessment of the nature of Singapore society and what was needed for it to move up the economic ladder.

# Our test: Does it work?

For Lee, the definition of the problem presented no great difficulty. Indeed he was single-minded to a fault about what the purpose of the exercise was all about.

"We were not ideologues. We did not believe in theories as such. A theory is an attractive proposition intellectually. What we faced was a real problem of human beings looking for work, to be paid, to buy their food, their clothes, their homes and to bring their children up. So whatever the final outcome, we had the immediate responsibility of getting the economy going and getting jobs and incomes …

"I'd read up the theories and maybe half-believed in them. But we were sufficiently practical and pragmatic enough not to be cluttered up and inhibited by theories. If a thing works, let's work it, and that eventually evolved into the kind of economy that we have today. Our test was: Does it work? Does it bring benefits to the people? Our first objective was to get the economy going, to provide jobs, to feed the people so that people can live. We were not interested in theories. Of course, the prevailing theory then was that multinationals were exploiters of cheap labour and cheap raw materials and would suck a country dry.

"We had no raw materials for them to exploit. All we had was the labour. Nobody else wanted to exploit the labour. So why not, if they want to exploit our labour? They're welcome to it. And we found that whether or not they exploited us, we were learning how to do a job from them, which we would never have learnt. We were learning on the job and being paid for it.

"In fact, we were part of the process that disproved the theory of the development economics school, that this was exploitation. We were in no position to be fussy about high-minded principles. We had to make a living and this was a way to make a living."

It is important to understand the extent to which Lee then, and perhaps even more so today, was disdainful about the theoretical and the dialectic. It was easy to argue an intellectual case for this or that. But the real test was not the elegance of a theory or the logic of an argument. It was quite simply whether a thing worked or not. Has it worked elsewhere? What benefits, drawbacks did it bring? Lee and his colleagues learned very quickly that the choices for such a tiny place like Singapore, situated where it was and starting off with a low-skilled multiracial population, were quite limited.

"On our island of 224 square miles were two million people. We inherited what was the capital of the British Empire in Southeast Asia, but dismembered from the hinterland which was the empire. The question was how to make a living? How to survive? This was not a theoretical problem in the economics of development. It was a matter of life and death for two million people. The realities of the world of 1965 had to be faced. The sole objective was survival. How this was to be achieved, by socialism or free enterprise, was a secondary matter. The answer turned out to be free enterprise, tempered with the socialist philosophy of equal opportunities for education, jobs, health, housing.

# Taming the unions

A notable part of the Singapore system established early was the way trade unions were brought in line. This was no easy task considering that in the early years the unions led political

*In July 1965, Lee warned leaders of the Public-Daily Employees Unions Federation and National Trades Union Congress that the workforce would have to show discipline and not make excessive wage claims or he would have to enforce discipline for them. The run-in with the unions culminated in the passing of a new labour law in 1968 that restricted the unions' right to strike.*

activism in Singapore. Many unions had been infiltrated by communist and left-wing elements that used unions as front organisations. How did Lee turn the unions around and make them a force working with management and the government? He told the authors:

"You can break the problem up into two periods. The first period was '59 to '63, when we were having a political battle. We were linked up with the communists ... And their intention was not to get the economy cured and growing but to create more problems so there would be more unemployment, so the system would collapse. ...

"If you can read Winsemius' oral history which will be available one day, he recounted how every time he met these trade unionists, like Lim Chin Siong, Woodhull and Fong Swee Suan, their intention was not to cooperate and get the economy going, but to create

mischief to bring the economy down. ... Because if the economy got going, the system will prevail and communism will not take over. So ... endless strikes, go-slows, sit-ins, all sorts of demonstrations to block the economy and slow it down.

"Then after Malaysia, it began to clean up. If you call a political strike without taking a ballot, you get deregistered. Slowly, we enforced the law. And that took about ... until '66. 1966, '67 we were still having trouble, including our own government daily rated unions because they were infected ... by all these militant ideas ...

"The turning point came in two ways. First, our two years in Malaysia. People realised that if we want to be out of the communal grip ... we've got to put our house in order, we can't go back to the old ways, then we will be ruined ... So that was a critical turning point.

"The other turning point was, in 1968, the British decided to withdraw. ... we had to work hard and build up our own defences. And I think from then onwards, something happened in the population; they recognised that they were in trouble. ...

"I think from then onwards, we either made it or we didn't, and we made it. So I was able to move fundamental laws – giving the right to hire and fire, to manage, to promote, to transfer – back to the employers because the unions had captured all those rights. So I passed the Employment Act and I passed the Industrial Relations Act. I changed the structure to make sure that unions were a complementary part of the production process, not a disruptive part."

"Fortunately, an answer was possible, given the favourable economic conditions of the world in the 1960s. A hardworking people, willing and not slow to learn new tasks, given a sense of common purpose, clear direction and leadership – these were the ingredients that turned adversity to advantage. Instead of a capital city suffering from ever increasing pressure from the drift of population from the rural areas in search of jobs in the bright lights of the city, we were able to check the drift of rural people and regulate the flow to such numbers as were manageable and useful to our economy.

"We developed an economy in which the enterprise of American, European, and Japanese MNCs transformed British military bases into industrial facilities for manufacturing, and for servicing of ships, oil rigs, aircraft, telecommunications, banking and insurance. Manufacturing, which formed 11.4 per cent of the GNP in 1960, more than doubled to 25.4 per cent in 1977. When the British decided to withdraw from their bases in January 1968, British military spending constituted 12.7 per cent of Singapore's GNP in 1967. What threatened to be a major economic setback was converted into an economic opportunity, as military facilities and the technicians working them were released for productive civilian industries …

"What made Singapore different in the 1960s from most other countries of Southeast Asia was that she had no xenophobic hangover from colonialism. The statue of the founder of Singapore, Sir Stamford Raffles, still stands in the heart of the city to remind Singaporeans of his vision in 1819 of Singapore becoming, on the basis of free competition, the emporium of the East, on the route between India and China. There were then 120 people on the island. They lived by fishing. Within five years of its founding, there were 5,000 traders – British, Arabs, Chinese, Indians, and others drawn in by this principle of free and equal competition, regardless of race, language or religion. Had the Dutch who governed the then Netherlands East Indies accorded these same ground rules to what made Singapore different in trade and commerce in the Indonesian archipelago, Singapore might never have got started. These were our origins. So we have never suffered from any inhibitions in borrowing capital, knowhow, managers, engineers, and marketing capabilities. Far from limiting the entry of foreign managers, engineers, and bankers, we encouraged them to come.

"Singaporeans were smart enough to recognise those more enterprising than themselves. That was the key to our rapid development."

*(Speech at the 26th World Congress of the International Chamber of Commerce, October 5, 1978)*

And so foreign investors were courted with a liberal economic policy which included attractive tax and fiscal incentives. For instance, they could lease land and buildings cheaply and quickly while tax exemptions were given to companies which the government wanted to attract. Tariff protection and exemption from import duties were allowed under certain circumstances, and there was no restriction on the repatriation of profits and capital.

Foreign investors responded well to these incentives. From 1965 to 1975, the value of foreign asset holdings in manufacturing increased 24-fold, from $157 million to

# We are revolutionaries

When the Rotary Club invited Lee Kuan Yew, who was then an opposition member of parliament, to address its members, he turned down the request because the People's Action Party's political beliefs then ran counter to the interests of the club.

Modern-day readers would find it amazing that the party once could not see eye to eye with captains of industry and those who were generally successful within the establishment, as Rotary Club members were and still are. But the PAP was a revolutionary party then, formed with the objective of overturning the existing social order and replacing it with its own socialist beliefs. But having formed the government in 1959, Lee was also only too aware that the economic realities facing the country compelled the party to work within the limitations of what was essentially an entrepôt economy. He explained the party's economic and political objectives when he finally addressed the club in February 1960.

"A whole set of political principles and socialist beliefs have often been summed up in the PAP phrase, 'a more just and equal society'. By this, the PAP does not mean that all men are equal and will be rewarded equally. Men are not born equal in either physical or mental capacity. But a socialist believes that society as a whole will benefit, and there will be more happiness for more people, if all are given equal opportunities for education and advancement regardless of class or property. It therefore follows that even under the new social order there will be some men who are more successful than others, but with this fundamental distinction, that they have become more successful after free and equal competition and effort.

"The PAP is basically a revolutionary and not a reformist movement, and the social and economic forces which threw the PAP into power have not altered. Although it is not practical or possible to have a profound change of social organisation by a major shift in the relations between social classes because of the entrepôt island economy of Singapore, it is nevertheless important to remember that the have-nots, who form the mass of the workers – the underprivileged, the underemployed and the unemployed, are seeking a change in their position in society. A government of Singapore which represents these urges cannot modify its social programme or political principles without forfeiting the trust and confidence that have been placed upon it by the underprivileged. Such a government can trim its economic programme to fit into the limitations of an entrepôt island economy only if a strenuous effort is made to redress the economic balance by a redistribution of social and economic benefits."

*(Text of speech on page 343)*

$3,739 million. Hand in hand with this laissez-faire policy, the government played a strong interventionist role in key areas of the economy, especially in those ventures which the private sector was reluctant to enter. Wholly owned and partly owned industrial and commercial ventures were set up, either through the finance ministry or through statutory boards.

Throughout, Lee and the government were not afraid to learn from the experience of others: to try out new approaches and new ventures, to capitalise on the successes and learn from the failures.

"We had learned from the difficulties of other developing countries which had been ahead of us in economic development and industrialisation. As a result, today, textiles and garments constitute about 5 per cent of our domestic exports, compared to 50 per cent of Hongkong exports. We consciously sought more skill-intensive and less export-sensitive industries like machine tools, electronic meters, miniature ball-bearings. Such industries need workers who are literate and skilled in working machines. They can employ more managers, engineers, and technicians from our two universities and two polytechnics for the same 1,000 workers on the factory floor.

"We invested heavily in our younger generation since they were our most precious resource; education was universal and was both academic and technical and from primary to tertiary levels. Because we had a trained and educated workforce ready, industries needing such a workforce came and set up operations in Singapore. And because they employed more sophisticated and automated machines, they could pay higher wages. This raised general wage rates and forced the low-wage factories to do likewise, increasing productivity by using better machines, or to move to a low-wage country.

"The older factories, whose products had a high labour content – flour mills, sawmills, textiles, simple assembly of integrated circuits – stopped expansion in Singapore. Some have moved out, first to Malaysia, and later to Indonesia. Some have moved to Thailand. Others are planning to move to Sri Lanka and Bangladesh.

"Small Singapore shipyards are expanding abroad instead of in Singapore. Singaporean shipbuilders and ship-repairers are in joint ventures with Philippines, and are discussing terms with Bangladesh. Singapore entrepreneurs, like the MNCs, are caught in the cycle of change, as rising costs and keener competition force them to look for new low-wage countries with good workers and stable social and political conditions. Only then can they stay competitive. The government actively encourages this for the transfer of labour-intensive industries frees valuable land and labour in Singapore for higher skill and capital-intensive factories.

"Learning from scratch in the Singapore experience proved a costly business. For Singaporean entrepreneurs to go into industry when their past experience has been entrepôt trading, the least hazardous way is to choose an experienced and expert guide."

(*Speech at the 26th World Congress of the International Chamber of Commerce, October 5, 1978*)

# How many engineers does it take to run the economy?

*Getting the skills right: Engineering students at Singapore Polytechnic – the country's first – learning to repair a colour television in 1972.*

One key aspect of running an efficient and modern economy was in training the population in all the requisite skills required by the global economy. This meant producing enough engineers, technicians, draughtsmen, production operators, drivers and a hundred other types of artisans and skilled workers. For a small country like Singapore with a limited pool of workers, training them to have the right skills was even more important. Lee, ever the pragmatist, demonstrated his attention to practical detail when he addressed Singapore Polytechnic students in January 1972.

"I asked for some figures from the Education Ministry, and they said to train an ordinary academic secondary school student costs us $300 per year, per student. If you send that student into a secondary technical stream, that means he goes twice a week to some vocational centre where he learns to do technical drawing and metalwork, woodwork and so on, the cost goes up to about $420. You send that student to a vocational institute, his cost is $800 a year, which is more than twice that of the ordinary secondary academic school student because of the benches he requires, the space he occupies, the equipment that he must be supplied with. And you can, of course, take this on to tertiary institutions and, broadly speaking, we are subsidising the cost of an engineering student, the subsidy per year is between $4,000 and $5,000, and the subsidy on the polytechnic student is anywhere between $2,000 and $3,000 a year.

"Therefore, we are presented with a very difficult problem of priorities. How many engineers do you produce for a certain number of skilled workers and technicians? We have had endless arguments on the matter. If you follow the American system then you produce probably one engineer for every two technicians, which is what they do in America. And the engineers do the jobs of the technicians. They are more highly paid. Or you take the British system where there is a clear demarcation between the pragmatic trained technician and the engineer who is the theorist-cum-pragmatist, and the ratio works out to about 8 to 1.

"Well, for the time being, we have decided, not because we are convinced that the British system is right but because of the economics of it, that it is probably more sensible for us to produce more technicians than engineers. And as we progress, we will have to review this. In five years, we make a review and another ten years, we make a second review. And the guiding factors will be what is the best possible way, given our peculiar, almost unique circumstances, to mobilise our manpower and train them."

*(Text of speech on page 347)*

# How the world ticks

Lee's pragmatic approach, however, is not without some deeply held beliefs about what makes the world go round. How does a country improve its standard of living, what is it that lifts a country to higher levels of wealth? While there might be any number of economic theories to explain all this, Lee's account is interesting for the insights it offers into how a pragmatist like him explains the intricacies of economic development.

"I now know that a lot of the stuff I was reading about factors of production and exploitation of labour by owners of capital – that's exaggerated and often bunkum!

"Supposing the colonialists and the imperialists never came to Africa or never came to Singapore and we were left to our own devices, you and I would not be here today. Why should you come? Why should our forefathers have risked their lives in junks to come here? What for? To catch fish? To plant tapioca?

"Now, of course, having gone through this, having had practical experience of how the economy works, how the world has evolved and having read so much more now of economic history and futurology or futuristic assessments of the future, it's quite clear what works and what doesn't work. The history of man has been a history of his need to get access to more resources, to satisfy his needs as his population expands. So at any one time in a given state of technology for a given population, he soon multiplies to reach the maximum. That's the way human reproduction has been. You reach your maximum population when you can no longer have the resources to feed it because otherwise you just keep on multiplying.

"When you reach your limit, there are two ways out of that box that you are in. One is to reach new resources by either capturing territory or trading.

"To capture, you have to use force and you must win or you are captured. … And from the very beginning of time, tribes have gone on to capture more territory for resources to expand, so the more vigorous tribes expanded. And so big nations grew out of these tribes, and so the biggest of them with the best leaders captured the most territory.

"Or you trade, and what he has, you don't have, you take. And what you have and he doesn't have, you give. That enables you to get more resources and feed a bigger population.

"The other is a scientific breakthrough where a man's ingenuity is able to manipulate nature. So you build reservoirs, you save water. So a dry area, you can irrigate. You build dams … you get coal and you build power stations, and you save labour and you use machines. So it is technology and trade that has enabled the world to develop. There's a limit to what trade you can do if you stay put at that technology. But when you break through to a different level of technology, then you've got another breathing space, more areas to fill up.

"Supposing we never had the technology of highrise living, I think we would find no way to house three million people if we were confined to attap houses, right? One floor, you can't house three million people. But the technology of highrise with lifts, power, electricity, water, compaction of refuse, disposal of refuse, has enabled people to live comfortably on limited land. So two things have contributed to this transformation of the world – technology and trade.

"If you stop world trade today and say 'right, all countries will be self-supporting', I think everybody is going to get desperately poor in a very short while. You have an excess of apples which nobody wants to eat. And we'll have an excess of human beings whom nobody wants to use.

"But because the world works on the basis of exchange and improving your production by bringing in new technology, we are playing a critical role in directing the spread of finance to sponsor and seed these new projects, the ability to bring in people who are going to manage these new projects, to build a dam, the power stations, to repair things and so on. And we are providing a service that's helping these countries develop."

## What made Singapore work?

Having a clearly defined objective and a pragmatic appreciation of the workings of a modern economy would have counted for nothing if Lee could not make Singaporeans understand what was needed to make the grade and if he could not mobilise them. The key to achieving this was to put in place a system that would encourage the people to work hard for themselves and their families, and so ultimately for the economy. As always, he was characteristically blunt about these things, choosing to speak honestly and frankly to the people.

*Opposite: Lee Kuan Yew and Mrs Lee surveying the transformation of the island from Telok Blangah Hill in November 1989. Lee said he was "surprised that we have done it so quickly in one generation, from rags to riches … It's not been done, I think, by many people."*

"At international conferences they use fine words about the application of science and technology to industry, but seldom about sheer sweat and elbow grease. That is what makes Singapore work. Whatever the shortcomings, people do work.

"The … factor which helps us is that we have not got deep class divisions. Social mobility is half the secret of Singapore's success: from rags to riches, from riches down the ladder. When you have social mobility, then you haven't that animosity and antagonism. Looking back over the last decade, one of the reasons why the communists failed was that they worked in a class hatred which was not there. I am not saying it could not come. If we classify our society – and all the scions of the rich and successful go to separate schools, then they could develop a special accent of their own. One of the reasons for the antagonism of the British worker to management is that he is branded by his accent. You can make a million pounds but you are still Billy Butlin because you talk like one. The workers resent this and they take it out by denying the boss his full day's work. In Singapore, irrespective of your father's wealth, background or status, you enjoy the same opportunities from primary school to university.

"Let me put in a positive way what we want:

"First, a striving acquisitive community. You cannot have people just striving for a nebulous ideal. They must have that desire to improve, whether it is the scooter, the mini car, the flat, the fridge, the washing machine, the television set, better shoes, better clothes or better homes. You must equate rewards to performance because no two persons want to be the same. They want equal chances in order that they can show how one is better than

# What's wrong with being a bus driver?

*How to get more to join the Singapore Bus Service crew? This may be dismissed by some as a petty problem, but not to Lee, who brought it to national attention.*

Managing an economy is not just about grand plans. For Lee it meant persuading, rallying, sometimes even scolding the people. His standards were high, his ability to see the big picture widely acknowledged. But his great strength as a politician was his ability to talk to people using language and illustrations they could understand. On economic development, this meant putting issues such as their jobs, pay or relationship with their bosses in terms they could relate to. No issue was too trivial or routine for him if it was symptomatic of a bigger problem or if, by bringing it out into the open, it held out wider lessons for all. In this quintessentially Lee speech, he spoke of his surprise that Singaporeans were turning down good-paying jobs as bus drivers.

"Recently, we mounted an exercise to recruit drivers for the Singapore Bus Service. You know that we have got to have more buses to have a good bus service, and you need good drivers. So we thought that the National Serviceman who had learned how to drive a three-ton truck should be offered the opportunity. So we mounted three recruitment exercises …

"Ten years ago, if you introduced a man into the Singapore Traction Company or into a Chinese bus company as a driver, he would have been happy to have given you his one month's salary as commission. We circularised the posts. About 800 National Servicemen went on ROD [Run Out Date, the date their full-time National Service ends] between January and July. About 500 turned up to listen to the opportunities we were offering them. SBS produced a colour brochure, 'The Bus Way to a Secure Future' … You know how many applied? Seven the first batch, 34 the second batch, 20 the third. You know how many are working now? One driver and three temporary conductors training to be drivers. Remarkable! Whilst training you are paid $11.60 per day, one year, as recruits. Then $12.80. This bewildered me. I chased up the Central Manpower Base. I said, 'What are they doing? What marvellous jobs are they holding?' Because I got the monthly returns as to how many workers are retrenched, how many work permits issued. … in the last 18 months since the retrenchment started, 30,000 workers have been retrenched, 70 per cent women and girls. But I just took this year, January to July; of the 7,500 retrenched, 4,800 – nearly 4,900 – were women. In those same seven months, we issued 11,500 work permits of which 4,400 were for women. It does not square up.

"What happened to these National Servicemen? They had primary six and secondary two – the highest levels. Many of them were just sitting at home! Some had gone out into the reserves in January. Forty or 50 are still unemployed. They go in at 18; they finish at 20. They only have a class 3 for driving a three-ton truck. You have got to be 21 before you take a class 4 to drive a bus. Originally, in the second batch, eight went in. They were asked – whilst practising to drive a bus and waiting to reach the age of 21 – to sell tickets. They said *pai-sei* [shy]. They liked their passengers behind them and did not want to face each chap to sell a ticket. This is the new generation Singaporean."

*(National Day Rally speech, August 17, 1975; text on page 351)*

the other. This is a fact of life, which even the communists have had to admit. The constitution of Romania, a socialist country, says that each man shall be rewarded in accordance with what he contributes, not 'to each in accordance with his needs'.

"Next, we want forward-looking good management. The old family business is one of the problems in Singapore. It is not so with European or foreign enterprise. One of the reasons for our floating an industrial development bank [Development Bank of Singapore, now DBS Bank] is because of the sluggishness with which people change habits. They are accustomed to buying and selling. And business is kept in the family. They have done this for hundreds of years. And the idea of sinking money into an anonymous corporation run by professionals over whom they have no direct personal control is foreign to them. They are loathe to make this change. So we have to accelerate this process. Business management is a professional's job and we need professionals to run our business effectively.

"And third, easy social mobility. One of the reasons contributing to Japanese and German recovery was that their … capitalists, managers, executives, engineers and their … workers all suffered defeat and they were fired with a singleness of purpose: to put their country back on its feet. That made the miracle of recovery. If the Japanese worker and the German worker had felt that his job in life was to defeat his employer and deny him that profit because he was being kept one down by the employer's son going to a public school and acquiring all those graces in life which were denied the worker's son, then he was bound to be sluggish and inefficient."

*(Speech at an annual dinner of the Singapore Employers Federation, May 10, 1968)*

The structure Lee established to achieve those three aims he set out in 1968 had one simple objective: rewarding hard work and enterprise. For all the complicated theories which modern economics has spun over the last century or so about what governments can and should do to achieve growth, there seems none as important as this. Without a system of rewards, why would a population strive to achieve ever higher living standards?

"First, you must have a structure in your society which makes learning and hard work rewarding. In other words, to study, to learn, to be an effective worker, either a carpenter, a welder, or a computer programmer, or whatever. That must equate to success, to rewards.

"If you have a system where the chap who cuts corners is a man who gets rich and the man who studies hard is the chap who's a mug, then you will fail. And that's what's wrong in many countries which have not succeeded … So you must, first, have that structure in place. To do that, you need order, discipline. And that's what's wrong with the Philippines.

"Second, you must create conditions where capital plus knowledge can be matched with workers with the skills and at a price that makes it productive. So whether it is machines to build factories, to make tape-recorders or radios, or whether it is to run a department store, they need capital. You just don't have a Takashimaya out of nothing. Somebody has built Takashimaya over 160 years in Japan and accumulated all the techniques of how to have high-class marketing. And they have decided we have a structure here that's worth

# We don't understand management

Increasing the Singapore workers' productivity was a major preoccupation of Lee's. He knew it was the only way forward for Singapore and was determined to get everyone else to understand this, even if it meant being brutally frank, as he was in remarks made in August 1981, a classic Lee speech delivered by a tough-talking prime minister who wanted to put across a difficult concept in terms people could grasp easily.

"My meeting with the American, German, Japanese, Singapore National Employers Federation ... was most instructive. The most disturbing facet of my discussion, reading their submission, was that if we had to depend on Singapore entrepreneurs we would not have today's Singapore. It's a damning admission for me as prime minister to tell you this. But I think you should know that.

"... We may have been traders, but we do not understand management. Our managers do not understand productivity. Otherwise how can I get a submission from the Chinese Chamber of Commerce telling me, 'Why should we confine CPF being managed by employers, to only big employers of 300 or more employees? We, small shopkeepers, can also handle it.' I don't think they have the slightest clue ...

"The Germans made this point: 'The Singapore paradox ... it is well known throughout the world that the workers of Singapore are busy and industrious. One can easily see this when looking around the Kallang area – small marine wharves build ships with the highest skill. One finds this in any area where demand for performance matches the ability to perform and the worker concerned can identify with the fate of the enterprise involved.

"'Touring the shopping centres, factories, office buildings, one often observes that operators or clerks are not in the least interested in the fate of the enterprise; just chatting and being nonproductive. ... To be successful you must instil a certain high-fidelity, feeling in something. That means a sense of loyalty, a sense of trustworthiness – high-fidelity. ... Management's problem is that they should not forget that not only the brains and the hands but also the hearts of people should be working for the company.' That's well put – not only brains and hands but get the workers' hearts. ... That's exactly what the Japanese have been doing.

"[The Japanese made this point.] On the anniversary of the company, they invited the workers to bring all their families to come and celebrate. Nobody came! The family is not interested in the future of the company. So he said, 'Why is this? Maybe it's the wrong format. So all right, Chinese New Year we invited them. They all came. Well, that's progress.' His worker gets married, he turns up for the worker's wedding. He is interested in the future of his worker. ... And he says, 'It's very strange, you know, I was not introduced to the father-in-law, the mother-in-law and so on. We just sat around.' I said, 'Well, you know, we inherited the British tradition and British bosses never attend the weddings of their workers. They were probably honoured but embarrassed and at a loss what to do.'

"But the heart of the worker, that's what productivity is about."

(*Text of speech on page 355*)

operating in because their skills, their knowledge, their capital plus our labour and our consumers will make it profitable. So it must be a match. And if you don't create that, nobody will come in.

"And many poor countries don't have the capital. Now we have the capital. When we started we didn't have the capital. When we started earning, we started putting money aside through CPF [Central Provident Fund] and built up the capital. Now, we have the capital to go to China, or Vietnam, or Indonesia, or India or wherever. But these countries need a lot of capital from our side. We don't have enough to get China or India going. But America, Europe, Japan, they have the capital. And you've got to make it productive."

Of course, it helps tremendously if, together with a structure that rewards hard work and enterprise, the people working it are by nature hard-driving and intelligent.

"The critical factor? The quality of your people. Are they hardworking? Do they learn quickly? How well can they do the job?

"I think the critical advantage is the people. If we were lazy and not good at mathematics, conceptualisation and science, our engineers would not have replaced the Dutch or the Germans or the Americans, and these factories would be employing expats at very heavy costs and may never have expanded so well.

"But we were able to fill up those jobs, we were as good as the American or Dutch engineers or the Japanese engineers. Well, the Japanese don't think so, so they keep a lot of their top jobs still Japanese.

"But it is the quality of the population. First, have they got the capabilities to be educated to that level? Second, have you given them the facilities and have they made the effort?"

What was required then was a rigorous and sound education system which in the early years of a country's development must be geared to the needs of the economy.

"I think what is universally true of most new countries is that they inherited a system of education, which very often was carried on unthinkingly by indigenous independent governments for five, ten years with very serious repercussions for their own development and resulting in unemployment.

"You find countries like Ghana, for instance, which in West Africa has been exposed to contacts with the West for several centuries. Before the British, there were the Danes and the early slave traders. They are people who have acquired quite a degree of sophistication, the ones on the coast as distinct from the ones in the hinterland. And the British have produced among them Greek scholars, Latin scholars. The Vice-Chancellor of the University of Ghana was a Greek and Latin scholar. But they did not produce engineers, technicians who could have run the Volta High Dam for them. Or perhaps more relevant, they did not produce good scientists in agriculture, in fertilisers, in how to make their economy move from a relatively simple agricultural pastoral base into something more productive.

# Many little regrets, but no basic errors

Lee looks back on 30 years of economic progress with satisfaction and a little surprise, and he has few misgivings about the way the economy has turned out.

He told the authors that he was "surprised that we have done it so quickly in one generation, from rags to riches, in 30 years, slightly over a generation ... It's not been done, I think, by many people."

But, he added, "Surprised in the sense that it was an unexpected result? No, I think by '75, '76, when we overcame the first oil crisis ... we were on course and recovering ... It wasn't a fluke. We were on course, we had a trim economy, we had people, we had people in charge in MTI [Ministry of Trade and Industry], in Finance, who knew how to manage the economy. We had workers who were able and managers who were able to adjust.

"From then onwards, it was a matter of how fast we could go. We were already airborne, we had taken off. The economy had taken off. Had we still been on the ground waiting for the takeoff, and the oil crisis came, we may have had a more difficult time. ...

"There're many small regrets. Mistakes here, mistakes there. You know, like trying to do shipbuilding when we didn't have an iron and steel industry and we were buying steel plates from Japan or Korea at high cost. We could have saved ourselves the trouble.

"Somebody should have said to us: Look, this is only if you also have iron and steel and then you've got cheap raw materials – cheap supplies of basic materials, not raw materials. Because if you want to build a ship, you need a lot of steel sheets. And we couldn't go into iron and steel because we'd pollute the whole of Singapore.

"No, this was in the late '70s. So without iron and steel, how could we go into shipbuilding? We could have saved ourselves. We built several Freedom vessels and licensing from the Japanese, IHI, 10,000-, 12,000-tons – not worth it.

"Many little regrets, but no basic errors."

"At the other end of the scale are India and Pakistan – highly developed educational sectors, universities well-endowed and prepared. They got into a position where they were producing unemployed engineers because the economic development was not keeping pace with the engineers they were producing – the net result being, their doctors migrated. As British doctors migrated to America for better jobs, Indians and Pakistanis filled British hospitals.

"And the lesson is that everybody has got to take a hardheaded look at his own position, decide in the context of his own base, the potential that it has, what is the next step forward. And for us the most important single thing is, of course, the development of our human resources, exploiting our strategic location which makes possible certain industries."

*(Speech to Singapore Polytechnic students in January 1972; text on page 347)*

No one can deny today Singapore's economic achievements. The success has been achieved by a combination of hard work, a strong and determined leadership, enlightened economic policies, political stability and a culture which encouraged thrift and learning. And of course, Lee's almost single-minded determination to transform Singapore's economic base. Critics have sometimes attacked this aspect of the country's development, that it has devoted too much to the economy at the expense of its political and cultural development. Lee is completely unapologetic about this and is as convinced today as he was 38 years ago that for any government and people, economic development must be the number one priority.

"Absolutely. If not that, what are you talking about? You're talking about misery and poverty. You're talking about Rwanda or Bangladesh, or Cambodia, or the Philippines. They've got democracy, according to Freedom House [a human rights group]. But have you got a civilised life to lead?

"… People want economic development first and foremost. The leaders may talk something else. You take a poll of any people. What is it they want? The right to write an editorial as you like? They want homes, medicine, jobs, schools. No, no, no, there's no question about it."

# End of History? Asia's Just Beginning

6

*Opposite: As the drama of the pro-democracy protests at Tiananmen Square unfolded, Lee was convinced that these students would meet a tragic end.*

The world watched spellbound for five weeks in 1989, as China's supreme leaders stood powerless before a crowd of thousands of protesting students who besieged Tiananmen Square, demanding reform. As the crowds swelled and the students' cries rose in pitch, communist party leaders were split over how to deal with the unruly crowd – should they try to mollify the young demonstrators, or assert their authority through the proverbial barrel of a gun? The impasse dragged on, culminating in a statue of the Goddess of Democracy being erected in the square, an affront to those at the helm. To their early chants against corruption and inefficiency, as well as a lack of openness and democracy in the system, were added little doggerels and barbs directed at China's paramount chiefs, including Deng Xiaoping, the country's paramount leader. Students in the university campus threw bottles out of their windows, an obvious play on the leader's name, which sounds like the Mandarin words for "small bottle". On May 20, martial law was declared in parts of Beijing. Deng backed a military solution to the crisis. But popular support for the students prevented the armed forces from moving against them, prolonging the impasse.

Back in Singapore, Lee followed these developments with more than a casual interest. As events unfolded, he sensed that a firm reaction from China's leaders would soon come. At about midnight on June 3, the tanks started to roll.

"The students asked for trouble at Tiananmen. I was watching the TV every night, fascinated. And the slogans were changing. The early slogan was an attack on corruption and on nepotism and inefficiency, and that won the support of Zhao Ziyang and company. There's a strong body of opinion in the Communist Party which says, 'We've got to put this right.'

"Then as it gathered steam and more and more people joined them, it shifted. And it became an attack on individuals within the party, including Li Peng.

"In the final stages, the last 10 days, I saw slogans attacking Deng Xiaoping. When I saw that, I said, boy, this is it. This Chinese government, Deng Xiaoping as the leader, cannot govern if you can do that and get away with it, because the Chinese people will lose respect for you. I was convinced they were going to get whacked, and they were whacked."

Why was Lee so sure about the explosion that was to take place at Tiananmen? The simple answer is that he understood well the nature of Asian societies and the way in which they had been governed for centuries. Leaders in these societies were expected to lead. They were looked up to, and granted a high degree of respect and deference in recognition of their role in providing for their people and improving their lives. Good, honest leaders who were able to deliver the goods were considered worthy of the people's support. Those who were corrupt, ineffective, or unable to assert their authority were dismissed.

This basic principle of power and allegiance would shape Lee's political beliefs, leadership style and public persona more than any great tracts of political theories. As leader, he was firm. As the island republic's elected head of government, he was decidedly in charge. Critics and those who opposed him knew they would be countered without compunction. He once remarked that if he found an obstacle in the way of a policy or goal he thought needed to be achieved, he would not hesitate to run a bulldozer to clear the way. No one imagined for a moment that the remark was made in jest.

A more recent example was the case of Dr Catherine Lim, a Singapore academic. In 1994, she wrote a series of critical commentaries on Lee's successor as prime minister, Goh Chok Tong. Many believed she was unlikely to have penned the piece if Lee were still at the helm. The writer, it was widely thought, would not have contemplated taking Lee on in such a public manner. Lee too was of this view.

"Let me put it like this. Supposing Catherine Lim was writing about me and not the prime minister … She would not dare, right? Because my posture, my response has been such that nobody doubts that if you take me on, I will put on knuckle-dusters and catch you in a cul-de-sac … Anybody who decides to take me on needs to put on knuckle-dusters. If you think you can hurt me more than I can hurt you, try. There is no other way you can govern a Chinese society."

The nature of leadership and how this related to the needs, desires and aspirations of a people were matters Lee pondered from his early years in politics. Not for him the notion that all men yearned for democratic freedoms, prizing free speech and the vote over other needs such as economic development. Asian societies, he contended, were different, having evolved separately from the West over the centuries.

He made this point in a BBC interview in 1977:

"… I often wonder whether the foreign journalist, or the casual visitor like you, has fathomed or can fathom the mind of an Oriental. And I am having to look after Orientals, whether they are of Chinese descent or Malay or Indian or Eurasian or Ceylonese and so on. What's inside is completely different: Is this a good government that I can trust to look after me and my family, and will see that my children are educated and will have a job better than mine, and have a home better than mine? Is it fair or is it unfair and unjust, favouring its relatives, its friends; looting the public purse for its relatives, for itself so that ministers live in luxury whilst the masses live in squalor?

"Those are the crucial issues because those are the issues that have toppled governments in the Third World. You can ask any taxi driver – he is a most uninhibited Singaporean you can think of. You can ask any bartender in any hotel. He'll let off a bellyache. But at the end of the day, when he puts his cross, when election comes, he has given me and my colleagues over seventeen and a half years – come June, eighteen years in office … which I think is cause for some satisfaction."

*(Interview with the British Broadcasting Corporation, March 1977; text of interview on page 369)*

Firm, decisive, farsighted. Those were the hallmarks of Lee's political leadership. Some called his style authoritarian, even autocratic. He cared not a jot. Having studied the nature of the society he was charged with, he believed that "there was no other way" to lead his people forward.

"My idea of popular government is that you don't have to be popular all the time when you are governing … There are moments when you have to be thoroughly unpopular. But at the end of your term, you should have brought about sufficient benefits so that the people realise what you did was necessary and will vote for you again. That is the basis on which I have governed. If you want to be popular all the time, you will misgovern …"

# Journey from the Left

How Lee came round to these views about political leadership and governance is mainly a story about his experience operating the system in Singapore, and his observations about how it was working or, as was sometimes the case, not working in various parts of the world. He had begun his own intellectual journey through the political theories and ideas of his time in the 1950s, from a very different starting point as a democratic socialist. The manner in which he changed his views along the way is a fascinating story of how Lee, when confronted with the fact that reality and observation did not quite conform to ideology, plumbed decidedly for the former.

"The world that I lived in was a very unequal world, and unjust. The whites were on top. You might be a good doctor, but if you are an Asian, you would be under a white doctor who's not as good … The injustice of it all, the discrimination, struck me and everybody else. We became strongly against the system.

# How the PAP mustered the vote

*Lee's election poster during the 1972 general election appealed to the voters' trust in the PAP's performance.*

Lee's doubts about the viability of the democratic system in developing countries begs an ironical question: How is it his PAP government, which never shied from taking "tough and unpopular measures", was able to win decisively at the ballot box time and time again, over 10 elections. If the democratic system was as flawed as he believed, what explained the fact that the people of Singapore backed his party? Was the Singapore experience a counter to Lee's own doubts about democracy? Lee thought not. Rather, he believed Singapore and the PAP survived through a combination of fortuitous circumstances. The sharp shock delivered by the traumas of Singapore's early years as an independent state was a key to this.

"I'm absolutely convinced that if we had never had Malaysia, if the British had just given us independence, we would have failed because we would have continued with the stupidities, the excesses, the riots, the strikes, the go-slows, the ethnic quarrels over languages. And we would have decided on Chinese as the national language, or Chinese as one of the major languages or the major language, and we would have failed.

"But that two years' experience had a very salutary effect in bringing about a realisation that this was a matter of life and death. And if we did not pull ourselves together and rein ourselves in and stop these excesses, we would die. That was how it happened. It wasn't planned that way.

"We made it succeed by very unorthodox methods of mustering the vote. First, we won in '59 on anti-colonialism, and against corruption. Second, we won in '63 on merger and against communism. Third, we won in '68 on the basis of seeing the country through after British withdrawal. Then, because the people recognised that we were determined people, not self-seekers, trust was established, then we could pursue our policies. It was the luck of the draw. It could not be repeated.

"If that was not the issue in '63, we would not have been re-elected. We would have had turnover governments and Singapore would have petered out. If '68 did not turn out that way, we would also not have been re-elected. Supposing it had been differently played, Singapore would have gone the way of other countries."

"I sympathised with the underdog because, in a way, I was an underdog under that system. But I was a privileged underdog among underdogs because my family was comfortably off and I was educated. But I could understand how the other underdogs felt. I started off on the premise that if we helped them, then they could be like us. That was the premise which turned out to be only partly true …

"At that time, I could not accept communism … emotionally, I rejected it because it was coercive, it used methods which I disapproved of … A chap disagrees and you stab him and kill him. There is no give-and-take …

"Capitalism at that time was associated with the British … When I studied economics in Raffles College, I was taught by a white professor who was paid three or four times the Chinese lecturer, who was paid ten times the Chinese tutor … the system was just wrong. We had native capitalists, a few Chinese rubber merchants, bankers, shopkeepers, small-time manufacturers … But capitalism benefited the people with the resources and the power … We decided that capitalism was wrong. We rejected it.

"When I found in Britain this idea of doing it the democratic way, by argument, by the vote, by gradualism, by taxing the rich and helping the poor, it was so emotionally attractive and, conceptually, intellectually sound. That in practice it was wrong and it didn't work was not obvious at that time. We believed democratic socialism would achieve maybe 80 per cent of what the communists would achieve, but without the injustices, the rigours and the brutalities of communism.

"Over the years, we recognised the limits and the counterproductive effects of subsidies on the incentive to work, and on training and achievement which are necessary for the creation of wealth for everybody. We did not see that in the early stages. Furthermore, we did not see that you can have a system where the white man is not superior, but he competes on equal terms in his production of superior goods and services.

"Today, the new meaning that capitalism has acquired, which means entrepreneurship, raising capital, putting your ideas into practice, testing the market, if the market accepts your service or your goods, you have created wealth for everybody and for yourself. That was not the way I saw capitalism as a young man."

# I had seen so many fail

Lee's early dabbling with democratic socialism was to be tempered by his observations of how other developing countries had run aground trying to work a democratic system alien to their peoples. Such a system, he concluded, was premised on certain key underlying societal and cultural factors: strong government, leaders with a sense of duty, responsible opposition parties, a mature electorate prepared to endure pain for long-term gain as well as share the responsibility of administering the society. These were taken as given in many of the developed Western countries where democracies were in place. But many of these prerequisites, he felt, were nonexistent in the emerging states, thereby undermining his confidence that the system would take root there. Nor was he overly sanguine about the prospects for democracy in his native Malaya, and later Singapore.

# Me? Why, I am a liberal

Few people, if asked to categorise Lee and his political beliefs, would choose the word "liberal". But this was how he described himself in an exchange with the authors:

Han: How would you describe your political beliefs, if you were a democratic socialist in the '50s?

Lee: Today, I would describe myself as a ... [long pause] ... in perhaps European terms, between socialists and conservatives, I would put myself as a liberal. As someone who believes in equal opportunities so that everybody gets an equal chance to do his best, and with a certain compassion to ensure that the failures do not fall through the floor.

I would put myself really as a ... [pause] ... a liberal democrat. Not in the Japanese sense of the word, the Liberal Democratic Party. A liberal, in that I want to run the system as efficiently as possible, but make allowances for those who will not be doing well because nature did not give them enough, or they cannot make that extra effort.

Han: That might surprise some people, that you would describe yourself as a liberal.

Lee: A liberal in the economic sense of the word, you know. Not a liberal in the sense of the American word "liberal". The American word "liberal" means somebody who thinks that you should allow everybody to develop in his own way and do his own thing. So, that has a special meaning.

But a liberal in the classical sense of that word, in that I'm not fixated to a particular theory of the world, or of society. I'm pragmatic. I'm prepared to look at the problem and say, all right, what is the best way to solve it that will produce the maximum happiness and well-being for the maximum number of people. You call it whatever you like.

He had these doubts about the viability of democracy in developing states as early as the 1960s.

> "There are vagaries about the system of one-man-one-vote which make it an extremely hazardous system to run anywhere in the underdeveloped and the under-educated world … the system of cutting up the country in accordance with the number of adult citizens of given proportions, to elect representatives who then elect among like-minded people a Cabinet which then elects a *primus inter pares* among the Cabinet, is one which presupposes so many basic conditions which are often nonexistent. … They have all been superseded by systems which give power effectively to one man or a group of men, for an indefinite period.
>
> "Government, to be effective, must at least give the impression of enduring, and a government which is open to the vagaries of the ballot box … is a government which is already weakened before it starts to govern.
>
> "… if I were in authority in Singapore indefinitely, without having to ask those who are governed whether they like what is being done, then I have not the slightest doubt that I could govern much more effectively in their own interests. That is a fact which the educated understand, but we are all caught in this system which the British … export all over the place, hoping that somewhere it will take root."

*(Address to the Royal Society of International Affairs in London, May 1962; excerpts on page 365)*

Lee's observations of developing states which had been swept up by the democratic tide only to come crashing down in a wash of disappointment cautioned him against being overly sanguine about the prospects of democracy in his native country.

> "I had seen so many fail. They came into power with such promising circumstances and much optimism, but this failed. The preconditions were not there. These were underdeveloped societies that had no national cohesion to hold them together.
>
> "Burma became independent and failed. Ceylon ran into difficulties by 1955. Solomon Bandaranaike had been assassinated by 1959. India was not successful. Pakistan had several constitutions failed and suspended. The generals took charge, first General Ayub Khan and General Yahya Khan. Then General Zia Ul Haq. These are countries where the British had been, much longer than in Singapore. They had universities. We never had universities. Ceylon had two universities at independence – 1948. India had many renowned universities of standards equal to London University, approximating Cambridge and Oxford. Their standards of examinations were very tough. And they had very bright and able men in the Indian civil service. But the basic preconditions were not there – a cohesive, united people, with universal education and a broad well-educated middle class to provide stability.
>
> "I saw so many governments not working. The Africans started off with great fanfare; Ghana collapsed; Nigeria fell apart. What makes Singaporeans think they are different? Were we better educated? Were we more homogeneous? Did we have more of the factors which will make for a successful functioning democracy?

**"One-man-one-vote" is a relatively new electoral system. Many systems began with unequal votes, with extra votes sometimes given based on the amount of taxes paid, property owned or whether the voter was married. Today plural voting is virtually extinct, in line with the ideal that every man should have an equal right to safeguard his interest. In some countries there are unequal votes for elections to different chambers of the legislature.**

"Remember, when we started, we were not even one society, never mind a nation. We were several different separate societies brought together under the British, an accident of history. Our loyalties and roots were in different parts of China, India and the Malay archipelago."

For Lee, the task of governing Singapore within a democratic system was made doubly difficult as it was a society riven with ethnic and religious divisions, and made up of immigrants, the bulk of whom were poorly educated and unused to democratic procedures.

Indeed, he concluded that there were times when decisions could not simply be a reflection of the majority will. One example was the question of whether Singapore should adopt English or Mandarin as the primary language. Left to the popular will, the Chinese, who formed the majority of the population, and for many of whom the Chinese language and cultural heritage was a source of much passionate pride, would have rooted for Mandarin, he believed. But this would not be in the country's best interests if it was to survive in an increasingly technologically based and English dominated world economy. He therefore went against the popular sentiment of the times.

"We had to intervene. Take some of the major decisions we have made … the problem of resettling our population and trying to make it a more cohesive society. We never took a vote. Had we asked people in Kampong Kembangan whether they wanted to be resettled, the answer must be no. If they had to be resettled, then they wanted to stay together in the same place. Go to Lorong Tai Seng and ask the Hainanese there: Would you like to have a Malay as your neighbour? The answer is no. We decided that if we're going to make a nation, we can't have race riots every now and again. Something brews up and people kill each other on the basis of race as the jerseys they wore. So we simply said, 'Ballot for your flats.'

"People talk about consultation, top-down and bottom-up. These are theories, yardsticks worked out by Western political scientists who have never been presented with the raw, unpleasant, unmanageable facts of making something out of nothing.

"If we took a poll, we would never have had National Service. I simply decided, 'Introduce it.' It was necessary. After a while, everybody understood it was necessary. But it had to be fairly implemented. I can't implement National Service, and my children don't do National Service; that's a disaster!"

Were the views of the people then never heeded? To paint Lee's Singapore as a repressive dictatorship, as some have done, would be to grossly oversimplify the politics of the place. He was mindful of the need to win the people's hearts and minds. But unlike politicians elsewhere, he was adamant that he would do so on his terms and not just bend to the prevailing political winds.

"Discussion is necessary for any successful policy. You have to get acceptance. So even if you don't have a public debate, in the old days, we used to get the MPs to go down and sell the policy at mass meetings, at dinners, constituency groups and so on.

**National Service— After separation from Malaysia, a Singapore defence force was built almost from scratch. Singapore youths signed up for National Service at the Central Manpower Base when registration opened on March 28, 1967. The first batch of National Servicemen was drafted in July 1967.**

# Does the ice-water man understand his vote?

*Ice-water man. "Do you honestly believe that the chap who can't pass primary six knows the consequences of his choice when he answers a question viscerally, on language, culture and religion?" Lee would ask the liberal crowd who championed the right of the man in the street to have a vote on major issues.*

Although Lee was prepared to work the system of representative democracy he had been bequeathed by Singapore's colonial masters, he was not one to believe that matters of state could be settled by consulting the people through referenda or opinion polls. His experience over the years threw up many examples of how people would have plumbed for options which were appealing but might have had disastrous consequences. One of these was the choice of working language for multiracial Singapore.

Lee was in no doubt that the predominantly Chinese populace would have opted for Mandarin. But this would have upset the delicate racial balance in the country, upset its neighbours, and worse of all, hampered the people's ability to ride on the Western – and hence English-dominated – wave of technological progress.

"The big decision was made in 1965 … we had to make a decision. We decided to do it by evolution, not by suddenly deciding, 'Right, English is the working language and we'll also learn our mother tongues.' I think there would have been riots. The Chinese would never have accepted that. So we said, 'We leave things as they are. Don't change it. But parents can decide.' Whether you want to go to a Chinese school, where you learn English [as a second language], or to an English school and learn Chinese or Malay or whatever. Or to a Malay school and learn English, or a Tamil school and learn English.

"By that policy, we knew that over time it would lead to English as the working language, as the lingua franca. Indeed, it turned out that way. Parents would choose a language that offered their children knowledge useful in life, today's life, not yesterday's. … Supposing we had said, 'Let us all do English because it's the working language', I think we would have been in trouble. So we said, 'Choose yourself.' Parents chose. And the Chinese-educated language chauvinists were very, very angry and unhappy with us all those years.

"But there was no better alternative. Supposing we had chosen Chinese or tried to sponsor Chinese, how would we make a living? How would we fit ourselves into the region and into the world? We could not have made a living. But the Chinese then would have wanted it. And if we had taken the vote, we would have had to follow that policy.

"So when people say, 'Oh, ask the people!' It's childish rubbish. We are leaders. We know the consequences. You mean that ice-water man knows the consequences of his vote? Don't tell me that. That's what Western journalists write. No Japanese journalist believes them. No, these are realities. But the West is creating a myth in order that we will follow them. But they haven't got the Japanese to follow them. They will never succeed in persuading the Chinese to follow them. Taiwan will never be like America. Nor will South Korea. Not even Hongkong.

"They say people can think for themselves? Do you honestly believe that the chap who can't pass primary six knows the consequences of his choice when he answers a question viscerally, on language, culture and religion?

"But we knew the consequences. We would starve, we would have race riots. We would disintegrate."

"Every policy I was going to implement I made public, and I made sure that it was made acceptable. But I had consultations on my terms; I wanted accurate feedback to improve the policy and the presentation, not to encourage pressure groups who were out to make me reverse policy. I had a certain view of how to survive and a certain policy to implement to improve things. If I had to modify it to get it accepted, I would modify it.

"What people now mean by consultation is an imitation of what they see in America; pressure groups and lobby groups. So our gays are now fashioning themselves on the West … It's an unthinking adoption of Western patterns of development without any pruning and modification to suit our circumstances."

## Model democracies or cautionary tales?

Lee's experience, at home and abroad, was thus to lead him to the firm view that there was nothing inevitable about democracy. The system was premised on cultural and social assumptions which held in the developed societies of the West, but which were nonexistent in many developing countries.

In the course of several speeches in the 1960s and 1970s, he identified several of the factors underpinning the democratic system which were lacking in many developing societies. The most immediate of these stemmed from the fact that these states were at a stage when the government needed to extract maximum effort out of the people. Development required foregoing consumption, saving, investment, training; in short, a considerable amount of sacrifice and pain.

But the democratic pull went the other way.

"Where the majority of your population is semi-literate, it responds more to the carrot than to the stick, and politicians at election time cannot use the stick. So … he who bids the highest wins. … At a time when you want harder work with less return and more capital investment, one-man-one-vote produces just the opposite …

"Effective government … in an underdeveloped situation means a government that must improve investment rate, that must demand more effort for less return over a sustained period – certainly more than five years. If you can make the demand for a period of two years, produce the results after the fourth, have the results enjoyed by the fifth, then all is well. … unfortunately the process of economic growth is much slower and painful, and neither five nor ten years is an adequate enough period for the demands that you make on a population to be felt and enjoyed by the population. Therefore, the result would be – unless you had exceptional leadership and exceptional circumstances … to take the solution which is least painful. … the least painful solution is not to make undue demands on your population … not to increase investment rate and not to jack up your society …

"Then you are competing against people who not only promise not to maintain the investment rate, but … to spend what there is [already saved] in the kitty … and if an electorate is sufficiently naive to believe that these things can be done, you break the bank …

"... there is an inherent defect in working that system [of one-man-one-vote] when one has to engage in a protracted period of economic growth; and if you had worked this one-man-one-vote in England in the 18th century, you would never have got your industrial revolution. You cannot get your coal miner to say he is going to put in more effort for less in order to build the industrial sinews of the state."

*(Address to the Royal Society of International Affairs in London, May 1962; excerpts on page 365)*

To enable these new states to take off economically, Lee believed that what these countries needed was firm, decisive government, with the staying power to see through its policies, rather than one which would be assailed by the voters and in danger of being tossed out at the next election.

"One curious fact which emerges from the experiments in parliamentary democracy in Asia is that it works only when the governing party has a clear majority and is strong and decisive. Where a government is weak and has not got a clear majority or depends on coalition parties, then the system breaks down as it has in Indonesia, Burma and from time to time in Thailand."

*(Speech at the Legislative Assembly, March 2, 1961)*

He would return to this point year after year. In a talk to civil servants in 1962, he singled out the three necessary conditions for growth and stability.

"Authority has got to be exercised. And when authority is not backed by position, prestige or usage, then it has to defend actively against challenge. But let me explain this. I went to India ... Authority there is not challenged. Mr Nehru is there. He is there and has been there almost as long as the Himalayas. Nobody doubts that he is going to be there as long as he lives. And that immediately produces a stiffening effect ... on the civil service, on the administration, the people. There is the old boy, he is going to be there, never mind all that shouting going on, everybody knows he is the man to trust. ...

"He who exercises authority has got to exercise it with firmness, competence and fairness, and what is most important, with a degree of continuity. ... People expect the state of affairs to develop, change gradually, progress, then they make their calculations accordingly. So that is what is happening in India. But when they don't have this certainty, one day Tweedledum, the next day Tweedledee, everybody has a go at power – then pandemonium. And that is what we must never allow.

"... the three basic essentials for successful transformation of any society. First, a determined leadership, an effective, determined leadership; two, an administration which is efficient; and three, social discipline. If you don't have those three, nothing will be achieved. And that is one of the fatal effects of the democratic system. This business of seasonal change and your civil servants get rattled. They say, 'My God! I'll be in trouble, I'd better succumb. Why not look for something for myself, then whatever happens, I am all right.'

It's all these creeping doubts, this wavering, this wishing to cushion oneself from trouble, that brings a complete sagging of the whole machinery and helps to bring about chaos and collapse."

*(Speech to civil servants, June 14, 1962; text on page 362)*

Lee also came to the conclusion that governments did not necessarily enjoy more support among their people just because they were elected in a democratic process. There were unelected governments that enjoyed more public support because they had been effective in meeting their people's aspirations for a better life.

"Ne Win once was given a chance to run Burma and he made sense out of it. There is no doubt about it. When he took over '57, '58 he whipped the place temporarily into shape. Piles of rubbish on the road, everybody was building right on the roads. That could easily happen in Singapore. Politicians outdo each other in popularity. It's the easy way out. Build an attap hut over the road? Yes, why not? So next chap asks, why not a shop on the road? Yes, carry on. Politicians will supply you with water too. That's the end of progress.

"The General came in and smashed it all. He was not interested in being popular, he was interested in making sense. He ordered the troops out, cleaned up the streets, knocked the houses down, made new roads where they had been planned. When he came in this second time, there was no resistance for two reasons. One, he had proved himself the first time, and second, as the Opposition leaders told me, he was part of the leadership of the original revolution. So he was successful. And he is there to stay.

"Just like Nasser. Nasser makes sense. ... But there is not the slightest doubt that the government in authority is in authority. It is making a sincere, honest and dedicated attempt at transforming the country, brooks no nonsense from anybody and has popular support.

"We arrived at three o'clock in the morning. ... There were chaps in *galabia* [national dress]. They were sitting around the street corners. They cheered madly. They did not know who we were, what we were. Motorcycle sirens going, they thought, well, must be some official party, just give these boys a cheer! Everywhere that was so. Factories, street corners, every time we went out.

"And if you go by constitutional and jurisprudential [theories], that is a bad guide of popular support. There was no popular elections. But the government is popular. Why? Because it has given the people a sense of purpose, it has given them a sense of importance and it's making progress.

"... What was interesting to me, in all these countries, was the fact that there was an effective leadership. These were men in authority who had tremendous worth. They were not men who were diffident about what they were about to do, nor did they lack the nerve to do it. Nehru, Nasser, Tito – they are completely different men but they had these common characteristics."

# Scooting to success

To Lee then, good government was not so much about fine liberal slogans and championing the rights of the people, but more a practical matter of strong leadership which would deliver material progress and improve the people's lot. Voters, he maintained, knew who they could trust to deliver the goods, be it houses, schools, or motorbikes. He made this point in a speech to civil servants in 1962.

*Opposite: Lee, on swaying the voters: "My job as a leader is to make sure that before the next elections, enough had developed and disclosed itself to the people to swing them around. That's the business of a leader. Not to go follow the crowd. That's a washout, the country will go down the drain."*

"When I was in Italy in 1957, everybody – that was the age of the scooter – everybody had a scooter. Five years ago, all Vespas running around. This time I went there and the first thing I noted was all the scooters had been replaced by little Fiats, 600, 500, and chaps who've got Fiats don't go and embark on revolution. They are thinking of the next instalment, how to make sure that they've got the next instalment to pay the Fiat dealer. Yes, it's a fact. We went out to the country one Sunday … there must have been 100,000 families with the same idea. They also went out, everybody with a little Fiat or an Alfa Romeo … And everybody brought a little tent or a fishing rod. … if they were young they made love, if they were old they just sat down under the sun and sipped mineral water. But no revolution.

"… Men's minds turn to revolution when things are getting worse, not when things are getting better. That is fundamental. What we want to do here is to make things get better. And the reason why Barisan is not successful is because things are getting better. Supposing you have got no houses – you know the number of school children who are being registered, the number of chaps who are moving into flats in Singapore? These are the basic factors on our side, telling factors. Watch the Barisan branches, they opened like mushrooms. Now they are closing down one by one.

"Why? Basically, because there is progress. Houses are going up, chaps are earning money, there are lots of scooters around. Yes. Last year, they registered nearly 8,000 scooters, that's what they told me, ROV. It's no laughing matter. It's a small state; 8,000 scooters. You just imagine that. Three in the family using it, you've got 24,000 people kept happy. With 24,000 girlfriends, you've got 48,000 chaps happy. …"

*(Speech to civil servants, June 14, 1962, on page 362)*

The more pressing concern of peoples in developing countries was for improvements to their lives. Democracy and other liberal ideals could wait. In short, what they wanted was not so much liberal democratic government, but simply good government.

But just what constituted good government? To Lee, it was clear that this would vary from society to society and over time.

"All peoples of all countries need good government. A country must first have economic development, then democracy may follow. With a few exceptions, democracy has not brought good government to new developing countries. Democracy has not led to development because the governments did not establish the stability and discipline necessary for development. What is good government? This depends on the values of a people. What

Asians value may not necessarily be what Americans or Europeans value. Westerners value the freedoms and liberties of the individual.

"As an Asian of Chinese cultural background, my values are for a government which is honest, effective and efficient in protecting its people, and allowing opportunities for all to advance themselves in a stable and orderly society, where they can live a good life and raise their children to do better than themselves."

*(Address at Asahi Forum, November 20, 1992; text on page 376)*

Apart from noting the inherent difficulties of applying the democratic system in developing societies, or those where the social and cultural conditions underpinning the society did not exist, he also spent much time pondering just how the system could be adapted to make it work in these societies. How could the system be modified to make it work more effectively in the developed societies as well where, he contended, it was failing to deliver the goods?

One idea he floated was a return to the system of restricting the vote to those who were in a better position to exercise it wisely. Given his way, he would have assigned the vote, or additional votes, to those who contributed most, economically, in a society. They, after all, were the ones who generated wealth, paid taxes and kept governments in operation. They were the ones who would have to bear the burden of costly government initiatives. Why should they not have more say over who formed the government?

"How do people get a good government in a developing country? I believe we can learn a valuable lesson from the property and educational qualifications the UK and the US had in their early stages of democracy. This can work well in the towns where most people are educated. Moreover it will encourage people to get educated. In the rural areas, the educated are fewer. So more traditional methods of representation, like the village headman or chief, can be the basis of representation. Such an approach can be criticised as elitist, but the chances of getting a good government will be better."

*(Address at Asahi Forum, November 20, 1992; text on page 376)*

He elaborated on the idea in an interview with the authors.

"If you have a general vote, it cannot work. In fact, the general vote is not working in America today. They want entitlements, but they don't want to pay taxes. Does that make sense? It's not working in Britain. They don't want to pay more for fuel, but they want the health service to improve. Well, where does the revenue come from? Or in France. So much social support for workers. If you want jobs, you must lower the minimum wage. But the students went on strike. You say, okay students, you can ignore minimum wage.

"How do you work it? The system is malfunctioning at present in Britain, America, France and for some time even in Germany. They wanted reunification, but they didn't want to pay more taxes. And German Chancellor Helmut Kohl made the mistake of saying 'you don't have to pay more taxes'. He started borrowing from the money market. So interest rates rose and caused a recession throughout Europe.

"I would restrict the vote to the level of your contribution to the economy. If you are making no contribution to the economy, you are in no position to demand all this. Who makes what contribution? The British and the Americans built up their infrastructure and their capital in the years when they had the restricted vote. They did not have universal suffrage until late in this century. In America, not until '65, when they had the blacks registered in large numbers. In Britain, married women did not get votes and become equal until 1948 or so. That's when they cancelled the extra university seats. University graduates had extra votes. If you were a graduate of Oxford or Cambridge, you could vote for an extra MP. That system worked.

"But there was pressure, not from the masses but from liberal thinkers, who thought this unfair. Let's all be equal, when we are not equal and do not make equal contributions."

## Some men, more votes

To Lee, this quest for equality was a chimera, for it was manifestly clear that men were not equal. Nor was their contribution to society. Modelling the system on the pious hope that one could assume away these differences was to invite trouble, he argued.

Applying this argument to Singapore, he tossed up for discussion the idea that the voting system in Singapore be modified in 15 to 20 years' time to reflect the contributions of younger working voters with families. Looking ahead, he worried that the rapidly ageing population in Singapore would pose a problem for future governments, which might come under pressure from a growing elderly lobby to spend increasing amounts on pensions, health care and other benefits for them. This, however, would have to be financed by taxing the younger workers, who might chafe at the punitive taxes that would have to be imposed on them.

"The old are not going to die so early. They're going to live till their late 70s, 80s. They will need care, help, food, medicine. Medical science will keep them alive. This CPF [Central Provident Fund] minimum sum will not meet those needs. They would have gone on holiday and spent much of it. And two, three hundred dollars a month, how can that meet all the nursing care and medicine and other institutional support? So they will vote for people who will promise all this.

"Who will pay? The young who are working pay taxes. Those who are not working are not paying taxes. If you tax the young too heavily, they will migrate.

"In Britain, thousands of brilliant professionals have migrated. Doctors by the thousands. Numbers equal to half the annual intake of doctors every year. Those who are at the top of the profession leave for America. Then Britain took in doctors from India and Pakistan to make up for the migration. How can you have a good system? In our circumstance, if we don't watch out, they will also leave. Then what happens? The system cannot produce.

"I've been thinking about this for many years – how to make the system work, how to make it representative but not so skewed so that it becomes unworkable ..."

To him, the need to change the electoral system was not a question of principle but a practical one of having to adapt it so that it continued to serve the interest of society. In 1994, he proposed a change to the system to be made sometime in the future:

"It is not necessary to change our system at present. But, later, we may have to give more weighting to the people whose views should carry more weight because their contributions are greater, and their responsibilities are greater; in which case, we should consider giving those between the ages of 35 and 60, married and with families, one extra vote. Their contribution to the economy and to society is greatest at this stage of life. Also, they need to vote for themselves and also for their children. Their children have an interest that needs to be protected. Once past 60, their children would have grown up, and would vote for themselves. Then the parents should drop back to one vote. But during those critical years, 35–60, people who carry twice as much responsibility should have two votes. This will make for a more viable system and a more stable society.

"It is not going to satisfy the purists, who believe that big or small, all contributors to society should have one vote. But at the end of the day, we need a system that works, that enables representative government to function in an effective way."

*(Interview with Singapore reporters, May 8, 1994; extracts on page 384)*

But this was not the first time that he had proposed radical changes to Singapore's constitution and electoral system. Indeed, over the years, he introduced several innovative modifications to the parliamentary system to adapt it to the country's peculiar circumstances. He amended the constitution to provide for several MPs to be elected in teams, with each including a minority candidate. This was to ensure that Singapore's minority races were represented in Parliament.

"We used to have certain constituencies where the Malays were the majority of the voters. Now we face a fundamental problem after we resettled them. Do we rebuild these areas and rehouse Malays in these areas so that they will still be the majority, or do we expose and scatter them like the Chinese and Indians – ballot for their neighbours?

"Well, the Malay MPs thought it over. We decided, in the long term, it's better that we mix everybody up. So we did. No constituency has more than 30 per cent Malays as the ceiling. The result, a tremendous pressure to find Malay candidates who can fight against a Chinese candidate and still win.

"That's quite a problem because the electorate has changed. A young electorate is no longer interested about the party having a balanced slate. They've never faced a riotous situation where people run amok and butcher, kill, maim each other because they are berserk. Now there's no such situation."

*(Interview with journalists, October 9, 1984)*

# Want an opposition? Split the PAP into two...

Lee has toyed with the idea of splitting his own People's Action Party into two, with a more liberal wing to rival the conservative wing of the party. This, he believed, was the most likely way to bring about a stable two-party system in Singapore, given that the existing opposition parties were, in his view, not up to the task.

But, on balance, he concluded that it was better to keep the party intact, given the small and limited talent pool in the country. The PAP, he argued, would remain the mainstream party, commanding the political centre-ground, and scouring the country for talent to co-opt into its ranks. This made it virtually synonymous with the Establishment in the Republic. Opposition parties would play a role on the fringes to keep the ruling party on its toes, by offering the people a choice at election time, as well as by throwing up alternative ideas.

"The way to bring it about, if it were wise to do so, would be to have the People's Action Party divide into two wings. Then both wings are committed to certain basic and fundamental rocks on which the society will rest and can argue about peripherals – whether more should not be spent for social security or a more liberal view taken – liberal with a big 'L' – of how we spend our money in tempering the harshness of meritocracy and open competition, whether we don't give a little more padding to those who can't quite make it to the middle ranges or income brackets.

"That's theoretical ideal. Then the voter can switch sides without prejudicing the system. But to put this into practice in Singapore requires splitting the PAP – an extremely radical step. I don't suppose I will do it because it's not wise to ask a segment of the party, say, 'Look, you go form the opposition. Get out of office.' I don't know if my successors will. I think it's an unnecessary hazard because there are enough schisms in the society as it is. It's not something you can cement over – differences of race, Chinese, Malays, Indians, and different kinds of Chinese, and different kinds of Indians, and different kinds of Malays. They are real. They are abiding. And we've done a lot to make it more uniform or less stark a contrast. But if you are discerning and you go to a housing estate, they all look the same, but you can see that they lead slightly different lives.

"So with these kinds of deep, underlying, almost primeval urges, I don't really see a Whig-Tory seesaw, tossing power back and forth."

In 1984, in a surprising move which would have been unthinkable in most other countries, where parties are locked in a keen contest for seats, Lee introduced a scheme to give away parliamentary seats to several opposition candidates who had been defeated in the elections. The aim: to enable Singaporeans, especially a younger generation of voters, to "learn the limits of what a constitutional opposition can do". The new crop of government ministers would also gain from having sparring partners in the House.

"When my senior Cabinet colleagues and I look back at our early hectic years of governing Singapore, we realise how much we have benefited from having gone through a very hard school. We met street thugs. Had we not become streetwise, we would have been clobbered. Like dogs which are closeted in a bungalow behind fences, we would have been run over when exposed to treacherous traffic. From our perilous years in the '50s and '60s, a whole generation of Singaporeans, now all over 40 years old, were educated in a harsh political school. They were wise to the ways of an irresponsible opposition and did not vote for any in four successive general elections. They need no further lessons."

*(Parliamentary speech, July 24, 1984)*

Critics dismissed this as an attempt to thwart the rise of genuine opposition parties and candidates, since voters might be persuaded that they could vote PAP and still have opposition MPs in the House. Lee was not perturbed. For him it was a matter of course that the democratic system would have to be adapted to suit the country's needs.

"I have told my younger colleagues a long time ago that we should not make unnecessary changes to the constitution, but that they have to look ahead and keep in mind that no constitution can stay unchanged for all time. The nature of society will change, the external environment that Singapore faces will change, and we have to change. If you want one-man-one-vote or representative government to succeed, from time to time, you will have to adjust your system to make it more viable, and less volatile."

*(Interview with Singapore reporters, May 8, 1994; extracts on page 384)*

## An Asian alternative?

For Lee then, democracy was not an end in itself. Unlike Western champions of the liberal democratic system, who regarded the right to freedom and democracy almost as a birthright, he believed that there was nothing inevitable about the system. Nor, left to their own devices, were Asian societies likely to evolve such a system similar to that in the West. These countries had had the system bequeathed to them. It was left to Lee and other leaders in these states to find ways to work the system, modifying it along the way. At the end of the day, he believed, what mattered most was not what form the system took, but whether it worked to improve the lives of the people.

He summed up this view in a conversation with *Foreign Affairs* managing editor Fareed Zakaria in 1994. When asked by Fareed what he thought was wrong with the

# Opposition: Yes, but what kind?

*Opposition players in Singapore – (from top, left to right) Chiam See Tong from the Singapore People's Party, Ling How Doong and Cheo Chai Chen from the Singapore Democratic Party, and Low Thia Khiang and J.B. Jeyaretnam from the Workers' Party.*

Despite the hard line he took with opposition figures in Singapore, Lee was to say often that he was not against the idea of a parliamentary opposition. A good opposition could offer government ministers useful sparring partners, sharpen their skills and keep them on their toes.

But while acknowledging that there were merits to having an opposition, he would contend that those who aspired to the job in Singapore were not up to it. Worse, instead of contributing to the debates on policy, they often served to undermine the system by casting aspersions on its key institutions, such as the judiciary and civil service. Lee would force them to back up their constant charge that the judiciary in Singapore was "pliant" and under the influence of the executive, despite the judiciary being rated by foreign observers, such as the World Economic Forum, as one of the most efficient and least corrupt in Asia. Time and again, they proved unable to do so. Lee had little time for such an opposition.

"The PAP is not an ideological party – not 'either you believe in this or you're out'. No, we'll take all good minds who are honest and sincere about doing a job for the people. We'll argue, 'Look, these are the circumstances, these are the facts, what can we do?'

"Take Chee Soon Juan [Singapore Democratic Party leader]. If he is not exposed, that man will do harm. He's capable of doing harm.

"We didn't go for Chiam See Tong [Singapore Democratic Party founder, now with Singapore People's Party]. We don't have to. Cheo Chai Chen and Ling How Doong [both of the SDP], we have not. Low Thia Khiang [Workers' Party], we have not gunned for him. He keeps within a certain framework. He's playing politics. He goes on this cost of living committee, he knows he's in the wrong, that the figures are correct. But he still will not admit it. That's okay, he is not actively trying to undermine the system. He looks after his constituency, he attends every wake, every marriage – well, good luck to him. Can you run a country on that basis? But if you are a troublemaker, in the sense that you will do Singapore no good, it's our job to politically destroy you.

"Put it this way. As long as Jeyaretnam [Workers' Party leader] stands for what he stands for – a thoroughly destructive force – we will knock him. There are two ways of playing this. One, you attack the policies; two, you attack the system. Jeyaretnam was attacking the system, he brought the Chief Justice into it. If I want to fix you, do I need the Chief Justice to fix you? Everybody knows that in my bag I have a hatchet, and a very sharp one. You take me on, I take my hatchet, we meet in the cul-de-sac. That's the way I had to survive in the past. That's the way the communists tackled me. He brought the Chief Justice into the political arena.

"Even then, the foreign press keeps saying, 'pliable judiciary'. So I said, 'We sue. Prove it.' You mean to tell me I won my libel cases because the judges favoured me? Every case is documented – what the man said, what he said in reply to my claim and so on.

"That kind of an opposition, if you do not check, it will degrade the system."

American political system, he replied, "It is not my business to tell people what is wrong with their system. It is my business to tell people not to foist their system indiscriminately on societies in which it will not work."

He added, "The system of government in China will change. It will change in Korea, Taiwan, Vietnam. It is changing in Singapore. But it will not end up like the American or British or French or German systems. What are we all seeking? A form of government that will be comfortable, because it meets our needs, is not oppressive, and maximises our opportunities. And whether you have one-man-one-vote, or some-men-one-vote or other-men-two-votes, those are forms which should be worked out. I'm not intellectually convinced that one-man-one-vote is the best. We practise it because that's what the British bequeathed us and we haven't really found a need to challenge that."

To work, he argued, the system would have to be adapted to suit the social, economic, and cultural context of the societies in which it was to be applied.

"Each country in Asia will chart its own way forward. Every country wants to be developed and wealthy. They will adopt and adapt those features or attributes of successful countries which they think will help them succeed. If these features work and improve their rate of progress, they will be permanently incorporated. If they do not work or cause difficulties, they will be abandoned. It is akin to social Darwinism, a process of trial and error in which survival is the test of what works.

"Simply modelling a system on the American, British or West European constitution is not how Asian countries will or can go about it. The peoples of Asia want higher standards of living in an orderly society. They want to have as much individual choice in lifestyle, political liberties and freedoms as is compatible with the interests of the community. After a certain stage of advance in education and industrialisation, a people may need representative government, however chosen, in order to reconcile conflicting group interests in society and maintain social order and stability. Representative government is also one way for a people to forge a new consensus, a social compact, on how a society settles the trade-off between further rapid economic growth and individual freedoms.

"In Singapore, the British gave us their form of parliamentary government. Our problem has been how to maintain stability in spite of the destabilising tendencies of one-man-one-vote in a new society divided by race, language and religion. We have had to put political stability as the first priority. As we progressed to higher educational and economic levels, we have widened participation in decision making. But no Singaporean leader can afford to put political theory above the practical need of stability and orderly progress. On this, I believe I speak for most, if not all of Asia, at present."

*(Address to the Asahi Shimbun symposium, May 9, 1991; text on page 372)*

# Preconditions for democracy

*Violence in Pakistan. Lee is not convinced that the country has the right ingredients for democracy to take root and flourish.*

Lee argued often that democracy was not an inevitable form of government. Certain cultural and societal preconditions needed to prevail before it could take root. Where these were lacking, the system had to be adapted to suit the local circumstances if it was not to be doomed to failure.

"Take Pakistan. In 1988, after General Zia Ul Haq, the president, was killed ... Professor Elie Kedourie ... who has studied Pakistan, ... wrote: 'Civilian, constitutional government was proved to be inept, corrupt, and quite unable to arrange a Third World economy, or deal with the ills and conflicts of a divided society suffering from deep rivalries, mutual fears and antagonisms ... For such a style of government to be practicable and tolerable, it has to be rooted in attitudes to, and traditions of, governance which are common ground between the rulers and the ruled: the supremacy of law, the accountability of those in power and continuous intercourse with the public from whom they derive their authority; the sturdiness of civil society, and the practical impossibility for any government to ride roughshod for long over its innumerable and multifarious interests and associations. None of this, of course, obtains in Pakistan ... Here the ruling tradition was of Oriental despotism where the will of the ruler was law ... May it not be that a regime of elections, parliaments and responsible government is unworkable in countries like Pakistan, and that to persist in attempts to set up or restore such a regime must lead to continual tumults in the body politic, and successive interventions by the armed forces?'

"Six years ago, Mrs Imelda Marcos fled the country ... so did Eduardo Cojuangco. Yet they were able to return and contest in elections for president. They were among the top four candidates. The president, Fidel Ramos, got 5.3 million votes, Cojuangco got 4.1, and Mrs Marcos 2.3. In other words, had Cojuangco and Mrs Marcos combined, their votes could have beaten Fidel Ramos. A society where such remarkable events are possible needs a special kind of democracy. In other societies, when a dictator is overthrown, the wife and close collaborators would probably have been mobbed and lynched before they got away, and if they got away, would never return.

"... one simple but fundamental problem. The majority of the voters, both in the Philippines and in Pakistan, are peasants or farmers. The landlords control their lives and their votes. The majority of members elected into the legislatures of both countries are landlords. They have blocked legislation for land reforms without which there can be no fundamental change in the economy. They have also blocked moves to have the children of their peasants educated. They prefer to have them uneducated but loyal ...

"Neither country has a background for democratic government. There are no habits in the people for dissension or disagreement within a restrained and peaceful context. Murders and violence are part of every Filipino election. The lawlessness that is in Sind province, the shootings ... between Sindhis, Muhajirs, Pashtuns, Baluchis in Karachi bear witness to the absence of a civic society."

*(November 20, 1992; text on page 376)*

# The liberal crusade: end of objectivity?

To Western advocates of human rights and democracy who sought to pressure Asian societies into adopting the standards of the West, Lee counselled patience. As the world was drawn ever closer together, norms for decent behaviour would be established. Attempting to force Western standards on Asian societies not only smacked of cultural arrogance, it risked throwing these societies into chaos and confusion.

> "These contacts will influence their behaviour, because their values, perceptions and attitudes will change. There will be no convergence to a common world standard. But we can expect more acceptable standards where bizarre, cruel, oppressive practices will become shameful and unacceptable. We cannot force faster change, unless the advanced countries are prepared to intervene actively. If a target delinquent government collapses and the country breaks down, are the donor countries prepared to move in and put the country together again? In other words, re-colonise and create the preconditions for democracy?"
>
> *(Address at Asahi Forum, November 20, 1992; text on page 376)*

Even some Western societies, he contended, did not display an inclination towards the democratic ideal. Yet, inexplicably, many in the West continued to champion democracy as having universal applicability.

> "The West, led by America, puts the credo simply as democracy is universally good for all peoples, and that to progress, modernise and become industrial societies, they should become democracies. Now that the Cold War has ended, I hope it is possible for Western political scientists to write in more objective terms. Why has democracy not worked in most of these newly independent countries? In particular, why has an American-based constitution failed to work in America's only former colony, the Philippines? The Philippines experiment in democracy started with independence and elections in 1946. That experiment in democracy failed in 1972 with martial law, long before Marcos was ousted in 1986. A second American-based constitution was promulgated by President Aquino in February 1987. Whilst a constitutional commission was sitting to frame this constitution, four coups were attempted. In May 1987, elections were held for a Senate and a House of Representatives. This still did not settle the loyalty of the armed forces because three more coup attempts followed. …
>
> "When Western commentators are not writing to convert a Third World country to democracy, they are more objective. For example, when they discuss the Soviet Union, they say openly that democracy will not work. …
>
> "European historians ascribe Russia's lack of a liberal civic society to the fact that she missed the Renaissance (middle 15th to end 16th century) and also the Enlightenment (18th century). These were the two leavening experiences that lifted Western Europe to a more humane culture. Now if democracy will not work for the Russians, a white Christian people, can we assume that it will naturally work with Asians?"
>
> *(Address to the Asahi Shimbun symposium, May 9, 1991; text on page 372)*

# Huntington's U-turn

*Former critic of Lee Kuan Yew, Harvard professor Samuel Huntington, has since changed his views. "You'll be surprised. I've got good things to say of you," he told Lee about his new book.*

Singapore's system of government, which Lee had fashioned over the years, would go with him to his grave. So predicted Harvard professor Samuel Huntington. He argued that Singapore's clean and efficient system of government would not outlive its founder as it was not underpinned by democratic institutions and values.

The professor was just one of several Western commentators who had crossed swords with Lee. For many of these liberal critics, Lee was the arch spokesman for the argument that Asian countries would evolve their own representative systems, suited to their society's ethos, cultures, traditions and stages of progress.

Finding these views an apology for authoritarianism and repression, many of them gunned for Lee, and Singapore, believing he should not be allowed to succeed lest doing so lent credence to his views. So, when Huntington called on Lee at the Istana and informed him that his new book, *The Clash of Civilisations and the Remaking of the World Order*, would soon be published, Lee figured he could expect more of the same.

"During this visit, he said, 'My book is coming out,' and I said, 'I'm ready for it.' He said, 'No, you'd be surprised. I've got good things to say of you.' And he has," said Lee.

He came to know about the Harvard don in 1968 and met him regularly despite having crossed swords with him several times. In his latest book, the professor lauded the Singapore government's initiative to foster a sense of shared values among the Republic's multiracial community. He called it an "ambitious and enlightened effort to define a Singaporean cultural identity", noting that the five values drawn up as a moral anchor for Singaporeans in 1991 were shared by the ethnic and religious communities here and had helped to distinguish Singapore from the West.

To Lee, the observation indicated that Huntington had changed his view about the universality of American values and democratic practices. He now understood the rule for peace in a multi-civilisational world, having seen what had happened in Bosnia, Somalia and Rwanda. This rule for peace was based on finding common elements and expanding the values, institutions and practices which people had in common with others, Lee told reporters in December 1996, in an impromptu press conference called after an election rally. Praising Professor Huntington for having shown the courage to drop his previous assumption that Western civilisation and values were universal, Lee said, "In other words, he accepts that America cannot remake the world in its own image …"

Quoting from the book, published in 1996, Lee pointed out that the Harvard don now believed that although Western civilisation was unique, it would be "false, immoral and dangerous" to believe it was universal. He realised the world had to be accepted as it was, with different languages, cultures and religions. "Many other things follow, there will be differences in values, social systems, and their spillover into political systems."

Not surprisingly, these views earned Lee a fair deal of opprobrium from liberal critics. His opponents labelled him an eloquent spokesman for soft authoritarianism, or a "kinder, gentler" form of political dictatorship. Others saw his critique of the democratic system as a cynical attempt to entrench his ruling People's Action Party in power. He was unperturbed, believing he had history and the logic of the argument on his side. Besides, Singapore's success was his best riposte.

He was also to become a leading critic of the Western liberal notion that mankind had reached the "end of history", with liberal democracies being the ultimate social and political order for all societies. To him, this liberal triumphalism, brought on by the collapse of the Soviet Union and the end of the Cold War, was a pious myth to be taken with a liberal dash of salt.

His views, expressed with characteristic candour and forcefulness, provoked many equally strong reactions. One of these was from South Korea's opposition leader Kim Dae Jung, who argued that democracy was not alien to Asian culture. Its advance was being thwarted by Asian authoritarians of whom Lee was the most articulate. Noting this, a somewhat bemused Lee replied:

"Kim Dae Jung wrote in *Foreign Affairs* magazine, 'Democracy is our destiny.' They got him to write a counter article to my conversation and they want me to reply. I don't think it's necessary. He makes assertive statements. Where are the concrete examples that these things are going to happen? If it's going to happen, why are they so excited about it? All the authoritarians, all the contrarians will die away because it is an inevitable tide of history.

"The very fact that they're so vexed about it and try to demolish me shows a lack of faith in the inevitable outcome they predict. They say I am the most articulate of the authoritarians and giving them sustenance. Rubbish. If history is on their side, that liberal democracy is inevitable, then just ignore me. Don't give me publicity. Right?

"I don't believe that because a theory sounds good, looks logical on paper or is presented logically, therefore that is the way it will work out. The final test is life. What happens in real life, what happens with people working in a society."

# The Nature of Human Society

## 7

Bell curve—
Social commentator
Charles Murray and
Harvard psycholo-
gist Richard
Herrnstein, in their
book, *The Bell
Curve: Intelligence
And Class Structure
In American Life*,
argued that human
intelligence is
largely transmitted
genetically.

*Opposite: The young,
Lee believed, held the key
to the future. Education
was a priority for his
government. The
Cabinet believed initially
that equalising opportu-
nities would narrow the
gap between the haves
and the have-nots in
society. But over the
years, many among them
were drawn to the
conclusion that equality
of opportunities alone
would not always lead to
equality of results.*

When the controversial Bell Curve hypothesis was published in 1994, suggesting that some men and ethnic groups were less well endowed intellectually than others, it raised a shrill stir in American political and intellectual circles. The authors, Charles Murray and Richard Herrnstein, were derided as racists, bigots and pseudo-scientists. Critics charged that the book was unhelpful to efforts to improve race relations in the United States, or worse, part of a neo-Nazi plot to keep ethnic minorities down.

For Lee Kuan Yew, however, the book was unremarkable. To him, the hypothesis revealed nothing new. It merely confirmed what had long been commonsense knowledge – that not all men or all races were equally able. He had drawn this conclusion long ago, from his own observations of the differences in ability within a society and between differing cultures.

The uproar in the West, he believed, stemmed from a stubborn refusal of its politically correct intelligentsia to accept the facts which nature had decreed. The result: policies based on wrong premises, which were doomed to disappointment; grand hopes of levelling society failed to deliver results because they went against the grain of the inherent inequalities in ability among men.

Lee would have none of this. To him, government policy, be it on education, social spending or the search for talent, could not be a matter of wishful thinking.

"The Bell curve is a fact of life. The blacks on average score 85 per cent on IQ and it is accurate, nothing to do with culture. The whites score on average 100. Asians score more … the Bell curve authors put it at least 10 points higher. These are realities that, if you do not accept, will lead to frustration because you will be spending money on wrong assumptions and the results cannot follow.

"By the 1970s, when we looked at the old examination results and the present, and we saw the pattern in the housing estates – one-room, two-rooms, three-rooms, four-rooms, five-rooms – it fits exactly with educational attainments. That the more intelligent and hardworking you are, the higher your educational levels, the higher your income.

"Supposing we had hidden the truth and taken the American approach and said, all men are equal. Then they (the less able or well-off) will demand equal results. And when the results are not equal, they will demand more equal treatment.

"I decided if I didn't bring it out, my successors will face a problem of credibility. Because they can't bring it out, they will say we're trying to escape the responsibility. So I started giving it to the community leaders, then to the media leaders, then to the teachers – finally brought it out into the open. There's no other way. Not to come to terms with this is to deceive yourself and be pursuing policies which would bring no good."

To Lee, this delicate matter concerning the innate and differing abilities of people was not just of academic interest. His views about the nature of human society were of considerable importance as they would influence profoundly the social and economic policies he pursued in Singapore.

He held strong views on these thorny issues. As a pragmatist, he concluded that they would have to be faced squarely before leaders could decide how best to act so as to achieve the goals of development for their societies.

These ideas evolved as a result of his experience and reading over the years. They were not what he originally believed as a young man at Cambridge drawn to the ideals of the British Fabians, a group of left-wing intellectuals at the vanguard of the Labour Party at the time. They were convinced that inequalities in society stemmed largely from unequal opportunities. If economic and social disparities were removed, or reduced, they assumed that the gap between the haves and have-nots would also close. The concept seemed appealing and noble enough. But reality, he soon discovered, fell rather short of this sanguine belief.

"We were too young, and the experiment in Russia and in Britain had not gone far enough for us to see, which we now see clearly, that there is a limit to what you can do in society.

"With human beings, you can give everybody equal opportunities, but the results will not be equal because they are of unequal abilities. Some people run faster than others, some people can lift more weights than others, some people can play better music than others, and some people are better at mathematics and will score more in the sciences. And I think that has been, for Britain, Russia and China, the real breaking point of the system. For instance, the British Left believed, and we believed with them, in the '40s and '50s, that equal opportunities would bring about more or less equal rewards. We did not know about this Bell curve, that it existed in every population from time immemorial.

"Equal opportunities meant that in the first few phases, in the '50s and '60s, we were able to throw up engineers, accountants, doctors from the children of hawkers, taxi drivers, labourers because they were not given opportunities. And we drew our scholars – 60, maybe 70 per cent of our best scholars were from the very uneducated rungs of society.

"But over 30 years, we can see now that the educated marry each other, as was inevitable, and indeed in our case is not happening enough, to our detriment. The result is, today, out of 10, we're lucky if we get three from the lower-educated groups. Although the higher-educated groups are only about 20 per cent of the population, they provide us with 70 per cent of the scholars. It is a fact of life and you can't change it.

"You see, starting block, a marathon, get ready, all at the same line, fire, off you go. One hour later, you see the wide differences between those who are still steady, pushing ahead, and the stragglers struggling at the end. Two hours later, five, six, are in front, racing to beat the record. That's the problem of life."

# Diamonds in the population

Lee's realisation of this came in the early 1960s, shortly after he and his PAP colleagues had taken charge of the government in Singapore. The multiracial nature of Singapore society made any disparity in ethnic achievement starkly obvious. They showed up in the yearly school examination results, which he tracked closely.

He concluded that all societies displayed signs of what he termed a "population diamond". At the centre was the bulk of the people, of average intellect and abilities. Above this, IQ and competence levels rose to an apex. Below the centre, and in about equal proportion to the apex at the top, abilities tapered off, down to the educationally subnormal and mentally retarded.

Despite the difference in ability, he felt that all men were entitled to be treated equally and fairly, and accorded the same dignity and respect as citizens. The government's role was to train each individual to his maximum ability.

The most able in society would have to be drawn into the top rungs, given the most important jobs through a strictly meritocratic system. This group at the top – he guessed that they made up between 5 per cent and 10 per cent of the population in any society – was the yeast which would raise the lot of the entire society. These people would have to be thrown up by a meritocratic system – or sought out by the society's leaders – and nurtured from a young age. To them would fall the responsibility of the top jobs, both in government and the private sector. Lee dismissed suggestions that such a system was elitist. Rather, he contended, it was based simply on a pragmatic recognition that not all men were of equal abilities and talents. He once said, only half in jest, that to bring Singapore down, an aggressor need only eliminate the top 150 or so men on whom the country relied most for it to keep ticking.

The less able would also have to be helped, to enable them to do their best and keep up with the rest of society. But for all its good intentions, social policy, concluded Lee and some of his more pragmatic Cabinet colleagues, could never overcome the underlying limits in ability that nature had decreed. Nor should it raise false hopes that it could.

**Singapore's first Cabinet—** In 1959, the Cabinet comprised Prime Minister Lee Kuan Yew, Deputy Prime Minister Toh Chin Chye, and these ministers: Yong Nyuk Lin (Education), Ong Eng Guan (National Development), S. Rajaratnam (Culture), Ahmad Ibrahim (Health), Ong Pang Boon (Home Affairs), Goh Keng Swee (Finance) and K.M. Byrne (Labour and Law).

*Opposite: Lee and Dr Toh Chin Chye held opposing views on the subject of equality.*

# Cabinet clash: pragmatists vs "ideologues"

This, however, was by no means a unanimous view. In fact, it split the Cabinet down the line.

"We – Dr Goh Keng Swee, myself, Hon Sui Sen, Lim Kim San – we were the pragmatists. Then we had our, I won't say ideologues, but those who were more emotionally attached to this idea of making it more equal for everybody – in other words, more redistribution. I would say Dr Toh Chin Chye instinctively felt that way. And Ong Pang Boon too. Therefore, there was a certain benign tension in the Cabinet, and we argued these things. And the tension and the argument went on right till the end.

"For instance, Dr Toh was against Medisave. He thinks we ought to provide equally for everybody, rich or poor, like the British did and like China has done. I said, 'The British had failed. And you don't get equal treatment in China, you get the pretence of equal treatment.' So the debate was right at the fundamentals.

"We believed, all of us believed, I believed, when we started off in the 1940s, that differences between individuals and individual performance and results were mainly because of opportunities. Given better opportunities of nutrition, food, clothing, training, housing and health, differences would be narrowed. It was much later, when we pursued these policies in the '60s, in the '70s, that the reality dawned on us, the pragmatists.

"On this issue, even Rajaratnam disagreed with us. He believes all are equal and if we give equal chances, everybody will be equal. And he strenuously disputed that we start off being unequal. But some people can run 100 yards in 10 seconds, others will take 15 seconds, and you can do nothing about it. If you try to give all the same results, then nobody will make the effort to run in 10 seconds."

This posed an acute dilemma for the PAP, a democratic socialist party which rode to power on the wave of popular demands for a more just and equal society. How was a popularly elected socialist government to act against the prevailing egalitarian sentiment? Yet, going the other way was to risk disillusionment among a section of the party's supporters. More importantly, Lee and his more pragmatic colleagues knew that pandering to this was a futile attempt to overcome inherent limits imposed by nature.

"When we were faced with the reality that, in fact, equal opportunities did not bring about more equal results, we were faced with another ideological dilemma. What is it that you want? Equal results or equal opportunities? Between the two, we felt that in Singapore, if we were to survive, we could not go the way of equal results; we had to give rewards in accordance with your effort.

"Now, we did try wherever possible, wherever more would bring about better performance. Never mind if it brings about equal results. If better housing, better health, better schools can bring about better results, let's help them. But we know that we cannot close the gap. In other words, this Bell curve, which Murray and Herrnstein wrote about, became obvious to us by the late '60s."

**157**

# Unrepentant socialist

*Equal pay for unequal work is a surefire way to kill productive instincts, says Lee. On the contrary, a worker is motivated to work when he can earn more if he puts in the effort.*

Though a self-proclaimed social democrat, Lee recognised that the masses in society would require more than socialist zeal to drive them to their best productive effort. He concluded that, willy-nilly, individuals worked for themselves and their families. To shy away from this reality was ideological folly. Rather, the state would have to work with these instincts to help raise production and effort, and thereby improve the lot of the workers.

"Perhaps we have underestimated the human problems of finding the techniques of organising men for production, and of persuading men to accept the disciplines of modernised agricultural and industrial production, if we are to fulfil their dreams. …

"The capitalists make people work through monetary incentives which we call sweated and exploited labour. The communists do it by regimentation and exhortation and a systematically induced state of semi-hysteria for work, using both the stick and the carrot. The democratic socialist is less ruthless and consequently less efficient, torn between his loathing for regimentation and mass coercion and his inhibition to making more effective use of the carrot by his desire to distribute the rewards more fairly and equally too soon.

"I am an unrepentant socialist. But in my own state, I have to concede that because it takes a long time to inculcate the high values of public duty and sense of service to the community, performance has been best only when workers are offered high incentives for high performance.

"Our building programmes have progressed rapidly because we allowed the individual worker to earn as much as he can over his other workers by working as hard as he likes. Our lowest productivity level is in many sections of our own government services such as our publicly owned dockyards where managers are on salary scales instead of the profit-sharing and bonus schemes of private industry, and where our workers are on wage rates which apply equally between the proficient hard-working man and the mediocre and not so hardworking man.

"We have had to recognise these faults. It has not changed our belief in the basic tenet that no man should exploit his fellowman. We believe it is immoral that the ownership of property should allow some to exploit others. But in order to get economic growth we have had to base our policies on the principle, 'From each his economic best, To each his economic worth.' The ultimate ideal, 'From each his best, To each his need', can only be relevant after we have moved away from ignorance, illiteracy, poverty, and economic backwardness."

*(Speech to Asian Socialist Conference, May 6, 1965; text on page 387)*

# All men are equal, but how equal?

This crucial distinction between equality of opportunity and outcomes was to become a guiding principle in Lee's approach to policy-making in Singapore, whether in education or welfare.

"If you want equal results, you've got to go one step further and either discriminate against the high performers or give more and better training to the low performers, which was what a section of the Fabian Society recommended.

"They faced the same problem: the gap did not close although opportunities were equal. And they said, well, all the more reason why the best teachers should teach the least able to make up for the difference, and the good students should have the less able teachers because they don't require the able teachers.

"I read this in a Fabian pamphlet written by three schoolmasters. After that, I stopped my subscription, because they had gone mad!"

Lee was also to develop a deep mistrust of welfare policies, as practised in Western welfare states. These, he believed, had drifted away from their original socialist goal of giving every man, regardless of his social status, an equal crack in the game of life. Instead, they raised false hopes, and furthermore, by promising men equal rewards, they often resulted in some choosing to opt out of the game altogether. He was also acutely aware that Singapore's small, fledgling entrepôt economy could ill afford such indulgence.

"In Singapore, a society barely above the poverty line, welfarism would have broken and impoverished us. My actions and policies over the last 30 years after 1959, since I was first saddled with responsibility, were dictated by the overriding need that they would work. I have developed a deep aversion to welfarism and social security, because I have seen it sap the dynamism of people to work their best. What we have attempted in Singapore is asset enhancement, not subsidies. We have attempted to give each person enough chips to be able to play at the table of life. This has kept the people self-reliant, keen and strong. Few have wasted their assets at the gaming table. Most have hoarded their growing wealth and have lived better on the interests and dividends they earn.

"I subsequently read Frederick Hayek's book, *The Fatal Conceit: Errors of Socialism*. He expressed with clarity and authority what I had long felt but was unable to express, namely the unwisdom of powerful intellects, including Albert Einstein, when they believed that a powerful brain can devise a better system and bring about more 'social justice' than what historical evolution, or economic Darwinism, has been able to work out over the centuries."

Hayek, a leading conservative thinker and renowned critic of socialism, had dismissed as a "fatal conceit" the idea held by some modern-day intellectuals that human ingenuity could fashion a societal system which was more humane and fair than the invisible hand of the free market. Instead, he contended that an extended social order, such as the

# The road from serfdom

*The state of welfare today: French public sector employees protesting against the government's plan to cut welfare benefits.*

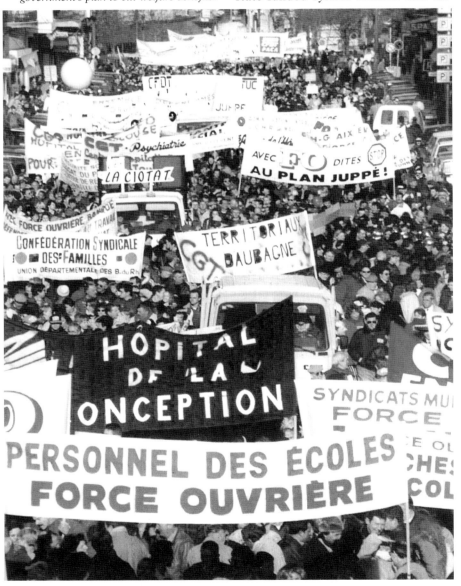

As a student in Britain, Lee witnessed the early years of the popular cradle to grave welfare state. Even then, he was to think the idea worthy, though somewhat misguided. Over the years, though, he would watch the early good intentions go awry as the state-funded system bloated and the pressure for ever more handouts mounted, sapping once vibrant economies of the enterprise and vigour.

"Welfarism, today, has a meaning which it did not have in the '40s and '50s. Welfarism today means the redistribution of wealth through subsidies that makes it possible for people to get many benefits in life with little effort. Therefore, it has led to the failure of society.

"At the time when I admired them, Britain was moving from the privations of war where hardships were shared – 'hardships' meaning shortage of food, clothing, housing, fuel – and it extended until several years after the war. They still had rationing for food, for clothes, and they were building houses, they had rent control, and they were beginning to solve the housing shortage by building council houses and so on. So it was seen as a logical extension of not only sharing hardships, but also sharing the benefits of peace.

"It was subsequently, in the '70s and '80s and '90s, that the effects of this redistribution of wealth, not dependent on individual effort, meant an economy which slowed down, and privation, or rather the lack of achievement and abundance, became apparent.

"Welfarism, when persisted in, brought about the results which have given welfarism a bad name today. But it did not start off in the '40s and '50s with that clear stark meaning. At that time it was about a fair and just society. Equal shares for all and equal chances for all. Many believed, as I did, that equal chances would bring about a more equal result, but it did not."

market system, was the result of a myriad of individual decisions. Each individual acted on the limited knowledge available to him, without being aware of the full consequences of his actions. Nor were the outcomes necessarily related to the intentions behind his decisions. The market mechanism caused a chain of adaptations and adjustments by men, each reacting to the multitude of signals from others in the system, to achieve order out of disorder. No superhuman being or committee could possibly possess all the knowledge held by these disparate individuals to work out a system that could do better, Hayek argued. Communist states, he added, had failed simply because they did not recognise or accept this human limitation.

Hence, Hayek contended, the systems evolved over the centuries were superior to any system men could devise. To him, traditions were not just arbitrary social rules. Rather, these had been selected through a competitive process: practices which were successful were perpetuated; those that were not were dropped. There was therefore a Darwinian process of social evolution, or trial and error, at work. Social norms and practices did not stem from some great mind, committee, god or underlying principle, which sanctioned some actions or men, he said.

Lee shared these sentiments. He was to warn voters often of the dangers of welfare policies which, however well-intentioned, might result in unintended consequences. He had seen how such policies had undermined the work ethic, giving rise to a culture of dependency among the people, when benefits became entitlements and the desire for equal opportunities was turned into a demand for equal results. This was to become a constant theme in his speeches and election rallies, as in a 1976 attack on the Workers' Party campaign slogan, "A Caring Society".

> "It's a good slogan, 'The Caring Society'. It's actually a crib, it's plagiarism from the British Labour Party's 'The Compassionate Society'. It sounds much better than 'caring'; it's 'compassionate'. You have compassion for the poor, for the disabled, for the less successful.
>
> "You know the end result? It's not to each man his worth. They are no longer seeking equal opportunities in Britain. What they want is equal reward, regardless of what your contribution is. That is a different game altogether.
>
> "So when I was asked in Australia 'Are you a socialist?' it is a loaded question, because they know I don't agree with the new Left. I said, 'Yes, perhaps an old-fashioned one.'
>
> "I believe in equal opportunities. I believe the human being wants an equal chance with his fellow human being, regardless of his father's wealth or status, in order that he can do his best, in order that he can compete and climb up to the top. And that is so whether you are in Moscow, Beijing, Washington or London.
>
> "You can't reverse human nature. When you try to do that, as the British Labour Party or a section of it has tried, then you bring a whole great people down.
>
> "They say, 'Ah, that's elitism!' Competitive examinations, the creaming of the best into special institutions where they are made to go faster, become high achievers and high performers for the society. They are penalised. Net result, the country suffers. Why should you try? In order that you will pay penalising taxes to keep the layabout happy?"

# Going with the grain

*Opposite: "In every culture, there is a desire to preserve your distinctiveness. And I think if you go against that, you will create unnecessary problems, whether it is with the Indians and their castes or with the Chinese and their clans. That is why, in the end, we decided we had to recognise facts." – Lee on how he came to realise the wisdom of harnessing ethnic ties, such as those in the Sikh community, which he would often praise for its spirit of self-help.*

Lee's approach to welfare then was to be based on a recognition of basic human nature: that individuals strove for their own advancement and that of their families. He believed that government policy should work in tandem with these human tendencies rather than try to counter them. The state should be wary of any initiative which would supplant, wittingly or otherwise, individual effort and responsibility. Nor could ties of care and concern between families and communities be "nationalised" or replaced by the state. The traditional family support systems would have to be maintained and fostered, as would the poor-law tradition which attached a certain sense of shame to state handouts.

"We live in different concentric circles. And your closest circle is your own family, then your extended family, then the clan and then your friends. One is your social, cultural or scholarly pursuits, or sports, recreation and so on. But when it comes to helping family members out, you've got to club together to help your family, because that's part of the culture that you have inherited.

"For survival, you will need protection, help, and succour, and that comes from your family. The only people who are going to help you when you are starving and sick and you need medicine and medicines are scarce, the only people who will sacrifice for you are your family. The big idea of altruism, when resources are scarce – that counts for nothing. But the genetic drive to protect your own offspring is a very powerful one.

"I saw that in the raw during the Japanese Occupation. Medicine was in short supply. Who would sacrifice? Your mother and your father; beyond that, your uncles, your aunts, your grandfather. Friends, maybe very close friends will help you, at the margins. So as part of that protective instinct, it's in the genes.

"And built into that is a certain cultural pattern, which varies from society to society. The Chinese culture is the one I know best. … the extended family network and the clan … they supported each other, for survival. It was a survival method worked out over thousands of years of war, devastation, floods, famines. Suddenly you're flattened by a typhoon – who helps you? You go to the government agency and ask for food? There is no agency. So this was the mechanism. I share your clan name, I will help you. So they transported and transplanted it here … it helps survival.

"The Indians have their own method. So do the Malays. The Malays: Islam and also the kinship ties … I don't think you can erase all that. That's for hundreds of years, or thousands of years. You can't erase it. Because I recognised it, I decided you cannot change this. Or if you tried to change it, you'd change it for the worse.

"For example, the Chinese communists had tried to dismantle families by separating them into communes, with husbands and wives sent to different parts of the country to work. When I read about it at the time, I thought it was all madness. And now they admit it was wrong. That not only was it wrong to try it, it has also failed. These were basic survival instincts, mechanisms. Both instinct and culture reinforcing each other and increasing the chances of survival.

# What I learnt from my gardener

Although Lee started out as a social democrat, his approach was never an ideological one. He recognised early on that the masses were driven by the desire to improve their own lot and that of their families, rather than by missionary socialist zeal. That being the case, Lee concluded that the socialist paradise of a society where each man was given according to his needs in return for his best effort had, at best, to be postponed. Put simply, unless workers were motivated to do their best, the state would lack the wherewithal to improve the lot of its people.

"I had a part-time gardener. He worked in the Health Ministry as an anti-malaria worker and turned up to tend my garden at 2 o'clock. How he was able to do that, I often wondered. He increased his duties over the years and was paid additional sums of money for cleaning the car, besides doing the garden. Then one day he started coming at 4 pm, instead of 2 pm, and was discovered to have taken on another garden near by.

"I was convinced that his whole purpose in life was to give the minimum to his major employer, the Health Ministry, in order that he could perform his other functions. All he had to do in his major job was to avoid the attention of the *mandore*. And all the *mandore* had to do was to avoid the attention of the overseer for not having discovered that such a man was not stretching himself. All the overseer's worry was to make sure that his supervisor did not catch him not catching the *mandore*.

"It is not by accident that our building trade is probably the most successful. Supervision is at a minimum, problems of discipline do not arise. A man is paid for performance: 'You complete this in accordance with a certain standard, you are paid the agreed price.' I am not suggesting that we could do this for all the complicated mechanical operations of modern industry. But we must recognise this urge, the instinct in our people to perform and give of his best only if he is rewarded better than the other who did not do as well. More and more, we must make this a cornerstone of our drive for high performance.

"It is not just the capitalist or free enterprise world that has had to recognise this hard fact. One of the most instructive journeys I had was the one to Eastern Europe in May last year. They understood that uniformity must mean a lowering of the effort. And in the many factories that I went to, the wages were not equal. They were paid in accordance with their performance. Further, if your performance needed special recognition and reward, there were all the social status symbols of the photographs on the driveway to the factory, and tickets to the ballet, the opera, and the hotel by the Black Sea. These brought forth high performance."

Mendaki—
A grassroots and community-based organisation started in 1982 to raise awareness in the Malay community of the importance of education and to help the underclass by holding tuition programmes. Other ethnically based self-help bodies like the Singapore Indian Development Association (Sinda), the Chinese Development Assistance Council (CDAC) and the Eurasian Association were set up later.

"That's why Chinese meet on Chinese New Year's Eve, to remind themselves of their obligations to each other and to recognise new entrants into the family circle. It's a cultural technique or method, so that in times of crisis you know who to call upon. And it has helped survival. When they came here, the government didn't care for them. They formed clan associations. They helped each other.

"That is an instinct of all human tribes or societies. In every culture, there is a desire to preserve your distinctiveness. And I think if you go against that, you will create unnecessary problems, whether it is with the Indians and their caste or with the Chinese and their clans. That is why, in the end, we discovered we had to recognise facts. And so I encouraged Mendaki to be formed because you could not get Chinese officers to enthuse Malay parents to do something about their children. But Malay leaders can. They share a certain common destiny. The Malay parents look at their leader and they talk the same language, they say, 'Yes, you have my interest at heart, so you're telling me all this. I'll listen to you.'

"I tell the leader? They say, 'Oh, you're prime minister, you'd tell me that.' But do I really share their fate, their destiny? Not quite so. So once I recognised that as a fact, I then built government policies around those facts."

## Everyone has a prize

The state's role was therefore to be a supportive one, working with basic human networks and instincts rather than supplanting them, wittingly or otherwise. But did this mean that it adopted a minimalist approach to government? What was it to do about the less well-off in society? Should it simply adopt a *laissez-faire* social policy, leaving individuals and their families to fend entirely for themselves? If that was the case, how could the state ensure that the less well-off continued to have a stake in society? What would hold such a collection of individuals together? Indeed, what made them a "society"?

Lee believed that to achieve a cohesive society, all citizens would have to be given a stake in the system.

"How do you organise society so that you encourage everybody to do his best, never give up, even if he can do only one-tenth of the course, but still, encourage him and give him something? I don't know what kind of 'ism' that will be. I mean, you have to think up some system to keep everybody in the race. It's a problem of social cohesion and performance.

"If you don't give the also-rans a chance to feel that they belong and they've not been discarded, then the society will have no cohesion. If you have too much cohesion, there's not enough rewards for high competitive performance and winning, then achievements will be low. So you've got to balance the two.

"How you balance it depends on the nature of your society and how much you're prepared to reduce in competitive excellence to achieve a national cohesion. If you have too much of it, you collapse. You may have all the cohesion in the world, everybody in Mao blue suits or grey suits, and you will fail, that's all."

# The yeast to raise society

*The "ideal" product – the graduate with intellectual discipline, stamina and compassion for society.*

Lee was not one who believed in the politically correct egalitarianism of his day. He argued that every society had a segment of its population – say, the top 5 to 10 per cent – which was exceptionally able. These people, like the philosopher kings of old, would have to be thrown up through a meritocratic process, or actively sought out, and put into the top positions in government and the private sector. To charges that such an approach was elitist, Lee would counter that doing so would help raise the lot of all in society, more so than a pretence that all men were equally capable or talented.

"Supposing now, I am given superhuman powers. I say, 'Look, here is Singapore with this limitation: 2 million people. What kind of schools, education would I have?' I will tell you what I think I would want to do if I were endowed with superhuman powers.

"I would like first, at the very top of your society, to rear a generation that has all the qualities needed to lead and give the people the inspiration, the drive to make it succeed. This would be your elite. If you go to any country, even young ones like Australia, they have special schools.

"What is the ideal product? The ideal product is the student, the university graduate who is strong, robust, rugged, with tremendous qualities of stamina, endurance and, at the same time, with great intellectual discipline and, most important of all, humility and love for his community; a readiness to serve whether God or king or country or, if you like, just his community.

"Every society produces this type or they try to. The British have special schools for them. They send them to Eton and Harrow and a few very exclusive private schools which they call 'public schools', then they send them on to Oxford and Cambridge. They have legends that the Battle of Waterloo was won on the playing fields of Eton. …

"We should try to do that. Not every boy is equal in his endowments in either physical stamina or mental capacity or character. But you want to try and get all those with the potential to blossom forth. That is your spearhead in your society. On them depends the pace of progress.

"This government at the moment – the whole of this administration – is running on I would say the ability and drive and dedication – not on the basis of what they get in salaries – of about 150 people. You remove these 150 people, if you can identify the 150; whoever wants to destroy this society, identifies these 150 people and kills them, the push will be gone. This is a very thin crust of leadership. This has to be spread quickly, more and more."

*(Speech to school principals, August 29, 1966; text on page 393)*

# Lessons from Lenin: the limits of government

Perhaps the clearest summary of Lee's view of how the art of government and policy-making had to be tailored to fit the nature of the societies they were meant for is seen in a speech he made in Parliament in 1991. This was the first time he was moved to intervene in a parliamentary session after stepping down as prime minister in November 1990. He rose to answer his old political adversary from the Workers' Party, Dr Lee Siew Choh, the former Barisan Sosialis leader, who returned to the House as a non-constituency MP in 1988.

"God did not make the Russians equal. Lenin and Stalin tried to. You are too long, they chop you down. … They tried it in China; it has failed. They tried it in Vietnam, boat people. In North Korea, total devastation. … Even in the capitalist West where they have tried throwing money at problems … You go down to New York, Broadway. You will see the beggars… Worse than in the '50s and in the early '60s, before the Great Society programmes. Why? Why did it get worse after compassion moved a president, motivated with a great vision of a society which was wealthy and cared for, could look after everybody – the blacks, the minorities, the dispossessed, the disadvantaged. There is more unhappiness and more hardship today and more beggars, more muggers. Why is that? Have we not learnt?

"Where are the beggars in Singapore? Show me. I take pride in that. Has anybody died of starvation? Anybody without a home left to die in the streets, to be collected as corpses?

"Because we came to the realistic conclusion that the human being is motivated by instincts that go down to the basic genes in life. And the first basic instinct is to protect yourself, and stronger than that, to protect your offspring so that there is the next generation. You kill that link, you have killed off mankind. They half killed that link in China by removing children from parental control to the communes, and disaster followed. We went with the instinct of the individual.

"Not all can perform in a free and equal society. Free chances, there will always be the losers. There is the altruistic streak in society. Individuals who have done well, who want to do something for their fellowmen, and we should use that. … You ignore that and substitute for the altruistic individual with that drive to do something for his fellowmen, a bureaucracy, and you have got corruption, inefficiency, and failure …

"I am proud of the ethos with which we have infused a younger generation of Singaporeans. We have given them the chance to stand up, be self-reliant, and be enough of a team, of a nation, so that all can perform at their best, and the whole group, including the losers, will not perish. And that is achieved by going with human instincts, going with basic culture, and making adjustments along the way for those who would otherwise lose."

*(Parliamentary speech during the 1991 Budget debate; text on page 390)*

Lee's views about human abilities thus shaped his policies over the years.

But he was also to worry about the future. If a society's human stock was a critical determinant in its success, how could it ensure that future generations were given a headstart? He worried that the nation's brightest were not reproducing themselves in

sufficient numbers. In a controversial speech in 1983, he noted that only about one in four Singapore men with tertiary education was marrying his intellectual equal. This meant that a large pool of graduate women were left unmarried, or marrying down, and having fewer children. On the other hand, less educated Singaporeans were spawning large families. To him, this signalled a dangerous trend which would diminish the quality of the nation's gene pool. While others would deride this as an attempt to tinker with the genetic makeup of society, for Lee it was little more than a forward-looking attempt to forestall societal problems.

*Opposite: "I never regretted my 1983 speech, although it caused a lot of unhappiness." As prime minister, Lee held a National Day Rally every August, when he would address the nation in his inimitable candid style, sharing his analysis of the past year and the years to come. In 1983, he caused a stir when he highlighted the country's declining birth rate and the tendency of its graduate women to remain single and have fewer children. This, he said, would lower the quality of the country's gene pool.*

"If you don't include your women graduates in your breeding pool and leave them on the shelf, you would end up a more stupid society. The men don't believe me. Every year, I produce them the results. You marry that kind of a wife, you get this kind of a result. They close their minds. I think we are not going to become as good a society as we were with each generation … This is the basic stock of success. If you don't have this, you can have the best human resources programme, but your human resource is poor.

"In the older generations, economics and culture settled it. The pattern of procreation was settled by economics and culture. The richer you are, the more successful you are, the more wives you have, the more children you have. That's the way it was settled. I am the son of a successful chap. I myself am successful, so I marry young and I marry more wives and I have more children. You read Hong Lou Meng, *A Dream of the Red Chamber*, or you read Jin Ping Mei, and you'll find Chinese society in the 16th, 17th century described. So the successful merchant or the mandarin, he gets the pick of all the rich men's daughters and the prettiest village girls and has probably five, six, seven, eight, nine, ten different wives and concubines and many children. And the poor labourer who's dumb and slow, he's neutered. It's like the lion or the stag that's outside the flock. He has no harems, so he does not pass his genes down. So, in that way, a smarter population emerges.

"Now, we are into a stage of disgenics – not eugenics – where the smarter you are, the more successful you are, the more you calculate. And you say, look, yes, for the good of society, I should have five children, but what's the benefit to me? And the wife says, What? Five children? We can't go on holidays. So one is enough, or at the most two. The people at the lower end – in our three-room flats, two-rooms – some of them have 10, 12 to 14 children.

"So what happens? There will be less bright people to support more dumb people in the next generation. That's a problem. And we are unable to take firmer measures because the prevailing sentiment is against it. But these are the realities. You cannot disapprove of it and say it's a pity that it should work that way. That's the way procreation has been structured by nature. And we are going about it in an obtuse and idiotic way."

For Lee then, while individuals were free to choose whom they married, their collective decisions would have a profound effect on the nature of the society in future. This was not something governments could choose to ignore. A society's human stock, the cultural traits its people were imbued with, and the ethos of the society, he believed, were crucial factors in its success. It is to these matters that we turn to in the next chapter.

# Culture, the X-Factor

8

*Opposite: A Japanese executive chef in Singapore's Shangri-La. Lee was an admirer of Japanese culture, believing that it was the Japanese instinct to do a job well, whether it was shoe polishing or being an ace chef, that had helped the country rebuild after World War II. "If you want to succeed, that is the kind of society you have to be ... whatever you do, do to the best of your ability."*

At the basement of the Imperial Hotel in Tokyo is a shoe polishing station manned by two elderly Japanese who, for 700 yen, will give you the shiniest pair of shoes you have ever seen. Their prowess with wax and brush was chanced upon by Lee Kuan Yew while on a visit to the city in 1994. He paid them this glowing tribute.

"I have never seen such a shine on a pair of shoes. No army shoes or pair of boots shone like the two that I saw there. What they did, including polishing shoes, they did well. That's the first thing I learnt about the Japanese. If you want to succeed, that is the kind of society you have to be. Whatever you can do, do to the best of your ability. They have succeeded!

"Another anecdote. I was in Takamatsu, which is on Shikoku island, after a Tokyo visit in the 1970s. This was a very small little hotel in Shikoku, the capital of the province. The governor gave me dinner. When it came to fruit time, the cook came out ... it was persimmon time because it was October. And he demonstrated his skills and peeled the persimmon in our presence and formed beautiful shapes on a plate and served the persimmon. He was an ordinary chef, but he did his job to perfection. It became an art. So I asked, 'How many years?' Three to five years as an apprentice to learn how to cut and do simple things. And he has become the chief chef after 15 years, but the pride with which he did his job!

"It's not just the person who can paint a beautiful picture who's an artist. In his way, as a chef, he was an artist and he gave pleasure. Well, there is something in the culture that makes the Japanese admire people who do their job well. ... If that's what you can do, okay, let's see how well you do it. And that has created a successful Japan."

Lee had long pondered why some people, or societies, were better – more skilled, hard-driving, predisposed to success – than others. Why indeed were some communities able to progress faster? How is it certain ethnic groups were more driven in the pursuit of material wealth? What explained the dominance of some races in the upper echelons in societies, or in certain professions? Why did they emerge ahead of other ethnic groups in multiracial settings? Was it in the genes, a product of history, or both?

These were not just the philosophical musings of a curious intellect. They were practical matters Lee believed had to be addressed if a society was to succeed and stay ahead. The answers to these questions were crucial if one were to understand the forces working with, or against, a people in their effort to improve their lot. He had to know. And he believed that any government that was interested in achieving better standards of living for its people would also have to face these issues squarely, touchy and thorny though they may be.

He grappled with these questions for many years. What was it, for example, that made the Jews renowned for their shrewdness and intellectual prowess? Why were Jews from some backgrounds more successful than others? One answer was suggested to him by an American Jew he met.

"I've always wondered: why are the Jews so extraordinarily smart and why are the European Jews smarter than the Arab Jews? If you look at the Nobel Prize winners, they tend to be Ashkenazi Jews, not Sephardi Jews. (I was reading a book called *The Jewish Mystique*. It was recommended to me by a Jewish banker, an American Jew, a top American banker.) Its explanation, I did not know this, was that from the 10th to 11th century in Europe, in Ashkenazim, the practice developed of the rabbi becoming the most desirable son-in-law because he is usually the brightest in the flock. He can master Hebrew, he can master the local language and he can teach it. So he becomes the son-in-law of the richest and the wealthiest. He marries young, is successful, probably bright. He has large numbers of children and the brightest of his children will became the rabbi and so it goes on. It's been going on for nine, ten centuries. The same thing did not happen among the Sephardis, they did not have this practice. So one had a different pattern of procreation from the other, and so we have today's difference. That was his explanation.

"The Catholic Church had a different philosophy. All the bright young men became Catholic priests and did not marry. Bright priests, celibate, produce no children. And the result of several generations of bright Fathers producing no children? Less bright children in the Catholic world.

"In the older generations, the pattern of procreation was settled by economics and culture. The richer you are, the more successful you are, the more wives you have, the more children you have. That's the way it was settled."

Closer to home, Lee noted similarly striking differences between the various ethnic groups in multiracial Singapore, as well as among various subgroups within each race. Looking around him in the Singapore Cabinet, he found a disproportionate number of Teochew Chinese, whose ancestors hailed from villages in southern China, as well as Hakkas, Lee's own dialect group. He did not believe this was pure chance.

Teochew—
The second most
prevalent Chinese
dialect group in
Singapore, with
212,600 speakers.
Top on the list is
Hokkien (465,500)
and third is
Cantonese
(203,400).

"Look at the number of smart Teochews there are … just count them. Teo Chee Hean, Lim Hng Kiang, George Yeo, Lim Boon Heng. Is it a coincidence? In a Cabinet of 15, how do you explain that? For that matter, the Hakkas consider themselves very special too. They are tough, resourceful, they were latecomers who got squeezed to the mountainous areas of the south when they came from the north. They were the only Chinese group that did not bind their women's feet, because they lived on hilly terrain, had to make a living and couldn't afford to have women with feet bound. You also have more Hakkas in the Cabinet than are represented in the population. They are supposed to be harder-working, tougher and therefore higher-achievers. So there are these differences even within the races."

## What the porters told Lee

Lee's observations of ethnic and cultural differences began as early as his student days in Cambridge and were to continue throughout his life during his many travels abroad.

"I visited Europe during my vacation (as a student) and then saw India, Pakistan, Ceylon, Indonesia, Japan, Germany … You look for societies which have been more successful and you ask yourself why. On my first visit to Germany, in 1956, we had to stop in Frankfurt on our way to London. We had [earlier] stopped in Rome. This languid Italian voice over the loudspeaker said something … And there were Italian workers trundling trolleys at the airport. It was so relaxed, the atmosphere and the pace of work.

"Then the next stop was Frankfurt. And immediately, the climate was a bit cooler and chillier. And a voice came across the loudspeaker: *"Achtung! Achtung!"* The chaps were the same, porters, but bigger-sized and trundling away. These were people who were defeated and completely destroyed and they were rebuilding. I could sense the goal, the dynamism.

"Then Britain – well, they were languid, gentlemanly. With welfare, the British workers were no longer striving. They were getting West Indians to do the dirty jobs as garbage collectors, dustmen, conductors. They were still drivers because that was highly paid, the conductors were paid less.

"So one was looking for a soft life, the other was rebuilding and pushing. That made a vivid impression, a very deep impression on me.

"I also visited Switzerland when I was a student in '47, '48, on holiday. I came down by train from Paris to Geneva. Paris was black bread, dirty, after the war. I arrived at Geneva that morning, sleeping overnight. It was marvellous. Clean, beautiful, swept streets, nice buildings, marvellous white pillowcases and sheets, white bread after dark dirty bread and abundant food and so on. But hardworking, punctilious, the way they did your bed and cleaned up your rooms. It told me something about why some people succeed and some people don't. Switzerland has a small population. If they didn't have those qualities, they would have been overrun and Germany would have taken one part and the French another, the Italians would have taken another part. And that's the end of them.

"… the Japanese. Yes, I disliked their bullying and their hitting people and torturing people [during the Japanese Occupation], a brutal way of dealing with people. But they have admirable qualities. And in defeat, I admired them. For weeks, months, they were made, as prisoners, to clean the streets in Orchard Road, Esplanade and I used to watch them. Shirtless, in their dirty trousers but doing a good job. You want me to clean up? Okay, I clean up, that's my job. None of this reluctance, you know, and humiliated shame. My job is to clean up; all right, I clean up. I think that spirit rebuilt Japan. It was a certain attitude to life. That assured their success."

These impressions had a lasting impact on Lee. They confirmed in his mind the idea that there were profound forces which shaped, and continue to influence, the qualities of peoples. To understand these, he believed one had to delve deep into history, as well as the collective memories of a community.

"If you read the history of East Asia, South Asia and Southeast Asia, you will find that a different culture developed in East Asia, primarily from China, that slowly spread over the whole of East Asia – Korea, Japan and Vietnam. Up to 800, 900 years ago, Vietnam and Korea were part of China. And even when they were not part of China, they were vassals or tributary states that acknowledged China as supreme. They all used the Chinese script. Vietnam used the Chinese script. The Vietnamese have Chinese names. You can render their names into Chinese … an Italian priest came along and romanised it. And the Koreans too, they still use Chinese script. And the Japanese.

"Buddhism was an overlay. When Buddhism got imported from India into China, and into Japan from China, from Dunhuang where the Buddhist caves were, Buddhism was transformed. It is not the difference between Mahayana and Hinayana Buddhism. The difference was there in East Asian culture, already in being, when Buddhism was imported slightly more than 2,000 years ago. So Buddhism underwent a change and it became Mahayana Buddhism to fit in with a different culture. Even in their meditation techniques, between the Chinese and the Japanese, there's a slight difference. Because when Buddhism reached Japan, it underwent another transformation, it got 'Japanised'. I have been to these Buddhist temples. Zen Buddhists, theirs is a stricter discipline. There is a certain Japaneseness about it.

"But throughout East Asia, because they were influenced by China and probably not just by culture alone, there must have been a lot of similar genes, similar stock, probably the physical makeup was not very different, so they were very intense types, hard-driving, hard-striving people. Whereas if you go to India, you'll find sadhus, holy men, people who abjure the world, who go around giving land away or begging from the rich to give to the poor. It's a totally different culture. There's the sort of Gandhi saintliness. It's not the model in China. In China, the model is either *Three Kingdoms* or Shui Hu Zhuan, *Water Margin*, the kind of hero who forms a robber band and kills off wealthy people. You don't go begging from the wealthy to give to the poor. You just kill the wealthy and take from them.

"So it is a completely different philosophy to guide a man in life. The Indians have a more tolerant and forgiving approach to life. More next-worldly. If you do good, then in the next world you'll get rewarded."

These observations led Lee to conclude that nature and nurture had combined to produce distinct "tribes" or ethnic groups which were different in their genetic and cultural makeup. Some of these were more predisposed to success. At one time, he contended that as much as 80 per cent of this was due to nature. Later, rather than become embroiled in the ongoing nature versus nurture debate, he would assert that whatever the relative importance of the two factors, there was no denying one central fact: that, willy-nilly, culture was a key determinant of the success of certain groups over the years. In this regard, not all men or cultures were equal, Lee believed, contrary to the politically correct cultural relativism of the day.

> "I started off believing all men were equal … I now know that's the most unlikely thing ever to have been, because millions of years have passed over evolution, people have scattered across the face of this earth, been isolated from each other, developed independently, had different intermixtures between races, peoples, climates, soils.
>
> "You take the American Red Indian. He is genetically a Mongolian or Mongoloid, the same as the Chinese and the Koreans. But they crossed over, according to the anthropologists and the geologists, when the Bering Straits was a bridge between America and Asia. But for a few thousand years, in Asia, they had invading armies to-ing and fro-ing, huge infusions of different kinds of genes into the population from Genghis Khan, from the Mongols, from the Manchus, God knows how many invasions. And in the other, isolation, with only the buffaloes, until the white men came and they were weak and defenceless against white men's diseases and were eliminated. So whilst they were identical in stock, origin, they ended up different.
>
> "I didn't start off with that knowledge. But by observation, reading, watching, arguing, asking, that is the conclusion I've come to.
>
> "This is something which I have read and I tested against my observations. We read many things. The fact that it's in print and repeated by three, four authors does not make it true. They may all be wrong. But through my own experience, meeting people, talking to them, watching them, I concluded: yes, there is this difference. Then it becomes part of the accepted facts of life, for me."

## The cultural X-factor

But being "part of the accepted facts of life", as Lee put it, did not mean that these observations were only to shape his intellectual map of the world about him. More importantly, they were to influence profoundly his thinking on the best approach to economic and social development. Understanding the cultural forces at work in the region where Singapore was situated was a significant part of the process of transforming it into the economic dynamo it is today. Without such an awareness of the cultural ethos at work, government policies were doomed to either failure or raising false hopes, Lee believed. In other words, to succeed, a society's leaders would have to know the nature of the people they were charged with.

# If we get swine fever, we'll tell the world

The remarkable thing about Lee's belief in culture as an important factor for success is his willingness to bring it out into the open even though he knew it might cause offence in multi-racial Singapore. To a large extent, few others could have done it – be so brutally frank and yet cause no violent reaction among the population. Singaporeans have come to accept his style and indeed expect no less from him.

"We must have a tightly knit society, less exposed and more secure. To survive and keep standards up requires constant effort and organisation. If you slacken, if you give up, then the drains will clog up, traffic will snarl up, there will be flies, plague and pestilence.

"In other parts of the world, when their pigs suffer from swine fever, they hush it up. They pretend they do not have it. Net result: all pigs get infected, the position becomes permanently chronic. We can do likewise. But we will become permanently a chronic society: sick. So when we get swine fever, we announce it, alert everyone so that we can arrest the spread of the disease and bring back normalcy. This is what is required of this community: all the time, that push, that thrust to counter the natural sluggishness which this climate tends to build into our physical system, and, all that while, we must have an awareness of the realities of life.

"We can build the industries. We have what sociologists call a highly 'achievement-orientated' type of society. For every boy, every girl here tonight, there are fathers and mothers egging them on to perform better than the other pupils in school. Not all societies have this. In many societies, they are quite happy just to sit down under the banyan tree and contemplate their navel. So when there is famine they just die quietly. Here, they will not die quietly. If there is no food they will do something, look for somebody, break open stores, do something, plant something, and if they have to die, they die fighting for the right to live.

"We have done well for two years, better than I have dared to expect two years ago. But, let us have a sober appraisal of the problems ahead. ... there is nothing which we cannot solve, given a little time.

"A good, striving, hardy people cannot be kept down."

*(Speech at joint Alexandra and Queenstown community centres' National Day celebrations, August 15, 1967)*

Lee identified culture as a key factor in the success of societies in a speech in 1967. He added then that, fortunately for him and for Singapore, culture was in its favour.

"I think you must have something in you to be a 'have' nation. You must want. That is the crucial thing. Before you have, you must want to have. And to want to have means to be able first, to perceive what it is you want; secondly, to discipline and organise yourself in order to possess the things you want – the industrial sinews of our modern economic base; and thirdly, the grit and the stamina, which means cultural mutations in the way of life in large parts of the tropical areas of the world where the human being has never found it necessary to work in the summer, harvest before the autumn, and save it up for the winter.

"In large areas of the world, a cultural pattern is determined by many things, including climatic conditions. As long as that persists, nothing will ever emerge. And for it to emerge, there must be this desire between contending factions of the 'have' nations to try and mould the 'have-not' nations after their own selves. If they want that strongly enough, competition must act as an accelerator, and no more than an accelerator to the creation of modern, industrial, technological societies in the primitive agricultural regions of the world.

"I think Asia can be very clearly demarcated into several distinct parts – East Asia is one: it has got a different tempo of its own. So have South Asia and Southeast Asia. I think this is crucial to an understanding of the possibilities of either development for the good or development which is not in the interest of peace and human happiness in the region.

"I like to demarcate – I mean not in political terms – demarcate them half in jest, but I think half with some reality on the basis of difference in the tempo according to the people who know what these things are. I mean East Asia: Korea, Japan and mainland China and including the Republic of China in Taiwan and Vietnam. They are supposed to be Mahayana Buddhists. And then there is Cambodia, Thailand, Burma, Ceylon, which are supposed to be Hinayana Buddhists. According to the Hinayana Buddhists, if the bedbug disturbs you then you take your mattress and shake it off; there is that compassion not only for the human being but for the bedbug, and you give it another chance and you let it off. Either it finds its way on to some other creature or it finds its way back to your bed. But watching the Japanese over the years, I have not the slightest doubt that is not what they do. And I think this makes some difference. I am not talking now – isms or ideologies. It is something deeper. It is part of the tempo, the way of life."

*(Speech to Foreign Correspondents Association, March 21, 1967; text of speech on page 396)*

Lee believed it was precisely the underlying culture and values of the East Asian societies that had prevented them from being kept down. These cultural traits were the secret X-factor behind the so-called East Asian economic miracles.

Could other societies repeat their experience by emulating the economic policies they had adopted, as had been suggested by a 1994 World Bank report on the East Asian economies? Lee thought not. Unless the necessary values – hard work, thrift, an emphasis on education – were present, simply emulating the economic policies would not suffice to take others down the East Asian road to material progress, he contended.

In an interview with *Foreign Affairs* in 1994, he noted that the World Bank report had shied away from giving the cultural factor its full weight as a necessary condition for economic development.

"If you have a culture that doesn't place much value in learning and scholarship and hard work and thrift and deferment of present enjoyment for future gain, the going will be much slower. But the World Bank report's conclusions are part of the culture of American and, by extension, of international institutions. It had to present its findings in a bland and universalisable way, which I find unsatisfying because it doesn't grapple with the real problems. It makes the hopeful assumption that all men are equal, that people all over the world are the same. They are not. Groups of people develop different characteristics when they have evolved for thousands of years separately. Genetics and history interact …

"Now if you gloss over these kinds of issues because it is politically incorrect to study them, then you have laid a land mine for yourself. This is what leads to the disappointments with social policies embarked upon in America with great enthusiasm and expectations, but which yield such meagre results. There isn't a willingness to see things in their stark reality. But then I am not being politically correct."

## Is culture destiny?

Having identified culture as a key determinant in the success of the society, Lee believed that governments had a role to play in creating the right cultural ethos which would help it get ahead materially.

Although he stressed the importance of culture and values he did not believe a society's rate of progress was predetermined. Culture, while a factor in success, did not fix its destiny. Nor was culture immutable. Ebbs and flows were found in the story of almost all societies, when underlying cultural tendencies gave way to other influences. Societies could also be shaped and imbued with traits which improved its chances of success. This, he believed, was the task of its leaders.

Governments could not change the peoples they were charged with. Nor should it pretend that it could by promising to make good the unequal endowments that nature had bestowed on them. What it could do, however, was foster the environment and tenor of society to help the people achieve their best.

"Genes cannot be created, right? Unless you start tinkering with it as they may be able to do one day. But the culture you can tinker with. It's slow to change, but it can be changed – by experience – otherwise human beings will not survive. If a certain habit does not help survival, well, you must quickly unlearn that habit.

"So I've got to try and get Singaporeans to emulate or to adopt certain habits and practices which will make Singapore succeed. If you go and act like the Italians and wander around gradually, take your own sweet time, trundling luggage, you are not going to have a good airport that can compete with other people in the world. You've got to hustle and bustle, now, get on with it! Clear the baggage quickly!

# Chinese or Singaporean? The ping-pong test

*Lee launched the Speak Mandarin campaign in 1979 to help Chinese Singaporeans preserve their mother tongue and to counter the erosion of traditional values.*

While the majority of Singaporeans were Chinese, Lee was ever mindful of the need to fashion a multiracial community in his fledgling state. The Chinese, while proud of their cultural heritage and keen to preserve the traditions which had helped them succeed, would have to be ever-mindful of the sentiments of the ethnic minorities in Singapore, as well as the Muslim communities that surrounded it.

"The past week of ping-pong was an interesting and important experience for Singapore. The question is: has the majority of our young people learnt that, although nearly 80 per cent of them are ethnic Chinese, they are Singaporeans? Or are they bemused enough to think that, being ethnic Chinese, they can identify themselves as members of a potential superpower? It is tempting to indulge in a sensation of greatness, without having to undergo the hardships and sacrifices of the people of China and, at the same time, as Singaporeans, enjoy the freer and better life here.

"When I watched the ping-pong on television the first night, I was slightly bewildered and angered. Instead of giving support and encouragement to our players, who were up against world-class opponents, a part of the crowd booed whenever our players played badly. I was also told that about 40 persons shouted slogans, wishing Chairman Mao long life. But there was no response to this from the bulk of the audience.

"However, from the second night on, there was no more booing. Instead, there were cheers whenever the visitors or our players acquitted themselves well in any rally.

"No one can ask of Singapore Chinese not to be ethnic Chinese. And it would be unnatural not to feel pleasantly reassured that, as Chinese, we are not unequal to other major ethnic and cultural groups in the world; that the Chinese, either because of ethnic or cultural attributes or both, are not inadequate and can make the grade, whatever the political system. But there are many people who are interested to know whether this ethnic, cultural and linguistic affinity will make us susceptible to manipulation through tugging at the heartstrings of our people and making them more Chinese-orientated and less Singaporean.

"After the past week, my assessment is that a portion can still be manipulated. But, unlike 10 years ago, the majority are now Singaporean. The situation should get better with each passing year. The orientation in our schools and the experience of the last 20 years have brought about this change.

"I believe a definite majority in Singapore are aware that our future, our destiny, depends on our ability to discern our collective interests and to protect these interests. For neither China nor any other country or government will protect us or our interests, just because we happen to be ethnic Chinese."

*(Speech at the Hong Lim PAP branch 15th anniversary celebration dinner, July 14, 1972)*

"But I would say that if you had come to Singapore airport in the 1960s and you come to Singapore airport today, you would know that something has happened in the meantime and the place and the people are different, they are more effective.

"Today, supposing your last stop was Bombay and you land in Singapore, I would think you'd be a bit grateful that your bags are handled so rapidly. There you are, here, take it. You are through customs in a shot."

# When different cultures mix

But identifying culture as the hidden X-factor that had helped certain societies do better than others raised a very thorny issue. These societies, such as Japan or Germany, were homogenous ones. How then would this cultural factor manifest itself in racially mixed societies? Lee was candid about his assessment of multiracial Singapore. He told the authors, "I have said openly that if we were 100 per cent Chinese, we would do better. But we are not and never will be, so we live with what we have."

But what happens when people from differing cultures are mixed in a multiracial context? Would not the more hard-driving group streak ahead of those which placed less emphasis on the pursuit of material wealth? And how would the government of a nascent multiracial state deal with such a tricky problem?

Lee's Malaysian experience in the early 1960s made clear to him the explosive nature of ethnic grievances, especially when there was a twinning of the ethnic and economic divides.

"One of the problems which has worried me is the uneven rate of development within the community, because the Chinese, Indians, Ceylonese and Eurasians progress at a faster rate than our Malays. If we do not correct this imbalance, then, in another 10 to 20 years, we will have a Harlem, something not to be proud of. So from politics I have had to go to anthropology and sociology to seek the reasons for this."

*(Speech to Southeast Asia Business Committee, May 12, 1968; text of speech on page 398)*

As with many other questions that Lee turned his mind to, he would look up authorities, either through his reading or in face-to-face meetings, for possible answers. These he would ponder to help him make up his mind. In the case of the crucial question of why some ethnic groups performed less well than others, he was to cite, in a speech in May 1968, the work of sociologist Judith Djamour, who did research on the Malays in Singapore in the 1940s and 1950s.

She argued that Singapore Malays and Chinese "certainly appear to have different cultural values. Singapore Chinese on the whole considered the acquisition of wealth to be one of the most important aims in life, and almost an end in itself; they are indefatigable workers and keen businessmen. Singapore Malays, on the other hand, attached great importance to easy and graceful living."

This view, Lee found, appeared to be supported by that of Bryan Parkinson, a Fellow at the Centre for Southeast Asian Studies at the University of Hull. In the January 1968 issue of *Modern Asian Studies*, he attributed the cultural differences between the Malays and Chinese to their having different "maximising postulates", or in other words, different ideas of what success meant, although neither view might be considered superior to the other. Parkinson wrote:

"This desire to succeed is no more absent from rural Malay society than it is from any other, but to the Malay success means something different from what it does, for example, to the Malaysian Chinese. The Chinese seem to regard success as being the improvement of their economic position even if this requires fundamental change or innovation. The Malays seem to regard success as doing what their forebears have approved and practised, but doing it as well as they can. Wealth and economic advancement are desired by the Malays, but not at the expense of renouncing utterly the traditions and traditional occupations of their forebears to which they have grown accustomed. …"

The upshot of this was of crucial significance. As Parkinson argued,

"There is nothing irrational about Malay values, and to criticise them in terms of other values is reprehensible. But if the values of the Malays remain basically unaltered, and there is no reason in Malay terms to explain why they should alter, then it is likely that economic advance for them will remain relatively low."

This was the worrisome conclusion that Lee was to reach. Given this background, he recognised that while efforts could be made to alleviate the situation and narrow the economic gaps between the races, the innate differences in aptitude and ability could not be wished away. Nor were the gaps likely to be bridged easily, or any time soon.

"This poses an extremely delicate problem. We tried over the last nine years systematically to provide free education from primary school right up to university for any Singapore citizen who is a Malay. This is something we don't give to the majority ethnic group – the Chinese. They pay fees from secondary school onwards. We don't find it necessary to do it for the other ethnic minorities, because broadly speaking, they are making similar progress as the Chinese. All are achievement-orientated, striving, acquisitive communities.

"The reluctant conclusion that we have come to after a decade of the free education policy is that learning does not begin in school. It starts in the home with the parents and the other members of the family. Certainly the adoption of values comes more from the home, the mother, than the teacher. This means change will be a slow process. It can be accelerated in some cases by our judicious intermingling of the communities so that, thrown into the more multiracial milieu we have in our new housing estates, Malay children are becoming more competitive and more striving."

*(Speech to Southeast Asia Business Committee, May 12, 1968; text of speech on page 398)*

# Singapore's Malay dilemma

*Members of the self-help group Mendaki help to motivate Malay youth in Singapore to "shift gears" and make their lives a success.*

Lee believed that government efforts could help communities improve their lot and help narrow the inequalities between various ethnic groups. But he was never under any illusion that the economic or ethnic divide would soon be bridged.

"I think we are foolish if we believe that these things can be wished away. There are deep and abiding differences between groups. And whatever we do, we must remember that in Singapore, the Malays feel they are being asked to compete unfairly, that they are not ready for the competition against the Chinese and the Indians and the Eurasians. They will not admit or they cannot admit to themselves that, in fact, as a result of history, they are a different gene pool and they do not have these qualities that can enable them to enter the same race.

"So there is a sense of being imperilled, endangered, running in a race in which they are bound never to win, or very few can win. You have this sense of being a deprived, a sat-upon minority. That has been handled sensitively and I think more than fairly. We have made concessions, given them free education when everybody else has to pay, given them land for mosques when everybody else has to buy their land for the temples or churches.

"I do not believe that that solves the problem. We have diminished the problem by making them live together, scattered in the estates and at least they know that their neighbour is not a demon. You know, a Chinese neighbour can be just as friendly, although you will not borrow their kitchen utensils because there's pork in the kitchen, but otherwise they are quite normal human beings. So it helps. But you will never dispel that sense of distinctiveness.

"At the very beginning, the Malays were not hardworking, nor were a lot of the Indians. We encouraged them to keep up. I'm not sure whether they will not feel a little resentful, but I mean this is part of history. I know that it took a long time before the Malays accepted that they had to work hard because it was not in their culture.

"Well, let me give you my experience. I was making a visit last week to some families who have upgraded, people with children who are in either late primary or early secondary school. And I moved from one flat to another flat, upgraded. One of the three families was a Malay family. And he's bought an executive flat, beautiful marble floor. All he had was 'O' levels in Malay language in Maju School, and his wife too. But he has learnt English. His wife is now working as a receptionist in some big firm of accountants. This chap had been working for an American firm making computer parts and selling them. Now, he's decided to branch out on his own and he's selling them in Malaysia and he's formed a company with a Bumiputra partner. And he is acting just like a Chinese. You know, he's bouncing, running around, to-ing and fro-ing. In the old culture, he would not be doing that.

"I'm not saying all of them have become like that. But here is one who has moved, shifted gears and has made his life a success."

# I did the exact opposite

Having arrived reluctantly at the conclusion that the gap in performance between races would not be eliminated simply by providing the less well off with a head start through better educational and life opportunities, Lee did what would have been unthinkable to most politicians elsewhere – he went public, airing his observations and concerns before the whole country.

Not for him the race-blind approach, which sought to gloss over ethnic differences, whether out of political expedience or ethnic guilt. For Lee, that was an exercise in self-deception, or worse, raising false expectations. Nor would he brook programmes such as affirmative action schemes which he saw as misguided attempts to hobble the more adept in society so that others might catch up. This, he felt, would only hold the whole society back.

"I did the exact opposite. Once I discovered that special tuition, special food and all this did not produce the necessary result, I looked up the prewar records and I found the same weaknesses in mathematics and so on. So I decided: first, inform the leaders and the elders and inform the teachers, then publish it. So please, let there be no misunderstanding. This has nothing to do with discrimination or lack of support or whatever. It's a profound problem.

"The reasons why I did this are simple ones. This way, we are going to get results. The other way, we are going to confuse people and you're going to get wrong results. Now, I suppose maybe it's too touchy a problem to say this openly, but to pretend that we are all equal and therefore I am not in it because you have discriminated against my caste, so I need a quota – it's going to lead to very unhappy consequences …

"I do not believe that the American system of solving the problem stands any chance. First, they deny that there is a difference between the blacks and the whites. Once you deny that, then you're caught in a bind. All right, if we are equal, then why am I now worse off? You have fixed me. The system has fixed me. So they say, right, let's go for affirmative action. Lower marks to go to university, and you must have a quota for number of salespersons or announcers on radio or TV. And so you get caught in a thousand and one different ways. And you say, since the army is now 30, 40 per cent blacks, you must have so many generals, so many colonels, and so on.

"I don't know how they have got into this bind, but I think that is not realistic. You don't have to offend people because they are not as good as you. I mean I'm not as smart as an Israeli or many Chinese for that matter. But that doesn't mean that I'm not to be treated as equal in my rights as a human being.

"The only way we can all really be physiologically equal in brain power and everything else is to have a mélange. All go into a melting pot and you stir it. In other words, force mixed marriages, which is what the people in Zanzibar tried. The blacks wanted to marry all the Arab girls so that the next generation, their children, will be half-Arab. But I don't think that's a practical way nor will it solve the problem. And you can't do that worldwide, you can – maybe you can do that in Zanzibar. In the process, you diminish Zanzibar.

Because whereas before you had some outstanding people who can do things for Zanzibar, now you have brought them down to a lower level.

"So my attitude now would be a very practical one of saying that we are equal human beings. Whether you can run 100 yards in 20 minutes, 20 seconds or 10 seconds, you've got a right to be here. But that doesn't mean that because you run at 20 seconds, I must run at 20 seconds. Then we'll all get nowhere."

# When cultures ebb

But if culture and values could change over time, what was there to stop them from retrogressing instead of altering for the better? Could societies lose sight of their values? Might those traits which built a society be superseded by others which were less favourable to its continued success?

In this regard, Lee was to worry often that rising affluence among Singaporeans was producing a generation which was increasingly "soft". Parents were indulging their children with their newfound wealth. Lee worried that the hard-driving virtues of the coolies and labourers who had built up the country might become displaced by the more languorous ways of their children, spoilt, ironically, by the fruits of their parents' efforts.

*Opposite: Lee kicking off a sepak takraw game in Tanjong Pagar. "When I was a little boy, I changed the screw, the pin of my top … or I caught fighting fish, went into monsoon drains. … Now they are sitting down, watching television and given teddy bears and little toys."*

"The danger is very real and very present because parents who have got through a hard life give their children what they'd missed – comfort, all the sweets, all the toys, all the jeans and fancy shoes which they wish they had had when they were young. That breeds a certain attitude of mind in the young which is not very good for them.

"They ought to begin to learn to do things. When I was a little boy, I changed the screw, the pin of my top. You buy a top, a wooden sphere, pear-shaped. And you change it [the pin] from a nail to a screw and you sharpen your screw and you put thumbtacks on the back of the top to armour-plate it, then you fight other people's tops. So it was a game but in which you contributed something into what you were doing.

"Or I caught fighting fish, went into monsoon drains. Along Changi Road, there were rubber estates in what is now Kampong Kembangan. In those ditches, you could get fighting fish. You went home and bred them. Some became fierce. Some were washouts, they ran away. But you were doing something.

"Now, they are sitting down, watching television and given teddy bears and little toys. Of course, because of that danger, we keep on physical activities in school, discipline, we try to counteract that. But you see the obesity, it's great. It's born out of ignorance. Parents think they're doing their children good. But in fact they're harming their children."

But the community's traditional values faced a threat not only from within. Being a highly open society, Singapore was constantly exposed to other cultures. Lee feared that Singaporeans, subject to a barrage of Western values, through the media and travel, could lose the cultural traits that had underpinned the country's success. Socioeconomic changes, unleashed when more Singapore women were drawn into the workforce, had

# Singapore too Westernised?

*Young people at a disco, a scene repeated in many nightspots. But more important than their "Western" exterior, Lee felt, was whether they retain the Asian core values.*

When a group of Hongkong professionals, who met Lee in 1984 to discuss the Hongkong problem, told him that, in their eyes, Singapore was a very Westernised country, his antennae immediately shot up. Hongkong, by comparison, they said, was a very Oriental society. Of all Singapore's long-term problems, this question about how its values would change with affluence and modernisation is perhaps the most vexing for Lee. He knows that the nature of Singapore society will change in time, that change is inevitable. But will it be for the better? He shared his concern with Singaporeans in this speech to students at the two local universities in 1988.

"I met a group of Hongkong professionals who were extremely uneasy, and we discussed a scheme that would make it possible for them to consider using Singapore as a perch in case of need, and continuing to work in Hongkong. At the end of their stay, when I met them, they said, 'You are a very Western society, we are very Chinese.' I said, what's the difference? They said, 'Your people, right down to ordinary workers, they look so Westernised, their behaviour is extremely Western. We are very Oriental.'

"… As I met friends, looked up their data, I discovered that this casual remark had profound significance. This was '84. It's the software in the younger generation which will determine whether Singapore continues to thrive, to prosper, to be a dynamo as it used to be, as it has been, or whether it will plateau like so many Western societies, like Europe or Britain, where they've just lost steam. They don't see the point of striving and achieving any more. They're just comfortable and they're happy. And the Europeans in particular, more than the Americans, they feel comfortable with an enlarged community in 1992. They can afford some protectionism. It does not matter if world trade becomes too fierce and too competitive for them. Life could go on, for at least some time. …

"What is it that we should consider core values? I don't think how you dress, whether you wear shorts or ties or open-neck shirts, or wear your hair short or long, makes the slightest difference. Unless it's a manifestation of an inner urge. But these core values, I believe, are basic. Do you consider your basic relationships to be fundamental? The human relationships. What Confucius described as the five critical relationships. Mencius epigrammatised it in this way … 'Love between father and son, one; two, duty between ruler and subject; three, distinction between husband and wife; four, precedence of the old over the young; and five, faith between friends.' Father and son, ruler and subject, husband and wife, old over young, faith between friends. In other words, the family is absolutely the fundamental unit in society. From family, to extended family, to clan, to nation.

*(Speech to NUS/NTI students, August 22, 1988; text on page 406)*

also left them with less time to nurture their children and pass on traditional values as had been done in the past.

Lee would lament this development time and again. He believed that efforts would have to be redoubled to help Singaporeans maintain their traditions and values if the society here was to keep the cultural "X-factor" that enabled it to thrive. Nothing, in this regard, was more important than preserving the family as the most basic and fundamental unit of society. A society able to do so would find half its problems solved, and would not require government, with its unwieldy bureaucracy and its tendency to succumb to corruption and lobby groups, to intervene. Indeed, he would place blame for much of the social ills of the West on the break-up of the family unit.

Lee therefore moved to enshrine the family as the "basic building block in society" and as one of Singapore's Shared Values. These cultural signposts had helped the country along its way in the past and would be vital guides in the tumultuous times of cultural confusion ahead as it became more international and cosmopolitan.

"... to succeed, we must decide, yes, this is a problem, we are under assault, what is it we want to keep? ... Have we changed? Let's go through some of the basic core values.

"Strong family ties? Yes, but only the immediate family, the nuclear family, father, mother, children. It does not include grandfather, uncles, cousins. They're remote. They live somewhere else, in some other flat, perhaps near by and they can leave the baby with them. But the links are not as close as when I grew up.

"I grew up in a big extended family home. A rambling house in Siglap, Katong. I grew up with a wealth of cousins ... There were five households – grandparents and four married sons and daughters and their children. So the relationship was a close one until, just before the war, we set up home on our own. But because the years of childhood were years of living in an extended family, the bonds are close.

"Marriage pattern? Altered beyond recognition. The arranged marriages are gone. Children are better educated than their parents. They decide the parents' ways and tastes and choices are not acceptable. The result, you all know.

"Relationship with authority? Ruler and subject by and large still abiding. But the older generation is more deferential, respectful of ministers, of officials, than the younger generation. I'm not saying it's good or bad. It's just an observation. ...

"Thrift, hard work, faith between friends? Hard work, yes; thrift, with CPF, less so. Faith between friends – I have not noticed deterioration, but with time, with mobility, we may get what Alvin Toffler once described as "the disposable society". As you move up, you dispose of your furniture, your old wives, your old clothes and you acquire new ones and you dispose of your friends too. ...

"By and large, it's a problem still at the top. Only the highly educated have that degree of bi-culturism where they are more Western than Eastern. At the middle and in the lower ranges, it's still very much an Asian society. The Western habits, songs, dances, whether it's a disco or Swing Singapore, their dress styles or their fast foods, that's just a veneer. But if it

# Religious Harmony Act: "We were headed for trouble!"

*Buddhism now attracts more and more followers among the younger and better-educated, a result, said Lee, of the greater proselytisation in polytechnics and universities.*

Freedom of worship is enshrined in the Singapore constitution. By and large there have been few problems keeping the religious peace since independence in 1965 despite the multi-religious composition of the people. But a new law passed in 1991, to pre-empt future problems from overzealous groups out to convert others to their faith, makes it an offence to proselytise in a way that would cause disharmony among the religious groups. Lee explains why it was necessary.

"Religion is at the core of any culture – and Islam and Catholicism are two of the most exacting religions which command your way of life. Just like Judaism does. If you read the Talmud, what you should do, what you can eat, what you can't eat, who you can marry, who you can't marry, when you have sex, when you should not have sex and so on, it's all laid down in the book. It's an injunction. ...

"So I would say that if we had a majority who were either Catholics or Muslims, then Singapore would never have developed in this way because the majority would demand that the minority comply, or at least do not publicly show a different way of life ... But the majority happen to be Chinese Taoists, Buddhists. And Buddhism is a very mild sort of, not an exacting religion. Ancestor worshippers, Confucianists. So it was a very relaxed situation, so long as we live and let live. Now don't go and force him into your religion. If you want to convert, don't do it in an aggressive way. And don't convert a chap who already belongs to a religion that's fiercely against conversion. Avoid that. So we have succeeded.

"But when the Christians became very active and evangelical, ... wanting to convert the Muslims, and the Catholics decided to go in for social action, we were heading for trouble! So the Buddhists reacted. And this Japanese group, Nichiren Soshu, very active group – huge Buddhist groups were growing rapidly in our polytechnics and universities and in reaction to all these Christians – they were being threatened. We would have headed for trouble quite unnecessarily. We've just got out of one trouble – communism and Chinese chauvinism and Malay chauvinism – and you want to land into another? Religious intolerance? It's just stupid. Stay out of politics. The Religious Harmony Act was passed; after that, it subsided.

"You cannot begin converting others and taking a tough line and expect others not to react, because they are losing their followers. You use the church for political purposes, the other religions will also enter the political arena, or they will lose out. So, as I told the Catholics and the Christians, 'The Muslims must react. The Buddhists are reacting. And I will help the majority because the Buddhists are in the majority. And do you want that?' So they stopped and agreed.

"Well, it's part of the law, and it will be enforced if anybody breaches it. But if you ask the human rights groups, that's a violation of human rights, we should allow everybody to do what they like. Free speech and free conversions, then you'll have an enlightened society. I do not accept that as the happy conclusion or outcome."

seeps down, if we are not conscious of what is happening and we allow this process to go on unchecked, and it seeps down, then I believe we have a bigger problem to deal with, where the middle ranges will also be more Western than Asian. ...

"I would hate to believe that the poor, ragged, undernourished Chinese coolie and the equally ragged Malay peon and driver and Indian labourer had the inner strength to build today's Singapore, and their children with all the nice mod clothes, well-fed, all the vitamins, all the calories, protein, careful dental care, careful medical checks, PT, well-ventilated homes, they lost that inner drive."

*(Speech to NUS/NTI students, August 1988; text on page 406)*

Preserving the society's cultural ethos was not just a matter of culture. For Lee, it was a question of survival. Singapore society succeeded because it was quintessentially Singaporean. Lose that, and all would be lost.

"We could not remain what we were, but we cannot change totally or we will be destroyed. If we change so thoroughly that we lose the qualities that have ensured our survival as a community or as different communities, what will guarantee us that American or British culture will see our survival with their atomistic approach to life? I don't think we'll survive."

# First Order, then Law

While American teenager Michael Fay lay in Singapore's Queenstown Remand Centre in April 1994, waiting for his sentence of six swift strokes of the *rotan* to be meted out, his parents and lawyers, as well as human rights activists and newspaper columnists in the United States, unleashed a verbal lashing at Singapore and its leaders.

The punishment, ordered by a Singapore court which convicted Fay of vandalising cars in the city state, was cruel, draconian, barbaric even, they charged. Lee and his ministers were portrayed as hardline autocrats, evil dictators, harsh neo-Confucianists. They were even likened to Nazi chief Dr Paul Goebbels, who revelled in human torture.

Meanwhile, Lee was on a two-week state visit to Australia and New Zealand. As the charges grew wilder by the day – there were allegations of public canings in downtown Singapore, of women being whipped for littering and other incredible tales – Antipodean journalists saw their chance for a story that might make world headlines. They sought Lee out at press conferences and public events, demanding to know why the boy had to be flogged.

To Lee, the matter was a simple case of crime and punishment. Vandals and other criminals had to be taught not to repeat their misdeeds. Better yet if they were deterred from committing their anti-social acts through the certainty that the law would seek them out relentlessly and inflict tough justice. This included a mandatory death penalty for drug trafficking, murder, armed robbery or kidnapping, and caning for vandalism, violent rape and molest, and the unlawful possession of a weapon. Lee was unapologetic about this tough-minded approach. This, he asserted, was how he had managed to keep Singapore's once gangster-ridden streets safe.

"If anyone thinks it is barbaric, well then, please don't bring your 18-year-old to Singapore. And if you do bring him, please warn him about the consequence," he said of the caning of Fay at a meeting of the National Press Club of Australia, drawing applause.

He went on to recount how an American journalist working on a documentary in Singapore had told him that she had gone for a jog in the streets around her hotel at Singapore's Marina Bay at 2 am. She said she "would have been mad" to do that in the United States, he noted.

"Why was she able to do that? Because we have established a certain security and personal safety," said Lee. He later added, "I think, with right-minded people, or people I consider right-minded, it is a plus. You know that if you come to Singapore, your life, body, limb, properties will be quite safe."

The documentary, Lee recalled, had featured several people who had been caned, including one who had been given 15 strokes for gang rape. The offender had said that "every stroke was a stroke of hell", which he would remember always. Would he do it again? "Never, not in my life," the criminal had replied. Lee concluded, "The punishment is not fatal. It is not painless. It does what it is supposed to do, to remind the wrongdoer that he should never do it again. And it does work."

## Order under the heavens

To Lee, the upshot of the Fay case was clear: tough measures had to – and would – be enforced by the authorities to maintain order in society. Not for him the fashionable liberal ideas of modern-day penology, which sought not so much to punish as to reform criminals, and where crimes were explained away by blaming it on some failing of the system or society. He believed instead in the old-fashioned ideas of guilt and responsibility. Deterrence was to be a key aspect of the legal system he fashioned for his fledgling state.

He dismissed as wishful thinking the Western liberal notion that all human beings, if left in the state of nature, would naturally be kind and gentle, forgiving and compassionate, and that only the evil of the system made them vicious and criminal. Even as a law student in Britain, about 40 years ago, he had thought that the new branch of criminology written by reformist sociologists and lecturers would not do Singapore much good.

> "I've always viewed them with a certain bewilderment, and I've watched what has happened to the countries that have implemented the theories. I am waiting for the day when even they will see the light. Human beings, regrettable though it may be, are inherently vicious and have to be restrained from their viciousness.
>
> "If these people said to us, cancel whipping and you will be a better society, we will underwrite this exercise in human liberty, then we would abolish effective punishments and treat criminals the way Americans do."
>
> *(Press conference in New Zealand, April 1994)*

However, Lee was well aware of the economic and social price that his people would pay if such a system failed. Foreign firms, he argued, would withdraw their investments at the first sign of disorder in the streets. Singaporeans, too, might send their money and their families to safer havens abroad.

Lee's first priority was therefore to establish and maintain order in Singapore, which in the late 1950s and early 1960s was a smouldering hotbed of communal and communist activities, quite a world apart from the urbane city of today. In this regard, he believed that more important than all the fine liberal pronouncements of individual rights and liberties was the government's responsibility to ensure the individual his fundamental freedoms. In short, this meant that people must be safe, and have opportunities to obtain food, shelter, education and jobs so that they could maximise their potential. This would also assure investors of the country's stability and security.

This philosophy towards law and order appeared to be shared by the vast majority of Singaporeans, perhaps because of their Asian culture. In Oriental societies, Lee believed, people looked to the authorities to establish "order under the heavens". Good rulers were those who could do so effectively and fairly.

Put another way, the people conferred on their leaders a moral authority to act in the community's collective interest. Leaders who failed to do so, or who acted unfairly or arbitrarily, risked losing their moral sway with the people. Indeed, the importance of maintaining its authority in the eyes of the people was stressed several times by Lee during the Fay episode. He said repeatedly that, had the government backed down in the face of American pressure to rescind Fay's sentence, it would no longer be able to impose similar punishments on Singaporeans. Nor could it govern effectively thereafter.

This was in stark contrast to the approach in the West, where government or state interference in an individual's life was discouraged and kept to a minimum. Having fought to free themselves from overly powerful governments, Americans believed passionately that their leaders' power should be fettered by checks and balances. Instead of restraining individuals, people should be left to their own devices, free to exercise their rights and responsibilities, and to look after their own concerns and interests.

Such a sanguine view of the way human communities worked, Lee believed, could not be applied to his native state, a fledgling multiracial society riven with ethnic, communalist and ideological divides. His people, the bulk of whom were the children of immigrants from the lower rungs of societies in Asia, had yet to cultivate the finer social graces that made state sanctions unnecessary, he maintained.

"Mine is a very matter-of-fact approach to the problem. If you can select a population and they're educated and they're properly brought up, then you don't have to use too much of the stick because they would already have been trained. It's like with dogs. You train it in a proper way from small. It will know that it's got to leave, go outside to pee and to defecate.

"Unfortunately, when I was in Britain in 1946, I compared Singapore to Britain, and found we were very ill-behaved, ill-trained. They were well-trained, they were polite, they were honest, what I saw of the British in the south, in London, in Cambridge, in Devon and Cornwall where I went for my holidays. We did not have 300 years of cultivated living and training.

# Corruption – a way of life

Lee took a very tough stand against corruption, especially the taking of bribes by officials for favours. He made clear that no one, not even top government officials or ministers, was immune from investigations into their financial dealings. Several were in fact charged and convicted when it was discovered that they were on the take. Lee also believed that, to help fight corruption, civil servants and political leaders would have to be paid well, so that there would be less likelihood of their succumbing to temptation.

Explaining his hard line in a speech to the Singapore Advocates and Solicitors Society on March 18, 1967, he said, "We live in an area where to be corrupt is a way of life. And there are scales starting from 20 cents for this and 40 cents for that, to two dollars for this. There are rates for the job. You know it, I know it. What is most important really for us is that because it is a way of life for others around us, it has to be understood.

"What is your answer? I say unless you are able to give our civil servants that pride in their standards and reward them for being able to maintain those standards, the standards in the end will be undermined."

In this regard, Lee believed that government leaders would have to set an example. They would have to be aboveboard and seen to be so. They should also not indulge in lavish living. As he explained to the authors: "We needed a civil service that was responsive to our goals. The most important thing was to make sure that they stayed honest. A civil service that is dishonest is a disaster to us. ...

"And that's one of the reasons why we were forced to take over, because we could see that another four, five years of the kind of government that Lim Yew Hock was running would have become more thoroughly corrupt.

"First, we had to set the example. If the ministers were taking something on the side, his personal secretary must know, right? So, we have got to set an example, not only in being uncorrupt, but also in being thrifty and economical, and not travelling in grand style. The previous government was living it up. They knew they were not going to last long, so they lived and travelled as best as they could. Enjoyed it while the going was good. We wanted to trim the cost of government, so we ran a very spartan government. No wastage, no lavish entertainment, no big offices. We set the tone, the example, they followed. They responded to it.

"We had the Corrupt Practices Investigations Bureau already set up in the 1950s. And I knew it was an effective organisation. We knew that this outfit was an important way to ferret out and punish those who broke the rules. So we helped fund it and built it up."

*(Interview with the authors and speech to the Singapore Advocates and Solicitors Society, March 18, 1967; text of speech on page 414)*

"So they could leave piles of newspapers at tube stations, and you have a coin box and you take the newspaper and put your sixpence, 12 pence, and take your newspaper and even manage your own change. I was most impressed by that. And the buses: people would go up and pay the conductor as they were running out if the conductor had not given the ticket. But of course, it's a different Britain now. Partly because of different education, no discipline at home, in the schools, and partly because immigrants have come in, and the whole atmosphere has changed and the people have changed.

"No, we were not that kind of a society. We had to train adult dogs who even today deliberately urinate in the lifts. What do you do? That would not happen or would not have happened in the Britain that I knew in the '40s and '50s. It's a standard of behaviour of people which springs from cultivated living over a long period and training of children in a certain way, so that they are considerate to other people. You tell me how long we take to reach that kind of a state. Maybe another hundred years of constant effort.

"We don't have that luxury. I cannot wait 300 years. And we're already into highrise living and you have them behaving like this, throwing things out of the window, killing people and messing up the place. How can you put up with that?"

# Laws to fit the society

To Lee, a community's legal framework was very much tied to its cultural ethos and makeup. The genteel live-and-let-live liberalism of the British legal system, he argued, as early as the 1960s, would have to be adapted to fit the unpolished nature of Singapore society in the 1950s, if order was to be maintained. A wholesale and unthinking transplant of British laws and norms, many of which were alien to its colonies, would only bring chaos.

"Our architects learn of classical forms of Grecian colonnades and the Roman forum, of the grace and beauty of Christopher Wren's St Paul's, buildings of beauty and grace built out of marble and sandstone, of ancient Greece and ancient Rome and not so ancient London, to fit the style and climates of their time and their people. But then architects have to come back to Malaya and mould from granite and cement the buildings to fit our people and our climate.

"There is a gulf between the principles of the rule of law, distilled to its quintessence in the background of peaceful 19th century England, and its actual practice in contemporary Britain. The gulf is even wider between the principle and its practical application in the hard realities of the social and economic conditions of Malaya. You will have to bridge the gulf between the ideal principle and its practice in our given sociological and economic milieu. For if the forms are not adapted and principles not adjusted to meet our own circumstances but blindly applied, it may be to our undoing. You must bridge this gulf quickly if you are not to spend the first few years of your practice after graduation floundering in confusion.

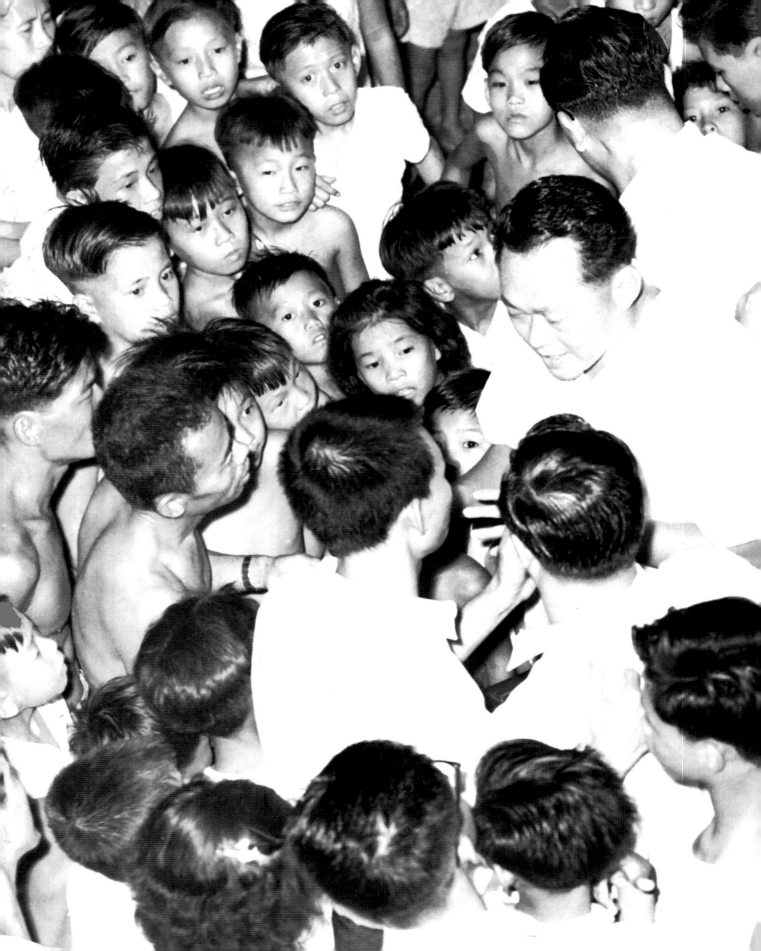

*Opposite: Laws must fit society. Lee was acutely aware of the nature of the society he was charged with in the 1960s – a racially mixed population, largely of immigrant stock, the bulk of whom were uneducated. In such an environment, he believed, the fine legal principles he had learnt as a student would have to be adapted to suit the society.*

"The rule of law talks of habeas corpus, freedom, the right of association and expression, of assembly, of peaceful demonstration, concepts which first stemmed from the French Revolution and were later refined in Victorian England. But nowhere in the world today are these rights allowed to practise without limitations, for, blindly applied, these ideals can work towards the undoing of organised society. For the acid test of any legal system is not the greatness or the grandeur of its ideal concepts, but whether in fact it is able to produce order and justice in the relationships between man and man and between man and the state. To maintain this order with the best degree of tolerance and humanity is a problem which has faced us acutely in the last few years as our own Malayans took over the key positions of the legislature, the executive and the judiciary."

*(Speech to the University of Singapore Law Society, January 18, 1962; text on page 411)*

His experience in working with people from all walks of life was to confirm this view. A liberal approach, he felt, was doomed to failure, as it was out of sync with the ethos of the people and the times.

"My practice of the law has influenced my approach. Training of the law has led the British to what they call 'the redemption theory'. Let's redeem the criminal, quite forgetting the harm he has already done to the victims who demand some justice be done.

"But what I saw of the criminals whom I defended, what I saw of them in the prisons when I used to see them on remand, left me in no doubt at all that to deal with these people you have to be quite strong and firm or they'll draw circles around you. I knew the whole story and the real story, and I had to defend somebody who was in the wrong. And I know that this chap, unless properly punished, is bound to repeat it."

He had made this point in 1966 when introducing a controversial Bill to make caning mandatory for vandalism:

"I know how strongly the professionals and the penologists are against caning. But we have a society which, unfortunately I think, understands only two things – the incentive and the deterrent … A fine will not deter the type of criminal we are facing here … But if he knows he is going to get three of the best, I think he will lose the enthusiasm."

## The jury is out

A telling example of the way in which his experience as a lawyer was to shape his view of how the legal system should be framed was his reaction to a case he handled in the 1950s, which left him with a sinking feeling about the pitfalls of a jury system. Such a system, found in Anglo-Saxon societies, would not work when transplanted to Asian ones, he concluded.

*Opposite: "I went home feeling quite sick, because I knew I had discharged my duty as required of me, but I knew I had done wrong."
– Lee, as a young barrister, after winning his first murder trial, which led him to believe that the jury system would not work in Singapore.*

"I never forget my first case, when I was assigned to defend four murderers. Remember the famous jungle girl case in Singapore in 1950, '51?

"A Dutch woman was running away from the Japanese, gave her daughter to a Malay woman to look after. She came back after the war, reclaimed the daughter. The Chief Justice, then an Englishman, pending hearing of the case, sent the girl who had been converted into Islam to a convent to be looked after, and hell broke loose. The police force mutinied. Malays and Muslims took out their knives and a lot of white men, just because they were white, nothing to do with the case, were killed. These four men were accused of killing a Royal Air Force officer and his wife and child. They were travelling on a bus from RAF Changi down to town.

"I was assigned – I had no choice. My job was not to ask them whether they were guilty or not because I knew what the position was and so did they. All I did – and it was my first case – was to work on the weaknesses of the jury – their biases, their prejudices, their reluctance really to find four Mussulmen [Muslims] guilty of killing in cold blood or in a heat of great passion, religious passion, an RAF officer, his wife and child. I did the simple tricks of advocacy – contradictions between one witness and another, contradiction between a witness and his previous statement to the police and the preliminary enquiry – and after a long submission by the judge, the four were acquitted.

"The judge was thoroughly disgusted. I went home feeling quite sick because I knew I'd discharged my duty as required of me, but I knew I had done wrong. I decided when we became the government, we will not allow this foolish, completely incongruous system which will never take root here, because no juror will take upon himself the onus of saying, 'Yes, he will go to jail.'

"... The Anglo-Saxon tradition of trial by jury may be good for Anglo-Saxons or the descendants thereof. It never really worked for non Anglo-Saxons. ... The French don't have it. They are Latin. I think the idea of 12 random jurors sitting there and deciding whether you ought to go to jail or not or whether you ought to pay damages or not, it's completely alien."

*(Interview with the British Broadcasting Corporation, March 5, 1977; text on page 419)*

# No witness, no trial

Similarly Lee would argue, somewhat controversially, that notions of absolute rights to freedom for individuals would sometimes have to be compromised in order to help maintain public order and security. He was not averse to suspending the right to habeas corpus, or an open and fair trial, for known criminals or political agitators. These people threatened the peace and could stall social progress, but could not be put away for lack of evidence as witnesses were too cowed to come forward to testify against them.

He contended that the liberal idea that societies had to be founded on law and order, while sound, could only be applied once a certain measure of order had been established. In its absence, the idea that simply passing laws would bring about order was sadly another pious liberal hope.

# Why have you detained men without trial?

In a feisty exchange with BBC interviewer Ludovic Kennedy in March 1977, Lee defended his decision to jail communist sympathisers and agitators without a trial. He dismissed Kennedy's suggestion that this was an about-turn from his position when he first entered Parliament in 1955, when he argued against detentions without trial.

Kennedy: Prime Minister, what do you say to the fact that some people have been detained in prison here for something like 13 years without trial. Is that justice?

Lee: It is outside the laws of the courts. It's legislation which the British passed when they were faced with a communist insurgency – a revolt. Same laws, the same ones, I suspect, are now in operation in Ulster. There are three of them – you are right – 13 years since 1963, really coming to 14. Two of them are doctors. ... And the two doctors know that all they have to do is to say, "I renounce the use of armed force to overthrow the government and therefore do not support the Malayan Communist Party in their attempt to do so", and they will be released. And they refused to do that.

Kennedy: But are you saying, Prime Minister, in a strong and prosperous society that you have here now in Singapore – the last election you won the biggest victory ever, you got all the seats in Parliament – that if you release these three people, you couldn't contain them?

Lee: No, that's not the point. We can release these three people. We released one – Dr Poh Soo Kai – as a trial to see what would happen. We released him in 1972 after we won the last elections with nearly as good a majority – 69 per cent of the electorate. And what did he do? He gave medicine and treated a known, wanted, injured terrorist. There is now evidence by a lawyer, at present under interrogation, who has gone to a magistrate and made a confession, on his own. Now, we have to get him struck off the rolls. But that's not all. He also gave large quantities of antibiotics and other essential medical supplies to couriers, to send them to terrorist forces in the jungle, all in the course of the four years he was out – from 1972 to 1976.

Kennedy: So these other two will have to stay there, forever?

Lee: No.

Kennedy: Until they sign your document?

Lee: No, they don't have to sign a document. All they say is: "I renounce the use of force. I do not support the Malayan Communist Party in their use of force to overthrow the government." But if they believe, as I think they do, that this is inevitable, that there will one day be a great victory parade and they will be on the rostrum where all the local Lenins and Maos will be – well, then they stand firm on principle and wait for tomorrow.

*(Text of interview on page 419)*

"In a settled and established society, law appears to be a precursor of order. Good laws lead to good order, that is the form that you will learn. But the hard realities of keeping the peace between man and man and between authority and the individual can be more accurately described if the phrase were inverted to 'order and law', for without order the operation of law is impossible. Order having been established and the rules having become enforceable in a settled society, only then is it possible to work out human relationships between subject and subject, and subject and the state in accordance with predetermined rules of law.

"And when a state of increasing disorder and defiance of authority cannot be checked by the rules then existing, new and sometimes drastic rules have to be forged to maintain order so that the law can continue to govern human relations. The alternative is to surrender order for chaos and anarchy. So it is that we have to allow the use of extraordinary powers of detention, first in the case of political offenders under the PPSO [Preservation of Public Security Order], and next in the case of secret society gangsters under the Criminal Law (Temporary Provisions) Ordinance.

"It must be realised that if you abolish the powers of arrest and detention and insist on trial in open court in accordance with the strict laws of evidence of a criminal trial, then law and order becomes without the slightest exaggeration utterly impossible, because whilst you may still nominally have law and order, the wherewithal to enforce it would have disappeared. The choice in many of these cases is either to go through the motions of a trial and let a guilty man off to continue his damage to society or to keep him confined without trial.

*(Speech to the University of Singapore Law Society, January 18, 1962; text on page 411)*

# Talking tough, taking action

Over the years, Lee and his government would take several measures which were designed to implement their brook-no-nonsense approach to crime. These included detaining communist agitators as well as passing laws which made activities deemed inimical to public order a crime.

Concerned about rising crime rates, the government amended the Penal Code in 1973 to introduce stiffer sentences for various crimes. New laws were also brought in, which prescribed the death penalty for those who used guns in crimes, for example. In 1984, noting a trend towards more lenient sentences being meted out by the courts, and a corresponding rise in the number of robberies, housebreakings and thefts, the Penal Code was amended again, with minimum sentences set by the legislature for various crimes.

More recently, apart from stiffening sentences further, the government has also taken steps to help the courts convict criminals. These included removing an accused person's right to silence, as well as accepting the testimony of a co-accused person in a trial. It also moved swiftly in the face of a proliferation of cross-border smuggling of arms and a rise in the number of armed robberies in the region. The Arms Offences Act was amended to allow the courts to presume that anyone who uses or tries to use a firearm in a crime intends to cause injury. The penalty: death.

# Ballots and bullets

Lee battled the communists and communalists in the 1960s to establish order and internal security. While he welcomed a contest for the right to form the government through the electoral system, he sensed that the communists were not so much interested in running the system as replacing it. He did not hesitate to lock up communist agitators and their sympathisers. Moving the Preservation of Public Security (Amendment) Bill in the Legislative Assembly, Lee argued that he would not brook anyone seeking to seize power with bullets while putting up a front of trying to win at the ballot box. He also told MPs that the best counter to communist attempts to instigate unrest was through economic growth and the spread of material prosperity to the masses.

"Let me be the first to remind this House that the ultimate answer to the communist challenge is not provided by this type of legislation giving the executive emergency or extraordinary powers.

"Ultimately it is the economical, social and political conditions and the battles on these planes that decide whether Singapore, and indeed Malaya, will grow from strength to strength as a democratic state in which the more tolerant features of human civilisation are preserved whilst the economic need and necessities of the people are rapidly met, or whether a more totalitarian system will succeed the democratic state to cater for these economic needs.

"These powers can only provide a temporary damper against those who set out to wreck the democratic state. The principles which guide this government in the exercise of its primary functions as a government have been enumerated by the Deputy Prime Minister. I would like to harken back to what I said on behalf of my party last year: 'Within this democratic system, everyone has the right to compete, to preach his political views, but the competition must be for the purpose of working the system, not of destroying it. These powers will not be allowed to be used against political opponents within the system who compete for the right to work the system. That is fundamental and basic or the powers will have destroyed the purpose for which they were forged.'

"At the same time we state quite categorically that we believe in the democratic system, that we will allow full competition within the democratic system, but competition for the purpose of destroying the democratic system will be resisted."

*(Parliamentary speech on the Preservation of Public Security (Amendment) Bill, October 14, 1959)*

Apart from tough laws, it is also the likelihood that criminals will be pursued and punished that has served as a strong deterrent against crime. The result: low and even falling crime rates in Singapore. The 1993 World Competitiveness Report ranked Singapore top for the confidence its people had that they and their property were protected. Its score of 9.5 out of 10 surpassed even Japan's 9.1 figure. In a survey in 1994 by the Singapore Press Holdings' Research and Information department, 99 per cent of those polled said they felt safe living in Singapore. In contrast, in a poll in the United States by *Newsweek* magazine, more than seven out of 10 Americans surveyed – and half of the children polled – feared that they or their families might fall victim to a violent crime.

Many Singaporeans appear to agree with the government's tough approach towards crime. By majorities of between 80 per cent and 99 per cent, they welcomed the use of caning as punishment for major crimes. The findings bear out a similar survey by *The Straits Times* in 1986, in which caning was also endorsed by large majorities: rape (97 per cent), attempted murder (82 per cent), drug trafficking (79 per cent) and robbery (63 per cent).

# A lawyer's limits

But Singapore's deviations from the legal practices elsewhere were not taken lightly. Nor were they a matter of expedience. Perhaps it was because of his legal training that Lee scrupulously kept to the constitutional framework of his fledgling Republic. Unlike other powerful leaders, who sometimes found it more convenient to bypass the law and legislature, he would pay heed to the legal limits of his, and his government's, powers, despite their overwhelming majority in Parliament.

"It might be good fortune, perhaps, that not just I alone but some of my colleagues were brought up in fairly liberal traditions. We don't have to be lawyers to understand right, wrong, good, evil. This is basic and fundamental in the values of a people. And I think even if the Minister for Law and myself were to go wrong, you will have some consolation, Mr President, in the knowledge that quite a number of my colleagues are men imbued with some of the values, some of the traditions of an open, of an equal, of a tolerant society.

"You cannot maintain that kind of a society unless you are prepared to practise it yourself. In other words, your style must be open. You must yourself be tolerant. And, most important of all, you must be able to ensure, insofar as you can, that your successors – even though they may not be of the same political colour as you are – are imbued with this value.

"Let us not deceive ourselves that we can do all these things just because we believe in democracy, the rule of law and the certainty of the law.

"You know, we have paid a very heavy price. We have departed in quite a number of material aspects – in very material fields from the principles of justice and the liberty of the individual, in particular – in order to maintain these standards, in order that there shall be a Bar; that there will be judges who will sit in judgement over right and wrong; that police

# The West beats up Singapore

*Scuffles among parliamentarians in Taiwan, a democracy which the Americans have deemed to be "freer" than Singapore's. But, in Lee's view, countries like Taiwan and South Korea have not proven that they are indeed better societies.*

Lee's readiness to go his own way, against the hectoring of Western liberal politicians and columnists, led to Singapore making the headlines often as an "authoritarian, dictatorial, over-ruled, over-restricted, stifling and sterile society". He was unmoved. The taunts, he argued, stemmed from Americans' sense of cultural superiority and inability to accept that a tiny island could choose to organise itself in a way contrary to its own views about how societies should be organised.

"For America to be displaced, not in the world but only in the Western Pacific, by an Asian people long despised and dismissed with contempt as decadent, feeble, corrupt and inept, is emotionally very difficult to accept. The sense of cultural supremacy of the Americans will make this adjustment most difficult. Americans believe their ideas are universal – the supremacy of the individual and free, unfettered expression. But they are not. Never were.

"In fact, American society was so successful for so long not because of these ideas and principles, but because of a certain geopolitical good fortune, an abundance of resources and immigrant energy, a generous flow of capital and technology from Europe, and two wide oceans that kept conflicts of the world away from American shores.

"It is this sense of cultural supremacy which leads the American media to pick on Singapore and beat us up as authoritarian, dictatorial; an over-ruled, over-restricted, stifling and sterile society. Why? Because we have not complied with their ideas of how we should govern ourselves. But we can ill afford to let others experiment with our lives in this small island.

"The American ideas are theories extracted from the American experience. They have not been successfully transplanted to a non Anglo-Saxon society like the Philippines, although America ruled it for 50 years. And now in America itself, after 30 years of experimenting with the Great Society programmes, there is widespread crime and violence, children kill each other with guns, neighbourhoods are insecure, old people feel forgotten, families are falling apart. And the media attacks the integrity and character of your leaders with impunity, drags down all those in authority and blames everyone but itself.

"American principles and theories have not yet proven successful in East Asia – not in Taiwan, Thailand or South Korea. If these countries become better societies than Singapore, in another five or 10 years, we will run after them to adopt their practices and catch up."

*(Global Viewpoint, September 1995)*

will produce witnesses and that witnesses for certain crimes shall require corroboration and evidence shall be in accordance with the Evidence Ordinance. …

"There are 720 criminal law supervisees – men on whom the due processes of law were unable to place even an iota of evidence. But for the fact that they are required to stay at home by night, I think life would be less what it is in Singapore, for their nocturnal activities can make your motorcar outside a less useful vehicle of transportation, among other things.

"This is true. We have had to adjust, to deviate temporarily from ideals and norms. This is a heavy price. We have over a hundred political detainees, men against whom we are unable to prove anything in a court of law. Nearly 50 of them are men who gave us a great deal of anxiety during the years of Confrontation because they were Malay extremists. Your life and this dinner would not be what it is if my colleagues and I had decided to play it according to the rules of the game.

*(Speech to the Singapore Advocates and Solicitors Society, March 18, 1967; text on page 414)*

# No end to violence

Whatever the justification, however, Lee's tough stance would attract criticism from liberal commentators abroad. They portrayed Singapore as an Orwellian state, with Lee cast as Big Brother, ever-ready to hector and punish his people into compliance with its all encompassing laws. Singapore, the joke goes, is a "fine" city. Others harped about it being "squeaky clean".

Lee was unmoved by these barbs. His confidence that he had taken the right course of action was bolstered perhaps by his experience of societies riven by violence and lawlessness abroad.

The rising cycle of violence was not limited to developing countries, but was a mounting problem in developed ones as well.

"Violence is part of the daily ration in the underdeveloped world. But it has spread now to the established, developed world. Violence has also become a daily recurrence.

"It is said that the Americans always had that streak of violence in their historical makeup. It was part of the saga of their Wild West. Now, in addition to Vietnam, there are riots, burnings, shootings and bombings in American cities. I was at Harvard last October. The SDS, Students for Democratic Society, bombed the Harvard International Centre. Why? I did not know. I do not think the mad bombers really know why they perpetrated this mad act of destruction. A booster dose of violence has been injected into the veins of American society as the two million American draftees have gone and returned from Vietnam.

"The blacks coming back from frontline combat duties in Vietnam are militant. Having learned how to fight with M16s, hand-grenades, mortars, tanks and helicopters, they exploit these techniques and tactics in America's cities in their battle for equality. The whites also are now prone to violence. The result is mad bombings in New York and other big American cities.

"I attended the 25th anniversary of the United Nations last October. It was bedlam. Every head of mission had a security squad clamped on him. And when President Nixon came down to speak at the UN, 3,000 Secret Service agents descended on New York from all over America and covered the whole of the UN building and its precincts. This was not a joke. Bombs could have exploded.

"Strange, but perhaps unavoidable, with instant television through communication satellites and other mass media, this mood for violence has been transmitted across the Atlantic into Britain. Twenty-five years ago, when I learned British constitutional law, my lecturers used to tell me how different, how tolerant and non-violent British society was. The British brought about change peacefully, unlike the French, who always sought change through violence and revolution. Hence, British laws were liberal and made sacrosanct the rights and liberties of the individual.

"How different Britain is today. It is the right of the government to govern that sadly needs protection. …

"We also have some who espouse the compassionate line, but for mercenary reasons. When we introduced the Bill to abolish the jury, one lawyer in the Bar Council delegation said to the select committee that since juries were reluctant to convict a person of murder, we should abolish the death penalty but not abolish the jury! There was a sad imbalance in his sense of moral priorities, a distortion of one's distinction between right and wrong."

*(National Day event, August 30, 1971)*

# Which way to safe streets?

For Lee then, the art of government, which included maintaining law and order in society, was a question of balancing the interests of individuals with the collective good of society. This sometimes required compromises and deviations from liberal ideals, he argued in an interview with *New Perspectives Quarterly*, in 1995.

"Good governance, even today, requires a balance between competing claims by upholding fundamental truths: that there is right and wrong, good and evil. If everyone gets pornography on a satellite dish the size of a saucer, then governments around the world will have to do something about it, or we will destroy our young and with them human civilisation. …

"The ideas of individual supremacy and the right to free expression, when carried to excess, have not worked. They have made it difficult to keep American society cohesive. Asia can see it is not working. Those who work a wholesome society where young girls and old ladies can walk in the streets at night, where the young are not preyed upon by drug peddlers, will not follow the American model."

Instead, Lee believed that the alternative approach he espoused, where governments laid down clear laws and enforced them firmly but fairly, was better designed to help achieve a stable society, as well as go some way towards moulding a responsible citizenry. Singapore's experience was telling.

"I am surprised that people are surprised that it works. Why should you be surprised that it works? The other way, we would still be where we were.

"Today, I'm not saying we're litter-free. Especially in areas like the public corridors in housing estates where nobody can see them, they just throw away the litter. But in the public places where they can be seen and fined, they've stopped. Now, there's no reason why they can't also stop for their own passageways, but they don't, right? We haven't reached that stage yet.

"I would hope, one day, standards reach that point where, instead of punishing one in 100, you may have to punish one in 10,000. But I would not dare to make such a prediction when this will be, because it depends upon how the policy evolves and whether it is pursued with vigour and with subtlety, so that each generation is able to produce better results with their children."

# 10

# Minding the Media

*Opposite: The first prime minister of independent Singapore, swamped by reporters as he leaves the Governor's Residence soon after the PAP won the 1959 elections.*

**1968.** Richard Nixon had just been elected the 37th president of the United States and was announcing his Cabinet line-up live on television. For Americans, this was not just a significant political event but, at least for some, also the first opportunity to have a go at a new president. It was quintessentially American television, but it would make quite an impact on one Singaporean viewer. Immediately after the announcement, the CBS network rolled in a panel of experts to pronounce on the new Cabinet, with daggers already drawn.

Lee Kuan Yew, then on a visit to the United States, watched the proceedings, both amazed and amused. He would recount the episode often in years to come, including at a talk to pressmen in Singapore in 1972.

"As Mr Nixon presented his first Cabinet, CBS had a panel of very quick, agile and nimble minds, ready to go. The moment Nixon was over, this panel of demolishers came on. They included John Kenneth Galbraith of *The Affluent Society*. He has a very felicitous turn of phrase which, if turned against you, can be quite waspish.

"He and most of the others began to shoot every one of Nixon's team down. It made quite an impact on me. The Governor of Massachusetts, a Mr Volpe, was appointed Secretary for Transport. The Governor had been voted for, and had won his election. Most probably he would have beaten Galbraith if ever Galbraith stood for election against him. Galbraith said, 'As for Governor Volpe, Massachusetts can well do better without him when he goes to Washington.' I am paraphrasing him. I cannot convey the derisive nuances.

"This panel did not know who would be in Mr Nixon's team, or what job each member would be doing until it was announced that night. The panel had no time for considered judgements. The attitude was one of showbiz: 'Right, let's have some fun.' They shot the Nixon team down like clay pigeons – or so they thought.

"But in the end Mr Nixon won in spite of a hostile press and TV. I was interested to see how *Time* magazine quickly switched over support from McGovern and hailed the victor.

"Now, if in a developed society they can have such disorders aggravated, if not partly caused by the mass media, commentators and journalists in developing countries should not unthinkingly toss poison and pollution into the pool."

*(Speech to the Singapore Press Club, November 15, 1972; text on page 431)*

That spectacle of television theatre was to reinforce Lee's view of the power of the media to so adroitly and cavalierly mock and debase a political leadership that had just been elected by the people. Who were these pundits to scoff at the people's chosen leader and his team? On whose authority did they speak? Who gave them the mandate? he wondered.

## Reaching for the knuckle-dusters

Over the years, Lee would keep close track of the outpourings of the press, domestic and foreign, watching for such poison being tossed into the political pool in Singapore. He noted the lines they were pushing, the social trends they backed, the causes they upheld.

"Every morning, my task begins with reading five, four now, newspapers. It can be tiresome. I note the scurrilous, the scandalous. I can live with that. But when any newspaper pours a daily dose of language, cultural or religious poison, I put my knuckle-dusters on. Do not believe you can beat the state."

*(Speech to the Singapore Press Club, November 15, 1972; text on page 431)*

The knuckle-dusters were to be used not a few times over the years.

Lee's antipathy to some sections of the press, notably the English-language press, which had backed the British colonial authorities against his fledgling party in the 1950s, was coloured by his early years as an opposition politician. But that notwithstanding, his attitude towards the press was based firmly on the view that, being unelected and bearing no responsibility to the people, journalists, columnists and commentators had neither a role nor the right to lead the country in directions contrary to that envisioned by its elected leaders. This view he formed fairly early on in his political career. It was a belief that was to be reinforced by his experience in dealing with the press, at home and abroad, over the years. Many a time, he would haul journalists or their editors over the coals, or take newspapers to task.

Although this raised eyebrows abroad, he was unapologetic. A fledgling state, he would contend, could not adopt a *laissez-faire* attitude to the press. Bitter experience had shown what happened when, unwittingly or otherwise, the media had swayed popular sentiment and roused political passions. Issues of race, language and religion, all of which smouldered beneath the surface, especially in Singapore's early years, were easily stoked. Several times, these had boiled over, spilling blood in the streets.

"In 1950, the publication of a photograph in a Malay newspaper of a Muslim girl in a convent, with the Virgin Mary in the background, caused riots. It was known as the jungle girl case. A Dutch girl, given to a Muslim Malay woman to look after, as the Japanese overran Southeast Asia, was rediscovered by her Dutch mother. She claimed her return. The girl had become a Muslim convert. The court, presided by an English judge, ordered the girl to be sent to a convent pending the outcome of the trial. There were four days of rioting. Some 50 Europeans were slaughtered and many more maimed by Malay and Indian Muslims. Their sin was to be European Christians, like the judge. The police, then mainly Muslims, just looked on.

"And again, on July 21, 1964, a sustained campaign in a Malay language newspaper, falsely alleging the suppression of the rights of the Malay and Muslim minority by the Chinese majority, led to riots in which 36 people were killed and many more injured, during a Prophet Mohammed's birthday procession. …

"I used to believe that … with higher standards of education, these problems will diminish. But watching Belfast, Brussels and Montreal, rioting over religion and language, I wonder whether such phenomena can ever disappear."

*(Speech to the International Press Institute, June 9, 1971; text on page 425)*

Foreign events, too, he was aware, could tug at the heartstrings of Singaporeans, who still held strong sentiments for their ethnic kin in their countries of origin. To him, denying this was sheer folly. These passions would have to be managed, and the ethnic communities in Singapore made aware that their lot lay with Singapore, not elsewhere.

"12,000 Sikhs from Punjab form one of the smallest communities in Singapore. They are split into contending factions, reflecting the contest between contending groups in the Punjab, of which they have heard on radio and have read in Punjabi language news-sheets. A recent fast to death by a Sikh leader in the Punjab to get Chandigarh given to the Sikhs generated tension among Sikhs in Singapore. True, nearly 60 per cent of the adult Sikhs were born and bred in the Punjab and emigrated to Singapore after their cultural values were settled. I believe, and hope, the second generation Sikh will be different."

*(Speech to the International Press Institute, June 9, 1971; text on page 425)*

# No free market of ideas

Given the potent mix of race, language and religion in Singapore, Lee believed that the Western notion of the press as an independent "fourth estate" to check and balance the government, and operating in a free market of ideas, could not be applied to this country.

"From British times, the Singapore press was never the fourth estate. And in Singapore's experience, because of our volatile racial and religious mix, the American concept of the 'marketplace of ideas', instead of producing harmonious enlightenment, has time and again led to riots and bloodshed."

*(Speech to the American Society of Newspaper Editors, April 14, 1988; text on page 438)*

# The media's role

*Lee in Helsinki for the 20th Assembly of the International Press Institute in 1971, joining other world leaders in discussing the role of the mass media.*

Lee has always been very concerned about the media's role in shaping popular attitudes, especially in developing countries. At the International Press Institute in Helsinki in 1971, he set out the essence of his approach in dealing with the press in Singapore.

"We want the mass media to reinforce, not to undermine, the cultural values and social attitudes being inculcated in our schools and universities. The mass media can create a mood in which people become keen to acquire the knowledge, skills and disciplines of advanced countries. Without these, we can never hope to raise the standards of living of our people.

"If they are to develop, people in new countries cannot afford to imitate the fads and fetishes of the contemporary West. The strange behaviour of demonstration and violence-prone young men and women in wealthy America, seen on TV and the newspapers, are not relevant to the social and economic circumstances of new underdeveloped countries. The importance of education, the need of stability and work discipline, the acquisition of skills and expertise, sufficient men trained in the sciences and technology, and their ability to adapt this knowledge and techniques to fit the conditions of their country – these are vital factors for progress. But when the puritan ethics of hard work, thrift and discipline are at a discount in America, and generally in the West, the mass media reflecting this malaise can, and does, confuse the young in new countries.

"We have this problem in a particularly acute form in Singapore. We are an international junction for ships, aircraft and telecommunications by cable and satellite. People from the richer countries of the West, their magazines, newspapers, television and films, all come in. ... It is impossible to insulate Singaporeans from the outside world. One consoling thought is Arnold Toynbee's thesis that crossroads like the Lebanon benefit from the stimulation of ideas and inventions from abroad.

"Western investments in industries in Singapore mean importing Western machinery. With the machinery come Western engineers and managers, and their families. They live in Singapore, reinforcing by personal contact the impact of Western mass media. To take in Western science, technology and industry, we find that we cannot completely exclude the undesirable ethos of the contemporary West. This ethos flakes off on Singaporeans. So we must educate Singaporeans not to imitate the more erratic behaviour of the West.

"Few viewers and readers of the mass media in new countries know of the torment amongst Western intellectuals. Some Americans question where their bureaucratised science and technology, their military-industrial complex, are leading them. Even fewer read of the torment of American intellectuals who question the wisdom of exporting this science and technology to the impoverished people of the underdeveloped world, when it has wrought such havoc on America, dehumanising an opulent society. But the underdeveloped have no choice. Whatever the side effects of importing Western science and technology, not to do so will be worse.

*(International Press Institute, June 9, 1971; text on page 425)*

As he saw it, the press could also be manipulated by foreign powers out to influence developments in the country. The ideological and strategic contests among the major powers in the region resulted in their being prepared to spend time and money to gain influence in countries throughout the region. To do so, they were not averse to whipping up passions over the airwaves, or to setting up newspapers through proxies, to stir up sentiments over issues of culture, language and ideology. He would not brook this.

"My colleagues and I have the responsibility to neutralise their intentions. In such a situation, freedom of the press, freedom of the news media, must be subordinated to the overriding needs of the integrity of Singapore, and to the primary purposes of an elected government. The government has taken, and will from time to time have to take, firm measures to ensure that, despite divisive forces of different cultural values and lifestyles, there is enough unity of purpose to carry the people of Singapore forward to higher standards of life, without which the mass media cannot thrive."

*(Speech to the International Press Institute, June 9, 1971; text on page 425)*

Ultimately, it was Singapore's elected leaders who bore responsibility for the well-being of its people, he would contend. The people had backed the government to improve their lot. His government, in turn, to honour the people's trust and meet their expectations, was not one to hesitate to clear any roadblocks in its way, including a querulous and interfering media, whether foreign or local.

The *Eastern Sun* closed in 1971 after the government published details of a black operation involving a communist intelligence service through its front organisation in Hongkong. The *Singapore Herald* folded the same year after it was taken to task for adopting a virulently anti-government line in its reporting and for having questionable foreign funding. That year also saw the arrest under the Internal Security Act of three senior journalists from the *Nanyang Siang Pau* for playing up communist propaganda and instigating Chinese chauvinistic feelings.

The Newspaper and Printing Presses Act of 1974 provided the legal framework for greater government control, including the right for it to decide who would own newly created management shares which conferred voting rights 200 times greater than that of an ordinary share. The Act was amended several times subsequently, giving the government powers to restrict the circulation of publications which it deemed were engaging in Singapore politics, or which refused to grant it a right to reply to their articles on Singapore.

These actions were to set the bounds within which the media, both local and foreign, would have to operate. While not seeking to nationalise the press or subject it to direct state controls, as had been done in some developing states, Lee would grant the pressmen a fair deal of freedom, but clearly on his terms.

FACE
THE
NATION
CBS NEWS

**Asian Wall Street Journal—** Its circulation was slashed from 5,000 to 400 a day in 1987 after it refused to publish in full the Singapore government's reply to one of its articles criticising Sesdaq, the second securities market here. It stopped circulating here in 1990 when the government amended the Newspaper and Printing Presses Act (NPPA) to require publications to obtain an annual permit if they had circulations above 300 and covered Southeast Asian politics and current affairs. But it reversed its stand in 1991, obtained a licence and was allowed 2,500 copies.

# The liberal critique

But would not such government controls stifle the free flow of information and ideas? Would this not breed corruption and abuse of authority? Indeed, could a capitalist free market economy thrive in the absence of a free market of ideas?

The Singapore government's management of the press would receive widespread criticism from the West over the years. Western commentators would come to acknowledge Singapore's economic achievements and Lee's role in pulling it off in such a short time. But they could not accept his conception of how the press should operate in a free and democratic society, often labelling Singapore's press laws draconian. Its media they would lambast as being neutered, pliant and sycophantic. Lee and his government's stand towards the media was portrayed variously as an attempt to check criticism, stifle democracy, and even to maintain the People's Action Party domination of the political scene in Singapore.

Indeed, in March 1987 the US State Department deplored the Singapore government's move to restrict the sale of the *Asian Wall Street Journal* in Singapore. It had done so after the newspaper refused to grant it the right of reply to one of its reports which proved erroneous. In an *aide-mémoire* sent to the Singapore Foreign Affairs Ministry, the US argued that the press should be free to publish or not to publish what it chooses, however irresponsible or biased its actions might seem. The logic of its case was that where the media was free, the marketplace of ideas would sort the irresponsible from the responsible and reward the latter.

Lee would counter that, far from weeding out the irresponsible from the responsible, the marketplace of ideas in a multiracial society could, and did, lead to riots and mayhem. Events had proven this to be the case only too painfully.

What was striking was that the Singapore electorate was by and large prepared to go along with this tough stand towards the media. Few voters, surveys showed, rated press freedom high on their list of priorities. The notion of the press as a fourth estate of government, out to check the executive at every turn, was not one that held much sway with the people, who looked to the authorities to bring material progress and development. Nor did the people accept the Western conventional wisdom that only an adversarial press could do its job credibly. The American idea of a press which is free to publish anything even if it was irresponsible or biased finds little sympathy in Singapore.

This was a fundamental difference in outlook on the role and scope of the media from that taken in the West. The American mistake was to assume the universality of its system and values, Lee would assert in many interviews and speeches over the years.

> "… the US model is not a universal standard. The media in other countries play different roles. These roles have grown out of their different historical experiences, political systems and national temperaments. They represent equally valid functions which the press fulfils in different environments.
>
> "A more appropriate model for the Singapore media would be the BBC World Service, which reports events impartially, but provides an interpretation from a definite perspective

# Perry Mason in Cairo?

*Actor Raymond Burr, appearing in his well-known role as the lawyer Perry Mason.*

As a tiny island-state, bereft of resources and a natural hinterland, Singapore could ill afford to cut itself off from the outside world in an attempt to shield itself from alien cultural influences. The flow of trade and technology from the West, Lee recognised, would bring with it Western mores and values. This point was made strikingly to him while on a visit to the Middle East in the 1970s.

"You have to fill television time. You open your station at 5.30 pm. It has got to be kept going till midnight and on two channels. It costs thousands of dollars, creative minds and good supporting technicians to make a good feature. So it is easier to fill up by buying programmes, usually American or British. I have seen Perry Mason in Cairo, speaking Arabic. ... Here was a country absolutely against the American system and establishment. But they faced the problem of filling time. There are many such popular series. But these programmes convey the whole ethos of the producer society.

"Similarly with newspapers. They have got to fill the pages. What is easier than to buy features? Some features are good. I enjoy reading James Reston, even though from time to time I disagree with his views. But many features are of indifferent quality, and some are positively bad.

"The most dangerous part of the mass media is its power of suggestion. People are imitative. If nobody had reported hijacking, or how easy and successful hijacking can be, there would not have been so many hijackings. I believe the Pilots' Association was right that if you want to cut down hijackings,

then report all the hijacking failures, and block out all the hijacking successes, particularly how they were successfully executed. The craze spread by imitation, until the impossible happened – they hijacked a Soviet aircraft. That took some doing. Obviously, despite the Iron Curtain, the ideas leaked through.

"This brings me to Singapore. I read a recent series in the *New Nation*. It was imitating what the Western journalists are doing. It was ostensibly respectable. First, a serious study of homosexuality. Then a protracted series on lesbianism. Then unwanted babies.

"The Lord Chief Justice of Britain said, in a recent case on pornography, that if anybody showed the muck in a case before him to his daughters, he would take the man and wring his neck with his own hands. How did it come to such a pass? By a gradual, insidious process of suggesting that this is all right, that there is nothing wrong with it. It has led to 'anything and everything goes'.

"Fortunately for us, the *New Nation*, *The Straits Times*, or for that matter the *Herald* and the *Eastern Sun*, they did not, and do not, have the same impact on our population. The Chinese or the Malay press and, in a more limited way, the Indian press, in the mother language, makes much more emotive and powerful appeals. They pull at the heartstrings. That is why in the case of [the Chinese language] *Nanyang Siang Pau*, though I did not twist their necks, we took firm measures."

*(Speech to the Singapore Press Club, November 15, 1972; text on page 431)*

– in the BBC's case, the point of view of Western liberalism. The BBC broadcasts in Singapore on FM, 24 hours daily. It was a service meant for the British community including their troops stationed in Singapore. When they departed in 1971, I personally asked them to continue it as a service to Singaporeans.

"Another model is the Japanese media, which also stay out of partisan politics, but go beyond plain reporting to shape public opinion to help build up a national consensus on important issues. …

"Thus while the US model of the role of the press is good for the US, as a universal standard, its applicability has not been proven. …

"Singapore's domestic debate is a matter for Singaporeans. We allow American journalists in Singapore in order to report Singapore to their fellow countrymen. We allow their papers to sell in Singapore so that we can know what foreigners are reading about us. But we cannot allow them to assume a role in Singapore that the American media play in America, that of invigilator, adversary, and inquisitor of the administration. If allowed to do so, they will radically change the nature of Singapore society, and I doubt if our social glue is strong enough to withstand such treatment."

*(Speech to the American Society of Newspaper Editors, April 14, 1988; text on page 438)*

Besides, he noted, the approach which was so heavily criticised by Western liberals was not so different from that practised in some of their own countries. Was there not an element of different strokes for different folks in their positions? he would ask.

"No foreign television station claims the right to telecast its programmes in Singapore. Indeed America's Federal Communications Commission regulations bar foreigners from owning more than 25 per cent of a TV or radio station. In other words, only Americans can control a business which influences public opinion in America. Thus before Rupert Murdoch purchased the independent TV stations of the Metromedia group in 1985, he first took up US citizenship. If a mighty nation of 240 million finds such safeguards necessary, what about a plastic, unformed society like Singapore?

"As for the US print media, in 1976 the South African Ministry of Information was negotiating covertly to buy the *Washington Star* to soft-sell apartheid. When the story broke, a storm broke out in Washington and the purchase fell through. Americans were outraged at this South African attempt to soft-sell apartheid in America's marketplace of ideas. But apartheid is patently abhorrent. If the marketplace of ideas automatically separates the good from the bad, and rewards the good, why this outrage at an attempt which is doomed to fail? When America reacts in this way, is it surprising that Singapore feels it cannot take chances with the offshore press taking sides on Singapore's domestic debate?"

*(Speech to the American Society of Newspaper Editors, April 14, 1988; text on page 438)*

# No cocker spaniel

Lee's government was to develop the position over the years that circulation in Singapore by foreign newspapers and journals was a privilege granted by the Singapore government on its own terms. These were, namely, that they should report developments in Singapore "as outsiders for outsiders". That is, they should not become a partisan in the country's domestic debate. If they found these conditions intolerable, they were free not to sell their papers in Singapore, he argued.

Over the years, he was to confront the powerful Western media on numerous occasions, restricting the circulation of international magazines such as *Time*, *The Economist*, and *Asian Wall Street Journal* when they failed to publish replies from the Singapore government to correct inaccuracies in their reports. This, he maintained, was the only way to ensure that he retained the right of reply, which these publications preached, but practised more in the breach.

But would this not stop the flow of information to Singaporeans and foreigners residing in the Republic? Would this approach not be at odds with the country's often-stated desire to become a hub for information, finance and technology?

He anticipated these criticisms. Curbing a paper's circulation, he countered, would not deprive Singaporeans access to information. He offered the proscribed publications free access if they would circulate without advertisements. This sent a clear message: no stoking of political controversy in Singapore for the sake of boosting circulation.

To reinforce his point, he went so far as to move a Bill in Parliament to grant immunity from the country's copyright laws. This was to allow Singaporeans to make any number of copies of the gazetted publications as they chose. Copies of these were also made available at public libraries. This, he argued, showed that the curbs against the foreign publications were not an attempt to stop the flow of information, but rather to stop publishers from seeking to profit by reporting on Singapore events with a certain twist to the news.

Despite the barrage of media criticism that these moves attracted, he remained adamant that right was on his side.

"The media slams, sloshes, jabs me, pokes me. You expect me to enjoy it and be passive and roll over like a cocker spaniel? Or do you think from time to time, using words, not using violence, I turn the probe on them. The moment they recognise that I have the right of reply, they lose their sharpness, they lose their willingness to give that slight twist because they know that I'll put it right. I think that's fair."

*(Interview with the British Broadcasting Corporation, June 14, 1995)*

He was also to acquire a formidable reputation for taking errant journalists and publishers to court to put right articles which impugned his integrity and that of the system in Singapore. He believed that any suggestion of the sort had to be squashed if it was not to take root insidiously. Referring to one of his many court cases against a foreign commentator who had cast aspersions on his leadership and likened it to a dynasty, he said:

"If I had not taken him to court and asked him to prove what he said and offered myself as a plaintiff and a witness for him to throw his accusation to my face, I would not be able to look at my voters, my electorate, in the face. …

"How do you prove one side right and the other side wrong by writing letters to each other? You are English. You know the fundamental rule of proving the truth. You meet face to face. You confront fact with fiction, truth with lies and the judge or the jury decides. …

"If you don't challenge it, there are any number of crazy, idiotic, vicious people who are out to get me down, who're going to spread it and say, 'Read this, he's done nothing about it. It must be true.' But I've done something about it and the story can't take off. I have sued 15 or 20 times over the last 30-odd years and they come back with the same story that I have been plundering the place, I've enriched myself, and if I had not stopped it each time on its tracks, I would not have survived or enjoyed the reputation that I think I do enjoy, that I'm prepared to stand up and be scrutinised."

*(Interview with the British Broadcasting Corporation, June 14, 1995)*

This no-nonsense approach was to win Lee many critics. They charged that he had resorted time and again to intimidation of the press to curb dissent at home and criticisms abroad. This, his critics claimed, would undermine the emergence of a civil society in Singapore, prevent democratic institutions and instincts from taking root, and keep the people in check. Lee was unmoved by such attacks. On the contrary, he argued that a free press, in its eagerness to fault and check its leaders and institutions – as well as its drive to boost its sales by whipping up public controversy and political intrigue – had overstepped itself. The result was a general debasing, even demolition, of the very institutions which these liberal commentators claimed to champion.

"Is it not more entertaining to have a plethora of opinions so that everybody is entertained and gets the spice that he wants? I'm not sure that the end result in Britain has been a great improvement over the years.

"As a result of press circulation and the desire to titillate and satisfy the cravings of an ever-jaded population, you have demolished the monarchy. You have degraded your members of parliament and your ministers with stories of sleaze and sexual peccadillos. You have downgraded your courts and made them look less than fair. You have demoralised your police force. Even the Church of England no longer has that same aura of authority and wisdom.

"I'm not sure that this is a better Britain. I think the Britain that I knew after World War II was better. I am not saying that Britain should remain unchanged, but there were certain fixed positions. What do you want a monarchy for if you don't want to regard it with some esteem? Of course, all kings have had their weaknesses …"

*(Interview with the British Broadcasting Corporation, June 14, 1995)*

Lee would therefore argue that despite the media barrage against Singapore, the country would have to assert its "right to be ourselves". It would have to chart its own course regardless of the criticisms that this might draw from the liberal Western press, which sought to fashion developing societies in their own image. To taunts in the Western media about Singapore being "authoritarian", a "dictatorship", or just plain "boring", or even jibes which likened Lee to Iraqi leader Saddam Hussein, he would reply:

"If I were a Saddam Hussein, then I would be a pariah which, unfortunately for them, I am not. I have access to any of the leaders I would like to meet in Europe, in Asia and indeed in America. And I think we should have the courage to withstand their assaults but only because we are open to scrutiny and will withstand microscopic examination. We shall proceed, and in the end, I believe we will be able to justify ourselves to the world."

*(From the stand during a defamation suit against the International Herald Tribune,*
*quoted in Straits Times, June 13, 1995)*

# THE MAN BEHIND
# THE IDEAS

# I Did My Best

Four thirty on a Saturday afternoon and the Istana is quiet save the steady, sleepy sound of cicadas snuggled deep in the trees on the sloping lawns. The Istana, Malay for "palace", stands on what was once part of a massive nutmeg estate belonging to a British merchant named Charles Robert Prinsep. In 1869, Governor Harry Ord, who was in charge of Singapore from 1867 to 1873, acquired the land and built Government House on it. The stately white building, a mix of Ionic, Doric and Corinthian orders, was constructed by Indian convicts from Bencoolen in Sumatra.

Over the years, other structures were added to the grounds. One of them, Sri Temasek, is the official residence of the prime minister of Singapore, though no prime minister has ever lived in it. There is also the Istana Annexe, Istana Villa and Istana Lodge. The main Istana building houses the president's office, while the Istana Annexe serves as the prime minister's office.

On the second floor of the Annexe, all is busy on this humid afternoon. Plainclothes security officers tread the narrow carpeted corridors, buzzing each other periodically over their walkie-talkies. In a brightly lit room, a secretary works at her computer, one ear peeled to an intercom linking her to an adjoining office where Lee Kuan Yew works.

It is an L-shaped room with an attached bathroom. It is free of personal paraphernalia. No family photographs decorate his table, no personal mementoes line his walls.

He sits behind a desk, his back to a computer. A low cabinet next to it is stacked with books and files. A wood-panelled wall camouflages the door to the room where his two secretaries work. A teak table for eight stands four metres from his desk, a jade dragon jar in the middle.

Lee works in this office six days a week, from about 10 in the morning to 6:30 in the evening, when he puts his work aside for his daily exercise in the Istana grounds. He has been known to come back to the office on Sundays and public holidays.

He is about 1.8 metres tall, and slim. His trousers, which are usually in light hues, are loose, and he tugs at the waistband frequently. He is at least 10 kilograms lighter than when he was in his forties. His shirts are well-pressed though well-worn, and he wears a windbreaker, usually beige, when he is in the office.

At 74, his hair is white. The once wiry black mop has thinned considerably over the years, accentuating a broad, high forehead under which small, piercing eyes stare. His face is pink in tone, the skin mostly unlined, though tiny creases crisscross the skin on his eyelids. His nails are neatly trimmed.

Even in a private setting, he is a forceful personality. His facial expression changes quickly and his hands often chop the air to emphasise a point. His voice rises and falls according to his emotions. He is quick to show impatience, and slow to smile. He has never suffered fools lightly.

Who is this man who, more than anyone else, has shaped the history of modern Singapore? Who is the person behind the personality Singaporeans regard with awe, respect, love, fear or hate? How would he describe himself? How does he see his 40 years of political life? What is his role now? What is his family life like? And what are his dreams and fears? Lee revealed his personal life in these interviews with the authors, weaving in events that took place 40 years ago as if they had happened only yesterday.

*Keeping fit has always been part and parcel of Lee's life. After his first operation to open up a narrowed artery, in 1996, he said that regular exercise had saved his life. If not for his healthy lifestyle, he might have been hit by heart problems years ago.*

# I have to be taken seriously

Asked to describe himself, Lee is careful and takes his time to answer the question.

"I would say that I'm very determined when I set out to do something. First, I've got to decide whether something is worth doing. If it's not worth doing, well, I'm not prepared to spend the time over it, to make the effort. Then I just coast along, it doesn't matter whether it succeeds or doesn't succeed, it's of no consequence.

"But if I decide that something is worth doing, then I'll put my heart and soul into it. I'll give everything I've got to make it succeed. So I would put my strength, determination and willingness to see my objective to its conclusion. Whether I can succeed or not, that's another matter – but I will give everything I've got to make sure it succeeds. If I've got to get good people, I get good people. If I've got to change tack, I will change tack. But the objective is the same. The presentation may change … If you have decided something is worth doing, you've got to remove all obstacles to get there."

What others think of him – many commentators have had a field day writing about him, and coffeeshop gossip about his life constantly hovers in the air – is water off a duck's back. He has always relished a fight with his critics for, as he noted in April 1975 in an interview with New Zealand journalists, "criticism or general debunking even stimulates me because I think it is foolish not to have your people read you being made fun of". He also puts it this way:

"I have never been overconcerned or obsessed with opinion polls or popularity polls. I think a leader who is, is a weak leader. If you are concerned with whether your rating will go up or down, then you are not a leader. You are just catching the wind … you will go where the wind is blowing. And that's not what I am in this for.

"Between being loved and being feared, I have always believed Machiavelli was right. If nobody is afraid of me, I'm meaningless. When I say something, to make it easier for me to govern, I have to be taken very seriously. So when I say 'please don't do that', you do it, I have to punish you because I was not joking when I said that. And when I punish, it's to punish publicly. And people will know the next time, if you want to do that when he said 'no, don't do it', you must be prepared for a brutal encounter.

"… My job is to persuade my flock, my people, that that's the right way. And sometimes it may be necessary not to tell them all the facts because you will scare them.

"What the crowd thinks of me from time to time, I consider totally irrelevant …

"The whole ground can be against, but if I know this is right, I set out to do it, and I am quite sure, given time, as events unfold, I will win over the ground. … My job as a leader is to make sure that before the next elections, enough has developed and disclosed itself to the people to make it possible for me to swing them around. That's the business of a leader – not to follow the crowd. That's a washout. The country will go down the drain!"

# How I get my ideas

Lee has never shied from borrowing ideas from other countries if they could benefit Singapore. He believes it is important for leaders to read and be interested in how other societies function. He related this to the authors:

*Drivers waiting in line for their cars to be inspected, after Lee implemented vehicle testing, an idea he got from one of his many trips abroad.*

"Way back in the early '70s, when Japan had trouble with the Minamata disease and pollution was a problem in Tokyo, I decided that we, as a small country industrialising rapidly, had no choice but to tackle the environmental problem right from the beginning. Retrofitting would be a disaster because they (foreign companies here) are all multinationals. Having approved them, how do you get them retrofitted?

"Anti-pollution came directly under me. It started off as a part of the Prime Minister's Office. I created that unit. I discussed it with the officials, and I started reading up on it. Then in my travels, I watched what other countries were doing – the way they sited their factories away from inhabited or residential areas, their anti-pollution controls for traffic. For instance, I was in Boston in 1970. There, I saw cars all lining up at garages. I asked, 'Why are they lining up at the garage?' and they said, 'Once a year, you must have a garage to certify that your car is up to certain standards, the emission, the brakes, etc., or you can't renew your licence.' I thought, why don't we have such a rule? Ours, you just wait until the car breaks down. When I came back, I said, 'Look into this.' So we started Vicom [Singapore's first vehicle inspection company].

"Long before a problem became acute, because we were travelling along the same road that these more advanced countries had travelled, I pre-empted the problem before it got out of control. We started putting pressure on diesel taxis puffing away fumes. Buses – endless problems! We had seven or eight bus companies until 1974. The problem was not solved until the 1980s. We had already started monitoring the towns, in Jurong.

"But more than reading, it's a frame of mind, it's an interest in the things around you that matters, and taking note of the happenings in other countries when I travel. When I travel, yes, I occasionally go to plays in London and New York or an exhibition. But I'm watching how a society, an administration, is functioning. Why are they good? ... And the ideas come from not just reading. You can read about it, but it's irrelevant if you don't relate it to yourself or Singapore's problems, which I constantly do."

# The makings of a leader

Lee has strong views about what makes a good and effective leader, what qualities are important and will make a difference to the way a country is run.

"You need, besides determination, all the other attributes that will push a project along. You must have application, you must be prepared to work hard, you must be prepared to get people to work with you. Especially for political leaders, you've got to have people work for you and work with you. You've got to enthuse them with the same fire and the same eagerness that pushes you along. I think that's a very big factor in leadership.

"At the end of the day, you must also have idealism to succeed, to make people come with you. You must have that vision of what is at the bottom of the rainbow you want to reach. But you must have a sense of reality … to feel when this vision is not practical, that it will ruin us.

"For example, people don't live the same lives. I can eat caviar every day, or at least George Lien can or Robert Kuok can. The world cannot. We therefore are entitled to the same level of medical services? No way. There may be only one such surgeon in the world who can do it. That surgeon will be flown, or you will fly to meet that surgeon. For everybody? No. So you've got to find something practical.

"Therefore, right from the word go, I decided, you are entitled to medical treatment such as we can afford as a society, basic medical treatment; all frills above that, if you can afford it, then you buy the frills.

"For heart transplant or liver transplant, you need a whole team of surgeons, anaesthetists, rejection experts. You can't do that for everybody. There must be a practical streak in your judgement. I had that, or we would have failed.

"[But] a leader without the vision, the idea to strive to improve things, is no good. Then you'll just stay put, you won't progress."

He also saw the importance of reading and exchanging views with experts.

"You must read. It's one way of getting information. But you've got to read what's relevant, not only what you're interested in. My wife reads Jane Austen. She was a student of English language and literature so she likes to read books in which she had found joy as a student. I wouldn't read Jane Austen, not because I don't admire her style, but because I would not have the time.

"Novels? Very occasionally. I would read Tom Clancy. He imagined this kind of Third World War scenario, clash with the Soviets and so on, and the kind of battles that would take place. There was one particular novel which I'd read and enjoyed. But, of course, that was also related to my work because I have to approve all these high-tech defence equipment.

"I suppose there are times when I get so tired and browned-off with certain problems, I want to take my mind off them, so I'll read something totally different, about South American tribes or whatever. Occasionally, I would read little biographies or autobiographies. There's

*Opposite: Lee as a young man studying in England. He had given this photograph to his wife-to-be Kwa Geok Choo.*

one about an English lady in Kashgar. My wife would have read it, she'd say, "Oh, this is interesting!" It's a totally different world. It transports me for one, two hours to a different world. Unless the book is riveting, I don't read it from cover to cover. I'll read it and if I see something else, I'll pick it up.

"You must not overlook the importance of discussions with knowledgeable people. I would say that is much more productive than absorbing or running through masses of documents. Because in a short exchange, you can abstract from somebody who has immense knowledge and experience the essence of what he had gained. In a one-hour exchange over dinner with some people who are knowledgeable in certain fields, you get the hang of a particular problem.

"Let's take a recent example. We had this Economic Development Board meeting with this international advisory group. I posed them this question. We are now using our knowledge and our capital and our expertise to help develop these countries – China, Vietnam, India, Myanmar – and help entrepreneurs from developed countries to go in with us, using our knowledge and our contacts to get these countries up. But after 20 years, 30 years, maybe less, they have caught up with us. And these MNCs, after five, 10 years, they get to know the place, they don't need us anymore. So what's our relevance?

"And George Fisher of Kodak was a very thoughtful man. He said, in the end, you have to own knowledge, property, like … Kodak owns the technical knowhow and the name Kodak. Even if you can find out how to make films nearly as good as Kodak, you don't own Kodak. He said, 'Perhaps you should buy into these companies and co-own them, then bring some of them over here and have R&D both here and in America or whatever.'

"You've got to start thinking ahead. You can't just say, okay, let's regionalise and we'll make a lot of money 20 years up. I'd be dead, but my children will not be dead, my grandchildren will be there, they've got to find a role for themselves.

"Then the Shell man, van Wachem, he's a retired CEO and now he's just chairman. He said, 'There are certain things where you cannot predict what is possible.' And he said, nobody – not even he – would have believed that Singapore in the age after the oil crisis, after '73 when oil-owning countries took over their own oil fields, could become a refining and a petrochemical centre. But we have, we are an entrepôt in oil and in petrochemicals …

"How do you extrapolate that? He has given me an idea of how something has developed in a way which he could not have predicted. He is in the oil business. He did not predict this. So we cannot be discouraged. In our way forward, things will happen which will offer us opportunities, which we will seize and can hold only if we remain alert, and on the ball, and competitive. In other words, finally, [what matters is] the quality of your manpower or quality of the teamwork behind the managers and your infrastructure."

# I can live frugally

When he decided to enter politics in 1955, Lee knew that he had to prepare himself for a life of uncertainty. He set about this in a characteristically practical manner.

"When I went in, I had to be comfortable with my own self, that I can live with failure. And failure means it has failed, the communists have won and I'm in deep trouble. Either I have to flee, or they will brainwash me, break me. I don't think they will just kill me because by that time, I would have become a prominent fellow, they want to use me like they used Henry Pu Yi, the last emperor. They brainwash you and break you. And I knew all that! I prepared myself for the possibility of failure, for the possibility of being able to live with failure. In other words, if you want a soft life, better not get into this.

"So I led a pretty disciplined life; if the worst came to the worst, I could survive. I don't need caviar for breakfast, or for dinner, or for supper. I can live on soya beans. I can live quite frugally if I need to. It became a way of remoulding my life in a direction or in a way which would withstand a sharp attack on it.

"Even today, I would still drive my car in the Istana grounds. If tomorrow I have no driver, I can just pick up my car and drive. Occasionally, on a Sunday, I drive myself outside the Istana. I carry my own bag as a matter of principle, because otherwise, for 30, 40 years, with everybody pushing chairs for you, your limbs will atrophy.

"And I was very keen that that shouldn't happen to my children, that nobody pushed chairs for them. If a ball fell down and the Istana boy wanted to pick it up, I would stop him and say, 'No, that's his ball. Ignore him. He will go to the drain and pick it up.' They had to learn that, and I think they have benefited from it."

Politics also meant he had to give up a potentially well-paying career as a lawyer, which one of his brothers went into.

"When I decided to go into politics, Bashir Malall, the man who ran the *Malayan Law Journal*, came to see me. He wasn't a lawyer, but he was a lawyer's clerk and he knew a lot about law. Had there been night courses, he would have been a very good lawyer. His son and I were schoolmates, so he knew me as a teenager. He liked me.

"I was doing well then as a lawyer in Laycock & Ong – '54, '55 – but I was getting involved in politics, all those unions and clan associations. He said to me, 'Make your name at the law first and make your fortune, then go into politics', which was what people of his generation did. That was conventional wisdom. You make a name at the law, you make your fortune, then you go into Congress politics, as in India.

"He didn't understand that something dramatic had happened to my generation, that making a fortune, playing safe, doesn't add up when the system is wrong. I was dead set against the system. But going into politics meant a hazardous, peril-fraught career. It's not a career, it's a vocation. You're taking a plunge, no return. And if you fail, you pay for it with your life. The communists, if they fix you, they fix you good and proper."

But, he admits, he had the luxury of allowing his convictions to rule his decision as his wife, Kwa Geok Choo, was herself a successful lawyer.

"My great advantage was I have a wife who could be a sole breadwinner and bring the children up. That was my insurance policy. Without such a wife, I would have been hard-pressed. To be fair, I was able to make these decisions because I had this fall-back position, I was insured."

In 1970, when the pay of other ministers was raised from $2,500 a month to $4,500, he chose not to raise his pay of $3,500 as he wanted Singapore to first ride out the rough economic times caused by the British withdrawal. Explaining his move, he said then, "I am able to do this only because my wife is a practising solicitor with an adequate income. But it is unrealistic to expect the next prime minister, one qualified for the job, to discharge the functions of this office for the present salary."

## Money is not important

He points out that money has not been a determining factor in his life.

*Lee and his bride in 1950. "My great advantage," said Lee, "was I have a wife who could be a sole bread-winner and bring the children up. And that was my insurance policy. I think without such a wife, I would have been hard-pressed."*

"Supposing I had been differently constituted and I had stuck to the law like my brother. At the end of the day, he has got millions of dollars worth of shares and houses. Maybe I could have the same, but where does that get me? I suppose he would be worth a hundred million dollars, I could be worth two hundred million because of our double income, my wife and I. But where does that get us?

"It makes no difference really whether I've got one million or a hundred million or one billion dollars. What can I do with it? I'm not going to change my way of life. So I could buy myself a big house and a big car and a yacht and a private aircraft.

"It's a matter of what is enough. And I pitched what is enough at a very basic level – well, 'basic' for my class. If you ask me to live today in an HDB three-room flat, and I had to eat at a hawker centre every day, that would be a real problem. But at the time I started, in the '50s and '60s, I think if you tell me to live off the hawker centre, I could. Now probably with age, my digestion is no longer able to cope, and I have to be careful what I eat."

Lee believes that education, more than money, is important. That is what he grew up believing and he cannot understand why other politicians amass fortunes.

"I can understand a person wanting to have, in today's Singapore, a house, a car. Projecting myself back as a young man, I would probably need about $10 million – $5 million to buy a house, the things that would go with the house and education for the children. So if I have another three, four million in the bank and income from it, and three, four hundred thousand dollars annual income, that's the kind of life that I as a non-politician would probably aspire to if I were in my 30s. That I can understand.

"But what I cannot understand to this day is why Marcos looted the place clean. What was the point of it? … I find that not understandable. He ate very frugally. I've had meals with him. He had stomach problems and was very careful what he ate. So wherever he went, he would have his own white rice whenever possible and his own kind of food. And he would eat two bananas because they helped him sleep – two of a special kind of banana, Filipino bananas because they were good for his sleep. And he had a presidential car and a presidential plane, and Malacanang palace. His clothes were not $20,000 clothes or $10,000 clothes. So why?

"I suppose they needed money to buy and sell people, to get things done. He probably wanted to set his children up, but they already had enough. So cleaning up the shop and leaving the Philippines with a $27 billion debt is something I do not understand. What could he do with it? But obviously, he found something worthwhile …

"And in the same way, I don't understand why some of our neighbours do what they do. I can only believe that, as young people, they were deprived and hungry. And they imagined that if you have all this wealth, you will be very happy. And having got started, they believe that they can make their children and grandchildren happy, which is a fallacy. They are building up unhappiness.

"My philosophy, I'm not sure whether it is valid today, but it was valid in my generation – if you've got an education, if I give my children a good education, the rest is up to them. That's the way I grew up because my father was the son of a very rich man. He lost everything. And my mother always told me, my father, he only passed his Junior Cambridge at SJI, then he stopped … When the fortunes were lost, all he could do was to be a storekeeper with Shell company. Whereas his friends, who were also children of rich men, were lawyers or doctors. One of them is Richard Chuan Ho Lim, whose children are William Lim and Arthur Lim. They were family friends. They always used to tell me, 'Get yourself a profession. Be educated. Then even if you are poor, you'll make your way up.'

"And that influenced my thinking, I suppose. So my responsibility for the three children, which I'd placed with my wife, was to get them educated. As it turned out, they won their own scholarships, so good luck to them. That's enough."

Lee's determination to do what he considers the right thing and the strength of his convictions has meant that he has had to make many unpopular decisions. He approaches this philosophically.

"In many cases, it cannot be helped. I don't consciously go out to make enemies of people. But when we are on opposing sides, we have to fight. You fight for your cause, I fight for mine, it cannot be helped. But you shouldn't extend that beyond the person involved.

"For instance, the Plen. A few years ago, Eu Chooi Yip approached Goh Keng Swee in Beijing and said, would we help the Plen's son? His son was born when he was on the run in Indonesia, and was brought up in Changsha with the whole lot of other children of communist cadres from the Malayan Communist Party. The son is a bright fellow and he won a scholarship to Qinghua University, and was working in a research institute. He wanted to get out because he didn't belong.

Eu Chooi Yip— Former Malayan Communist Party leader. Barred from entering Singapore in 1967, he was allowed to return in 1991 on compassionate grounds, after agreeing not to engage in any political activity here. He was a consultant on China affairs in the Institute of East Asian Political Economy before he died in 1996.

"I don't know whether it's the society or the system, or maybe both. If you are not a China Chinese, you are separate, different. They treated him as a foreigner. They gave him special privileges, but he was never one of them. His girlfriend was a fellow Malayan. He wanted to come here. Goh Keng Swee spoke to me, I looked at it … I had the Internal Security Department check on him, whether he is a communist. If he's a plant, then we're looking for trouble. They were convinced that he was not, so we let him in. Now, he's working for one of our research organisations. That's all right. So the Plen wrote to me and thanked me from Haadyai."

Being a politician has also made him more wary of people, especially those who might use their relationship with him for their own gain.

"I've got used to that and I think I'm pretty sensitive in discerning who's on the level and who's wanting to get something out of me. One of the qualities that you need to have to last as a leader is you must be good at that, otherwise you get taken for a ride. You must be able to smell people out.

"It's a difficult thing to describe. I think it's being sensitive. I discussed this with the people who did our Shell system of appraisal for recruitment and promotions. And I asked them whether some people are naturally good at it, at interviewing and appraising. They said, yes, some people are better than others.

"It's got to do with being able to interpret body language. Watch the chap, his voice, whether he is dissimulating, what's his real position, the tone of voice, the tic in his face, his body position or whatever. You can see into a person and through a person.

"And the best two persons I have met with very high sensitivities will be Tan Teck Chwee who was chairman of the Public Service Commission … he's very sharp … and Lim Kim San. I'm not sure if he's as good now because, as you get old, your faculties, your sharpness of eye and ear, like your sensory capabilities, diminish. But he would shake hands with a person and recoil from that man. He once said to me, of Khaw Khai Boh, who was the head of our Special Branch and who became a minister in the Malaysian government, 'When I shake his hand, I feel I want to wash it.' You know, the oiliness of the man and the viciousness of the man – he just sensed it. It's a gift.

"And I think I may not be as sharp as Tan Teck Chwee, maybe not even like Lim Kim San. But I'm not far behind. I can tell a person who's on the level and whom I can trust and whom I cannot and won't.

"Dr Goh Keng Swee cannot do that, he's always making mistakes. He's very brainy, very thorough, very methodical, but lacking here. And I don't know why. He doesn't see through people. The person has got to work with him, then after he's thoroughly disappointed, he gets rid of the man."

# I would do a lot for a friend, but …

As prime minister, he has had to take tough action against friends. When President Devan Nair, a long-time ally, was found misbehaving because of alcoholism in 1985, for example, he had to be removed from office. Then, in 1986, he let the law take its course when National Development Minister Teh Cheang Wan was discovered to be accepting bribes.

*Opposite: Lee was already courting Kwa Geok Choo before they left for studies in Cambridge, England.*

"Let me put it in a simple way. I would do a lot personally for a friend, provided what we set out together to do is not sacrificed. We set out to get this place up. If I sacrifice that now, we are doing harm to what we've been trying to do; that cannot be done.

"But if you need a hundred thousand dollars, I'll sign it out of my own resources or raise the money. Good luck to you. And that's a different matter, that's a personal relationship. But that personal relationship cannot be transmuted into a concession that will jeopardise state interests. That cannot be done because that's what we're trying to establish – a system where people act in accordance with certain principles.

"The purpose is not just to be righteous. The purpose is to create a system which will carry on because it has not been compromised. I didn't do that just to be righteous about Teh Cheang Wan. But if I had compromised, that is the end of the system."

Lee acknowledges that if Singapore had been under another person, the manner in which the country was run would probably have been quite different.

"The best example of what actually could happen is when I had to discuss with Goh Keng Swee what happened if I got knocked down by a bus and he took over. And he told me, 'Frankly, I can't run it your way. I've got to change the method, but I will go in the same direction. I will get there, but a different way.'

"He could not do it my way. He didn't have my temperament. He is as determined as I am – but he could not do the things my way because he's not so good at interpersonal skills. So he would have to do it through another route."

Although politics has been a way of life for Lee for more than 40 years, he is not so sure that he would walk the same path if he had been born later. Needs and motivations are changing, he says, and the young who might have gone into politics in his time today see little need to enter public life.

"Supposing I had been born in a different era, in '73 or '74 in Singapore, and I'm now 21, 22, what would I do? I would have got a scholarship, judging from what I did the last time, I think I would have got a scholarship and gone off to study abroad.

"I'd come back. The environment is different, the future is different, I would not be so absorbed in wanting to change life in Singapore. I'm not responsible for Singapore … I've done my National Service, I'm willing to do my reservist training. Why should I go

# On Mrs Lee and the children

*The Lees with their three children, from left, Hsien Loong, Wei Ling and Hsien Yang.*

Mrs Lee Kuan Yew is often by Lee's side at official functions and trips. What influence does she have on him? He revealed this to the authors:

"Not in political matters. In political matters she would not know enough to tell me whether this is right or wrong. But she would tell me whether she would trust that man or not. That's a gut feeling. And often she is right because she has got an intuitive sense of whether the chap is trustworthy and friendly or unfriendly.

"She did tell me that she didn't think Malaysia would work … She didn't think it would work because, she said, 'You know the way they do things and we'll never change them.' So I said, 'Well, that doesn't mean we need to be like them. And we'll have to work with them because somebody must represent the Malays. And we will not be able to represent the Malays for a very long time, so we would have to find a way of working with them.'"

Lee is also known to be close to his sons – Deputy Prime Minister Hsien Loong and Singapore Telecom chief executive officer Hsien Yang – and only daughter, Wei Ling, a doctor. He told the authors that he took pains to ensure that they grew up living normal lives.

"When I took office, they were very young. They were seven, five and two years old in '59. So first thing my wife and I decided was we should not move into Sri Temasek, which was the official residence, because that would be a very bad thing for them. You'd get an inflated idea of who you are, what you are, with all the servants around and the gardeners. So we decided to stay put [at their Oxley Rise house].

"And all the time we've tried to make them have a sort of a normal environment which was equal to the kind of life I led before I was prime minister. And I believe that's been to their advantage."

He said they got used to being the children of the prime minister after a while. "I don't think it went to their heads. They were treated in school just as another student. And they were not difficult students. So, there was no reason for them to throw their weight around.

"I suppose in her [Wei Ling's] case, it was more difficult because young men would shy off her. But that's not the only reason, that she's my daughter. She's also a bright student and it didn't help that she became the Honours student of her year, as a doctor. The doctors just stayed away, so she has had to pay a price for it. But the boys didn't have the same problem. I suppose being a prime minister's son did not make them less marriageable."

*Lee with Hsien Loong during a Pulau Ubin visit in June 1960.*

and undertake this job and spend my whole life pushing this for a lot of people for whom nothing is good enough? I would seriously think of other jobs.

"Given this kind of a Singapore, I'd ask myself: What they need is a real bad setback and then they'll understand how damn fortunate they are. Then they will learn. Let the setback take place first, then I'll enter politics. And in case we don't recover from the setback, I will have a fall-back position, which many are doing – have a house in Perth or Vancouver or Sydney, or an apartment in London, in case I need some place suddenly, and think about whether I go on to America.

" I had lunch with Lim Kim San. And he said, 'No, no, you won't enjoy life. There's no meaning.' I said, 'Don't say that, Kim San. If I ask you now, and you were 40 years old, to enter politics, would you do so?' And he said, 'No, I don't think so.' I said, 'That answers my point.' Whereas in 1963 he gave up his business – pawnshop business, sago business, director of UOB, to take on this job after working for HDB from '60 to '63. If he were 40 years old, would he do it now? I don't think so.

"… I was the product of the times. That Japanese Occupation brought the whole world crashing down. I understood what power was about. From that, it all happened. If I am back again aged 21 or 22 in today's Singapore, I don't think I will undertake this work voluntarily. At that time I felt such a compelling need to do something.

"… I don't think my younger son feels any compelling need to change Singapore. He's quite happy, he has done his job. He took his SAF scholarship, he did his job. Now he's joined Singapore Telecom – do a good job of it. Go into politics? Lose all weekends going around meeting people. He sees his brother, he sees no reason why he should do it. The brother, I believe, may be different, because he is older by about five and a half years. He went through the race riots in 1964 and 1969. At the time of the riots – '64 – he was already 12, 13, in Catholic High School. He remembers the separation. So he has a different outlook. For him, Singapore was in peril and life was perilous. He got drawn into it because I took him around when I went on my constituency tours … He followed me in the afternoons and early evenings. As dinner time approached, I would send him home. Singapore is a small island, it takes just half an hour to go home. So he got drawn into it."

## Stepping aside

On November 28, 1990, Lee handed over the reins of government to Goh Chok Tong. The event was televised, and many observed that he looked emotional. Since then there has also been talk about whether he has really relinquished power and whether his influence behind the scenes has diminished. To him, all this misses the mark completely. Those who indulge in such idle speculation, he said, do not understand what his stepping aside as prime minister meant to him and the country.

"I had prepared for it for a long time, so I was impatient for it to take place … The Western press, they write up these things projecting their reactions into me, that to give up power was a disastrous loss of authority and so on. Whereas my approach was totally different.

"I had a job to do. I had come to the conclusion by about '76 that my most important job was to get a team that could carry on the work, otherwise we would fail. We'd been trying since '68 to get capable successors. We fielded Chiang Hai Ding, Wong Lin Ken in '68. In '70, Augustine Tan. All bright PhDs. They couldn't do it. You need more than a capacity to write treatises or argue logically. You need practical minds, tough characters who will push a policy through.

"By '76, I was getting very anxious. Hon Sui Sen had a profound influence on me. We were close friends from Japanese days. … One day, he told me that he wanted to retire after the next elections. I said, 'How can you do that? You're still young.' He said, 'No, I'm not.' He said, 'You know, when these chairmen and CEOs come to see me, they are not just looking at me, they are looking for who will be taking my place. Because their investments are going to go on a long time – 10, 15, 20 years, and I won't be here. The Americans have a succession system in place. At 65 you're out, and you've got to find a successor before then for the Board to confirm. So they were looking around and watching the younger team. They're watching you too,' he said to me. 'You are still okay,' he said, 'but, you know, they are looking beyond your lifetime.'

"So I spent a long time hunting for good men, working out a system that will produce a team of good men, comparable, at least as competent as what I had in place. They may not be as tough and tough-minded, or as imaginative or creative because that's in the luck of the draw. But they must be able to run the place. They must first know the problems. So we set out head-hunting.

"I set the target at 1988, when I would be 65, believing that the sooner I give up, the younger I will be and the more active I can be to make sure that the team succeeds. I'll be around to make sure that the team can succeed. The later I give up, the older and slower I will be, the more risky its success.

"When '88 came, Chok Tong wasn't confident of taking over from me and dealing with our immediate neighbours, Suharto and Mahathir. He felt he would be at a disadvantage. So he said, 'Better give me two years; meanwhile I can get a feel of the job.' Meanwhile, I had been passing over more and more of the work to him. And I said, 'What do you think? What's your view?' – pushing him to make decisions and then supporting him. Or if I disagreed, I would explain the reasons.

"So when 1990 came, he wanted me to stay on for the 25th anniversary of Singapore's independence, for a sentimental reason, 1965 to 1990. So I finished my term in August and he was ready to take over by November, after I'd tidied up some odds and ends.

"My job after that was to make sure that an error which is avoidable because of my experience should not be committed if I can help it. I think the team in place is functioning. And I believe, without me, it can function as well. That is a triumph!

"The Western correspondents don't understand that this is a completely different approach to the problem of succession. For him and his team to fail, it's my failure. I brought this team together. If they succeed, it is I who brought about the success. It's a very serious business, of ensuring the continuation of good government."

*On November 28, 1990, Lee relinquished the reins of government to Goh Chok Tong. "I had prepared for it for a long time, so I was impatient for it to take place. ... For him and his team to fail, it's my failure. I brought this team together. If they succeed, it is I who brought about the success."*

It was for this reason, he says, that he went public in 1988 to give an assessment of whom he thought could best take over from him. He had rated Tony Tan his first choice, even though Goh Chok Tong was then First Deputy Prime Minister.

"When I went public to say, 'Look, this is my assessment,' I did that deliberately to make sure people understood that this was an open exercise, that they, Goh's peers, had chosen him. In other words, having chosen him, they have to support him. I had not appointed him. If I appointed him and they disagreed, they could withhold support and he would not succeed ...

"Having seen what went wrong, particularly in the communist countries, and even in Britain, where Churchill handed over to Anthony Eden, Eden failed and Macmillan picked it up – I did not believe that if I appointed the leader, they would give him the same wholehearted support. So I forced them to decide amongst themselves. I had said to them, 'Look, my assessment is as follows.'

"This was after the 1984 elections. I watched them run the elections and I watched their press conferences. I said the most decisive leader was Tony Tan. He would say yes or no and he would stick to it. Goh Chok Tong would try to please you. You can see him in a press conference, even today. If he sits back and talks to his Cabinet, then he comes out with a firm position, after long discussion. But if you engage him in a press conference, you might get him to make some concessions.

"You will never get Tony Tan to do that. You won't get me to do that. You can talk to me till the cows come home; if I have decided that this is no go, it is no go. You may be unhappy, but I am quite convinced, after six months, maybe after six years, you will know that I was right. But he [Goh] has one advantage – he has their support. They've got to support him because they elected him. And I think that that was a wise move. I made it public to let people know that the choice was that of his colleagues.

"There was a reason and method behind what people thought was a casual passing of judgement. I was seriously placing the weight on the shoulders of his colleagues. They have worked with me, I have pointed out this is right, that is wrong.

"I thought at that time that Deng Xiaoping made a mistake getting rid of Zhao Ziyang. Maybe he had compelling reasons, I don't know – must have been powerful reasons. After working with a man for 30, 40 years, why knock him down like that?"

Does he miss being the prime minister?

"Frankly no. Supposing I'm prime minister, I have to attend to all the day-to-day problems, I've got to go to all these conferences, Asean summit, Apec, visit so many countries. I have done all that for so long. What's the point of it? I have outgrown it. I don't hanker to go to an Asean summit or an Apec summit, or to have a state visit to America or Britain.

"I've been through all that. I have been the guest of honour at formal dinners, state visits – from President Johnson to Nixon, to Ford to Reagan and Bush. Well, that's enough!

"The prime minister has to work with Clinton. It's not my job. He's a younger man. Supposing I were the prime minister and I had to deal with Clinton, I would find it quite an effort dealing with a Vietnam War generation, a man who was against the Vietnam War. I was for the Vietnam War and had encouraged the president of the United States, both Johnson and then Nixon."

On his role as senior minister and his life now, Lee sees himself as a guardian to the younger team running Singapore.

"At 70-plus, what do I need? Time to reflect. I need enough to keep me engaged and interested in life. What is it I want to do? What can I best do with the balance of my time? I don't know how much time I've got left. If, let's say, I have another five or 10 years – if I am lucky, and am like my father more than like my mother, who died when she was 74. But it's 10 years in which my energy levels will be declining, year by year.

Zhao Ziyang— Chinese premier and party chief handpicked by Deng Xiaoping to be his successor. His star fell swiftly and he was sacked in 1989 for sympathising with pro-democracy student demonstrators in Beijing's Tiananmen Square. He was barred from attending Deng's funeral in February 1997.

"What I'd like to do now is to give this government the benefit of my experience in avoiding mistakes. I can't tell them what to do as their great achievements, their great breakthroughs. That's for them to work out with younger Singaporeans. But I know that certain things are sure paths to trouble, so avoid them.

"It's not by accident that we got here. Every possible thing that could have gone wrong, we had tried to pre-empt. That's how we got here, that's why we have substantial reserves. Because if we don't have reserves, the moment we run into trouble, who will lend you money when you've got no gold mines or oil fields? We've got nothing. All we have is this functioning organism which requires brains, specialised skills put together in a very intricate form, with inputs from many nations and their experts in financial services, manufacturing, tourism, all sorts of economic activities put together. It's not easy to replicate.

"I consider this as the best contribution I can make, the most worthwhile thing to do."

# I've been a lucky man

Lee describes himself as an agnostic, but he appreciates that there are those who regard religion as a main pillar of life. Others, like himself, are guided by certain personal beliefs.

"I was brought up as an ancestor worshipper, Taoist, Buddhist – the traditional Chinese family. If I visited a funeral wake of a Chinese family, I would perform the necessary rituals with joss-sticks in respect. At home, after some years, around the 1960s, we stopped the rituals in memory of my grandfather on certain days like Qing Ming, with the offerings, candles, joss-sticks.

"If you ask me, 'Is there a God?' my answer is 'I don't know.' But I do know that those who believe in God – like Hon Sui Sen and his wife – they derive great strength and comfort from their religion. They do not believe that this is the end of the world. Their behaviour and their hopes do not end with this life. That gives them enormous reserves of stamina and serenity of mind.

"I would not dismiss religion as so much superstition. The communists have failed in stamping out religion because it is part of human nature.

"I don't think I have ever, in times of great danger or peril, gone down on my knees to pray, or gone to the temple and hoped for some miracle. I do not believe strength comes, necessarily, from a belief in God. You must have some belief in a philosophy, in an idea, in a concept.

"It is a question of faith which, in the case of the communists, had nothing to do with God. It is a question of faith, the belief that something is right and they're going to do it. So if you ask me, what is my faith, I'll say, well, I believe certain things are worth doing and let's do it … People are made that way."

Would he describe himself as a happy man?

*Lee with his extended family at a Chinese New Year's Eve reunion on January 22, 1993. The family network and the traditions they uphold have always been important to Lee.*

"Ask a man in his 70s like me what is happiness, and I would say a certain serenity of mind, a certain satisfaction with having done things which were worth doing and in not having more than one's normal share of tragedies.

"Everybody goes through the vagaries of life. I am fortunate that I escaped death at the hands of the Japanese and death and injury in a nasty accident when my car turned over at Thomson Road, at Caldecott Hill, near Radio Singapore. It was a bad turn. It's no longer there now. There was a deep ravine on the side with iron waterpipes. And on a very rainy day, this was in '51 – I was going to play golf at the Island Club. The car just skidded and then rolled over two times, but landed on soft grass and soft earth! If I had hit that pipe, that would have been the end of both of us, and my wife was expecting her first child then. So I think it was deliverance.

"Taking everything into account, I've been a lucky man. My son is not so lucky, he lost his wife. Quite inexplicable. She was a doctor, should have known that she was having heart trouble because she was feeling pains in her neck. But too late. And by the time the attack took place, doctors could do nothing … And he got lymphoma. That's the luck of the draw and he has to live with it. So if you compare my fate with his, I am luckier. But in the end, he will have to be the stronger person.

"Life has an unfair, unpredictable quality about it and you must take it as it comes. But then, that's not what I would have thought if you had asked me when I was 30 years old. Now it's a different perspective. How many of my generation are alive, never mind being fit and mobile and still *compos mentis?*"

Lee said his greatest personal achievement is his family.

"I'm very happy that I've got a good, happy family. I've got a happy marriage, I've got three children I'm very proud of, I can't ask for more. That's my personal achievement."

Of his political achievements, he pointed to a thriving Singapore.

"What I have to show for all my work is Singapore, and Singapore is still working. It would have been better if we had Singapore as part of a successful Malaysia. I still believe that, but it wasn't possible, so that's that."

Would he live life differently if he had to do it all over?

"Among those of my generation, very few are alive, very few have been as fortunate as I have been, very few have taken the risks I have taken and survived. Why do I want to live my life all over again?

"A golf pro once demonstrated a trick shot. He took an egg, put it on a tee and he took a sand wedge. And he said, 'I'll hit that tee, snap it and the egg will drop on the grass unbroken.' And he did it. He snapped a tall wooden tee and the egg dropped down unbroken. I wanted to see how actually it was done. I thought he turned the blade, so the blade snapped the tee, and did not touch the egg. So I said, 'Do that again.' He said, 'No, I may not be as lucky the second time.'

"I think I will give you that answer. I may not be as lucky a second time in so many things. … All I can say is, I did my best. This was the job I undertook, I did my best and I could not have done more in the circumstances. What people think of it, I have to leave to them. It is of no great consequence. What is of consequence is, I did my best."

# IN HIS OWN WORDS: SELECTED SPEECHES AND INTERVIEWS

Lee Kuan Yew's first election campaign was not in Singapore, for the People's Action Party, but in England, for the Labour Party during the 1950 British general election. To help his friend, David Widdicombe, the Labour candidate for Totnes, Devon, he drove a lorry, making the rounds in the constituency and stopping by the gates of factories, delivering speeches on the back of the vehicle. This speech, in early February 1950, focussed on how he saw the electoral fight between Labour and the Conservatives.

# If I were an Englishman

If I were an Englishman, I would not have to explain my presence on this platform for it is the right and indeed the duty of every Englishman to take sides in a general election. You may well wonder what a Chinaman should be doing here. You have important domestic issues to discuss that should not concern any foreigner. Let me say at once that I am not a foreigner. I am a British subject from British Malaya. And I am here because your vote on February 23 will affect me and 7 million other Malayans some 8,000 miles away. It is your Colonial Office here which decides our fate. It may be that some of you could not care less what happens to a lot of ignorant and illiterate natives. But, unfortunately, what happens to my ignorant fellow countrymen, and what they do, is going to affect you in England.

From Malaya, Britain gets more dollars every year than she gets from Marshall Aid. It is the country that produces the world's rubber and more than one-third the world's tin – two raw materials which America does not have and must import. Malaya's dollar earnings are so important to Britain that Sir Stafford Cripps obtained a promise from President Truman to keep down the American production of synthetic rubber in order that America will buy more Malayan natural rubber. If Britain loses Malaya her dollar gap will rip open. That would mean a heavy cut in your imports of food and raw materials, consequent unemployment and a steep rise in the cost of living.

Since Labour came into power four years ago I have often criticised their colonial policy and administration; and your Labour candidate, whom I have known since I came to this country three years ago, has received his full measure of what I thought were the faults of Britain's colonial programme. But when it is a choice between Labour, a party with a social conscience, and Conservative, a party without one, we in the colonies have no difficulty in deciding which is the better. To the Tories, the colonies are just areas for

> When it is a choice between Labour, a party with a social conscience, and Conservative, a party without one, we in the colonies have no difficulty in deciding which is the better.

very profitable investment. Every other week you will notice in the *Times* the 50–60 per cent dividends, such dividends as you never see anywhere else in the world. To them, we are just a lot of natives providing their younger and less able sons with a decent career and a comfortable pension on retirement. They had and still have no plans for helping the less fortunate peoples in the Empire to a better standard of living and a greater degree of self-government. Indeed they say quite openly that they do not intend to liquidate the Empire. And to them the giving of self-government to the non-European peoples would be the liquidating of the Empire. What they refuse to see is the fact that the Asiatics and African peoples in the Empire have grown up politically and are no longer content to be governed from Whitehall, no longer happy about being developed by big capitalist interests. There was no socialist government in Holland after the war. They wanted to go back to the glory of their prewar empire. They refused to face the facts of postwar nationalism in Asia. So they engaged in a bitter and costly war in Indonesia. Now, after three years of it, they have had to admit defeat.

I searched through the Conservative Party manifesto for some statement of policy on the Empire. All I found was a vague generalisation about "promoting the welfare of the Empire". And here is where they give a hint of their true colours: "Both Britain and America will gain to the advantage of all." All, that is, except the colonial peoples themselves.

Nationalism has come to stay in Asia, and we believe it is only the Labour Party that is honest enough to face the facts. Labour has a colonial policy. It had one in 1945 and its four years' record in Malaya is impressive. Reforms long overdue have been carried out in the midst of postwar difficulties and shortages. The Tories talked for years about the need for a university in Malaya. The Labour government last year founded the University. The Tories had long groaned about the white man's burden to the coloured peoples – but they did little to help these coloured peoples to help themselves. Under a Labour government the first social surveys have been carried out in Malaya and the first social welfare services started. The Tories gave four scholarships a year to students to study in England. The Labour government has now more than 200 Malayan students on scholarship in English universities, studying medicine, law, the sciences and social welfare. The Tories squashed trade unions in colonies before the war just as they have squashed them here before the war. I myself am not a state or government scholar and I have nothing to gain by speaking for the Labour government. I say these things because they are the truth and because they are not so generally known in this country.

We have confidence in Labour because we have seen Labour carry out its last election promises. We have no confidence in the Tories. They have not promises at all. They merely string out general phrases. Remember Lord Woolton's broadcast last Saturday: "Stand by the British Empire and Commonwealth." But he did not say what he proposed to do in specific terms and I have grave suspicions of what he might have meant when he went on to say that he was going to "develop the vast untapped resources of the Empire". Mr Churchill said at Sevenoaks, "And all that great Empire must be raised, and roused, to a sense of its grandeur and its strength." Does anyone here really believe that the

The Tories squashed trade unions in colonies before the war just as they have squashed them here before the war. I myself am not a state or government scholar and I have nothing to gain by speaking for the Labour government.

British Empire is asleep? This Empire needs no rousing. Have we all not heard of the recent troubles and riots in West Africa, of the terrorists in Malaya, and have we so quickly forgotten the civil disobedience in India when the Tories were in power before the war? This Empire, far from wanting to be roused, needs tact and a good deal of understanding. And we in the colonies know that it is only Labour that is fully alive to our difficulties and our aspirations to self-government. If you want to keep Malaya in the Empire, and keep the dollars that Malayan tin and rubber earn within the sterling area, more dollars than Britain gets from her export drive, then keep Labour in office.

There are some of my fellow countrymen who would like to see a Tory government back in office – not because they have any faith in a Tory government, but because they know that with a Tory government which thinks in terms of the world of yesterday, with a government determined to repress and suppress the nationalist spirit of colonial peoples, a government determined to bring back the grandeur and might of the 19th century empire, unrest will mount and disorder will break out. And in the mood of discontent and violence more will go over to the extremists and the communists. Then the Malayan Communist Party will be strong enough to drive the British Army out of the country. You all know about the bandits and terrorists in Malaya. But let me tell you that behind these virulent outrages there lies a tightly-knit communist organisation. How far their bid for power succeeds or fails will depend on how far they can get the genuine nationalist aspirations of the people behind them. A Tory government determined, like the French government in Indo-China, to thwart the nationalist aspirations of the people will send all moderate nationalists over to the communists – and this indeed is what has happened in Indo-China.

With a Labour government in Britain these extremists have so far failed to get any appreciable support from the people, for we believe that from Labour Britain we can get what we want by constitutional and orderly methods.

I have met many students in this country from India, Pakistan and Ceylon. I have not met one of them who believes in the sincerity of Tory proclamations of equal Asiatic partnership and cooperation within the Commonwealth.

There are over 300 of my fellow countrymen studying in this country. We are all unanimously agreed that a Tory government back in office would mean more trouble out in the East. My hope and our hope of a peaceful solution of this pressing colonial problem is in Labour.

To those who are still open to reason and argument I say that if you value fairness and social justice not only to the people of Britain but also to the millions of British subjects in the colonies, return another Labour government. But even if you care nothing for fairness or social justice to the colonial peoples, then for the sake of your own self-interest, your own economic well-being, for the sake of the dollars you get out of Malaya and your other colonies, return a government that has the confidence of these peoples, who will then gladly cooperate with and be happy to grow up within the British Commonwealth and Empire.

If you want to keep Malaya in the Empire, and keep the dollars that Malayan tin and rubber earn within the sterling area, more dollars than Britain gets from her export drive, then keep Labour in office.

**255**

This is probably the most important political speech Lee Kuan Yew made in his early years as a student in Cambridge. He was speaking at the Malayan Forum, a political grouping of Singapore and Malayan students formed by Goh Keng Swee, Tun Razak and Maurice Baker. In this speech, in January 1950, he analysed the political situation in Malaya, the race problem there, and the coming battle with the communists. His message: the English-educated, especially those like him, studying in England, were the best placed to assume power from the British. But ultimately the battle would be with the communists, in a struggle which he predicted would be a violent one.

# The returned student

## Platitudes and controversy

This is not a learned paper with carefully garnered and marshalled facts, buttressed by an impressive mass of statistics. Rather it is a personal evaluation of the political problems facing us, and a personal interpretation of the lines along which we should act if we are to rise up to the situation instead of waiting passively for events to overtake and overwhelm us. Its purpose is to stimulate rather than to inform. Many of my propositions may be controversial, but where it is a choice between platitudes and personal convictions, I feel it is my duty to state my convictions vigorously, for one great obstacle to a rapid and orderly political development of Malaya has been and still is the Malayan habit of ignoring unpalatable facts and avoiding unpleasant controversy.

## Crumbs from the table, British and Japanese

The superior social and economic position of the returned student is a fact in Malayan society. Whether this privileged position enjoyed as a class is justifiable is quite another matter. But it is the inevitable accompaniment of the supremacy of the British in the country. The English in Malaya forms the ruling caste. He has superimposed on the people his language, institutions and way of life. His is the model of perfection, and the closer an approximation to his standards the individual Asiatic attains the better his social and economic position. That is beyond controversy. In the few years the Japanese were the ruling caste, there were already signs that the nearer one was to being a Japanese, the better off one was going to be in a Japanese-dominated Malaya. Had they stayed long enough, I have no doubt that those of us who could speak Japanese, who behaved like the Japs and who had been educated in Japan would have been the most favoured class of

I feel it is my duty to state my convictions vigorously, for one great obstacle to a rapid and orderly political development of Malaya has been and still is the Malayan habit of ignoring unpalatable facts and avoiding unpleasant controversy.

Many of us will remember the unhappy spectacle of English-speaking, Western-educated colleagues suddenly changing in their manner of speech, dress and behaviour, making blatant attempts at being good imitation Japs.

Malayans. For they would have been the most acceptable to the rulers, who because of their economic and military hold on the country, could dispense extra privileges. Many of us will remember the unhappy spectacle of English-speaking, Western-educated colleagues suddenly changing in their manner of speech, dress and behaviour, making blatant attempts at being good imitation Japs. Indeed some were sent to Japan so as to be better educated, to enlighten their ignorant countrymen in Malaya and doubtless also to become the privileged class, second only to the genuine Japanese himself. It is pertinent to note that the Malayan student returned from Britain ceased under Japanese domination to occupy that second-class status, except in so far as it was impracticable to dispense with his services for the time being.

It is four years now since the British have returned. For them, nothing could be better than to revert to the pleasant orderly society of 1939. Once again the English-educated are given their old privileges; and of this English-educated class, the returned student forms the uppermost crust.

## Our eminent neighbours

It is relevant to observe the part this class (the returned student) has played in British-dominated India, Dutch-dominated Indonesia, and American-dominated Philippines. In the brief space of four years, we have seen the emergence of six Asiatic countries to national independence: India, Pakistan, Burma, Ceylon, Indonesia, Philippines. Malaya now finds herself the only remnant of colonial imperialism left in Southeast Asia surrounded by these new Asiatic national states. The only other fragment of colonialism left in Asia is French Indo-China, and at this very moment, we are watching the last desperate French attempts to salvage what little they can from that unhappy country for the French national income.

In all these new Asiatic states, it is the returned students who have led the fight for independence. The Indians, Pakistanis, Ceylonese and Burmese returned from England, the Indonesians returned from Holland, the Philippines returned from America – they have formed the spearhead of national movements. We now see as prime minister of India, Pandit Jawaharlal Nehru, educated at Harrow and Cambridge; as premier of Pakistan, Mohamed Liaquat Ali Khan, educated at Oxford; as premier of Burma, Thahin Nu, educated at Cambridge; as premier of Indonesia, Dr Hatta, educated at Leyden University, Holland; and last but not least, as leader of Viet Minh, Dr Ho Chi Minh, educated at Paris, where he first joined the Communist Party.

## What might have been

If this should conjure visions of future greatness in any of us, I hasten to add that the pattern of events never quite repeats itself, and there are cogent reasons for believing that this pattern will not do so in Malaya. Had there not been the difficult racial problem in Malaya, had there not been a Chinese community almost as large as Malays, had the population been six million, all Malays, I venture to suggest that British imperialism in

Malaya would be well on its way out. But the facts being what they are, we must accept British rule for some time, time during which we can attain a sufficient degree of social cohesion, and acquire a sufficient degree of civic and political consciousness among the various races of Malaya. This time is vital if we are to avoid a political vacuum that may otherwise follow British withdrawal from Malaya.

## And what is

Returned students in any British colony fall broadly into two classes:
  (1) the rich man's son
  (2) the impecunious government scholar
The first, on returning home, finds himself better equipped to be a bigger and more efficient capitalist entrepreneur. The second finds himself linked up with the colonial administrative system, given positions second only to the Englishman, who must necessarily in a colonial system always be at the top. But they will be better off than their fellow Asiatics who have not been to England. Hence both groups, on returning to Malaya, find themselves a part of the vested interests of the country, both somewhat reluctant to dislodge the system under which they enjoy these advantages.

## British dilemma

It is significant that Colonial Office policy since the war has been to increase the number of scholars sent to England. This is no doubt, in part, a sincere attempt to carry out Labour's election programme of 1945, when they promised that the colonial peoples should be helped to self-government. But I think there is equally no doubt that this policy is also intended, to a large extent, to ally the potential leaders of a potential Malayan nationalist movement with the existence of British rule in Malaya. These men and women, if left frustrated and underprivileged in Malaya, would turn their energies to the overthrow of a system where they are not given the opportunity to attain what they feel is their rightful due from society. So it is that empires exist, that one nation by economic and military supremacy is able to dominate another and to continue to keep it subject for a long time afterwards, although there is no intrinsic superiority in individuals of the master over individuals of the subject race. But no matter how enlightened a colonial policy, it must finally end. That is the British dilemma. To quote from a learned treatise by a professor of anthropology at London University who was in Malaya before the war, and whose book *Malay Fisherman* was published before the British re-occupation, at page 306:

> "Quite apart from any disorganisation resulting from the war, and from any conservatism, apathy and suspicion that may be met, there are two major political and economic issues that have to be faced. One is the question of the kind of relations which should exist between Chinese and Malays in Malaya; the other is the question of the place which the British wish to occupy. With postwar reconstruction should certainly come a more positive policy for Chinese-Malay relations in the Malay States, giving more definite political opportunities to

These men and women, if left frustrated and underprivileged in Malaya, would turn their energies to the overthrow of a system where they are not given the opportunity to attain what they feel is their rightful due from society.

The two things we the returned students can help to decide are: firstly, how soon and orderly the change will be, and secondly, whether we shall find a place at all in the new Malaya.

the Chinese and more enlarged economic assistance to the Malays. It does seem evident that the old Colonial system, with a comparatively small group of Europeans as the dominant power, is a temporary historical phase; that with the advance of modern technology and education there is almost bound to be ultimately a transfer of responsibility to the major groups resident in the country."

## The sun must set

Empires never last for ever. Either the master and subject races finally merge into one unified society as in Britain, where the Welsh and Scots, once English-dominated, now form part of one political society, enjoying equal rights with the English. Or the empire ends with the subject races violently resisting and finally emerging as a separate national and political entity as in the case of the Irish Republic, India, Pakistan and Indonesia. The indefinite continuance of the subjugation of one race over another is only possible where the subject race is inherently, both mentally and physically, inferior. Anthropologists are unable to prove any innate superiority of one race over another. This scientific fact and the historical fact that no empire has been able to last more than a thousand years is, I think, no mere coincidence.

We in Malaya are now seeing British domination after over a hundred years enter its last phase. Colonial imperialism in Southeast Asia is dead except in Malaya, and our generation will see it out. No sane man, whether he be English, Malay, Indian, Eurasian, or Chinese, can honestly study the situation in that part of the world and not come to the conclusion that either with or without the opposition of the Western-educated intelligentsia in Malaya, British imperialism will end. The two things we the returned students can help to decide are: firstly, how soon and orderly the change will be, and secondly, whether we shall find a place at all in the new Malaya. At the moment it is clear that the only party organised to force the British to leave, and to run the country, is the Communist Party. They are not merely so many bandits, shooting and being shot at in the jungle, and creating terror for the sake of terror. Theirs is a tightly knit organisation making their bid for power.

## A greater evil

It is this element of international communism which I fear will make the pattern of development that has unfolded in India, Burma, Ceylon, etc. unlikely in Malaya. In all these countries the leaders from the educated classes, the returned students, had time to organise and were already organised, like the Indian Congress Party, before international communism became a force in the political life of these countries. But this does not mean that communism is not a force in these countries. It is, right now, the biggest threat to the newly established national governments of Asia.

How far these governments can counter the appeal and force of communism will depend on how far they are bold enough to carry out social reforms in the teeth of their own vested interests. That is another feature in the political development of our neighbours: the active support of native capitalists in the national aspirations of their fellow countrymen.

But it is abundantly clear to Malayan vested interests, and that would include Chinese and Indian commercial interests, the Malay royal families, and the professional classes, that with the disappearance of the British Raj must also disappear the great inequality in wealth of the peoples of Malaya. For any independent Malayan government to exist, it must win popular support, and to gain any popular support it must promise and do social justice. Indeed, and this is a fact important enough to warrant repetition, the continued existence of the new Asiatic states depends upon whether they are able to carry out long overdue reforms; whether they can, without the communist religion, do all that a communist state can do for the masses.

## The lesser evil

We, the returned students, would be the type of leaders that the British would find relatively the more acceptable. For if the choice lies, as in fact it does, between a communist republic of Malaya, and a Malaya within the British Commonwealth, led by the people who despite their opposition to imperialism still share certain ideals in common with the Commonwealth, there is little doubt which alternative the British will find the lesser evil.

Despite the general political apathy that exists in Malaya there are many who are awakening to the critical position Malaya is in, both internally and in relation to the rest of Southeast Asia. If we, who can become the most privileged part of the local population under British rule, openly declare that British imperialism must go, the effect would be immediate.

But if we do not give leadership, it will come from the other ranks of society, and if these leaders attain power, as they will with the support of the masses, we shall find that we, as a class, have merely changed masters. The difference between the British, Japs and the new masters who will arise if we remain unorganised will be a difference only of degree and not of kind.

## What we must do

The first problem we face is that of racial harmony between Chinese and Malays. The second is the development of a united political front that will be strong enough without resorting to armed force, to demand a transfer of power. To both these problems, we the Malayan students in England, whatever our race and creed, can make a substantial contribution. If we who are thought of as the intelligentsia of Malaya cannot make a sincere start right now towards a solution of these problems, the future is grim. No class in Malaya is better equipped to lead a Malayan nationalist movement. The common man in Malaya rightly or wrongly associates intelligence and ability with an education in England, perhaps for the reason that such an education makes possible a greater and more rapid acquisition of wealth in a British Malaya.

We, the returned students, would be the type of leaders that the British would find relatively the more acceptable.

We must break the soporific Malayan atmosphere and bring home the urgency of the problems facing us. We must break down the belief that we are inferior and will always remain inferior to the Europeans.

We have already seen the birth of Malay nationalism, we are seeing the first movements of a Malayan Chinese nationalism. There is no doubt that the other racial groups will also organise themselves. This may be a prelude to a pan-Malayan movement, or it may be the beginning of serious dissensions and communalism that may end in another Palestine. The prerequisite of Malayan independence is the existence of a Malayan society, not Malay, not Malayan Chinese, not Malayan Indian, not Malayan Eurasian, but Malayan – one that embraces the various races already in the country. Were it possible to eliminate the non-Malay population by deporting them to their country of origin, there would be no danger of another Palestine. But even the most extreme Malay nationalist will concede that the Chinese, Indian and Eurasian population already in the country cannot be excluded by this simple process. Irresponsible communal leadership will bring disaster. Since, therefore, the non-Malay communities must be accepted as part of the present and future Malaya, it follows that unity must be attained.

We can study with profit the solution Switzerland has found for her racial problems. Here is a national state with three large racial groups – French, German and Italian – and a fourth small group, the Romansch, able to maintain its unity and independence through all the strain and stress of two world wars, when French, Germans and Italians were fighting on different sides. Whether we have the Palestinian or Swiss pattern emerging in Malaya is still in the balance.

## A challenge

The present political situation is rapidly changing. Colonialism with its fantastic discrepancies in wealth and power will end whether or not we do anything. It is not a question of our fighting for independence in the way the Indian Congress Party fought for theirs. It is whether we are to play any part at all in the political life of the country. There is still time for us to organise ourselves into a force in the country. But the final question is what each individual returned student will do when he goes back to Malaya, for in the last eventuality, any party, any society, any body politic, consists of individuals.

There can be no leaders without a body to lead. There can be no body to lead if there is no cohesion. As single individuals, any Malayan nationalist who attempts to propagate ideas that would lead to the end of British Malaya would be considered undesirable by the British authorities. Their main interest is to prolong British control of our country. For them Malaya means dollars. Losing Malaya would mean a big widening of the dollar gap with consequent loss of essential imports to Britain and resulting unemployment. We must be prepared to see that whatever the political label of the British government in Britain, be it Conservative, Labour, or even Communist, British colonial policy in Malaya may remain unchanged in its fundamentals. A British Labour government may sincerely believe in socialist, egalitarian principles, but no British government can of its own free will give independence to Malaya and face the British electorate unabashed when the British cost of living index has gone up by some twenty points.

## Our opportunity

But our trump-card is that responsible British leaders realise that independence must and will come to Malaya and that, therefore, it will be better to hand Malaya to leaders sympathetic to the British mode of life, willing to be a member of the British Commonwealth, and what is most important, willing to remain in the sterling area. For the alternative is military suppression, a policy which another imperialist power has found impossible in Indonesia. We may take heart in the knowledge that no one can concede more graciously an already untenable position than the English. Our duty is clear: to help to bring about social cohesion, and to bring home to even the most diehard imperialist that his is an untenable position.

What actual steps we take when we get back will depend on the political temper at that time. Whether we can openly advocate and propagate our views or whether we should be more discreet and less vociferous is something that can be answered only when the time comes. Only if a spirit of cooperation and political independence is infused among our fellow Malayans can pan-Malayan political parties really exist, and Malayan leadership emerge. We must break the soporific Malayan atmosphere and bring home the urgency of the problems facing us. We must break down the belief that we are inferior and will always remain inferior to the Europeans. If every returned student makes known his convictions to his own immediate circle, the cumulative effect will be tremendous. A small pebble dropped in a pond can cause extensive ripples. Without the countless unnamed Indian patriots who did their share in awakening a sense of national pride and dignity and independence, there could have been no Congress Party, no Gandhi, no Nehru and no Indian Republic.

## Order or chaos?

If we fail to fulfil our duty, the change that still will come must be a violent one, for whatever the rights and wrongs of communism, no one can deny its tremendous appeal to the masses. Whatever our political complexion, from deep blue Tory to bright red communist, we must all remember that we are not indispensable in this struggle for freedom. But we can affect the speed and orderliness of the change. What the individual returning home chooses to do is a question of personal inclination, economic circumstances, and political convictions. But if the majority of us choose to do nothing, choose to believe that Malaya can be insulated from the nationalist revolts that have swept the European powers from Asia, then we may find that there is no place for us in the Malaya that is to be after the British have departed.

> If we fail to fulfil our duty, the change that still will come must be a violent one, for whatever the rights and wrongs of communism, no one can deny its tremendous appeal to the masses.

Lee Kuan Yew contested the general election in 1955, Singapore's first under a newly constituted legislative assembly. The People's Action Party fielded four candidates and three won. Lee won in Tanjong Pagar, a seat he has held for 42 years and 11 general elections. In this campaign speech on March 21, 1955, he spoke about the ugly face of colonialism and what the PAP would do to correct the situation.

# Colonies are out of date

There is something wrong with Malaya, something rotten with the colony of Singapore. You know it and I know it. We've known it for a long time. We are a colony and colonies are out of date. Colonialism is on the way out but is not moving fast enough. We in the PAP intend to give colonialism a final push and sink it for good in Southeast Asia. But colonialism alone is not our enemy. Our enemy is the evil that colonialism brings. The colonial system is the rock on which rich men build their houses and colonialism is the swamp on which the poor put up their slums or their tumbledown attap shacks. Colonialism corrupts because quite a lot of them can do very nicely for themselves under the system. Colonialism looks after them and their profits very well.

Now we all know there is something wrong with Malaya. But for the past six years, all we have been able to do is to grumble to each other. Or, if we are too poor or too afraid even to grumble, we just suffer. Colonialism maintains itself by supporting capitalism and its emergency regulations, ostensibly aimed at communism, are very convenient for keeping shut the mouths of those who would like to destroy the system constitutionally.

What do we complain about? That we are governed by gentlemen in London. That others in London, not quite such gentlemen, are able to come here with their businesses and their rubber estates to squeeze profits out of us. Exploitation is the word.

The rulers from London, when they first came, perhaps, gave us better rule than we could then give ourselves. That is all done with. Now we are ready for self-rule. No man can be a full human being if he has to say "Yes Sir", "No Sir" to a boss who is boss because he belongs to the ruling race. And how can our workers fight for a fair wage, for a fair return for their labour when the white *tuan* or the Chinese *towkay* or the merchant from India is encouraged by the colonial system to make money out of the workers' sweat? We don't blame the *tuans* and the *towkays* making a good thing out of this country while they

> What do we complain about? That we are governed by gentlemen in London.

**263**

can. But now it is time for the workers to claim their rights, to claim a fair share for their labour, and we blame the colonial system which allows the rich to get richer, and the poor to have to make do with what they can get.

The time has come for Malayans to unite for we can't stop this exploitation unless we are masters in our own country. So that is the first thing that has to be put right. We've got to have independence. But what do we see today?

Civilian employees of the British army, navy and air force are kept outside the labour code of their own country, even the inadequate labour code of a colonial power. Over wide parts of the island the services enjoy almost extraterritorial rights. We have appalling slums. People packed in cubicles and dark, airless tenements. We see attap dwellers evicted and their simple houses pulled down. Most of the building that goes on in Singapore is by individual capitalists building for their own profits. Don't blame them. Blame the system that allows houses for those who can afford them while the poor live in blackness and squalor. We have not nearly enough schools. More are being built much too slowly. The government used to blame the high cost of materials but private buildings went on. A fine new cinema was put up. Our schools seem to aim at creating Malayans with an unhealthy respect for their colonial masters. Do we agree with our education policy? However, I won't go on.

You all know from your own experience of injustice, discrimination and exploitation. I have seen it face-to-face when I met employers over trade disputes in which various trade unions have been involved. So what are we going to do about it? I and a number of others – trade unionists, teachers, labourers, journalists, clerks, professional men – have formed a party, the People's Action Party, because we have watched for too long the antics of our so-called politicians and our so-called leaders. Till now the term "political parties" has been almost meaningless and in danger of falling into disrepute because till now this is the sort of thing that has happened. A few gentlemen get together and decide that it would be a good thing for their business, good for themselves or flattering to their self-esteem: the honourable Mr so-and-so to get a seat in the Legislative Council so that the self-interest may not seem too obvious. They go through the motions of forming a political party. But you and I are not deceived by these gentlemen.

At the last elections, only one in six of those eligible to vote registered, and of those only half bothered to vote. Need I say more? Political apathy towards the professional politicians, yes. But are the people of Singapore politically apathetic? I don't think so. Last Thursday, over 2,000 people came to our PAP election meeting. On Saturday, over 3,000 came and last night over 6,000 people flocked in from miles around just to listen to the PAP candidates. I must admit that there is political apathy towards the other so-called parties. One party brings along a lion to draw the crowd. Another party brought a fold-mattress, and very nice too. And another party seldom has meetings because it does not seem able to get anyone to come along and listen.

We formed a party because we felt that we must have a genuine political party rooted in the people. Our members are people of all races and they come from all classes of society. It was after we had formed the party that our members decided to contest these

*We in the PAP intend to give colonialism a final push and sink it for good in Southeast Asia.*

elections. Our helpers are all voluntary, ordinary workers like you and me – professional men, teachers, clerks, messengers, bus drivers, factory workers, hawkers. They come after their work to help because the People's Action Party is their party. The PAP will fight for complete independence and for the rights and dignity of the workers. We are contesting four seats in these elections. We do not like this new constitution. We are not content with streamlined colonialism. But we intend to put four men in the new Assembly so that the colonial government and its supporters can hear our voice, can hear our voice at first hand, and our voice is yours because we know you feel the same as we do about injustice, discrimination and exploitation.

Now here, briefly, are some of the points in our election platform which distinguishes us from the other parties:

Unity with the Federation. The PAP believes that immediately after the elections in Singapore and the Federation, negotiations should be started to bring about the unification of Malaya.

National Service. We shall seek to repeal the National Service Ordinance. We are not in principle opposed to conscription but we believe that only an independent government freely chosen by the people and responsible to them has the right to ask its citizens to die for it.

Emergency Regulations. The PAP seeks the removal of the arbitrary powers of arrest and detention without trial in open court, restrictions on the freedom of speech, assembly and association – all contained in the Emergency Regulations.

Trade Unions and Politics. The Trade Union Ordinance must be amended to permit trade unions to set up political funds. The Trade Dispute Ordinance must be repealed. This Ordinance is a copy of the English Trades Disputes Act introduced after the general strike in 1926 in Britain by a Conservative government to prevent trade unions from assisting one another by united strike action. It has now been repealed in England. It must be repealed in Singapore.

Education. There should be free and compulsory education for all children till the age of 16 and a comprehensive scholarship scheme for higher education.

Malayanisation of the Public Services. The Public Services must be Malayanised completely within the next four years. No new expatriate should be recruited on the permanent establishment.

Economic Control. The government of the people should have full control of its trade and the dollar it earns and the management and disposal of sterling balances and national savings. Measures like control of rubber must go.

Housing. We must create a housing authority for slum clearance and subsidise housing by interest-free government loans instead of the present interest-bearing loans from the government to the SIT [Singapore Improvement Trust].

Some of the other parties believe in some of these things. But the People's Action Party will continue to believe in all of them and to fight for all of them, long after the elections are over. If you believe in these things as we do, then vote for the People's Action Party.

Some of the other parties believe in some of these things. But the People's Action Party will continue to believe in all of them and to fight for all of them, long after the elections are over.

In September and October 1961, Lee gave a series of 12 radio talks on the struggle for independence, through merger between Singapore and Malaya. The talks were meant to clarify the political situation to the people of Singapore, and to explain why it was crucial for Singapore's survival to merge with the mainland. Lee also explained why the PAP had to work with the communists to drive out the British, and the workings of the communists. In this extract of the talk given on September 15, 1961, he sets out the communist challenge facing Singapore.

# The battle for hearts and minds

For years since the beginning of the Emergency in 1948, communism has been painted in terms of violence, terror, brutality and evil. There was violence, there was terror, there was brutality, and there were evil men. But that is not the whole story. For if it was as simple as that, the communists would have died and perished with the collapse of their armed revolt. It is because, together with these weaknesses, they have some strong qualities that they have been able to survive in spite of the collapse of their armed revolt. For the foreseeable future the communists have no chance of capturing power in the Federation or Singapore by force of arms. But they have been able to continue the struggle for the communist cause through new methods.

Many of their old supporters in the jungle have died or been banished. Some have drifted back anonymously into the towns. Only a hard core remains on the Malayan-Thai border.

But new recruits have been found. These are the idealistic young men and women, largely from the Chinese middle schools of Malaya, both the Federation and Singapore. These are new men fighting under different conditions, with different methods and tactics to create a communist Malaya. Partly by persuasion, mainly by fanaticism and faith that the future belongs to the communists, these new recruits are continuing the struggle. They press on, capturing the leadership of trade unions, cultural organisations and old boys' associations. Most important of all, they try to capture the power to manipulate the lawful political parties.

Past governments called this subversion. Because the Communist Party is illegal in Malaya none of its followers go about telling people that they are communists. Publicly they will always pretend to be democrats; privately they keep on recruiting as many effective persons as they can persuade to join them in the communist cause.

> There was violence, there was terror, there was brutality, and there were evil men. But that is not the whole story.

266

We now began to understand the meaning of revolution in terms of life and blood, liberty and incarceration, hate and fear, love and comradeship.

… My colleagues and I are of that generation of young men who went through the Second World War and the Japanese Occupation and emerged determined that no one – neither the Japanese nor the British – had the right to push and kick us around. We determined that we could govern ourselves and bring up our children in a country where we can be proud to be a self-respecting people.

When the war came to an end in 1945, there was never a chance of the old type of British colonial system ever being recreated. The scales had fallen from our eyes and we saw for ourselves that the local people could run the country. In fact the local people did run the country for the Japanese military administration. The Europeans had a better life in our country – more pay, bigger houses, bigger cars and a higher standard of living – not because they were more capable but because power and military might were on their side.

When that power went they were stripped literally naked as prisoners of war, and became ordinary people. It was the Japanese ten-cent storeman who, backed by Japanese military might, suddenly became the big boss who occupied a big house and had a better life.

## Revolt

Three years after the end of the Second World War a violent revolution started in Malaya. The communists, who were almost a nonexistent force in the years before the war, were allowed to arm themselves as a force just before the British surrendered. They went underground with those arms. Over three and a half years, partly with the arms they took underground and partly with more arms parachuted in by the Allies, they built up a tough little army in the jungles.

With the surrender of the Japanese, they came out into the towns. For the first time, the MCP emerged as a legally recognised political force in our country. But it was not for long. In 1948 they retreated to the jungles and the armed insurrection which the British called the "Emergency" started.

That was a fierce and grim revolt. The angry young men from the Chinese middle schools, who hated colonialism and the British, joined the communists to rid the country of British imperialism.

In those tough years, 1949 and 1950, we got our first taste of the practical realities of politics. We had learned the theories of socialism, communism and capitalism in books, and read the histories of revolutions. But we now began to understand the meaning of revolution in terms of life and blood, liberty and incarceration, hate and fear, love and comradeship.

## Realities of revolution

We have learned one important thing during the last decade: that only those count and matter who have the strength and courage of their convictions to stick up and stand up for what they believe in, for their people, for their country, regardless of what happens to themselves.

Parts of this narrative are concerned with friends of personal courage and deep political conviction who have gone over to the communist side. Because they have accepted the communist doctrine and dogma, they would have not the slightest compunction if the time comes to destroy us, the non-communists, if we do not bend to their will. On the other hand, other friends have been so disgusted by the stupidities of the leadership of the Communist Party that they abjured the communists and came over and joined us at great personal peril.

So the battle goes on for the hearts and minds of the political activists of the country. Some I will be able to tell you by name. Others I shall refer to by nicknames. But they are all real living people, men of my generation, fierce men on both sides. They will be listening to these talks, wondering how much I will disclose, whether I will take an unfair advantage over them. My colleagues and I, not being ruthless communist cadres, have different standards of conduct from theirs. With us, personal friendship and sentimental regard for old friends matter.

Lee realised that the only way the PAP could get rid of the British colonial masters was to join hands with the communist movement. All the other political powers of the day were, in his words, "dilettantes playing at politics". In this extract of a radio speech he gave on September 18, 1961, he spoke of how the communists operated, and their ability to tap the support of the masses.

# How I came to know the communists

Politics in Malaya was a deadly serious business. These are not clowns or jokers. They had decided to go with the communists.

This talk is largely a personal narrative. It will explain how I came to know the communists, what they are after in Malaya, who they are, how they operate, why we worked on parallel lines with them for many years and why eventually we have parted company over merger.

Let me take my story back to 1950 when I began to learn the realities of political life in Malaya. At that time every genuine nationalist who hated the British colonial system wanted freedom and independence. That was a time when only weak men and stooges came out and performed on the local political stage. Fierce men were silent or had gone underground to join the communists.

There were the Progressive Party and their feeble leaders. There were the clowns of the Labour Party [Labour Front] of Singapore. When I met acquaintances like Lim Kean Chye and John Eber and asked them what they were doing, why they were allowing these things to go on, they smiled and said, "Ah well! What can be done in such a situation?"

One morning in January 1951 I woke up and read in the newspapers that John Eber had been arrested, that Lim Kean Chye had disappeared and escaped arrest. Shortly afterwards a reward was offered for his arrest. Politics in Malaya was a deadly serious business. These are not clowns or jokers. They had decided to go with the communists.

So my colleagues and I pressed on, working with the unions. The only unions able to take fierce and militant action were those with no communist affiliations whatsoever. The postmen went on strike. I acted for them. We extracted every ounce of political and material advantage out of the dispute with the colonial government and got them maximum benefits.

The Post and Telegraph workers wanted their salaries to be revised and backdated. The dispute went to arbitration. We helped them and exposed the stupidities and inadequacies of the colonial administration. The whole of the government civil service was organised to revolt against non-pensionable expatriation pay for the benefit of a few white men.

You remember my colleagues, Dr Goh Keng Swee and K.M. Byrne, organised a fight against the European half of the civil service. So we went on organising the workers in their unions, rallying them to fight the British colonial system for freedom, for a more just and equal society.

Meanwhile, I had got in touch with the people who were detained in the same batch as John Eber. They were the English-educated group of the Anti-British League, a communist organisation. The ABL relation to the MCP is like that of the volunteer force to the regular professional army.

I was instructed to act for one of them. I came to know and like him. Subsequently, in 1953, he was released from detention. We became friends. He told me that he was a communist. I will call him Laniaz. He is still a most important communist cadre spreading propaganda on behalf of the communist cause.

Through him I came to know Devan Nair, who was the most determined ABL member I have ever known. Subsequently, I discovered that Devan Nair was in fact on the way to being a full-fledged Communist Party member.

We became comrades in the united front in the unions and in the PAP. Devan Nair knew I was not a communist; he knew that I knew he was a communist. In 1956 he landed in jail together with Lim Chin Siong and company. After spending a great part of his life with the Malayan Communist Party, he came to his own conclusion that their leadership was inadequate to meet the needs of the revolution in Malaya.

Determined and dedicated though they were, they had their shortcomings and were unable to make the necessary changes in policy and approach, to create a national-based movement for their communist cause.

Devan Nair is now on our side. On the other hand, S.T. Bani, assemblyman for Thomson, who was not a communist and who had for several years worked together with me in the unions, competing against the communists, decided some time late last year to throw in his lot with the communists. He had been won over to their side. So the battle goes on for the hearts and minds, first of the political elite of the population, and ultimately of the whole population.

Laniaz joined us, a core of the English-educated, to fight colonialism. We were all non-communists other than Laniaz – Dr Toh, Dr Goh, K.M. Byrne, Rajaratnam and myself. We organised and worked in the unions, recruited cadres of our own in the English-educated and Malay-educated world. We drew up plans for the setting up of the party.

> We helped them and exposed the stupidities and inadequacies of the colonial administration.

## Riots

Then one day in 1954, we came into contact with the Chinese-educated world. The Chinese middle school students were in revolt against national service and they were beaten down. Riots took place, charges were preferred in court.

Through devious ways they came into contact with us. We bridged the gap to the Chinese-educated world – a world teeming with vitality, dynamism and revolution, a world in which the communists had been working for over the last 30 years with considerable success. We, the English-educated revolutionaries, went in trying to tap this oil field of political resources, and soon found our pipelines crossing those of the Communist Party. We were latecomers trying to tap the same oil fields. We were considered by the communists as poaching in their exclusive territory.

In this world we came to know Lim Chin Siong and Fong Swee Suan. They joined us in the PAP. In 1955, we contested the elections. Our initiation into the intricacies and ramifications of the communist underground organisation in the trade unions and cultural associations had begun.

## The underground

It is a strange business, working in this world. When you meet a union leader you will quickly have to decide which side he is on and whether or not he is a communist. You can find out by the language he uses, and his behaviour, whether or not he is in the inner circle which makes the decisions. These are things from which you determine whether he is an outsider or an insider in the communist underworld.

I came to know dozens of them. They are not crooks or opportunists. These are men with great resolve, dedicated to the communist revolution and to the establishment of the communist state, believing that it is the best thing in the world for mankind. Many of them are prepared to pay the price for the communist cause in terms of personal freedom and sacrifice. They know they run the risk of detention if they are found out and caught. Often my colleagues and I disagreed with them, and intense fights took place, all concealed from the outside world because they were communists working in one united anti-colonial front with us against the common enemy, and it would not do to betray them.

Eventually many of them landed in jail, in the purges in 1956 and 1957. I used to see them there, arguing their appeals, reading their captured documents and the Special Branch precis of the cases against them. I had the singular advantage of not only knowing them well by having worked at close quarters with them in a united front against the British, but I also saw the official version in reports on them.

Many were banished to China. Some were my personal friends. They knew that I knew they were communists, for between us there was no pretence. They believed that I should join them. They believed that ultimately I would be forced to admit that what they call the "bourgeois" democratic system could not produce a just and equal society, and that I would admit that they were right.

We, the English-educated revolutionaries, went in trying to tap this oil field of political resources, and soon found our pipelines crossing those of the Communist Party. We were latecomers trying to tap the same oil fields.

On the other hand, I used to spend hours arguing with some of them, trying to prove to them that whatever else happened in China or Russia, we were living in Malaya and, irrespective of communism or democratic socialism, if we wanted to build a more just and equal society in Malaya, we would have to make certain fundamental decisions, such as being Malayans, uniting the Chinese and Indians and others with the Malays, building up national unity and national loyalty, and rallying all the races together through a national language.

## MCP strength

The strength of the MCP lies in the propagation of communist theories and ideals to recruit able and idealistic young man and women to join them in their cause. Our able young men on their side can, by working in a union, fighting for better pay and conditions of service for workers, get thousands of workers on to their side.

Let me explain this. In 1953, I became legal adviser to the Naval Base Labour Union, fought their case and won the confidence of the committee and the men. They were looking for a union secretary. I introduced to them S. Woodhull, a person I had then known in the University of Malaya Socialist Club for one and a half years. I knew that he was anti-British and anti-colonial. I also knew he was reading Marxism and that he was initiating himself into the mysteries of world revolution. But he was not a communist or a member of the ABL [Anti-British League] although they were grooming him for recruitment. He was then prepared to work for a cause. On my recommendation he became secretary to the union.

He worked hard and by 1955, two years afterwards, he had organised, with the help of a handful of dedicated noncommunist activists like Ahmad Ibrahim and a few communist ground workers in the union, 7,500 workers in the Base. He had organised them into a coherent force which would listen to him, not because the workers believed in socialism or communism, but because the workers knew him to be a trustworthy and industrious man who worked with me for them.

In this way, the communists, although they had only a few hundred active cadres, could muster and rally thousands of people in the unions, cultural organisations and student societies. By working and manifestly appearing to work selflessly, and ceaselessly, they won the confidence and regard of the people in the organisations. Having won the confidence and regard, they then got the people to support their political stand.

The strength of the Communist Party lies not in their mass as such but in the band of trained and disciplined cadres, who lead the masses into communist causes, often without the masses knowing they are communists.

> The strength of the Communist Party lies not in their mass as such but in the band of trained and disciplined cadres, who lead the masses into communist causes, often without the masses knowing they are communists.

# Why the British misled the communists

Let me tell you how and why the British deliberately misled the communists and manoeuvred their open-front workers into a false position.

… Over a period of several months, at luncheons, cocktail parties, dinner parties and other social occasions, the UK Commission officials dropped hints to Lim Chin Siong and his friends, and even generally to businessmen and sharebrokers, both local and British, giving everyone the impression that they considered Lim and his friends reasonable and sensible people. Slowly Lim and his friends were led to believe that if they were to obtain power by constitutional means, so long as the military bases were left untouched, the British would be quite happy to let them run this island.

Lim was putting on his best act. He was pretending to Lord Selkirk [the British Commissioner-General for Southeast Asia] and his officials that he and his friends like Fong Swee Suan were just like Toh Chin Chye and myself. They were also PAP non-communist socialists, only they were in the more radical wing of the PAP.

Selkirk and his officials had no doubts that Lim was the most important open-front communist leader. But they pretended to believe Lim's act, that he was a genuine non-communist socialist. The British went out of their way to be nice to Lim and his friends, encouraging them to believe that there was no constitutional difficulty to their taking over the present government or forming the next one.

On the other hand, the British pressed us as the Singapore government to curb and contain the subversive activities of Lim and his friends. We were therefore puzzled when we found that Lim and his friends were absolutely confident that they could take over and run the government. We could not understand how they came to believe this when on the other hand we were being pressed to take action against these same people. It was only after the Anson by-election, two days before the motion of confidence in the

Assembly, when we found that Lim Chin Siong and his friends were in conference with the UK Commissioner at Eden Hall, that it dawned on us that this was a deep ruse which had been going on for some time.

So long as Lim and his friends believed that they could not assume power without getting into trouble, they would play it quietly and not give trouble to the Singapore government, particularly a PAP left-wing government. So long as they did not attack the Singapore government, the British could not get the government to go out of its way to suppress Lim and his communist friends. So the British led Lim and the communists to believe that they could take power. Once Lim and the communists believed this they became bold. First they pressed us to change our policy. We refused, and then came the attack by the communists on the PAP.

Lim and Fong said they went to tea at Lord Selkirk's residence for social friendliness. Unfortunately, Woodhull later admitted that they went to see Lord Selkirk "to clarify the situation".

… What the British wanted to achieve was to get the communists to come out into the open on their own, attack the PAP and be purged in retaliation. Lim Chin Siong, the communist open-front leader, was helped by Woodhull and James Puthucheary, and also by sympathisers like Francis Wong, editor of the *Sunday Mail*. Francis Wong was also testing the ground at the UK Commission and having confidential discussions over lunch with UK Commission officials.

By June they all became convinced by the British that constitutional rights were open to them and that they could assume power. The green light had been given. They could out-left the PAP. In this way, they blundered into their conflict with the PAP.

The British have great experience in dealing with such delicate situations. Whatever embarrassment our exposure caused them, they have said absolutely nothing, and thereby saved themselves further embarrassment.

So the British led Lim and the communists to believe that they could take power.

# Clowns and crooks

There were the mild and feeble political parties, like the Progressive Party, the Labour Party [Labour Front], and a whole host of funny ones. Clowns and crooks passed off as leaders of the people.

You may ask: If the communists are such a danger to our society, why did we work with Lim Chin Siong and his communist friends in one anti-colonial united front? This and other questions have to be answered. However uncomfortable the truth may be to me and my colleagues, you must know it.

I have told you how in 1953 we came to make our first communist contact with Laniaz. That was a time when the British, in fighting the communist insurrection, also suppressed all nationalists who attacked them. The result was that all those who were anti-British either kept quiet, or quietly threw in their lot with the communists underground to down the British.

So in the open constitutional arena there were no lawful parties of any significance, with people fit or willing to lead the anti-colonial fight. There were the mild and feeble political parties, like the Progressive Party, the Labour Party [Labour Front], and a whole host of funny ones. Clowns and crooks passed off as leaders of the people. Emotionally, we felt more sympathetic with the communists who were sacrificing their life and limb to down the British and get them out of the country than with these comic and crooked men.

Laniaz himself did not originally start off as a communist. He started as a nationalist. Slowly over the years he drifted more and more with the men who were fiercely fighting the British. They happened to be communists, and he joined them. In this same way we also drifted into the same communist company as Laniaz had done. Laniaz was anti-British as strongly as we were. We knew he wanted to establish an independent communist Malaya, and he knew we wanted to establish an independent democratic Malaya. But neither of our two different objectives would ever come to anything as long as the British were here. First we had to get rid of the British to get independence. That was a common objective.

We came to the conclusion that we had better forget the differences between our ultimate objectives and work together for our immediate common objective, the destruction of the British. Whether you wanted a democratic Malaya or a communist Malaya, you had first to get rid of the British.

This broad anti-colonial united front was an inevitable phase in the history of our struggle for freedom. Before India got her independence, there was a time when Nehru and the Communist Party of India formed a united front against the British to fight for independence. At a time when the colonial ruler made no distinction between the communists and the non-communists who opposed him, it was only logical and indeed inevitable that both the communists and the non-communists should come together to achieve their common objective.

But we never forgot that once the British were out of the way, there would be trouble between us and the communists as to what kind of Malaya we wanted to have in place of the old British colonial Malaya. We were quite clear as to what we wanted – an independent, democratic, socialist Malaya, which by democratic means could bring about a more just and equal society. On the other hand, they wanted a communist Malaya. This is what the communists mean when they say "seeking concord whilst maintaining differences". They know the difference between our ultimate objective and theirs. But they say let us not argue about these differences, let us seek concord on the common objective of fixing the British, and on that we were agreed.

## Vested interest

We have now fallen out because we have disagreed on our next objective. We want merger and independence. The communists do not. They have a vested interest in continuing the anti-colonial struggle so that under cover of anti-colonialism they can advance communism. They want the anti-colonial struggle to go on and on, meanwhile using Singapore as a base from which to undermine Malaya.

The second question that you may ask is: now that we all know Lim and his friends are up to no good, why do we not take immediate steps to deal sternly with them?

The answer is: because if we take immediate steps to deal sternly with them, we shall lose the open argument of who is right and who is wrong. This is a battle for the minds of the people, for the people's support for what we believe is right for the country.

We must convince you, the people, that what we propose, independence through merger with the Federation, is in your best interests; that the communist aim to frustrate immediate merger is only for their own communist selfish advantage, and that deliberate prolonging of the anti-colonial struggle in Singapore, to use Singapore as a base from which to undermine the Federation, will bring trouble to all of us.

To take immediate action is to lose to the communists in the battle for the people's support. Singapore is a multiracial city with four major language groups – the Chinese-speaking, Malay-speaking, Tamil-speaking and the English-speaking. The Malay-speaking, Tamil-speaking and English-speaking groups are quite certain that Lim Chin Siong and

*We were quite clear as to what we wanted – an independent, democratic, socialist Malaya, which by democratic means could bring about a more just and equal society. On the other hand, they wanted a communist Malaya.*

his communist friends are up to no good, and consider that they should be put away and not allowed to do mischief. But we have to convince the Chinese-speaking not only that Lim and his friends are communists, working under instructions from the communist underground, but also that what they are doing is not good for all of us in Singapore.

We must carry the opinion of all the people, including the Chinese-educated, with us. To do this we must bear in mind two things. The first is that to take stern action against the communists while Singapore is still a semi-colony with ultimate power still vested in the British would be to open ourselves to smear and misrepresentation that we are just stooges of the British and have acted to preserve British interests.

## Proxies see Selkirk

British power is supreme in Singapore. The sovereignty of Singapore is still vested in the British. In the last resort, it is they who have the final say on what happens to Singapore.

We know, and the communists also know, that in the last resort the British must take action on their own to protect their military and other interests. The communists fear this and for that reason their proxies went to see Lord Selkirk, the UK Commissioner, in Woodhull's own words, "to clarify the situation".

The last government under Tun Lim Yew Hock took massive action against the communists. The government failed in the eyes of the people. They failed not because they had taken action against the communists, but because their action was deliberately misconstrued to the people by the communists as having been done under instigation by the British. As a result, the government lost out.

The second thing we have to bear in mind is this. It is unwise to take stern immediate action against subversion in the unions, cultural organisations, old boys' associations and even in the universities' student clubs, because the action will be very largely against the Chinese-educated who have penetrated the leadership in these unions and associations.

Unless there is a clear distinction made between the communists and the non-communists amongst the Chinese-educated we would merely create resentment against the government and sympathy for the cause of those detained.

## An important distinction

We must therefore make a clear distinction between the Chinese-educated and the communists. As Fong Swee Suan, Chan Chiaw Thor, Woodhull, Devan Nair and James Puthucheary have stated in their letter to me, nearly all communists in Malaya are Chinese-educated. But not all Chinese-educated people are communists. To purge the communists we have to be careful that we make it clear that we are not purging the Chinese-educated. This is a trap into which we must never fall.

The last government fell into the communist trap of allowing themselves to be presented as anti-Chinese culture and Chinese education. When they purged the communist student leaders to immobilise the handful who were responsible for the "stay-in" strike, they had to flush out of Chinese High School and Chung Cheng High School

To purge the communists we have to be careful that we make it clear that we are not purging the Chinese-educated. This is a trap into which we must never fall.

thousands of non-communist Chinese-educated students. The Labour Front government helped the communists to convince the people that the government had purged Chinese education. We cannot afford to make this same mistake.

Hence the vital importance of getting a constitutional guarantee on local autonomy on education which will enable the Chinese to carry on their education from primary school to Nanyang University; otherwise the communists will make trouble over this to prevent merger.

Our conflict is with the communists, most of whom are in the Chinese-educated world. But this does not mean we quarrel with the Chinese-educated, for that is exactly what the communists want us to do.

### Fair and equal place

Our duty is to bring the various linguistic groups together to build up a united, tolerant society in which all the races and all the language groups will live in peace. We must give the Chinese-educated a fair and equal place in our society and convince them that their best interests lie with the nationalist and democratic side.

So in spite of all the misunderstanding the communists and their supporters are trying to create amongst genuine and sincere Chinese educationists over the recent proposed change in the Chinese middle schools from the present six-year system of three years for junior middle and three years for senior middle, to a system with four years for Secondary School Certificate plus two years for post school certificate, we have been patient and always open to reason. In this way, we prevent the communists from making people believe that we are anti-Chinese education and carry with us the support of the neutrals who form the bulk of the people in the Chinese-educated world.

We must give the Chinese-educated a fair and equal place in our society and convince them that their best interests lie with the nationalist and democratic side.

Why was Lee Kuan Yew so determined to make Singapore part of Malaysia, and why was the Malayan Prime Minister Tunku Abdul Rahman so apprehensive of the idea? What made the latter change his mind? Lee answered these thorny questions in this speech at the Royal Society of International Affairs in London in May 1962, in which he also spoke about the communist threat in Singapore.

# What does Malaysia mean to us?

The alternatives are so unpleasant as to be quite unthinkable, and, because they are so unpleasant, I have not the slightest doubt that Malaysia will succeed.

Malaysia – what does it mean to us? What does it mean to you? What does it mean to the outside world? To us, who do not want to see Singapore and Malaya slowly engulfed and eroded away by the communists, it is an absolute must. The alternatives are so unpleasant as to be quite unthinkable, and, because they are so unpleasant, I have not the slightest doubt that Malaysia will succeed.

When the federation of these five territories or some grouping was first suggested by Mr Malcolm MacDonald many years ago it was welcomed by people who were then considered weak, reactionary stooge elements of British colonialism. Red-blooded people like myself and the communists scoffed at this fanciful plot to try and delay the political advance against the British colonial system in Malaya and Singapore. Well, that was more than a decade ago, and times have changed. In that time several things happened. First of all, Communist China emerged as a real force in the whole area. Secondly, the fringes of Southeast Asia became more and more unstable – Indonesia, Vietnam, even Burma. Thirdly, within the last decade the realities of power politics came home to the young nationalists of Southeast Asia; and it came home vividly with the Sino-Indian border conflict. There was the Bandung Conference, and the warm afterglow of fraternity and solidarity of Afro-Asia – just because we were Afro-Asians – vanished; the reality of power was brought home. I think anybody who has not been to the area for ten years and gone back, the one marked difference they would find between the 1940s and the 1960s is the fact that in those ten years everybody graduated into first-class Scouts – no longer tenderfoots. One has not just joined the Boy Scouts, one has found out about pathfinding, and how it is necessary to have a good compass.

Now, why am I now solidly in favour of Malaysia? I have spent the last three weeks talking to a few people whose names and repute carry weight in the Afro-Asian world, and in the non-communist world generally, to convince them that this is no longer a British plot, that this is our scheme, amended and somewhat different, but nationalist and not colonialist. I think it would be useful if I were to tell you how it began, what the position is now, what I think will happen in the immediate future, and what I think the long-term prospects are.

Officially, Malaysia began when the Tunku, the prime minister of the Federation of Malaya, came down to Singapore to make a speech to some foreign correspondents in May of last year, and he said he was all in favour of closer economic and political association between Malaya, Singapore and the Borneo territories; a fateful pronouncement, because for the first time he acknowledged that he had to have economic and political association with Singapore. Since 1955, when he was somewhat aghast at the boisterousness of the people in Singapore, his policy has been one of systematic isolation and the cutting of all ties between Singapore and the Federation in the fond belief that the British could look after Singapore.

## Persuading the Tunku

I spent a great deal of time and effort between 1955 and 1959, when I assumed office, trying to convince him that in the long run he had to reckon with Singapore, and that it was easier if he included us in his overall calculations and started on the basis of Singapore as part of his overall problems than if he tried to pass the problem-child over to the British. I will tell you that I was amazed and astonished at the turn of events which, between 1959 and 1961, helped me to bring home to him the realities of the position. Of course, the British, in their own pragmatic way, also helped, but I would say that nobody, however well-informed, could have foreseen the rapidity with which events developed in and around Malaysia. I certainly did not, because I had envisaged an unpleasant time trying to contain an almost uncontainable situation in isolation from Malaya. But, fortunately, our enemies made a number of mistakes which helped us: first in convincing the Tunku that Singapore mattered to him, that the British could not look after Singapore for him indefinitely, that he had to come to terms with Singapore, and that the best way of coming to terms with Singapore was to come to terms with Malaysia in the context of Southeast Asia. That is really the heart of the matter with regard to Malaysia. The Tunku never thought about the Borneo territories. He never imagined that he would be a sponsor of a plan that would form a viable broadly-based nation in Southeast Asia comprising these five British possessions. His attitude between 1955 and 1959 was one which is not unnatural in people who have just inherited tremendous problems of their own, of just minding their own business, and he had a lot of business to mind in Malaya. He was doing well, and he saw no reason why he should undertake problems, the nature of which he did not like and the prospects of providing solutions to which he was uncertain of.

All of you are well-informed on Malaya and Malaysia, and all of you, no doubt, can read between the lines of what politicians often leave unsaid, but, because I am talking to an audience not of immediate political flavour, I think I can afford myself the privilege of

Since 1955, when he was somewhat aghast at the boisterousness of the people in Singapore, his policy has been one of systematic isolation and the cutting of all ties between Singapore and the Federation in the fond belief that the British could look after Singapore.

talking between the lines, which is perhaps what you would like. Let me now explain to you why we are in the present position:

I will not pretend to try to explain British policy, because there are people more competent and more knowledgeable than I am, but whatever the policy was designed to achieve it certainly helped me, because it convinced the Tunku that he had to come to terms with immediate realities – that was Singapore. It has got 1.6 million people of which 1.2 are Chinese, 200,000 Malays and about 200,000 Indians, 2,000 Eurasians and others. After his experience in Malaya he was convinced that Singapore was not an easy place to govern, because the communists are able to manipulate Chinese sentiments, Chinese feelings and love of Chinese things, such as language, culture and civilisation, to much greater effectiveness than anybody else, certainly to much greater effectiveness than he and his colleagues.

But in the course of the first 18 months we were able to convince him and his colleagues that if he allowed the Singapore situation to continue in isolation to Malaya he would create a position where it was worthwhile to make a political appeal based on the Chinese alone. Because if 70 per cent of the people in Singapore are Chinese, and you can win the majority of the 70, you can win political power on the basis of one-man-one-vote, and whatever he tried to do with his 2.5 million Chinese in the Federation, as long as a contrary cause was going on in Singapore, he would fail to win over these 2.5 million Chinese in the Federation, because they are one people and one political situation; what happened in the Federation had its effect on Singapore and vice versa. The argument convinced him, and he was coming round to the view that it was better to move ahead of events, hence that momentous speech when he casually mentioned closer political and economic association. We responded, we welcomed it, and we said that if Malaysia helped merger we were all in favour of it, and that led off a chain of events which has completely altered the outlook in Malaysia for the next decade.

Briefly, the reactions were as follows: the communists, being over-suspicious, believed that we had already reached an agreement with the British and the Federation – in fact, we had not – to create this federation called Malaysia. For various reasons they decided that they would force the fight into the open and stop it, and that very act accelerated the whole process and brought home to the Tunku and his colleagues the dire necessity of having Malaysia, or of being undermined by a communist-manipulated situation from Singapore. An Independent Television man interviewed the Tunku in April of this year; he casually laughed and asked the Tunku how Malaysia was going, and the Tunku said, "I do not know – I hope all is well." He was at that time somewhat angry at what was going on in Borneo. The man asked him, "What happens if Malaysia does not succeed?" and the Tunku replied, "I would be the most happy man in the world." That is true; without Malaysia he would feel a sense of relief without these problems; with Malaysia he would feel that it was the lesser of the two evils, but he has not got the answer to some of the many problems he will inherit. These are the immediate problems:

> The man asked him, "What happens if Malaysia does not succeed?" and the Tunku replied, "I would be the most happy man in the world."

## The racial mix

In Malaya today there are 3.4 million Malays against 2.5 million Chinese against 0.8 million Indians. A society which is not completely integrated. Part of the Chinese are English-educated and would fit in with the Malayan scene – anything between 30 and 40 per cent. The balance are not English-educated, and half of that balance will probably have their loyalties tied up with the country of the origin of their ancestors. The Indians do not form a sizeable force, nor do they constitute any problem. The Tunku has been doing well because the Malayan Communist Party has been sufficiently unwise to pursue a policy which rallies all the forces in the Malay world around him, and leaves the forces in the Chinese world who are not for the communists no choice but to reach a working basis with whoever leads the Malay majority.

Let me explain this: 99 per cent of the Malayan Communist Party is Chinese. They have fought for the last 17 years, since 1945, to establish a Soviet republic based on the efforts and sacrifices of the Chinese. They cannot conceive of a situation in which communism can come to Malaya without their efforts; and they use the obvious and the simple method of winning more people over to communism by pointing to the illustrious example of China. The result is that they win more recruits from the Chinese into the Malayan Communist Party and present communism to the non-Chinese in Malaya as Chinese imperialism, and so they get themselves more and more isolated in this Chinese world.

The Malays watching this have a tremendous fear that their position will be jeopardised, and, therefore, playing around their traditional leaders – and the Tunku is an extremely shrewd and able leader of his people, have kept all the traditional forms of leadership. He himself is the son of a Sultan, a traditional leader of his people; and he has proved over seven years that his leadership over the Malays is likely to be undisputed for a long time, and certainly for as long as the Malayan Communist Party pursues this stupid policy of augmenting their strength on the basis of the prestige and reputation of China, making an appeal only to the Chinese.

But with Malaysia the Tunku inherits different problems. In the first place, if he had merger with Singapore without Malaysia he is quite convinced that enormous differences will arise, because the population of Singapore is 1.2 million Chinese; plus the 2.5 million in the Federation, this will make it 3.7 million as against 3.6 million Malays. I am not saying this is a desirable method of computing, but I am saying that this is basic political arithmetic which weighs in the minds of political leaders – communist, non-communist and anti-communist – because of the situation. Therefore, he is adamant that with merger – which he sees no escape from – he must have Malaysia. For then he will have 1 million Malays, Dusuns, Dayaks, Muruts and others, to add to the 3.5 million, which will make it 4.5 million, and the Chinese would be 3.6 million plus 400,000 in Sarawak and North Borneo to make it roughly 4 million. In other words, merger without Malaysia lands him in a situation which he fears: a Chinese-led communist party may in the extreme manipulate Chinese sentiments to a point where the Chinese with electoral weighting

Malaysia is the answer, because that would more or less maintain the present balance of the communal forces in Malaya.

can upset a constitutionally elected government. Therefore, Malaysia is the answer, because that would more or less maintain the present balance of the communal forces in Malaya. The communists know this; they are resigned to merger because they understand that it is impossible to have an independent Singapore, but they want merger alone without Malaysia because they believe that what the Tunku fears is right, that they have got the power with China communists to manipulate the Chinese to a point where they might be able to constitutionally upset the government.

## Why Malaysia must succeed

My next thesis is, I do not think the one-man-one-vote system is going to endure in Southeast Asia for various reasons which I shall discuss briefly, but the present generation of leaders in this particular phase envisage a continuance of the one-man-one-vote system and see in this a workable solution to prevent any communist manipulation of Chinese sentiments on behalf of the communists. Now, are they right? It is very difficult to say. But we have certainly got a better base and a better start with Malaysia than without Malaysia for this one simple reason – that the Chinese, being an extremely practical-minded people, never embark on a gamble which they do not think is likely to succeed. Therefore, if you start with Malaysia they will not ever embark or allow themselves to be persuaded to embark on a scheme to capture power which they may otherwise be tempted to do.

So, in my estimation, the way in which events have developed between May and now have been such as to have heightened the conflict and the cleavage between the China Chinese and the rest of the community. But the China Chinese are not communists – that is important. They are for themselves with all their prejudices and pride in their ancient culture and civilisation; and if we start off from a situation in which they are not going to win anyway by pursuing a Chinese line, I think we stand a very good chance of pulling a considerable proportion of them across to the other side, away from the communists, and that is what I think people like me can do if given a chance. You can govern Malaysia without the Chinese because you will have a situation where the Chinese are not a majority, but you will not govern it well; because 40 per cent, though they may be of Malaysia, are the 40 per cent that makes the Malaysian economy tick. That is a fact which, fortunately, the Federation leaders understand; the Tunku and all his colleagues understand this, and there is no desire and no inclination on their part to start on any anti-Chinese crusade, as was attempted by the Indonesians. Therefore, I say that the prospect of Malaysia failing presents such awful consequences that I am pretty sure it will succeed because it is in our power to make it succeed. The only thing which I think is necessary before it succeeds is a considerable amount of common sense, first in the British who run the administration in Borneo and who have considerable influence amongst the population there through chieftains, trade associations and so on, a certain amount of reasonableness from the Federation in acknowledging that Borneo is, after all, 1,000 miles over the sea, and that the local population has got aspirations of its own, local

We have certainly got a better base and a better start with Malaysia than without Malaysia for this one simple reason – that the Chinese, being an extremely practical-minded people, never embark on a gamble which they do not think is likely to succeed.

ambitions which they want to be fulfilled with their own men, and the planning to bring it into being without much fuss and bother.

I do not envisage the present period of gestation coming to an otherwise but happy conclusion. No doubt there will be a great deal of trouble from time to time as adjustments are made in attitudes and approaches to resolve the problem of good government in the new Federation of Malaysia. But I believe it will come about before June 1963.

In this hard-hitting speech to the Malaysian Students Association of New South Wales at Malaysia Hall in Sydney on March 20, 1965, Lee spoke bluntly and frankly about Singapore's problem in its 18-month merger with Malaysia: the PAP was for a more open and competitive economy while the Malay leadership in Kuala Lumpur was intent on continuing the status quo and preserving special Malay rights. These differences would lead eventually to separation.

# Preserving Malay special rights

*The man, the boy who is admired in a Malay community is the person with the social graces, a good athlete; not necessarily the intense individual.*

One of the problems we discovered in about six years of trying to implement our education policy in Singapore is that the Malay is not basically a money-conscious man. He does not seek gold as tenaciously as the immigrants. The immigrants came here seeking gold, fulfilment, success.

If you go to any school in Malaysia you will find in the immigrant communities, particularly amongst the Chinese and the Indians, a tremendous emphasis on education and high performance. This is not necessarily so amongst the Malays. The man, the boy who is admired in a Malay community is the person with the social graces, a good athlete; not necessarily the intense individual. Now this creates a very difficult problem of adjustment when they both have to live in the same milieu and work in the same society, having to cooperate with each other and to find an equitable way of distributing the fruits of that society.

I do not believe the problems that we are confronted with are Malay special rights and Malay as the national language. Nobody quarrels with that. Nobody in his right mind quarrels with that. The problem is, special rights and Malay as the national language will not by themselves resolve the basic imbalance in economic development between Malays and non-Malays.

I could speak to you today in Malay, if my Malay were good enough and you could understand me. I do not see how that can resolve the problem of low income, or the padi crops, or their poor rubber. There's no nexus between the two. We could have a bit more national pride if today we sat here and your Australian friends had to sit back and probably listen to us through the aid of an interpreter. And I think in the end it is necessary. There must be that *amour propre* in a nation. We can't always live on a borrowed language. But at the same time, the problem that is arising because of these economic and social problems of imbalance between indigenous and immigrants have not been resolved – quite a number of politicians who are unable to explain the failure of their economic and social policies pick upon national language and Malay special rights as an explanation for why they are not doing well.

This is a very dangerous situation. You can give as many jobs as you like, reserve as many taxi licences, contract licences, bus licences, the right to operate factories; the Indonesians have tried the whole gamut. Finally, they have taken over everything. They have only got themselves to take over now. But I suggest that the day they do that, the day they get a grip on themselves, that day they begin to tick. You cannot resolve these problems of economic development, which require skills, technical skills, managerial skills, organisational methods, by just making speeches, and when you fail because your policies were inadequate you give xenophobic slogans as an excuse. This is a very grave problem for us, for it could very easily happen. You read – well, many of you can't read because it is in Jawi – the *Utusan Melayu*. Now we are taking the trouble every day to translate all these important statements that they are making, feeding to the Malay peasantry, a philosophy which in the end if it goes unchecked must lead to the same reckless xenophobic slogans which we have heard from our neighbours.

No society which has this imbalance can be altogether at ease. The eight years that have passed from 1955 to 1963 were unique in that really what happened was a Western-educated Malay leadership, traditionalist by birth, conservative by temperament, continued the laissez-faire policies of the old colonial government and with good rubber and tin prices ended up with a considerable degree of public development, public construction, which is monuments, museums, roads. But because the economy is based on the profit incentive, it produced successful response in the towns and in the urban areas and has not been equally successful in the country.

The urban areas are largely occupied by peoples of immigrant stock, Chinese and Indians and others, who respond to high rewards. They work hard for high pay, they work harder to get overtime, in fact they make a point of making sure there is overtime in order to make money. So you see, they understand the profit incentive. Having bought a scooter, they save to buy a refrigerator. Having got a refrigerator, they want a television set. Having got a television set, they buy the flat they're living in.

But not so in the rural areas. It's the people who are not accustomed to this money economy who do not acquire wealth just for the sake of acquiring wealth, and are therefore afraid of transition, education, adjustment, to a highly monetised economy that must take place. And in fact it's already taking place in a very unfortunate way, because as development in the country does not keep pace with development in the towns the young men are drifting from the country into shanty areas around the big towns, looking for jobs. And if they don't find the jobs to satisfy them subsequently, there will be a great deal of social unrest.

So having told you what I think is the real problem, I will ask you now to view what you have heard in the newspapers, some of it even in the Australian newspapers, against this background. What do you get coming out from Malaysia? A great deal of noise,

You can give as many jobs as you like, reserve as many taxi licences, contract licences, bus licences, the right to operate factories; the Indonesians have tried the whole gamut. Finally, they have taken over everything.

disharmony, discord, competition, it would appear, between the PAP and the Alliance, competition between the present government and my colleagues and I who want to form the next government – so they say.

But is that really the cause? Is it really true that we are that shortsighted, unable to see what is in our own long-term interests? But it does give us a lot of anxiety to see men who are faced with enormous problems – which can only be met by forward planning, economic programmes, to meet these problems of imbalances, and education, to try and close the gap – explaining away all these failures on the basis of race, special rights, national language.

It is not the PAP or my ambition to capture power that is causing them concern. I may not be alive in 20 years' time. Or, if I am alive, I may no longer be interested in politics. Or, if I were interested in politics, more active, more competent, more able leaders may have emerged. But the ideas that we represent, the thesis that we propound that this is a Malaysian nation or it will break, that thesis is unanswerable. This is the problem which we want them to face now, and not to hide behind all this xenophobic talk of race, language, religion.

We are prepared to accept Malay as the national language. We do not quarrel with Malay rights in the constitution. But we go further, and say that they will be unable to solve the imbalance in economic and social development, even with all these safeguards, unless they begin forward planning.

I'll give you instances of things they could do which they are not doing and which we are going to bring into the forefront in the next few years to their great discomfort.

You've got agriculture as the basis of Malay livelihood – padi, rubber, fishing. The last budget, 1964 for 1965, had $16,000,000 set aside for the Ministry of Agriculture, half of it for payment of staff in the Ministry. So you had $8,000,000 for expenditure. You know, in Australia and New Zealand the farmers are the best, the most well-off section of the community. They are in the higher income brackets. And in America, even more so. Why are they not in Malaysia?

Many reasons. All right. All the past historic reasons why in fact agriculture was backward. But must it always remain like that? Can you not have crop-seed selection, research into what are quick cash crops, fertilisation, marketing boards to cut off the profits of the middlemen? So many other things could be done. And most important of all, education. If the man is not educated he is unlikely to be able to adopt the scientific techniques which alone can ensure him a better life. In other words, we propound the thesis that you must increase that man's capacity to earn, not slip him a gold coin. Slipping him a licence, or giving him a gold coin, will not solve his problem. He gets a licence to run a bus company. He does not know how to run a bus company. He then gets a Chinese or an Indian to run it for him, and he gets a percentage cut. How many bus licences can you give? One hundred bus companies running around in Malaysia, or make it 200; 200 families who have benefited from it have resolved Malay poverty? I don't think so. Ali gets the licence, Baba runs the company. So, you know, people get very cynical in Malaysia. They call these Ali Baba. And this will never resolve this imbalance.

Ali gets the licence, Baba runs the company. So, you know, people get very cynical in Malaysia. They call these Ali Baba.

They attack our policies. Why? The Singapore government came under systematic attack for having persecuted Malays, driven them out of the cities as we redeveloped the city, oppressed them. Really, was that true? In September 1963 for the first time, three Malay constituencies voted for a non-Malay party, the PAP, and Malay communal parties, UMNO candidates, lost. Would they vote for us if we were oppressing them?

But this is the core of the problem, isn't it? Because if we can win over the Malays by intelligent economic and social programmes in Singapore, so we can in Malaya. And if we begin to do that, then the whole structure of the communal parties and the basis of power of the Alliance is shattered. That is why they mounted this campaign, not intended primarily for Singapore but for Malayan Malays who do not know Singapore, to tell them quite falsely that when Malays voted for a non-Malay party they became persecuted and dispossessed. So the lesson is, always vote for a Malay party, you see?

Supposing you stood up, a Chinaman stood up in Kuala Lumpur, and said "Chinese Unite" and banged the gong. If you had not been appointed by the Malays to go and bang that gong, you would be in some very big trouble. They would say, "Ah, high treason!"

I'll give you an instance where I think this is utter folly. I have met a number of Dayaks, very high government officials from one of the Borneo states. One was in the radio business, broadcasting. There was a conference, I think in Sydney, for Common-wealth broadcasting technicians, or whatever it was, and Sarawak was supposed to send one, he was supposed to send one. And you know, in Malaya they used to have the old practice that all the Malayan delegations that went overseas put on the songkok as a kind of uniform. I don't think any harm is intended by this. But I am pointing out this example as a moral to what we should be on the lookout for, and how they are doing themselves, and doing Malaysia, and doing all of us enormous harm. The Dayak was told to put on this songkok. He was going to represent one of the Borneo states. And he said, "Look, the constitution of Malaysia says that Islam is not the religion of my state, and I refuse to put this on because I am a Christian and I refuse to be a Muslim." And he did not go. And he is a very bitter man. His junior, who is a Chinese, decided, you know, it doesn't matter. Just put on the songkok. So he came to Sydney for a fortnight. I hope he found Sydney much cooler than I'm finding it now.

What is happening now is that the more you try and emphasise Malay-ism, even unconsciously, the more you are generating anxiety and insecurity in the non-Malays. So I tell you quite frankly – as a Malaysian, not as a Chinaman – never say "Chinese Unite". It's stupid. Sure to lose. You understand what I mean? Morally, it is wrong. But I go one step further. Practically, it is stupid politics.

The problem that faces all of us is this. Do we make this nation work? Do we begin to integrate these communities? Racial integration in the sense of admixture, intermarriage, I think is unlikely to happen to any large degree for various reasons. One, the Malays are Muslims. They are non-pork-eating. The Chinese are non-Muslims, and they are pork-eating. Second, Muslims are required, when they marry, to have their spouse become a Muslim. Chinese are reluctant to be converted, even without any physical mutilation,

> Supposing you stood up, a Chinaman stood up in Kuala Lumpur and said "Chinese Unite" and banged the gong. If you had not been appointed by the Malays to go and bang that gong, you would be in some very big trouble.

The Chinese in Malaya, feeling a bit irksome under all these restraints, after Malaysia they look at the Chinese in Singapore and the non-Malays, and they say, "Well, that's what I like."

just in order to be a spouse. These are problems and genuine problems. So it is likely that, racially, for a long while to come Malaysia will continue to have distinct racial groups.

But what we can create is a socially and intellectually integrated community, feeling, thinking, reacting as Malaysians. And you do not get that by saying Malays Unite, Chinese Unite, Indians Unite. You begin to get that by telling them all that they share a common destiny, that if things go wrong everybody will suffer. If things go right, it is the job of the government to see that everybody benefits. On that basis, you build a nation. On that basis, you have an enduring foundation for what could be one of the most prosperous and satisfying communities in Southeast Asia.

Malaysia is new, 18 months. But the problems are not new. The problems were always there. The biggest mistake was that of separating Singapore from Malaya in 1945. I think the British were shortsighted when they did that, believing that thereby they could always hold Singapore in perpetuity, an island without a hinterland, economically not viable, they could manipulate and hold as a base forever. It took us from 1945 to 1961, 1962, before they were convinced this was wrong, that in fact this was one political situation. But we lost 18 years. And in the 18 years, development took place in divergent directions in Malaya and in Singapore.

If Malayans had learned to live with each other right from the very beginning instead of this artificial political segregation, the situation would be less acute today. The immediate problem with Malaysia is this. The Chinese in Malaya, feeling a bit irksome under all these restraints, after Malaysia they look at the Chinese in Singapore and the non-Malays, and they say, "Well, that's what I like." You see? Not unnaturally, because there is free competition, the best man for the best job. No privileges, licences, tenders or any other perks – a highly competitive society. It was a free port, an open society, a competitive society, and it produced a great deal of talent and a great deal of drive, and a great deal of prosperity.

On the other hand, the Malays in Singapore, looking at their counterparts in Malaya, seeing them getting these licences and these jobs, they said, "That's what I want after Malaysia." So probably you've got your Division Two Officer thinking he's going to become a Permanent Secretary or Under-Secretary in a couple of months' time. And then he discovered that this was not possible, that in fact this was not the case in the constitution and so on for Singapore. And there were, in any case, these problems.

I do not say these problems were artificially created. There was a genuine problem of adjustment. When this problem was put into the pressure-cooker: one, by Confrontation – the Indonesians telling the Malays that they are being bled dry by the Chinese and the Indians and the British, that Tunku is a stooge, selling out to the Chinese Indians and the British; two, local extremists, our own Malay extremists, began to work feelings up that they were being persecuted. What do you expect would happen? And this did happen. And if it continues, the third, the fourth or the fifth one must end up in widespread disaster. You can never put Humpty-Dumpty together again. And the only salvation I see is that everybody now understands this.

In the months leading to Singapore's separation from Malaysia in August 1965, charges and counter-charges were made by both sides over who was responsible for the deteriorating relationship. Matters became so volatile, there was even talk of the Kuala Lumpur government detaining Lee. How true was this and how would Singapore react to it? Lee answered these questions in a press conference on May 22, 1965.

# What will all this bickering lead to?

**QUESTION:** Mr Lee, it looks as though there is divergence of views between you and the central government about the concept of Malaysia. Quite recently, the Grand Alliance of the Opposition Parties was formed. Is there any likelihood of a delegation going to Tunku Abdul Rahman to restate your idea about your concept of a Malaysian Malaysia, or you are just satisfied with airing of views in the Parliament?

**LEE KUAN YEW:** Well, first of all I want to put the record right. This is not a Grand Alliance of Opposition Parties. I read the manifesto issued by the convention. It's a convention of non-communal parties who stand for a Malaysian Malaysia. Do not start using terms with which people for convenience label this group because then we are likely to mislead ourselves. This is not a grand opposition just to oppose the Tunku or the Alliance. We are not interested in opposing anybody. This is a rallying of all non-communal parties. In other words, put it in another way, all multiracial parties, parties that accept Malaysians without distinction of race. First condition, we do not classify people as Malays, Chinese, Indians and then those who are not Malays, Chinese or Indians, well, they are out. They have no party to join. So, some people feel sorry for them and they say "Right, we will form another one which all the smaller groups can join"; like the Singapore People's Alliance changes its name to something or the other. That is fundamental number one.

What are these non-communal groups coming together for? To establish not a new government, but to establish the acceptance of the fundamental concepts written into the constitution of Malaysia. This is not my interpretation. This is another error: to believe that this is the interpretation of the convention. Read the fundamental provisions of the constitution of Malaysia and the Malaysia Agreement. And what is the conclusion

> This is not a grand opposition just to oppose the Tunku or the Alliance. We are not interested in opposing anybody. This is a rallying of all non-communal parties.

Look, if people do not want a Malaysian Malaysia and they are prepared to use extra-constitutional methods to ensure that there is no Malaysian Malaysia, then I say, better let us know now …

we must draw from it? That we are all Malaysians, regardless of race, religion, creed, colour. There are some provisions: Article 159, for instance, which says Malays and indigenous people can have special provisions made by the Yang di-Pertuan Agong about jobs in the civil service and about the dispensation of licences and land in the states of Malaya, Sabah and Sarawak; not in the state of Singapore. But that is not a fundamental part of the constitution. Otherwise, it would apply to all of Malaysia, and it would be in the fundamental provisions. That is a provision in the constitution. But the fundamentals you will find spelt out in the first few clauses: right of all Malaysians to assemble, to freedom of speech, to liberty of person and so on; liberty of association. It does not say that one group is more Malaysian than another. We are all Malaysians or we are not. I think this is what we want to establish beyond any doubt. After that, we can decide whether such a Malaysian Malaysia is better as a socialist country, a democratic socialist country, or as a capitalist country, or as a half-capitalist, half-socialist country or whatever it may be. But first of all, let it be a Malaysian Malaysia; and let there be a democratic representative system so that the will of 11 million Malaysians in the wider Malaysia, … let them express themselves from time to time, and let their representatives decide the destiny of the country.

QUESTION: You are quoted last night as saying that if there is going to be trouble in Malaysia, let it be now. Could you expand on this?

LEE: Yes. Reading the newspapers, particularly the two Malay-language newspapers or perhaps specifically, *Utusan Melayu* and *Utusan Zaman*; the Sunday edition of *Utusan Melayu* which has been called "Voice of the Malays" – mind you, this is not something we can take too lightly because when the prime minister of Malaysia, the Tunku, recently opened an extension to *Utusan Melayu*, he said this was the "Voice of the Malays". So we have got to take it quite seriously because once it is been so described by no less a person than the prime minister, we have to take it seriously. And what it has been saying over the last one year gives room for considerable doubt as to whether they accept Malaysia as a Malaysian nation. Reading the daily outpouring of appeals on the basis of race, "bangsa" you know: … "Bangsa" in Malay does not mean the nation, the people. "Bangsa" means race, and the appeals are not made to the people of Malaysia, "Kebangsaan Malaysia", but "Bangsa Melayu", sometimes without even mentioning "Melayu", just "Bangsa". What does that mean? Where do the other Malaysians come from? Where do they belong if they are not included in these appeals, and these slogans are meant to rally – must be – one section?

So, when I say "trouble" I mean, "Look, if people do not want a Malaysian Malaysia and they are prepared to use extra-constitutional methods to ensure that there is no Malaysian Malaysia, then I say, better let us know now because it is no use carrying on for five, ten years defending Malaysia … you know, meeting Confrontation, making sacrifices, vigilante corps, defence of our nation, defence of freedom and democracy; for whom? For Malaysia. Who is encompassed by the term "Malaysia"? Malaysians or just "Bangsa"?

**QUESTION:** What action do you think you will take on this? Is there any possibility that Singapore could secede from the Federation?

**LEE:** No, I don't think we want to discuss the consequential effects of our conclusion that, in fact, people are prepared to use extra-constitutional methods in order to see that Malaysia is not a Malaysian Malaysia. But once we come to that conclusion, that it is hopeless, that in fact there are people in high positions in UMNO for instance, high office in the party, governing party, who insist that this is not a Malaysian Malaysia, well, I would say that it is better we resolve these things and make other arrangements now than later. Now we are less along the road towards perdition than if we were to go on for five or more years.

**QUESTION:** Mr Prime Minister, do you include under extra-constitutional methods, the possibility of your arrest?

**LEE:** Well, amongst others. But I don't think … you know, it is one of these things which catches the news headline but really, is that likely to resolve the problem? Will the arrest of PAP leaders prevent the struggle for a Malaysian Malaysia from going on? Or do you think it will make it more acute? You can't stop at that, isn't it? I have been reading the proceedings of the last UMNO conference. You get Singapore UMNO delegates saying, "Take over television and radio from the state government." Why? Because we report faithfully what *Utusan Melayu* and *Utusan Zaman* say in *Malaysian Mirror*; you know, Mirror of Opinion, "What Others Say". Well, you believe that you can just stop at taking radio and television, or you think it will lead eventually to a complete suspension of constitutional and democratic government?

Do you believe that you can just arrest a few PAP leaders and then life in Singapore will go on with these leaders quietly stashed away, being fed, I hope, kindly and adequately, and all the other leaders will carry on and govern Singapore quietly and keep the workers happy, and factories will go up and all will be nice and happy? Or do you think, step after step, it goes on until finally, again you have no democratic or representative government and it is ruled by extra-constitutional methods? It must lead to that, isn't it? And when it leads to that, I say, what is the way out? Can they sustain that kind of a Malaysia? Can Australia, New Zealand afford to be associated in defence of that sort of Malaysia? Can Britain? Has she got the capacity of the Americans in Vietnam to sustain that sort of Malaysia? Because that is required once you move into that situation. A thousand miles of frontier on the Borneo border, 600 to 700 miles from Singapore to Perlis, a guerilla civil war restarts, the British can support that? First of all, will they want to support it? Secondly, assuming that they have to because they are committed, have they got the capacity to do that for one, two, three, or ten years?

Mr Prime Minister, do you include under extra-constitutional methods, the possibility of your arrest?

On one thing we cannot give way: a Malaysian Malaysia. Otherwise, it means nothing to us. It means nothing to me and to the other Malaysians who are here with me. Any other kind of Malaysia, I have no place.

QUESTION: Are you suggesting the guerilla war would start as a result of this, or there is a possibility …?

LEE: Where do you think it will lead to? Where do you think it will lead to? It must, isn't it? Once you have a revulsion of feeling, an antipathy against a regime, where do you think, the communists will come up? You mean they will just cheer and say, "Well, three cheers now the PAP is out of the way"; they will take over the constitutional stage and they will win the next elections and govern Singapore and keep Singapore happy? Or do you think they will mount, together as others mount, mount a campaign which must lead in the end to the complete dissolution of Malaysia? Is there any other possible consequence of such steps? If we sat down, as I hope others will … we do this very often, do this exercise amongst ourselves and say, "Well, if we do this, then what happens; if we don't want that to happen, then we cannot do these things." Therefore, we try very hard to be as patient and as forbearing as we can.

But on one thing we cannot give way: a Malaysian Malaysia. Otherwise, it means nothing to us. It means nothing to me and to the other Malaysians who are here with me. Any other kind of Malaysia, I have no place. I have therefore no stake in that kind of Malaysia, and I am not going to help defend, protect or advance its cause. Why should I?

QUESTION: Are you as pessimistic as you are projecting yourself to be about the future of Malaysia as such?

LEE: No. I am not all that pessimistic. I think I put my position and the position of my colleagues fairly clearly on May 1. I said the prospects are fair. And it is not bleak. I don't want to be dishonest and say that the prospects are rosy, that all is well, because we will be misleading people, and that's not the way to govern. You can't just lead people into believing things which you know to be false. But I say they are fair for one simple reason. As you yourself can see reading the proceedings of the recent UMNO conference, there are leaders in UMNO who realise what the things being suggested by some leaders, some extremist groups in UMNO, where these steps will lead if they were taken: arrest PAP leaders; take over radio and television; smack us down, do us in by extra-constitutional methods, or perhaps even within the constitution, in accordance with the law, but not in accordance with the spirit of democratic practice. You know, we passed the Internal Security Act, or we passed the Emergency Regulations here, not for it to be used against the democratic opposition but against undemocratic, unconstitutional opposition. And I would say that we are encouraged to read Dr Ismail Abdul Rahim (Malaysian Minister for Internal Security) state fairly clearly that as long as we express our views democratically and constitutionally and rally people's opinion democratically and constitutionally without resort to violence, he accepts that position as right. There are the hopeful signs: that some people have sat down and calculated where these steps which are being urged by extremist groups, where these steps will lead to, once you start on them.

QUESTION: It has been suggested recently that you and the PAP are creating racial discord in this country. So, what have you to say about it?

LEE: Well, can we really go back to how this all started? You can look up the old editions of the newspapers, starting from last March. If we want to be accurate from the point of time, the campaign started immediately we announced our intention to compete in the general elections in Malaya. And from then onwards, it has never stopped, this appeal to race in the Malay language only, and this attack that we are anti-Malay. How do we add to racial discord because we have pointed out the dangers of what this sort of appeal can lead to? How do we add to it? What have we done?

QUESTION: Mr Lee, when is the PAP as a national political party going to evolve a policy for the uplift of the Malays and the rural people in Malaysia as a whole, not just in Singapore?

LEE: Well, we had refrained from doing this for one and a half years now because we didn't really want to join issue with the ruling party, UMNO; and even in the last elections in Malaya, in April last year, we did not contest the rural seats. But I think a position has now developed in which we must make clear our stand not only to the urban areas but also to the rural areas: where we stand, what kind of Malaysia we want in a Malaysian Malaysia, one in which the imbalance of development between the rural areas and the urban areas must be altered, must be remedied.

I thought it was a useful beginning what happened after my visit to Australia, when I mentioned to some Malaysian students who asked me in Adelaide why we should agree to Malay rights, Malay special rights in the constitution for Malays and indigenous peoples in Malaya, Sabah and Sarawak. That the problem is not whether there are Malay rights or not but whether these Malay rights can really uplift the life of Malays generally, not just as a small group of people who become company directors or contractors or part-owners of transport companies, but Malays generally in the rural areas who are now drifting into the towns looking for jobs because rural development is not going at the same pace as urban development. And Malays are coming into Singapore looking for jobs. Last year, 10,000 Chinese and Malays came from Malaya into Singapore looking for jobs. We know that from the identity card change of address: 10,000 came down. You know, if we are exploiting Malays and being cruel to them, why should these Malays, about two to three thousand Malays come in last year from Kedah, from Muar, from Selangor?

Because rural development is not going at the same pace as urban development. It is happening in many countries throughout the world, this drift from the countryside into the towns. But in Malaysia, it is a particularly sensitive problem because, by and large, the Malays have been a rural people. They lead a pastoral sort of life: agriculture and fishing. I raised this question: I said, how much did they spend; last year's budget in December, how much for the Ministry of Agriculture? Eighteen million dollars out of a total budget of nearly $1,300 million; $1,300 million, you spend 18 million dollars, of which half goes to Establishment costs. They mention development estimates of over 100 million dollars, most of which are going into rubber research. Not the smallholder; the big estates get the benefit out of that: rubber research, replanting. Shouldn't we do something? Even in Thailand today, they are growing maize where they did not grow maize. They are exporting maize. Before, they grew only rice. Now, they have increased their rice population and grow maize, one of their main export products. We are importing their maize for our chickens. We cannot do that in Malaya? Surely this must be done. And a Malaysian Malaysia can only survive if it provides opportunities both for rural people and for urban people. In other words, you must create more equal opportunities for a full life for everybody.

Where I feel extremely frustrated is: every time we talk about this, they say, "Ah! I am attacking Malay rights." I am not attacking Malay rights. I am saying that these Malay rights which have been going on for so many years have not solved the basic problem of social and economic development in the rural areas. That what you have got to do if you want Malaysia to survive is to raise the earning capacity of the Malays; not give him a gold coin because if you give a chap just a gold coin to make him live a better life without teaching him how to earn that gold coin, we are all going in for more trouble. You give him a gold dollar today, you have got to give him a gold dollar next month because he has got used to a higher standard of living and you haven't taught him fertilisation, new crops, new seeds, new methods of irrigation, new marketing boards to ensure that he gets a maximum for the price of his products. You have got to give him a higher earning capacity which can come only with higher education, higher skills and better economic planning.

> Where I feel extremely frustrated is: every time we talk about this, they say, "Ah! I am attacking Malay rights."

In this speech on the widening Singapore-Kuala Lumpur rift, Lee took the battle into the heart of the Malay leadership when he spoke in the Federal capital during a parliamentary debate. Speaking sometimes in fluent Malay, he confronted them with attacks they had launched on him and challenged them to counter the PAP's ideas over how to uplift the Malay community. Following are extracts of his speech during the debate in the Federal Parliament on May 27, 1965, on the motion of thanks to the Yang Di-Pertuan Agong for his speech from the throne.

# Enemy of the people?

I would like, Mr Speaker, Sir, to read if I may what this same Malay press, the *Utusan Melayu*, was saying at the very same time that His Majesty was making the speech, and it is not what *Utusan Melayu* says that worries me but who *Utusan Melayu* is quoting from. Said *Utusan* of the 25th of May, headline, "LEE IS AN ENEMY OF THE PEOPLE OF MALAYSIA. Klang, 24th May, Dato Harun bin Haji Idris, Mentri Besar of Selangor, described Lee Kuan Yew as an enemy of the people of Malaysia and was endangering the peace of the country." In the same issue day before yesterday, this time it's *Berita Harian*, the Mentri Besar of Perak, Dato Ahmad bin Said, has called upon the Malays and amongst the things he called upon them to take note of is his statement: Lee Kuan Yew is now not only our enemy but he is also the most dangerous threat to the security of this country.

Now, Mr Speaker, Sir, I think no advantage is served by equivocation. This has been going on and I have got a whole file, it goes back to a campaign mounted immediately after we announced our intention to contest the last elections, it goes back one whole year. This is what the secretary-general of UMNO said in *Utusan Melayu* on the very same day, the 25th: the Secretary-General also called on the Malays to be more strongly united to face the present challenge; he stressed that the Malays should realise their identity, quote, "Wherever I am, I am a Malay. If the Malays were split the Malays would perish from this earth."

Now, Sir, I would like if I may to start with the oath which we all took when we came into this Chamber before we had the right to participate in debates; it is laid down that no Member shall have the right to participate as a representative of the people unless he swears this oath, and the oath reads, which I read myself, Mr Speaker, Sir, in the Malay language: "I … (full name), having been elected as a Member of the House of Representatives, do solemnly swear or affirm that I will faithfully discharge my duties as

"Lee Kuan Yew is now not only our enemy but he is also the most dangerous threat to the security of this country."
—Dato Ahmad bin Said

such to the best of my ability and that I will bear true faith and allegiance to Malaysia and will preserve, protect and defend its constitution." This is its constitution, Mr Speaker, Sir, published by the government printer with the authority of the Yang di-Pertuan Agong, compiled in the Attorney-General's Chambers, Kuala Lumpur.

What is it, Mr Speaker, Sir, that I or my colleagues or the other members in the Malaysian Solidarity Convention, what is it that we have done which deserves this denunciation as "enemy of the people"? A danger, a threat to security? We have said we believe in a Malaysian Malaysia. We honour this constitution because that was what we swore to do. And if I may just crave the indulgence, Mr Speaker, Sir, to remind Honourable Members of what they swore to uphold:

Part 2, fundamental liberties: Article 5, liberty of the person; 6, slavery and enforced labour prohibited; 7, protection against retrospective criminal laws and repeated trials; 8, equality – equality, Mr Speaker, Sir, political equality; prohibition of banishment and freedom of movement, freedom of speech, assembly and association; 11, freedom of religion; 12, rights in respect of education; 13, rights of property. But I will be fair to Honourable Members. There is also, as part of this constitution we swore to uphold, under 12, general and miscellaneous: Article 153, reservation of quotas in respect of services, permits, etc. for Malays; and just before that, Article 152, National Language.

We uphold that, we accept it. This is what we swore to protect, to preserve and to defend, and this is what we have every intention of doing, Mr Speaker, Sir, by every constitutional means open to us and given to us by this constitution, the basis on which solemnly and in good faith we came into Malaysia.

Sir, I think it is time we took stock of our position and we began to face each other on fundamental issues: where we stand in respect of Malaysia, what we propose to do to advance its cause, what we are prepared to do if in fact we are to be thwarted from our legitimate objective to get what was agreed in this constitution implemented. Therefore, I noted with regret that in spite of the protests we have made as Members of the Opposition, that grave constitutional matters require at least solemn deliberations of this House, we are still faced with standing orders which entitles the government to bring about radical and fundamental changes in the constitution, all within one day, one day's notice of the Bill, the intention of the first, second and third readings, if the government so chooses. Is this likely to protect, to defend, to uphold the constitution?

Sir, I would like to divide the opposition between loyal and not-so-loyal opposition. The Member for Batu reminded the House that I once said there was a gulf between them and us. There is still, Mr Speaker, Sir, perhaps not between him personally and us, because he is not really what his party represents. Parties like the Socialist Front, Mr Speaker, Sir, and PAS, parties which have, over a series of elections spread over 10, 15 years, almost abandoned all hope of ever achieving what they want to constitutionally; it is only those parties that then began to become disloyal.

## We don't intend to secede

I can give the Prime Minister and his colleagues this very firm assurance that we have a vested interest, Mr Speaker, Sir, in constitutionalism and in loyalty because we know, and we knew it before we joined Malaysia, that if we are patient, if we are firm, this constitution must mean that a Malaysian nation emerges. Why should we oblige the Member for Johor Tengara to get out of Malaysia? "Secede," says he, "I demand that we say so now." We tell him and all his colleagues now we have not the slightest intention of secession. Secession is an act of betrayal, to leave like-minded people like ourselves in Sabah, in Sarawak, in Malaya to the tender mercies of those who talk in terms of race: "Wherever I am, I am a Malay." I would have thought, Mr Speaker, Sir, if one were to say, "Wherever I am, I am a Malaysian," it would have sounded enormously more comforting to all of us and would have helped to consolidate the nation.

But let me assure him, he has asked and urged the Hon'ble Minister of Home Affairs to take action, he has been going on for some months now, but it's reaching crescendo – this was the 24th, the day before we met, *Utusan Melayu*, 24th: "Albar [Jaafar Albar, secretary-general of UMNO] challenges Kuan Yew: Don't be fond of beating about the bush. Lee asked to state openly his stand whether Singapore wants to secede from Malaysia." And it goes on to say: "If Lee Kuan Yew is really a man he should not be beating about the bush in his statements and should be brave enough to say, 'I want to secede from Malaysia because I am not satisfied.' But, said Albar, Lee did not dare say that because he himself signed the Malaysian Constitutional Agreement. Regarding Lee as 'the most stupid person he has ever come across,' Albar said that Lee entered Malaysia with his eyes open and the present Malaysia is the same Malaysia which he had endorsed. Why did he not think of all these before? Why only now have we regretted? Why? asked Albar in a high-pitched tone" – not I who said that, the *Utusan*, high-pitched note – "and his audience replied, 'Crush Lee, crush Lee …'

"Lee, continued Albar in a lower tone, was really like an 'ikan sepat' which cannot live save in muddy water. Several voices shouted, 'Arrest Lee and preserve him like entrails in pickle.' Dato Albar smiled for a moment and then replied, 'Shout louder so that Dr Ismail can hear the people's anger.'"

I want to make quite sure that everybody hears the people's anger.

Albar then went on – it is a very long piece, Mr Speaker, Sir, I leave that for Honourable Members who are interested and we can put them on the mailing list, those who do not read Jawi, we will put them on the mailing list and provide them with copies so that day by day they can follow the theoretical expositions of this ideological group – "Albar regarded Lee Kuan Yew as a frightened man chased by his own shadow." (What can I do about my shadow, Mr Speaker, Sir; it must follow me?) "Lee is like a traveller in the sands of the Sahara, said Albar" (Vistas of the Hydramaut, Sahara, Saudi Arabia.) "He looks to his left and sees the desert sands, to his right a vast emptiness and to his rear a wide open space, and he becomes frightened. To subdue his fear he shouts on top of his voice."

We tell him and all his colleagues now we have not the slightest intention of secession.

Well, Mr Speaker, Sir, I have quite a number of things to say, so I hope Members will forgive me if I say what I have to say in a fairly modulated way but I think sufficiently distinct and clear to leave nobody in any doubt as to where we stand.

Sir, I have no regrets about this document [holding the constitution in his hand]. It was passed in this House and in the old Parliament of Malaya; it was passed in the Assembly of Singapore. Why should we regret it? What we will regret very much, as was obliquely hinted in the address of His Majesty, "There would be an end to democracy" – the constitution suspended, brushed aside. Now, Mr Speaker, Sir, I think these are important matters which affect all of us. And therefore, by the time a campaign which has been going on for some months finds an echo, albeit an oblique one, in His Majesty's speech to us, it is worthwhile going into the credibility of this insinuation.

## Malay rule

"The trouble with us from Singapore is we are not accustomed to Malay rule."
—Dr Mahathir Mohamed

Mr Speaker, Sir, we all want peace, we all want Malaysia to succeed, and that is why we came into Malaysia, but if we echo "yes" in this pernicious doctrine, "Wherever I am, I am a Malay" – said Dr Mahathir yesterday, "The trouble with us from Singapore is we are not accustomed to Malay rule." That's why, the implication being we ought to be, Mr Speaker, Sir. The bigger English language newspaper for some reason or the other left it out, this very important passage, but the smaller English language newspaper very kindly put it out in script for us, so if I may just read this: "On the question of Malay privileges about which Mr Lee made so much play while in Australia and New Zealand, the saviour of Malaysia ignores the facts as they really are. We Malays are very sensitive but this is a total war declared by the PAP and even if it hurts our feelings it is wiser to demonstrate that in this land the privileged Malays, Ibans, Dayaks and Kadazans live in huts while the underprivileged Chinese live in palaces, go about in huge cars and have the best things in life."

I would have thought that was, if I had just read that without having heard Dr Mahathir say it yesterday, I would have thought it came straight out from Radio Jakarta, Mr Speaker, Sir. That is their line, that all the Chinese have got big houses and big cars. I can show Dr Mahathir any number of Chinese in very miserable hovels in Singapore where there is a housing programme, let alone any other part where they haven't got a housing programme yet.

## What Dr Mahathir said

[Quoting Dr Mahathir again] "It is, of course, necessary to emphasise that there are two types of Chinese – those who appreciate the need for all communities to be equally well off, and these are the MCA supporters to be found mainly where Chinese have for generations lived and worked amidst the Malays and other indigenous people, and the insular, selfish and arrogant type of which Mr Lee is a good example. This latter type live in a purely Chinese environment where Malays only exist at syce level. They have been nurtured by the British and made much of because they helped the British economic empire. They have never known Malay rule and couldn't bear the idea that the people they have so long kept under their heels should now be in a position to rule them."

Ominous words, Mr Speaker, Sir.

[Again quoting Dr Mahathir] "They have in most instances never crossed the Causeway. They are in fact overseas Chinese first – more specifically Chinese of the southern region as their mind sees China as the centre of the world – and Malaysians a very poor second, a status so utterly artificial to them that it finds difficulty in percolating through their criticisms."

What does that mean, Mr Speaker, Sir? They were not words uttered in haste, they were scripted, prepared and dutifully read out, and if we are to draw the implications from that, the answer is quite simple: that Malaysia will not be a Malaysian nation. I say, say so, let us know it now, why waste five-ten years' effort to build this, defend this – for whose benefit, Mr Speaker, Sir?

According to this sacred document, we are obliged on oath to uphold this for the benefit of all Malaysians and a Malaysian is there defined, but all Malaysians have a duty also defined there under the General and Miscellaneous provisions, to ensure that the development, preservation of jobs, licences and so on in Malaya, Sabah and Sarawak will go to Malays. Quite clearly a distinction between our political equality and our duty as part of that political equality to give special attention to the economic and social uplift of the Malays and the other indigenous peoples in Sabah and Sarawak. We accept that obligation and I was delighted when I discovered that the secretary-general of UMNO agreed in print that I had the right to determine the destiny of Malaysia.

While on that basis, I say there is ground for believing that the future of Malaysia is fair. Deny that basis, I say we don't need Sukarno and Confrontation to destroy us.

Now, I believe it would be helpful, Mr Speaker, Sir, if I were to spell out not for the benefit of the Prime Minister or the Minister for Home Affairs, because I think they have already sat down and worked these things out in their minds and therefore they speak with greater and wider circumspection. Is it really that simple that you can resolve these problems on the basis of stifling or negating your democratic constitutional opponents?

This is *Utusan Melayu* again, Mr Speaker, Sir, and the secretary-general of UMNO urged in the strongest possible terms that action should be taken now. Well, I am a frightened man according to him and therefore I see shadows. I think it would help if I could sort of work out the various logical consequences. Frightened even though I may be, we are still not bereft of our senses. There are two ways in which developments in Malaysia could take place – first, in accordance with the democratic processes set out in the constitution, and second, not in accordance with it, using extra-constitutional capacities and the administration of the Police and the Army.

We have calculated this before we came into Malaysia and we must accept the consequences, but let me spell out the consequences. First, Mr Speaker, Sir, I go back again to His Majesty's speech. Said he, "I would like to pay special tribute (not just a tribute – a special tribute)" and to those this special tribute was addressed were besides

> I say there is ground for believing that the future of Malaysia is fair. Deny that basis, I say we don't need Sukarno and Confrontation to destroy us.

our own Security Forces and the Police, the British, Australian and New Zealand Armed Forces.

Now, what does that mean, Mr Speaker, Sir? It means quite simply that if we are without assistance, airlanes between Malaya and Western Malaysia and Eastern Malaysia will be closed. The sea will be closed. We cannot carry troops on the *Mutiara* to go and fight in Sabah, can we? We know all that. We might be able to buy some, I don't know, perhaps, but let us be frank and honest to ourselves first, that Malaysia by itself hasn't got the capacity to be governed by force – it is as simple as that, and therefore that capacity must be borrowed from somewhere – the British, Australians, New Zealanders.

Well, Sir, I don't know the Australians and the New Zealanders as well as I know the British for I happened to have lived in that country for several years and therefore I took particular care and interest when I visited them recently to find out whether there was a possibility that such extraordinary aid can be given in order to hold Malaysia down. I will not talk about the governments because they are friendly governments – friendly to all Malaysians, which included me – and I will talk more pertinently of the people in these countries.

One battalion was sent to South Vietnam recently from Australia in defence of what the Australian Prime Minister called the survival of the democratic world and a very vociferous and articulate opposition disagreed profoundly. They may be right or they may be wrong, but of one thing I am certain – neither Australia nor New Zealand has got the capacity to play the role of the Americans in South Vietnam. Therefore, we ask – have the British got this capacity? Maybe for some time, but for all time? Because that is what it means.

Once you throw this into the fire and say, be done with it, it means that you do it for all time and history is a long and a relentless process. People born, people destroyed, and more are born and more surge forward. It is part of the story of the human race on this earth. Can it be done – will the British public be parties to that? Well, I am not talking about the British government, Mr Speaker, Sir. I am now talking of the British public when, whatever government it is – Conservative or Labour – it faces the same British public.

All right, so they want us to secede and leave our friends from Sabah and Sarawak, from Penang and Malacca and all the other parts of Malaysia at their tender mercies. We cannot oblige, Mr Speaker, Sir. We will not, we know the juxtaposition of strength and weakness on both sides. We are fervently of the opinion that if we give and take and accommodate, this can succeed, and there is no other way to make it succeed and we shall be patient, but I will tell Members on the other side why I think what they are doing is not likely to lead to success for them.

And if I may, in conclusion, spell out to all Malaysians where we stand, what we want to achieve and how we are going to achieve these things, then they will know what are their problems. Their problem is not that we are against Malay as the national language. We accept it: *Kita Terima Bahasa Melayu menjadi Bahasa Kebangsaan*. [We accept Malay as the national language.]

> Their problem is not that we are against Malay as the national language. We accept it: *Kita Terima Bahasa Melayu menjadi Bahasa Kebangsaan*.

[Lee continues in Malay.]

But let me remind members in UMNO, and I would like to draw this to the attention of the members in the MCA and their associates. This is a very dangerous thing, leading people to believe that if we just switch in 1967 from talking English in the courts, and in business, to speaking Malay, therefore the imbalance in social and economic development will disappear. It will not disappear. How does our talking Malay here or writing to the ministers of the federal government, both Malays and non-Malays, in Malay, how does that increase the production of the Malay farmers? The price he gets for his products, the facilities he gets from the government, fertilisation, research into better seeds, marketing boards. How does that raise him? In fact our worry is not with Article 153, which gives special reservations to Malays for jobs and licences. I am saying it is inimical to the country. What I am saying is that it has been in force now for 10 years with the imbalance between the rural and the urban areas widening.

The Minister for Finance is aware of this. He has the figures. He knows what is the rate of growth between the urban and rural areas. We have got visible evidence of that – that the Malays are drifting from the kampongs into the towns in Kuala Lumpur – shanty towns around the suburbs. And they are coming to Singapore looking for jobs. Malaya last year – on the change of identity card addresses, 10,000 young men came to Singapore looking for jobs. Equivalent to quarter of our birth rate of that generation – 20 to 25. We were having an annual rate of 40,000. One quarter added to our burden. Of that 10,000, more than 3,500 were Malays – more than 3,500 who *tumpang* with friends looking for jobs. Just solving these problems on the basis of Article 153? You are going to solve these problems on the basis of a Congress Economi Bumiputra? What does it say the Congress is going to do? "Intended to give opportunities to all those who are familiar with the problems connected with participation of the Malays and other indigenous population in the field of commerce and industry."

Let us start off with the Chinese and the Indians – the non-Malays first. What percentage are in commerce and industry as bosses or shareholders? 0.2 per cent, 0.3 per cent, that is the total. For one bus company – that is the simplest unit because I think everybody will understand it; it is a simple operation, it has been done very often, so everybody knows. One bus company, let us say there are 20 shareholders and they employ 2,000 workers – mechanics, fitters, ticket collectors, drivers, people who repair the buses, paint them up. Let us assume that out of the 4.5 million Malays and another 0.75 million Ibans, Kadazans and others. We create the 0.3 per cent shareholders, do we solve the problem? How does the Malay in the kampong find his way out into modernised civil society? If you create this 0.3 per cent, how does this create a new and just society? By becoming servants of the 0.3 per cent who will have money to hire them to clean their shoes, open their motorcar doors? We have not done this before because we tried to do it the friendly way. But I am afraid the time has come in which we have to state quite clearly what we think is happening, how we think these problems have to be tackled.

The urban rate of growth, the Minister of Finance, the Honourable Minister can confirm this. It is at least 2.5 to 3 times the rural rates over the whole population per capita. He has had discussions with my colleague Dr Goh and he knows why Singapore's per capita income is also higher. How can you lift this up? By trying to compete with Singapore as to who can build a better urban society?

It is the wrong objective. Surely by setting out to bring about a social uplift, change and progress in your rural areas. We never touched on these matters before, Mr Speaker, Sir, because we thought we would like to help members of UMNO with ideas and so on privately, but it is now necessary, because they will not listen to us privately, to state our position publicly.

Of course, there are Chinese millionaires in big cars and big houses. Is it the answer to make a few Malay millionaires with big cars and big houses? That is what Alliance means. Mr Speaker, Sir, I am sorry to say it, but that is how it works. How does that solve the ground problem? How does telling the Malay bus driver that he should support the party of his Malay director and the Chinese conductor to join another party of his Chinese director – how does that improve the living standards of the Malay bus driver and the Chinese bus conductor who are both workers of the same company? It is just splitting the workers up. We have taken some time before, we have come down to the bone and it cannot go on like this.

If we delude people into believing that they are poor because there are not Malay rights or because opposition members oppose Malay rights – where are we going to end up? You let people in the kampongs believe that they are poor because we don't speak Malay, because the government does not write in Malay, so he expects a miracle to take place in 1967. The moment we all start speaking Malay, he is going to have an uplift in the standard of living, and if it doesn't happen, what happens then? Oh, you say, well they are opposing Malay rights. We are not opposing Malay rights. We honour and support it, but how does Malay rights solve your Malay *rakyat*'s living standards? So wherever there is a failure of economic, social and educational policies, you come back and say, oh, these wicked Chinese, Indians and others opposing Malay rights. They don't oppose Malay rights. They have the right as Malaysian citizens to go up to the level of training and education which the more competitive societies, the non-Malay society has produced.

That is what must be done, isn't it? Not to feed them with this obscurantist doctrine, that all they've got to do is to get Malay rights for a few special Malays and their problem has been resolved. I don't see how that follows. So, Mr Speaker, Sir, we are posing to the Alliance government now the fundamental challenge. Not Malay national language, which we accept and agree, not Clause 153, which we accept and agree, implement and honour this constitution, but let us go one step further and see how you make a more equal society – by taxing the poor to pay for the defence of the country? Special rights or do you tax those who have in order to uplift the have-nots including many non-Malays, Chinese, Indians, Ceylonese and Pakistanis? There are many such poor people, don't make any mistake about that. I say, over the months, they will have to come across and meet us on this issue – development in the economy, in the social and educational sectors. Meet us, show to the people that Alliance has got the answers to this problem. If they

> Of course, there are Chinese millionaires in big cars and big houses. Is it the answer to make a few Malay millionaires with big cars and big houses?

haven't, don't stifle us, give us a chance to put forward an alternative, for we have an alternative which can work and has worked in Singapore and will continue to bear fruit.

We will wait and see – in 10 years we will breed a generation of Malays with educated minds, not filled with obscurantist stuff, but understanding the techniques of science and modern industrial management, capable, competent and assured: the family background, the diet – health problems, the economic and social problems that prevent a Malay child from taking advantage of the educational opportunities which we offer free from the primary school to university. We will solve them, we will meet them, because in no other way can you hold this multiracial society together if over the years the urban areas populated largely by people of migrant stock goes up and up and the rural areas remain stagnant.

Surely this is an unstable and unsafe situation? I would like to remind members of the government that they will find in the PAP and I hope in the members of the Convention – Malaysian Solidarity Convention – a loyal, constructive opposition, an opposition in accordance with this constitution. It is no use threatening us, that they are going to take away our local authority in Singapore and so on. It cannot be done unless you are going to use the guns and, as I have said, you haven't got enough guns and we are not going to allow them to get rid of the Member for Sarawak Affairs and the Member of Sabah Affairs. They are valuable parts of Malaysia, because you can put one hundred thousand troops in Sabah and Sarawak and they may never be seen or heard of again if the Ibans do not like it.

Let us be frank. We did this calculation carefully and methodically. There is no other way. It is not credible. You want a whole little Malaya, maybe; a whole Malaysia on that basis, no. The threat is not credible. The Minister for Sarawak Affairs has got a knowing smile. He knows they are headhunting people, Mr Speaker, Sir. Let me inform all these members here, we change this, we will change that, this solemn document says – 161H – you will challenge nothing of that sort without the consent of the state government and first you have to win a democratic election in Singapore, and we hold it quite democratically you know. They say nine days; all right, I promise them next time, a full real long spell on radio and television, the whole works. We never run away from open confrontation as our friends from the Barisan Sosialis can testify. We love it, we relish the prospect of a meeting of minds, a conflict of ideas, not of force. We are gentle people who believe very firmly in ideas.

We are gentle people who believe very firmly in ideas.

Six days after Singapore's separation from Malaysia, on August 14, 1965, Lee spoke to four foreign correspondents on the events leading to the split and whether there were any other options available. He also revealed that he had in fact offered to resign as prime minister after the racial riots in 1964, if doing so would help mend the rift.

# Prime Minister, what if you had been arrested?

**QUESTION:** Mr Lee Kuan Yew, Tunku Abdul Rahman has said that you were pleased and wanted to get out of the federation. And yet in your last Monday's press conference you broke down. Where, would you say, the truth lies?

**LEE:** Did the Tunku say I was pleased?

**QUESTION:** He said this yesterday …

**LEE:** Where?

**QUESTION:** He said you wanted to get out and that you are pleased to get out …

**LEE:** No, no, no. I haven't seen it in the press …

**QUESTION:** He said this at a press conference yesterday in Kuala Lumpur.

**LEE:** Well, I am sorry to hear that because I do not want to believe that the Tunku would utter something which is not the truth …

**QUESTION:** His actual words were …

**LEE:** He knows my positions; and he knew how close it came to a real collision … because my colleagues were not prepared to give way. You know, half my Cabinet were born and

**305**

bred in Malaya. Their families are there. You mean to tell me you can abandon them like that? And they are abandoned now. They are foreigners now. My colleagues fought with me against the communists. What for? To bring Singapore into Malaya in order to lift up Malaya: bring fresh air, social development, economic development.

I am not saying it is all purely personal, that it is just because they have got their families there. But they were born, bred, rooted there. They just happened to have come down to Singapore, which was the biggest city in Southeast Asia. And they made a living here and they finally became ministers here. You think you can face your Cabinet colleagues ... Let me put it in another way: supposing Mr Menzies were presented with an ultimatum by the American President that either Victoria gets out or the ANZUS Pact is not valid. You think Mr Menzies will be pleased and happy? It is easier for me. My family is here; born here, bred here. But half of my Cabinet have been born, bred there; their families are still there. How do they face their families? And they signed, you know. And I would not have signed unless they all signed. I am not the Tunku, I am not a prince. I cannot just sign on behalf of the government. The whole Cabinet had to sign it, and they signed with the utmost reluctance. And for them, when they look back at that moment, it will be a moment of anguish. It is going back on everything we fought for and believed in. And I do not care what anybody else says.

*It is easier for me. My family is here; born here, bred here. But half of my Cabinet have been born, bred there; their families are still there.*

**QUESTION:** Mr Lee, were there any reasonable alternatives that the other members of your Cabinet put forward at the time that looked as if they had a chance, other than complete secession?

**LEE:** I met the Tunku on Saturday the 7th at half past 12. I remember it distinctly. The appointment was supposed to be at 12 o'clock. I arrived. I waited for him for half an hour. Some of his ministers were there. We talked little nothings. He came and we went to a separate room. I said, "Tunku, is there no other way? Why not loosen it into a confederation? Give me common market. We will run all our activities ourselves. We will go slow in the rest of Malaysia. Give me common market; give me the right to take initiative in security matters so that the communalists cannot start riots in Singapore, and we carry on in Malaysia slowly: take it in 20, 30 years."

And he said, "No." I said, "My colleagues will not believe this." I said, "Will you see my colleagues ... Dr Toh?" Dr Toh was born and bred in Taiping; his family is there. Every year, he does a biannual pilgrimage. You know, Chinese families have reunions: Chinese New Year and some other moon festival. Dr Toh is not going to say "Yes".

For two million people moving forward faster and quicker, we abandoned eight million; abandoned them and left them in a slow and sluggish situation. And the Tunku did not want to see Dr Toh. But he wrote Dr Toh that letter and Dr Toh did not reply. ... One whole night we sat down and argued. It is all over. Never mind about that. We will talk about that later on. It is part of the history now of Southeast Asia ...

QUESTION: There seems to be some contradiction here though, Sir. And is it a fact, for instance, that Dato Jaafar Albar wanted to suspend the constitution and rule by edict and possibly to jail you; and in fact that the alternative that was suggested was either that you resign from here or separation?

LEE: Well, those who are unkind, those who do not like us will say that my colleagues and I were afraid for our personal safety and freedom and therefore we signed. But amongst my colleagues are quite a number who have been to British jails. Mr Jek, for instance, Mr Devan Nair. I do not think they were afraid of going to jail. But we sat down and calculated that if the Tunku really could not keep his ultras down … Going to jail means I become a martyr. I must come out. Mr Wilson, who is a personal friend, cannot see me languishing in jail forever. I do not think Mr Menzies, even though his political orientation is different from mine, but he is a human being … He knew that we were fighting for something which was valuable for Australia … He cannot see me languishing in jail. In one or two years, I would have come out.

QUESTION: This was the alternative then that as given …

LEE: No … We are not afraid of that. Let us say that they take over the government and rule by edict. Right? Some of my colleagues will be away. We will have a government-in-exile. We were prepared for that … Prince Sihanouk is a very personal friend of mine and Phnom Penh is very close to Malaysia. I would be in jail because I cannot run away. But quite a number of my colleagues who have got international contacts could run a much more effective campaign than the Indonesians and the communists ever can. But I tell you what deterred us: that in a moment of anger, race conflict takes place in Singapore. The Malays here are in a minority. The Chinese thinking that well, if this is it, to hell with constitutionalism, they will beat up some completely innocent people who have nothing to do with this … Troops come down; Malay troops come down, shoot the Chinese. Do you think it stays just in Singapore or do you think it spreads throughout Malaysia?

If I believed that we could go to jail … then demonstrations, mass rallies, resolutions, international telegrams, Socialist International, British Labour Party, Australian Labour Party, New Zealand Party: resolutions passed all over the place; and we come out and find Malaysia is still one whole … Then we would have come out to a Malaysia which was in one piece. You have got to calculate … I may be wrong. It may be that Singapore consists of docile people who could be cowed and brutalised into submission. But I don't think they could have … My estimation was that they would really give vent to their feelings. And if this spreads across the Causeway … The Tunku will have had it, too; because in that situation, the gentle, the charming, the soft-spoken leader has no place. And I want the Tunku to be there because I happen to believe – not because I like him – but I happen to believe that there is a little bit more chance of holding the multiracial situation together with him in charge.

> We are not afraid of that. Let us say that they take over the government and rule by edict. Right? Some of my colleagues will be away. We will have a government-in-exile. We were prepared for that.

QUESTION: Mr Prime Minister, we've dealt with the problem of separation and what would happen if you went to jail. But what about the situation if you personally were to resign? Do you think that would have helped the attitude between Singapore and Malaya? Do you think it would have made it any better? Kept the federation together?

LEE: After the riots last year they said that if I resigned there would be better cooperation. I told my colleagues if there's going to be cooperation in Singapore and Malaysia will prosper, let's do it that way. I was even prepared to serve under Dr Toh. And my colleagues, they've all got little computers and they do a bit of calculation. They don't play the thing by ear – take a stick or drop sand and read the palm. If I resign, whoever takes my place, whether it is Dr Toh or Dr Goh, will have to prove that he's not a stooge-man. And to do that he'll have to take a very firm line. In fact, much firmer, much harder – not just an apparently firm line – but concessions and a real hard line. And they decided it could not work.

QUESTION: And did you agree with this?

LEE: I think that's right. You see, Singapore knows all of us. We've been looking after Singapore now for nearly seven years. They know us as a very closely-knit group. They also know the individual idiosyncrasies or differences of style between the ministers. I do not think Singapore would believe that I resigned because I wanted to go back to the law and make money.

QUESTION: Then it was suggested, Sir, that you do resign, and you rejected this?

LEE: No, no. I didn't reject this. I was prepared to resign. But my colleagues could not accept it because they would be in a worse position. Mr Tan Siew Sin [Malaysian Finance Minister] openly said in Parliament that there can be no cooperation with Singapore as long as I am the prime minister of Singapore. Now this was said openly in Parliament. Do you think if I resigned, Singapore would believe that there would be cooperation, or that the former central government which has had its way and now has got its way [in this separation] – that they would keep quiet in the situation?

QUESTION: About the future of Singapore, Sir, as long as Confrontation continues, Singapore's economy suffers. If Confrontation does continue, how do you feel Singapore's economy can be assured?

LEE: Singapore has a very resilient, enterprising and resourceful lot of people. Everybody thought – and perhaps the Indonesians might have thought – that if they cut off their trade, chaps will be out in the streets hungry, and riot, and so on. But it never happened because they've got a great deal of grit and the will to survive and to work hard. We'll carry on. We'll survive.

> I do not think Singapore would believe that I resigned because I wanted to go back to the law and make money.

QUESTION: What do you think the chances are now, Sir, for the common market idea between Singapore and Malaysia?

LEE: Well, you know what the Agreement says. Annex "J", which were the provisions for a common market, has been cancelled … It was at Mr Tan Siew Sin's personal insistence that that clause be inserted in the Agreement. But the Tunku agreed to a clause that there will be either a joint council or committee for economic cooperation. I've told the Tunku that without economic cooperation, there will be growing troubles in Singapore … boys and girls passing out from schools, more than there are jobs for them. And the situation would be a bit less stable, a bit more volatile, and the bases will be that much more rickety. The whole thing is interwoven. I was glad that the Tunku assured me that he understood very clearly that there was a clear nexus between defence and security, and commerce or trade and industry. But we'll have to go slow. There must be a thaw first, because over the last one and a half years so many things have happened: attitudes have sort of hardened. We just want to take it easy for a while, and common sense, logic, the relentlessness of economics, must prevail.

It is the accepted wisdom now that Singapore's expulsion from Malaysia was the single most important factor in making Singaporeans want to put in the extra effort to succeed as an independent country. No one was more determined to lead them and prove the critics wrong than Lee Kuan Yew himself. Below are extracts of a fighting speech he made at the Sree Narayana Mission in Sembawang on September 12, 1965, just over a month into independence, to rally the people for the task ahead.

# On our own – but we will succeed

We will set the example. This country belongs to all of us. We made this country from nothing, from mud-flats. It is man, human skills, human effort which made this possible. You came, you worked – for yourselves, yes. But in the process, your forefathers and my forefathers who came here: we built this civilisation.

It is one of the few cities in Asia where you can get anything you want. You pick up the telephone: it works; and it not only works internally. You can pick up the telephone and speak to Delhi, London, Tokyo, Canberra – anywhere you want. Do you think you can do that just by shouting slogans? You can get any kind of cuisine you want, any meal. European food? You can get the best in any of the hotels in town. Chinese food? What kind do you like? There is Cantonese, Hokkien and Teochew. Indian food? There are South Indian, North Indian: anything you like. Malay food? You like Sumatran food, *nasi padang*? Where else in the world can you get this?

And I say, we will progress. I was sad not because Singapore was going to suffer: no. I was sad because by this separation, we could not help millions, several millions of our own people, our own countrymen – in Malaya, in Sabah and Sarawak – to progress with us. That was why I was sad. We could not help them any more. They have now got to help themselves. They have got to throw up their own leaders and they have got to take a stand. We cannot interfere.

Here in Singapore, in ten years, Geylang Serai will be another and better Queenstown [Singapore's first modern high-rise housing estate] – all the shacks will be demolished. I say that for Singapore because I do not think Singapore is boasting when it says it can do it. It will do it. But do you think in ten years the kampongs in Malaya will have Queenstowns? I do not think so. If you want that, then you must have the thrust, the ideas, the dynamism, the push, the tolerance of each other. That is why I was sad for

I was sad because by this separation, we could not help millions, several millions of our own people, our own countrymen – in Malaya, in Sabah and Sarawak – to progress with us.

Over 100 years ago, this was a mud-flat, swamp. Today, this is a modern city. Ten years from now, this will be a metropolis. Never fear!

them who are our people. Not just Chinese and Chinese, Indians and Indians. There are many Malays here.

Half of our police force comes from Malaya. Their families are left behind there. They will be quartered; they will live in modern civilised conditions. Their families will come down here and they will want to stay with them, and we will have to say "No" because there is a limit to what we can absorb. We have only got 224 square miles. It is a cruel thing to do this, but it has to be done. Some people wanted it this way. We could have helped them emerge, but it was not to be.

But I say to you: here we make the model multiracial society. This is not a country that belongs to any single community: it belongs to all of us. You helped build it; your fathers, your grandfathers helped build this. There was no naval base here, and it is not the British who built it. It was your labour, your father's labour which built that. My great grandfather came here and built. Yes, he came here looking for his fortune, but he stayed – my grandfather was born here.

Over 100 years ago, this was a mud-flat, swamp. Today, this is a modern city. Ten years from now, this will be a metropolis. Never fear!

Some people think that just because we are a small place, they can put the screws on us. It is not so easy. We are a small place in size and geography. But in the quality of the men, the administration, the organisation, the mettle in a people, the fibre … therefore, don't try. That is why we got booted out. If they could have just squeezed us like an orange and squeezed the juice out, I think the juice would have been squeezed out of us, and all the goodness would have been sucked away. But it was a bit harder, wasn't it? It was more like the durian. You try and squeeze it, your hand gets hurt. And so they say, "Right, throw out the durian." But inside the durian is a very useful ingredient, high protein … And we will progress.

Forty per cent – more than 40 per cent – of the purchasing power of the whole of Malaysia is in Singapore. We may be 20 per cent of the population of Malaysia, but purchasing power, the capacity to buy goods like microphones, clocks, drinks, fans, lights, television, transistors: the money is here because here they work. And if people do not want that 40 per cent – 44 per cent market – well, that is their business. We want to open the market with them, but if they do not want it we will make our own soap … We are buying soap from Petaling Jaya: Lux. You know, it is always advertised on TV: Lever Brothers. It is no harm. We buy the soap; it is good for them; it is good for us. We can make motorcars together for the whole of Malaysia. And never forget, if it came to the point then Lever Brothers may have to set up a soap factory here, because after all, nearly half the sales are in Singapore.

You ask *The Straits Times*: what percentage of their newspaper is sold in Singapore? True, we are only two million. But we have the highest literacy rate in the whole of Asia. Nearly half *The Straits Times*, if not more, is sold here. Here, everybody buys a copy. There, maybe one kampong buys one copy and everybody looks at it! It is true. We are talking now in terms of hard cash; the hard facts of life. And if people want to be hard to us, then we have got to survive. And we can keep this market to ourselves. But this is all shortsighted. Let us throw our eyes over the horizon into the future. What does Dr Ismail say: this will come back again. But under very different circumstances and different conditions.

You know and I know that anybody who says, "Go back to Malaysia on the same circumstances" will be called a lunatic, isn't it? We were patient; we were tolerant. We put up with it hoping that they would see the light. But we had to be firm. We could not give in. So as a result we are out.

History is a long process of attrition. It will go on. And one day, it will come back together. You see, this is not like a map and you can take a pair of scissors and cut off Singapore and then take it and paste it in the South Pacific and forget about it. It is not possible. This is part of the mainland of the continent of Asia. And that Causeway … You know, the Japanese blew it up; it was still rebuilt. It is part of history; and you are part of history. You are part of this place as much as I am. As much as Inche Othman Wok, my colleague, is. And I say that is the way it will be in the end.

I guarantee you this: there will be a constitution which we will get redrawn in which minority rights … You know, it is very easy in Singapore for people to stand up and if you talk, "One race, one language, one religion," there will be a lot of trouble, you know. We do not want that sort of thing. That is stupidity. So we are going to get the chief justices of India, Australia, New Zealand and a few others together with our own Chief Justice and a few of our eminent lawyers to draft "entrenched" clauses … You know, "entrenched": no government can just cancel the clauses. Entrenched, and enforceable.

If anybody thinks he is being discriminated against either for a flat or a scholarship or a job or for social welfare relief because of race or language or religion, he can go to the court, take out a writ; and if he proves that it was because of discrimination on the ground of race, language, religion or culture, then the court will have to enforce the constitution and ensure minority rights.

We are an equal society. You are equal to me; I am equal to you. Nobody is more equal than others. In some places, they say, "We are all equal." But what they mean is, they are more equal, you see – which makes life very difficult. But here, when we say "equal", we really mean it. We do not have to do it in Singapore. But we are thinking in terms of 100, 200 years, 1,000 years. You must help them emerge. And there is only one way: education and economic thrust.

> You are equal to me; I am equal to you. Nobody is more equal than others.

In this speech at a seminar on communism and democracy on April 28, 1971, Lee talked about the problems facing newly emerging countries like Singapore with no tradition of government and a shared sense of security. Worse, in Singapore's case, the number of people at the top who mattered was so small they could all fit into a Jumbo jet which if it crashed would mean the end of Singapore.

# Singapore's fate depends on 300 men

In your eleven and a half years in school, my colleagues and I have been trying to give you the kind of education which will prepare and equip you for your part in making Singapore a better place to live in. If you have done your share of work, including extracurricular activities, you will find life in Singapore a rewarding challenge.

For six years, 1959 to 1965, we planned on the basis of a Singapore which would be together with peninsular Malaya. On August 9, 1965, we became independent on our own. We had to make fundamental changes in our political, social and security policies. Most important of all, education had to be geared differently to prepare you for a different way of life. We knew that there would have to be considerable cooperation with Malaysia in security matters. But we knew economic cooperation would be slow in developing. There would be less and less entrepôt trade. We had to concentrate more on manufacturing, mostly for exports to world markets. So we would require fewer clerks and shopkeepers, but more technicians, engineers and executives.

I have put the subjects – politics, economics and security – in the order of their importance to your future. Without a stable political situation and a rational and realistic political leadership, there can be no economic development. There will be little investment in factories, few jobs, massive unemployment, and a dangerous internal security position. And without a thriving economy, you need not worry about defending the homes that you have not built, and the wealth that you have not created.

Unfortunately, this is too true of many new countries. The political situation is confused, and the support of a poorly educated people is sought by emotional appeals, not rational argument. After a new government is elected, its promises cannot be fulfilled. Then violence results from frustration.

New countries, like Singapore, face many problems: a lack of the instruments for effective government, not enough trained administrators, engineers, technicians, not enough capital, and scarce technological expertise. Further, poor organisation of whatever meagre trained manpower there is makes the problem worse. But given tough-minded and honest political leadership, these problems can be slowly overcome.

In established societies in the West, like Britain, a system of government has gone on unchanged, or changing only gradually, for over three centuries. They have developed a large number of people who, whilst fighting for their personal or sectional interests, have made a habit of putting their country's interests above their own. They have learned from experience that without national security and a strong economy, their own interests will be lost. They have developed the reflexes necessary for group survival as against individual survival. In times of grave crises – as in the Second World War – they joined to form a national government, sinking their party rivalries to make sure that the nation survived.

New countries do not have this continuing hard core of people to provide for continuity in political leadership. Worse, they do not even have enough political leaders with any understanding of their economy, and what to do to generate economic growth.

The first generation leaders are the men who had led their people to independence. They seldom understand that government means more than just mobilising mass support for protest against the injustices of colonialism. After independence they cannot deliver the goods. They had not learned about administration and economic growth. They are not able to create confidence in a government's promises and undertakings. They cannot get foreign investments to add to domestic capital. Then they have not educated and trained their young in the skills and disciplines which can use this capital and machinery to bring about the better life.

Worse, when the first generation leaders pass away, there are no successors who have made it a practice of placing the national interest above their own. They worry more about their own future than that of the people. They then decide to make provisions for their own personal future. The result is a further decline in the economy, and a deterioration of the social order.

In 1945 the British cut Singapore off from the Straits Settlements of Penang and Malacca, which were put into Malaya. The British wanted to hold us as a military base for as long as they could. They made a grave mistake. By 1963, when we rejoined Malaya in Malaysia, a way of government had become so established in Malaya that the changes and accommodation necessary, with Singapore as part of the Federation, were not acceptable to Malaysia.

We have to live with what has happened. Events which took place before you were born, in 1945, and again in 1948, when the Malayan Communist Party staged its revolt in an armed bid for power, have shaped our destiny. You have inherited the past, including the mistakes and the successes of those before you.

There is as yet no large core of people in Singapore to provide the reflexes for national, as against individual survival. We must make a habit of putting group interests first and personal interests next. Singaporeans must become more conscious that their very existence as a distinct people, in a poor and troubled Asia, depends upon our ability to react quickly and in unity to defend our interests.

There is as yet no large core of people in Singapore to provide the reflexes for national, as against individual survival.

Many are too young to remember how bad things were. They take for granted Singapore's orderly progress and continuing prosperity as the natural order of things. Those who do remember know that our present stability and prosperity have been built upon the cohesion, the determination and the planning of a small band of men. We are succeeding in creating a developed, albeit a small, nation. Singapore has a good chance of continuing to be a successful nation if the next generation understands the ingredients of success:

First, a stable political situation.

Second, a well-educated and trained population, ready to work and pay for what it wants.

Third, the ability to attract higher-level technology industries.

Fourth, better standards of life and in a cleaner, greener and more gracious Singapore.

Fifth, the competence of our defence forces to ensure that no one believes he can just walk in and take over what we have created and built.

The main burden of present planning and implementation rests on the shoulders of some 300 key persons. They include key men in the PAP, MPs and cadres who mobilise mass support and explain the need for policies even when they are temporarily inconvenient or against sectional interests. Outstanding men in civil service, the police, the armed forces, chairmen of statutory boards and their top administrators – they have worked the details of policies set by the government and seen to their implementation. These people come from poor and middle-class homes. They come from different language schools. Singapore is a meritocracy. And these men have risen to the top by their own merit, hard work and high performance. Together they are a closely knit and coordinated hard core. If all the 300 were to crash in one Jumbo jet, then Singapore will disintegrate. That shows how small the base is for our leadership in politics, economics and security. We have to, and we will, enlarge this base, enlarging the number of key digits.

It is strange, but true, that the fate of millions often turns around the quality, strength and foresight of the key digits in a country. They decide whether a country gains cohesion and strength in orderly progress, or disintegrates and degenerates into chaos.

In the Second World War, Winston Churchill and a small group of men around him gave a whole nation the courage and resolution to fight against insurmountable odds. He triumphed and Britain triumphed. Today, in Britain, a new generation of leaders is trying to find a similar formula for national unity and collective endeavour, for her position in the top league of major developed nations under vastly changed world conditions. This leadership consists of several men of ability and determination. But they must also have the capacity to inspire their people to unite for a national cause, to place trade union and sectional interests second to national interests.

De Gaulle succeeded in remaking France into a coherent nation after the shambles of defeat in the Second World War. The dissension between bickering political parties in the years from 1945 to 1958 resulted in the unhappy spectacle of unstable and short-lived coalition governments, with no long-term or consistent policies. Finally they were near civil war, as they got embroiled in Algeria for the sake of one million white French-

*If all the 300 were to crash in one Jumbo jet, then Singapore will disintegrate. That shows how small the base is for our leadership in politics, economics and security.*

Algerians. The recovery to the prosperity and progress France now enjoys owes a great deal to de Gaulle, his leadership, and the group of leaders around him who, even now after de Gaulle, chart the destiny of France.

Let me explain one special feature about Singapore. Our population is mixed. Even the majority community, 76 per cent Chinese, is composed of different groups: the older generation are dialect-speaking. Then we have the Chinese-educated and the English-educated. Next, we have Malays, Indians, Ceylonese and Eurasians. They have different languages, religions and cultures. It is not easy to get these various groups to see politics alike. But the government has to reconcile different views and get people to support policies to further the interests of all.

There can be few places in the world where it is necessary for senior Cabinet ministers to read three sets of newspapers every morning, one in Malay, two in Chinese and three in English. In the past few months, a Malay newspaper has been talking of nothing but Malay problems, and advocating "bumiputra" policies. One Chinese newspaper, on the other hand, has been playing up pro-Chinese communist news, and working up Chinese language issues. It is worth noting that this newspaper does not do this in its Malaysian edition. But the line taken by this paper has forced the other major Chinese paper to compete in drumming up chauvinistic and xenophobic sentiments. The English press, particularly one English language newspaper, financed by capital from obscure sources nominally from Hongkong, has been playing upon "with-it"-ism – permissiveness in sex, drugs and dress styles. On National Service, whilst giving lip-service support, this newspaper worked up a campaign to fault it on every count. These three newspapers set off three different pulls in three contrary directions. Unless checked, they will tear Singapore society asunder. Any government of Singapore that does not keep these divisive and disruptive activities in check is guilty of dereliction of duty.

We must get the next generation on to more common ground to build their future upon. We must give our children roots in their own language and culture, and also the widest common ground through a second language, on which all can compete equally.

Singapore's civil service is widely acknowledged as one of the best in the world – modern, efficient and clean. Much of the credit must go to Lee and his colleagues for providing the much-needed leadership, especially in the early years. In this speech at the opening of the Civil Service Political Study Centre on August 15, 1959, Lee spoke about the political challenge for civil servants.

# The trouble with the civil service

For several years, two of your ministers and I have been discussing the problems which a democratic socialist party, committed to a dynamic social programme, will have to face when it assumes power in Singapore. And one of these problems is the civil service through which we have to translate our policies. These two ministers were then your colleagues. They know the civil service as well as any one of you, for no one can accuse Dr Goh Keng Swee or Mr K.M. Byrne of not knowing the civil service in which they have spent the greater part of their lives.

I myself am not altogether ignorant of the persons who make up the higher echelon of the civil service. Many of you were my contemporaries in school, in Raffles College and, later, in England. It is because we understood the good qualities and the weaknesses of our civil service that we have anticipated fairly accurately the problems that would face us when we assumed office. We debated then the possibility of making the civil service politically alert and alive to the great changes that were taking place and the even more tremendous changes that will take place in the pattern of governments in Asia.

But although Dr Goh, Mr Byrne and I share a great deal in common with you in our educational background – the schools we went to, the colleges we attended, the courses that we took, the examinations that we passed – yet a great deal has happened since we left college. Since then we went through different social experiences, looked upon the same world through different looking glasses and saw different things. And in the end we began to think in different concepts and talk a different language, the concepts of political revolution and the language of the masses.

There were two causes which made people like Dr Goh and Mr Byrne change from quiet senior civil servants to articulate mass leaders. One is their innate character. The other is the social-political experience of the last 18 years since the Japanese invasion. And this Civil Service Study Centre is, in part, an attempt to telescope into a study course the main elements of the political and social forces which caused the postwar revolutions in Asia. If nothing else, you will at least understand what was the genesis of the forces that have shaken the British Raj under which nearly all of you were recruited, and under which you were guaranteed a lifetime of service with a pension at the end.

Some of you may be bewildered and perplexed by what you may consider the impatience with which we are asking for things to be done. If so, then I hope that at the end of your course in this Study Centre, if you do not share our impatience, you will at least understand it. You will at least appreciate why we consider it so vital, if the democratic state is to survive, for the democratic machinery to be in tune with the temper of the people and tempo of political change in the rest of Asia.

Whether an administration functions efficiently and smoothly in the interests of the people as a whole or in the interests of a small section of the people, depends upon the policies of the ministers. But it is your responsibility to make sure that there is an efficient civil service.

If you look around you in Southeast Asia you may be disturbed by the phenomena of newly independent countries passing from the first phase of democratic constitutions into military or semi-military dictatorships. Pakistan, Indonesia and Burma are grim reminders to us that the democratic state is not something which will look after itself just by the setting up of a democratic constitution. There are many reasons why in Southeast Asian countries like Pakistan, Indonesia and Burma the democratic system has broken down, and why in India and Ceylon it has, relatively speaking, succeeded. One of the reasons is that both in India and in Ceylon they had the administrators to run the machine of the democratic system. India had more civil servants than Pakistan. In Ceylon they had a long time to build up their civil service. And so, despite all the stresses and strains of racial religions and linguistic classes between Tamils and Sinhalese, Buddhists and Hindus, the administration did not collapse.

We cannot pretend to be as fortunately placed in respect of the civil service as the Indian government was when it became independent. But we are certainly in a much better position than the Indonesians who were practically without any civil service when they took over from the Dutch. For the Dutch did not believe that the Indonesians should be taught how to govern themselves.

My theme to you today is simply this: You and I have a vested interest in the survival of the democratic state. We the elected ministers have to work through you and with you to translate our plan and policies into reality. You should give of your best in the service of our people. Whatever your views on socialism, capitalism, liberalism, communism, whether they be progressive or conservative, your task and mine for the next five years are exactly the same: that is, to demonstrate that the democratic system can produce results. It is in our interest to show that under the system of "one-man-one-vote" there can be an honest and efficient government which works through an efficient administration in the interests of the people.

If we do not do our best, then we have only ourselves to blame when the people lose faith, not just in you, the public service, and in us, the democratic political leadership,

*Some of you may be bewildered and perplexed by what you may consider the impatience with which we are asking for things to be done.*

but also in the democratic system of which you and I are working parts. And when they lose faith, then they will look for alternative forms of government. And let us never forget that the communists are only too ready to offer the people more drastic alternatives in social revolution than the democratic system of government. It is our duty to see that the people are never confronted with such an alternative of despair.

I am confident that if only we can convey to you the tremendous challenge to the existing system that is posed by the expansion of the communist bloc and the communist revolution in China, and in particular the MCP [Malayan Communist Party] in Malaya, you will respond to the urgency of the task. The mass of the people are not concerned with legal and constitutional forms and niceties. They are not interested in the theory of the separation of powers and the purpose and function of a politically neutral public service under such a constitution. As far as they are concerned, in May 1959 they had a form of government under which if they exercised their vote, they would be able to elect their own government. And so they did elect their own government in order that there might be a better world for them and their children. If the future is not better, either because of the stupidities of elected ministers or the inadequacies of the civil servants, then at the end of the five-year term the people are hardly likely to believe either in the political party that they have elected or the political system that they have inherited.

The social revolution did not begin nor does it end with Malayanisation of the public service. For civil servants this was the most significant aspect of the social revolution that took place in Malaya: the expulsion of the expatriate European from positions of executive control in the civil service and your subsequent elevation to such positions. Some of you, like Dr Goh and Mr Byrne, played your part in the fight to remove an unjust system, but all benefited from the work and sacrifice of those who did, and the fight for fairness and equality to the English-educated elite in the civil service is over. But, as far as the mass of the people are concerned, their fight for fairness and equality is just beginning. Having got rid of colonial domination, and elected their own leaders to direct their own civil service, they want to see the beginning of their social revolution – more and better jobs, better houses for their families, schools for their children and the prospect of an even better future in a more just and equal society.

If the Civil Service Study Centre achieves nothing else but the awakening of your minds to problems which you may have overlooked before, if it opens your minds to political riders which you had formerly regarded from purely administrative eyes as tiresome problems, then it would have succeeded.

We know that the majority of civil servants are loyal and honest to the service – that you are prepared to do your share of work for what the state has promised you in return. But more than that, I am confident that if you could only see through the placid surface of constitutional change in Singapore to the revolutionary forces that are contending for supremacy beneath the constitutional façade, competing for the power to transform society after their own political philosophies and ideologies, then you will become as anxious as we are to bring about a more equal and just society within the framework of the democratic system and as quickly as possible. For there is no other way to preserve what we consider

> Let us never forget that the communists are only too ready to offer the people more drastic alternatives in social revolution than the democratic system of government.

good in the past other than by exorcising all that was bad in it. To do that in a situation where the mass of the people demand rapid and immediate results means tremendous burdens have to be carried, both by the political leadership and the administrative machinery. The purpose of this Study Centre is not only to stimulate your mind but also to inform you of the acute problems which confront any popularly elected government in a revolutionary situation. Most of these are problems that face the whole region. Once the problems have been posed to you, you will be the better able to help us work out the solutions to them, by making the administration more sensitive and responsive to the needs and moods of the people.

In formally declaring this Centre open, I ask you – having defined and analysed the problems that confront us – to join us in this task to work more effectively together in establishing a secure and healthy base for democratic institutions through which we hope to establish a liberal, just and happy society.

Lee set very high standards for his administration and did not pull his punches whenever he encountered sloppiness and incompetence. In this speech to senior civil servants at Victoria Theatre on September 20, 1965, he related how he found some wanting.

# Make sure every button works

Every morning the driver has instructions to take that telephone and to test-dial it. I want to make sure that when I want it and I pick it up, it is working. And that is what I want this government to do.

I caught a whole Works Brigade group. There was a slight drizzle and they all went into a house and disappeared. One hour after the drizzle, I looked around; I couldn't find them. I summoned them. Commander came out. Commander called the chaps out. They were all angry with the commander, not knowing what it was all about. Why were they disturbed in this way? Probably they were having a quiet game of cards. Finally, they took a count after a very leisurely line-up; six more missing. So chaps went around looking for them. The next day, the Director of the Works Brigade and that camp commandant turned up. And I put one big douche of cold water. So they woke up …

You know, I will not tolerate this. I went to a government bungalow the other day and I pressed the button and nothing happened. And I went to the kitchen and I told my son, "Press the button now" and he pressed and nothing happened. And I wondered how it was. Succeeding families had been living there – prominent government ministers and officers – without that being put right. I just don't understand. And the following day, all buttons worked.

Now, if I may explain that to you in a graphic way. When you have a button, there must be a purpose. When you click it, the light goes off. So that is what it is for. When you want the light on, you make sure you click it and it is on.

I have now, perforce – because I am travelling from place to place, looking after more than just my own ministry – to have a telephone in my car, which is something I dislike intensely. In my office, there is only one telephone, and I don't like three telephones to be buzzing around. And I don't allow them to buzz because it drives you crackers to have four, five telephones buzzing. And my telephones only show one light and a dull thud, and at any one time, I talk to only one person, and I flick on and off at will, which chap is priority, which chap waits. But you know, every morning the driver has instructions to take that telephone and to test-dial it. I want to make sure that when I want it and I pick it up, it is working. And that is what I want this government to do.

I have been to other places. I have visited about 50 different countries and been a guest of about 50 different governments. And you form impressions of these places. Some of them you leave with an abiding impression that this place is going to hum and spin like a top. I have been to such places, and I say "Well, this works!" Now, I can't tell you the places where it hasn't worked because I want to be friends with all countries. But I'll tell you about what happened in Jakarta since, anyway, they are not my friends at the moment. But I wish them well and I hope one day, all will be well.

I was put in a VIP bungalow which had just been put right for another prime minister who had just visited the place. And that night, it rained. And you know, I heard *tong, tong, tong*. The servants, of which there was an abundance, knew exactly where the pails should be put. And there were five pails. And I felt very sad, because it occurred to me that perhaps there were no more people who found it worthwhile – with the rupiah soaring like that – to learn how to climb roofs and put tiles in place. It is not worth the while. The best thing is to buy this and sell that and do this and cut that and do something else; probably to steal the wire off the telephone and sell it.

And I wanted to close the door and I did not know it was hinged … You know these old Dutch doors; they have a hinge so that they stay in place even if the wind blows. And the hinge came off and with it plaster from the wall. So I was gravely embarrassed and I said, "I am very sorry." The man said, "No, no, no trouble at all. We will put it right." So we went out that morning and I came back that evening. And I went to look at it, to see whether it was all right. From a distance I thought "Oh, it seems all right." But there was no knob for the hinge any more. It was just wall. I went closer … They had put a piece of white paper, pasted it and whitewashed the white paper. No, no. Those who accompanied me on that mission will remember that that was true. And we sat down and we said, "My God, this is trouble."

Now, this place will never be like that if for no other reason than because the people have got a habit of working. But I tell you: "I don't want just that. I want to make sure that every button works. And even if you are using it only once in a while, please make sure every morning that it works. And if it doesn't when I happen to be around, then somebody is going to be in for a rough time because I do not want sloppiness.

I do not ask of you more than I am prepared to give myself. And I say, it does you no harm whatsoever just to make sure that the thing works. And don't be too kind. If you want to be kind to your people, to our people, then you have got to be firm; and at times, stern to those who have a duty to perform, to see that the duty is performed.

I have not the slightest doubt that this Civil Service, having gone through what it has in the last seven years, will be more than equal to the task. And what is more, every year, we are going to take the best in.

I am tired of having first class honours graduates coming out, doing a bit of dabbling in the Attorney-General's chambers … They get a bit of money, then they learn a bit of the law and learn how to practise and after three years, they go out into private practice,

> We sat down and we said, "My God, this is trouble."

I don't want second-raters and the third-raters in and first-class men out-fighting us, because that is a stupid way of running the country.

leaving the second class honours man … The second class honours man goes to court to prosecute a case and the man defending is a first class honours man. Now if the law of evidence is loaded against the prosecution plus brains of the defendant being loaded against the prosecution, then thieves, rogues and vagabonds get away. That is not my idea of good government.

You know, the British ran this place with their men. But then they ran a different system. They recruited from Britain and they offered rich rewards when they retired. A fellow retires at the early age of 50 – and some of them live till 85 and we are still paying them pensions, big pensions.

We meet a different situation now. I am working out with my colleagues – the Minister for Finance and the other officers – a scheme which will keep good men in the service. I don't want second-raters and the third-raters in and first-class men out-fighting us, because that is a stupid way of running the country. I want first-class men prosecuting. I don't mind a first-class man defending because if you have got a first-class man prosecuting and a good officer who has prepared his IPs, Investigation Papers, you will get a conviction. Particularly if you also have a good magistrate on the bench …

I have watched all this, and this will not do. I watched specialists leave the hospital until finally my wife had to go to Mount Alvernia Hospital to get a former government surgeon to do an operation. It is stupid. I want them inside – better than those outside. That way, this place will hum. And I want those who believe that joining the government service means automatically you are going up the ladder, to forget it. Not with this government.

Those who have got the vitality and the grit and the drive and can climb up that rope, well, he goes up. Those who are sluggish and worse, those who have got ability but think that they have done their life's work by just passing an examination and getting a good degree and now they have got in through the PSC and they are sitting back and not blotting their copy book and so by affluxion of time they will become head of the ministry – I say, forget it.

This speech is included here to show the extent to which Lee went to improve the civil service – in this case, its standard of writing. He had gathered the top brass of the administration to lecture them on the finer points of writing plain, simple English and to impress on them the importance of doing so. The speech was made at the Regional Language Centre on February 27, 1979.

# Clean, clear prose

Ladies and gentlemen,

You may wonder why I have taken the trouble of getting you all together this afternoon. I have asked ministers, ministers of state, permanent secretaries, deputy secretaries and everybody who has to do with the drafting of minutes, memoranda, Cabinet papers and other documents that go up to ministers, to be present. But this is only the tip of the iceberg. The problem is much graver lower down.

First, the genesis of our problem. From about 1955, language became a sensitive, emotional, political issue. You remember the Chinese middle school student riots and strikes of 1954–55. We have allowed the education system to develop in accordance with the choice of parents. We offered them four streams. I was on the Commission of members of the Legislative Assembly. We recommended this. It was a politically wise recommendation.

When the PAP took office in 1959, we decided to select students for university scholarships and for jobs on the basis of their ability. We tried to eliminate the advantage of language skills because of better home environment and to diminish the disadvantages of a poor command of the English language for those from the Chinese stream or the Malay stream. We therefore awarded higher weightage to subject performance and ignored linguistic skills – how did you do in your mathematics, physics, chemistry, biology? How much intelligence does a boy or girl have? It was the right decision. As a result, we did not have bright students stuck in lowly jobs, and gradually the move into the English language grew into a swell.

Now we have removed language and education as political issues. Now we can openly discuss language as an important instrument of communication. We have decided that English shall be our working language. The price we have paid for identifying talent in

*This is only the tip of the iceberg. The problem is much graver lower down.*

the way we did, was a lowering in the standards of both spoken and written English. It will take 10 to 20 years to make up for the omissions of the last 20 years.

I could have put into a five-page note what I am going to tell you. But it will not have the same impact. The spoken word is always stronger, more emotive, and commands attention. The written word requires a practised, educated mind to extract nuances of meaning.

What I want to discuss is the importance of simple, clear, written English. This is not simple. Dr Goh gives every officer whom he thinks is promising and whose minutes or papers are deficient in clarity, a paperback edition of Gowers' *Complete Plain Words*. It presupposes that the man who attempts to read the book has reached a certain level of literary competence. The book, written words – just as my memo if I had attempted one – cannot convey to you the emphasis, the importance, the urgency, unless the receiver is a trained reader. And in any case, human beings are never moved by written words. It is the spoken word that arouses them to action. Arthur Koestler rightly pointed out that if Hitler's speeches had been written, not spoken, the Germans would never have gone to war. Similarly, Sukarno in print did not make great sense. According to language specialists, in face-to-face communication, 40 per cent of meaning is conveyed by words; 60 per cent is conveyed through intonation, gestures, the facial expressions.

The spoken language is better learned early; then you will have fluency. However, my thesis is that the written language can be learned and mastered at any age in life without much disadvantage. It is learned fastest when your written mistakes are pointed out to you by a teacher, friend, or senior officer who corrects you. That was the way I learned. When I was at school my compositions were marked. When my children were in school they simply got grades for their written work. Their teachers had so many essays that they never attempted to correct the compositions. This has contributed to our present deplorable situation.

I want to convince you, first, of the importance of clear, written communication; second, that you can master it, if you apply yourself. The use of words, the choice and arrangement of words in accordance with generally accepted rules of grammar, syntax and usage can accurately convey ideas from one mind to another. It can be mastered, even though you are not an Englishman. Then we will spend the rest of this afternoon discussing how we can help each other to master it. If I persuade you to want to master the skills in written English, then this meeting will have been successful.

When I was a law student I learned that every word, every sentence, has three possible meanings: what the speaker intends it to mean, what the hearer understands it to mean, and what it is commonly understood to mean. So when a coded message is sent in a telegram, the sender knows what he means, the receiver knows exactly what is meant, the ordinary person reading it can make no sense of it at all. When you write notes, minutes or memoranda, do not write in code, so that only those privy to your thoughts can understand. Write so simply that any other officer who knows nothing of the subject can still understand you. To do this, avoid confusion and give words their ordinary meanings.

Arthur Koestler rightly pointed out that if Hitler's speeches had been written, not spoken, the Germans would never have gone to war.

Our biggest obstacle to better English is shyness. It is a psychological barrier. Nobody likes to stop and ask, "Please, what does that mean?" or "Please tell me, where have I gone wrong?" To pretend to know when you don't know is abysmal folly. Then we begin to take in each other's mistakes and repeat them. We recycle and reinforce these mistakes, compounding our problems. Of course, this happens not just with us. It is worldwide. The Americans use English words and give meanings to them, never so intended by the British. Finally its usage becomes established. There are four times as many Americans as Britishers. They produce so many more books, films, and TV features that the American meaning of these words has overwhelmed the English.

But let us discuss simpler problems that confront us. The facility to express yourself in a written language is yet another facet or manifestation of your ability, plus application and discipline. It is a fallacy to believe that because it is the English language, the Englishman has a natural advantage in writing it. It is not so. He has a natural advantage in speaking the language because he spoke it as a child, but not in writing it. It has nothing to do with race. You are not born with a language. You learn it.

It is the same with Chinese. You have very able Englishmen like Giles and Wade who knew Chinese more profoundly than I think any one of us here. They spent their lifetime mastering the mysteries of the language. So Winstedt compiled the first Malay-English dictionary. And when I started learning Bahasa Indonesia, the Indonesian consul-general in 1957 presented me with an Indonesian-English dictionary by T. Wittermans, a Dutchman. And so Americans – whether they are of Dutch, French, German, Swedish, Italian, African, Japanese, or Chinese descent – born and bred in America suffer from no disability in their written English.

First, you must want to achieve it. I want you to, because without effective written communication within the government, there will be misunderstanding and confusion. Every passing year we shall more and more assess the worth of officers for their language competence. We cannot afford to overlook language incompetence. We ignored language competence in the past because it was too difficult a problem. It would have been unfair to those from the non-English medium universities. Now that Nanyang University is teaching in English we cannot afford to tolerate slipshod writing without grievous results. This is the price we have had to pay for inadequate bilingualism. However, those who have made it to university and the top echelons of the public service have no excuse for not being able to master the written language.

Let me just give a few recent illustrations of writing so sloppy that I had to seek clarification of their meanings:

First item: "With increasing urbanisation and industrialisation, we will require continued assistance particularly in the technological and managerial fields." I asked myself, "What have I missed in this? What has the first part about urbanisation and industrialisation to do with the second part about continued assistance? Why do we need more assistance particularly in technological and managerial skills because of increasing urbanisation and industrialisation?" It is a *non sequitur*. We need technological and managerial assistance anyway. The first part does not lead to the second part.

> It is a fallacy to believe that because it is the English language, the Englishman has a natural advantage in writing it.

Next time impress me with the simple way you get your ideas across to me.

Item from the Ministry of Education: "(It is necessary to study) the correlation between language aptitude, intelligence and values and attitudes to ensure that the various echelons of leaders are not only effectively bilingual but also of the desirable calibre." I read it over and over again. It made no sense. This is gibberish. I inquired and I was told, well, they were trying to find out how language ability and intelligence should influence the methods for instilling good social values and attitudes. Well, then say so. But somebody wanted to impress me by dressing up his ideas in many important words. Next time impress me with the simple way you get your ideas across to me.

Next item: "France is the fourth major industrial country in Europe after West Germany, Britain and Italy." Calculating backwards and forwards, I decided France cannot be the fourth. I queried. The reply was that France was fourth in terms of number of industrial workers. Now, China probably has the largest number of industrial workers in the world. In some factories they may have 14,000 workers when a similar factory in America would have 4,000. Does that make China the first industrial country in the world?

Item from the Ministry of Foreign Affairs, on North-South relations: "The Third World has the stamina to sustain pressure for the Common Fund. Progress will probably be incremental with acceleration possible if moderation prevails." Now what does this mean? By "incremental" the officer meant "slow". "Slow", I understand, but "acceleration possible", I do not.

If we do not make a determined effort to change, the process of government will slow down. It will snarl up. I have noted this steady deterioration over the last 20 years. I want to reverse it. If we start with those at the top, we can achieve a dramatic improvement in two years, provided the effort is made. Now I want to discuss how we can do it.

Let me explain my problems over learning languages so that you will know that you are not alone. When I made my first speech in Hokkien in 1961 during the Hong Lim by-elections, the children in China Street hooted with derision and contempt. I was unintelligible. I was talking gibberish. They laughed and jeered at me. I was in no mood for laughter. I could not give up. I just had to make myself understood. I could not, like David Marshall, get an interpreter – I would have lost. I had a Hokkien teacher follow me. He knew what I wanted to say. The ideas were there.

Let me emphasise this point. Before you can put ideas into words, you must have ideas. Otherwise, you are attempting the impossible. My ideas were there. My problem was how to say it in Hokkien. So my teacher would listen to what I had said in Mandarin. He knew what I wanted to say. The next day he showed me where I had gone wrong and how I could express myself. I made rapid progress.

Over successive election campaigns I reached higher and higher plateaux. He and I worked out this method. He would listen to me. Before I made my speech at a major place, I would first go to a minor function, a small street corner rally or a rural community centre gathering. There I would practise. My teacher would listen. He noted down my mistakes. My ideas he gathered from my Mandarin and my English speeches. He polished up my Hokkien, gave me new words and phrases, told me where I'd expressed myself wrongly so I made progress. If I had pretended I knew, or I had been shy to ask, I would have got nowhere.

The written English we want is clean, clear prose. I choose my words carefully – not elegant, not stylish, just clean, clear prose. It means simplifying, polishing and tightening.

I do not think the correct script that I have seen circulated of my Chap Goh Mei speech gives you an accurate impression of the effort required. I made the speech off the cuff. In that way I sensed the mood of the gathering and pitched my thoughts on a note and in a way which made my listeners receptive. Then it had to go into print. I had to pencil it through, to tighten, to clarify, so that in written form it would be clear and clean. Remember: That which is written without much effort is seldom read with much pleasure. The more the pleasure, you can assume, as a rule of thumb, the greater the effort.

So do not be ashamed that you have got to learn. I pencilled through my answers to the *Asian Wall Street Journal*. It was 45 minutes of questions and answers on tape. I took one hour and 30 minutes to pencil through. And yet when I reread it in the newspapers, I noticed a grammatical error, an obvious one, which I should have corrected. So this needs discipline.

So when you send me or send your minister a minute or a memo, or a draft that has to be published, like the President's Address, do not try to impress by big words – impress by the clarity of your ideas. Then I am impressed. I speak as a practitioner. If I had not been able to reduce complex ideas into simple words and project them vividly for mass understanding, I would not be here today. The communists simplified ideas into slogans to sway people's feelings, win people's hearts and settle people's minds, to get the people to move in directions which would have done us harm. I had to check and to counter them. I learned fast. The first thing I had to do was to express ideas in simple words.

How do you learn to do this? CSSDI [Civil Service Staff Development Institute] has only two trained persons who can help. There is Mr Roger Bell here, under the Commonwealth Fund for Technical Cooperation, and Miss Teo, who is also acting as my projectionist. That is the sum total of our teaching talent. This problem is similar to what we face in the joint campus. There we have about 1,800 English stream/Chinese stream students. Even those from the English stream suffer from poor English. There are about 600 from the Chinese stream, only 30 per cent with adequate English. Their teaching resources are stretched to the limit. The only way is for the students to teach each other. Those who know must help those who do not.

My experience is that attending courses helps but not as much as lessons tailored for you. You have written a memo. Somebody runs through it and points out your errors: "You could have said it this way." "This is an error." "This can be broken into two sentences, a full-stop here, a different phrase there." In other words, superiors and peers and even subordinates who spot errors should be encouraged to point them out. My PAs point out my mistakes; I tell them to. When going through a draft three or four times I am concentrating on and amending the meaning. So I miss the consequential mistakes in grammar. My PA who puts up a clean draft is not so hypnotised and by rereading the

That which is written without much effort is seldom read with much pleasure. The more the pleasure, you can assume, as a rule of thumb, the greater the effort.

phrases, spots these errors and sidelines them. I tick the corrections off, indicating "Yes, incorporate." If I do not do that, I will make more mistakes.

Let us discuss how to improve, how to teach each other. Of course the ideal is to get one instructor for one person. One Miss Teo can probably cope with four officers. In six months to a year, the four officers should show dramatic improvement. You have the ability. The problem is applying this ability to mastering grammatical roles and the meanings of words, and using them to put your ideas across. You did not learn it in school thoroughly enough. It will be painful at the start, but it has to be done. In short, how do we maximise teaching resources, by what methods? I want a free discussion on how we can help each other because there just is not the staff to teach everyone.

Three final examples on how urgent the problem is, from two papers coming before Cabinet on Thursday. The first is a very well written paper; the other badly written. But even the well written paper contained a repetitious phrase which confused me. Because it was well written I thought the repeated words must be there to convey a special meaning I did not see.

"If the basis of valuation is to be on a basis other than open market value as evidenced by sales, arbitrariness and protracted litigation would occur, thus tarnishing the credibility of government machinery." I ran my eye back over the opening words. I had to query: Do we lose anything if we dropped the words "to be on a basis" before "other" – "If the basis of valuation is other than open market value …" Answer came back – "No meaning is lost." And this was in a well written paper.

I will read extracts from the other paper. The writer had to explain why we must set up an institute. I read the paper and found it disjointed. It made no sense in parts. So I reread it. Let me read one part: "The need for such services is made more acute as at present, there is no technical agency offering consultancy services in occupational safety and health." I asked, "What's happening as at present? Why 'as at present'?" What the officer meant was: "There is acute need because there is no department which offers advice on occupational safety and health." We have taken in each other's mistakes. He had constantly read "as at present", "as of yesterday", "as of tomorrow", so he just stuffed in three unnecessary words – "as at present".

Next extract: "He recommended that a central autonomous body be set up to give clear direction, to coordinate and to strengthen Singapore's industrial safety and health efforts, to service industry and protect valuable manpower." I asked, "What is it we are going to do?" If the officer has no ability, I will be wasting my time. But he has ability. What he wants is sufficient application, to know the rules, to try and achieve the simple. And this is not simple.

There is such a thing as a language environment. Ours is a bad one. Those of you who have come back from a long stay in a good English-speaking environment would have felt the shock when reading *The Straits Times* on returning. I spent a month in Vancouver in October 1968. Then I went on to Harvard in Boston. For one month I read the papers in Vancouver. They were not much better than *The Straits Times*. They had one million people, English-speaking. But there was no sparkle in their pages. The contrast

> There is such a thing as a language environment. Ours is a bad one.

in Harvard was dazzling. From the undergraduate paper, *The Harvard Crimson*, to the *Boston Globe* to the *New York Times* to the *Washington Post*, every page crackled with novel ideas smartly presented. Powerful minds had ordered those words. Ideas had been thought out and dressed in clean, clear prose. They were from the best trained minds of an English-speaking population of 220 million!

Let us try to do better. We are not doing justice to ourselves. If you do not have the ability I would not be spending my time here. I know the ability is there; it has just not been trained to use the written word correctly and concisely. And it is not too late to start the training now. It is not possible to conduct the business of government by talking to each other with the help of gesticulation. You have to write it down. And it must be complete, clear and unambiguous.

I have discussed this with Head of Civil Service and PS (Prime Minister's Office). Dr Goh Keng Swee has sent his promising Mindef staff for training in batches of ten. They have improved. I believe if officers are prepared to point out each other's mistakes, those who know can help those who do not. It does not mean that the person who does not know is the lesser mind. It is not the case. If he had concentrated on learning the use of the written word in school, he would have developed the skills. How do we do it, gentlemen? I want to hear you.

> Every page crackled with novel ideas smartly presented. Powerful minds had ordered those words. Ideas had been thought out and dressed in clean, clear prose.

# How much is a good minister worth?

My generation of political leaders have become dinosaurs, an extinct breed of men who
went into politics because of the passion of their convictions. The problem now is a
simple one: How to select younger leaders when the conditions that had motivated the
old guards to sacrifice promising prospects of a good life for a political cause no longer
obtain in a completely different social climate. This change in climate is inevitable with
economic progress and a change in social values.

My generation of
political leaders
have become
dinosaurs, an
extinct breed of
men who went
into politics
because of the
passion of their
convictions.

In the '60s and '70s, as prime minister, I responded to this problem by a gradual
increase in pay to reduce the big gap with the private sector. But in the 1980s it no longer
worked. So in 1984 I decided to target ministers' salaries at 80 per cent of their private
sector counterparts.

I've spent 40 years trying to select men for big jobs – ministers, civil servants, statutory
boards' chairmen. So I've gone through many systems, spoken to many CEOs, how did
they select. Finally, I decided that Shell had the best system of them all, and the
government switched from 40 attributes to three, which they called "helicopter qualities",
which they have implemented and they are able to judge their executives worldwide and
grade them for helicopter qualities. What are they? Powers of analysis; logical grasp of
the facts; concentration on the basic points, extracting the principles. You score high
marks in mathematics, you've got it. But that's not enough. There are brilliant
mathematicians but they make poor executives. They must have a sense of reality of
what is possible. But if you are just realistic, you become pedestrian, plebeian, you will
fail. Therefore you must be able to soar above the reality and say, "This is also possible" –
a sense of imagination.

Then Shell has evolved certain other attributes – leadership and dynamism – a natural
ability that drives a person on and drives the people around him to make the effort. The
two psychologists who worked this out are Professor Muller, a Dutchman, and a Van

Lennep, whom I met because I was interested some 15 years ago. These qualities are really inborn. You can develop knowledge but if you haven't got them, you haven't got them, including the ability to be a good interviewer. Have you got that capacity to see through a person? Listen to his voice, hear what his words are saying but look him in the eye, watch his face muscle and you'll know that he is actually thinking the opposite. A good interviewer does that.

So, the first premise that I worked with is that, yes, they are interchangeable. But you must interchange them at an age when they are still flexible because the older you grow, the more set you are in your ways, then the less able you are to take on a new career.

I had to choose men from all sources and it was an extremely difficult job as the economy took off. In actual practice, my formula of 80 per cent did not work because income tax returns came for last year. By the time the Finance Ministry and the Public Services Division had adjusted them and worked it out into the salary scales and made sure that everybody's relativity was worked out, there was another one or two years, and so we were two to three years late. By which time, because we went through a buoyant period, private sector went on another 20 to 30 per cent. Under the new system the only lag will be because the income tax returns are late and analysis and review will only take another year, so it's two years behind time …

One corporate chief who was head of a think-tank some 15 years ago passed a scathing judgement on British Cabinet ministers – that of the 20-odd Cabinet ministers, he doubted if three would be CEOs of British corporations. Who's responsible for that? They are. They created that climate of opinion where so much hypocrisy exists and the public believes, yes, it's glory. Therefore, you do your job for the country. You end up with what they now call "sleaze". I spent a few days flipping through the English Sunday newspapers and they are just full of it. Contact men. You want to meet the minister? Give me sterling pounds 40,000 a year as a retainer, I'll arrange a dinner. But it's commonplace in Britain, where it never was. It only used to be Americans who did that. But hypocrisy has led to that same position.

Then, you know, the memoirs that people have written – Bob Hawke has a highly controversial, colourful piece. But of course it's not in the same class as Margaret Thatcher when it comes to pounds. Harper Collins paid her sterling pounds 2.5 million. That's an American publisher, and the London *Sunday Times* paid her, just for serial rights, a few million pounds.

For the past four years since I stepped down as prime minister, I've been studying the external economy and Singapore's place. Prime Minister wanted me to brainstorm and look ahead. I came to the conclusion that unless there was a major upset in peace and stability, which is not very likely for the next 10 years and probably for the next 15 and maybe even 20 years for this generation, this region is going to boom because it is taking off. It started off with the Korean War in the 1950s when the United States built up Japan. Then the Vietnam War – the United States had to source their supplies from Southeast Asia. From Japan, the industrialisation went to Korea, to Taiwan, to Hongkong, to Singapore. The Plaza Agreement in 1985 pushed up the yen so the Japanese had to

One corporate chief who was head of a think-tank some 15 years ago passed a scathing judgment on British Cabinet ministers – that of the 20-odd Cabinet ministers, he doubted if three would be CEOs of British corporations.

relocate their industries at the lower end. Then the Americans put pressure on the Koreans and on the Taiwanese and on us and pushed our currency up, so we in turn had to relocate. And now there is a web of cross-investments right across the Pacific, the western end. Unless we are fools and start going to war with each other, we are all going to boom.

## Why PAP ministers are sought after

The corporate world in Singapore knows that PAP MPs have been carefully selected. A PAP MPship is like a good housekeeping seal, a hallmark of character and integrity that adds value to a person. I instituted the practice. If you look through the MP lists from 1955 onwards, you will find that in 1955 we had two barbers, two postmen, clerks. But they were unionists, they were not ordinary people. But with rising standards, every election term, I had to move with the higher educational levels of the voters. This is a demanding electorate. Everybody strives to get up to the highest he can of the education ladder. And he wants somebody who is better than him to represent him. He doesn't want somebody he can talk down to.

So these people, PAP MPs, are sought after. But let me assure the House that the government enforces strict rules to prevent influence-peddling for the benefit of any person or company. But for that, Singapore will be just another of the governments in the Third World, which we are not. And it is important that we remain different because that is an enormous economic capital for us. Lose that and we may lose about 30 per cent of the rationale why we are different and why we attract different kinds of investments.

But I have had to recognise, and I have told the Prime Minister, you can't fight this. Now, a powerful wave has swept up our young and some of our not-so-young. There is an eagerness, almost anxiety, that they miss the escalator that is moving up and that can carry them to golden opportunities. And in fairness to the young, I will add this, with almost a touch of nostalgia for older and better times – it has swept up part of the older generation too. Because the old guards, they don't just die away. In Hollywood movies, you walk into the sunset and music and clouds. But in real life you live on, you become a little bit more infirm, you need medical treatment, and you have needs to meet. For example, Dr Goh Keng Swee. Recently he resigned from the Board of the Government Investment Corporation in order to avoid conflict of interest situations with the GIC when he advises several financial institutions on investments in Singapore and abroad which may also be of interest to GIC fund managers. That's quite a shift in the world. It's as if I suddenly decided that I'll join Henry Kissinger Associates. And the rewards are in, for key personnel, it's six, seven figures. Or I don't even have to leave Singapore. I could go back to Lee & Lee. I started the firm.

Recently, another distinguished former minister, old guard, part of my generation, was deputed by the retired MPs to see the Prime Minister, who told me of this. He was deputed to request that the commuted part of the pensions should be restored after twelve and a half years, as is the case with civil servants. It is not the case with ministers and MPs.

*In Hollywood movies, you walk into the sunset and music and clouds. But in real life you live on, you become a little bit more infirm, you need medical treatment, and you have needs to meet.*

I know what the old guards feel. They have seen me. I've said, "You know the rules of the game. You went in, these were the rules, these were the pensions." But they feel they've been short-changed because their fixed pensions have deprived them of their share in Singapore's growing prosperity. So the PM has to consider the matter. It is the same society, the same old guards who sacrificed. Some of them literally took their lives into their hands when they decided to stay with the PAP and not move over to Barisan in this House in 1961. But for several of them, the history of Singapore would be different and I would not be meeting and talking to you here. We may be in a completely different age and a different world.

Now, let me talk about the recruitment of ministers. In the last 14 years, only four ministers have been recruited from the private sector – Tony Tan from OCBC, Yeo Ning Hong from Beechams, Wong Kan Seng from Hewlett Packard and Yeo Cheow Tong from Le Blond. Indeed, the last two – Wong Kan Seng and Yeo Cheow Tong – were originally from the government: Kan Seng was in the Admin Service and Yeo Cheow Tong was in EDB. All other ministers have been recruited from the public sector, either the SAF or public institutions.

For the future, the position will be more difficult, and I believe the Prime Minister will be very fortunate if he can find one out of five ministers who will come from the private sector. He keeps on trying. He never gives up, he keeps on making friends, he keeps on inviting them to tea sessions. They keep on saying, "Next time, please, when my children are grown up." They could not afford to accept the offer he's made to them to become MPs and ministers of state or ministers.

## We must get a mix of ministers

Now, let me explain why it is important to have a mix of ministers from different backgrounds in the Cabinet. I'll give my personal experience and example.

Lim Kim San was and is a very practical man of business. He doesn't write speeches and books. Every time he has to make a speech I know it's a tremendous effort and he tells me, he says, "Must I make this speech?" I say, "Yes, you have to. It's your own constituency." But he has a lively, practical mind. That's why Singapore Press Holdings' profits have increased. He's gone in there, looked at the accounts, decided that the following changes will be made, costs will be cut, this will be amalgamated. And it has just jacked up profits, as I knew he would do.

We made him chairman of Housing and Development Board in 1960 when we formed HDB. It was crucial, life and death. If we failed, we would not be re-elected. This was the first year of office of PAP, remember? And there were a lot of zealous idealists who wanted to put theories into practice. One of them, a member of the PAP central executive committee, said, "We must be different from other builders. Other builders hire contractors who exploit workers. We will hire the workers direct, cut out the middleman, they'll be paid more and we'll be model employers."

Ong Eng Guan (Minister for National Development) ordered Lim Kim San to hire the construction workers direct. Kim San was nonplussed. He came to see me in my

*I believe the Prime Minister will be very fortunate if he can find one out of five ministers who will come from the private sector.*

So it is important for the PM to find younger generation Lim Kim Sans, people with different backgrounds who will sit down, cross-fertilise ideas, improve and sometimes block a plan which is theoretically marvellous but will not work out in practice.

office. He asked me a very simple question. He said, "Do you want me to build houses or do you want me to be an employer of construction workers?" He said, "If you want flats, then I know how flats are built. You leave it to me. I'll produce you the flats. If you ask me to hire workers, better look for another chairman."

"Let me explain," he said. "Every contractor has an elaborate supervisory system. He has his relatives. He has his trusted 'kepalas'. They in turn have each a gang and they know each person in that group and each person has got to produce results to deserve the pay. Now if I hire them all, including the 'kepalas' who don't know each other, you'll be lucky if you get half a flat for where you would have a flat." So I said, "Proceed!" All these ties of kinship and personal obligations ensured success. So I overruled Ong Eng Guan and he built the flats. One block was in my constituency, opposite the former Singapore Harbour Board Union House, Cantonment Road. It's still there. If that had not gone up, I may not have been re-elected because Nanyang University and all the Chinese middle school students targeted Tanjong Pagar to canvas against me. But they looked at the flat that was going up, they decided these little boys are not going to put up the flats, I was. That was why I came back to this House.

Later, I persuaded him to take part in the 1963 general elections and I made him Minister of National Development. On several occasions, his practical market approach to problems made a difference to the success of projects.

So it is important for the PM to find younger generation Lim Kim Sans, people with different backgrounds who will sit down, cross-fertilise ideas, improve and sometimes block a plan which is theoretically marvellous but will not work out in practice. It has a leavening effect. You need people with different backgrounds. Now if we keep to past practices, suppose we make no change, we just keep on tampering with the system, and every few years we come back here and have another long debate; I've had them every three, four, five years since 1972. Individuals in Singapore and corporate entities will flourish but Singapore will be depleted at its heart, at the core. And without this functioning core, you will not have your opportunities.

The Prime Minister is already 53, the Deputy Prime Minister is 43. This team will not last two election terms without considerable infusions of fresh blood. Three ministers have got two ministries each and ministers need 15 ministers of state as backups and they haven't got it. They've only got seven. And they need to be recruited in order that they learn on the job and become part of the team.

## The Singapore way works

If our solution – and I believe this one is a realistic solution and a sound one – works in five to ten years, the World Bank will again give us a citation as they did this year. And let me read what they said: "Not surprisingly, Singapore, which is widely perceived to have the region's most competent and upright bureaucracy, pays its bureaucrats best." When they use the word "bureaucracy", these are Americans, they mean ministers too. But they went on to say, "The monthly base salary of a full minister in Singapore ranges from US$13,800 to US$17,300, while a minister of state receives the equivalent of US$5,600 to US$7,600." They are saying, yes, it works.

I am pitting my judgement after 40 years in politics – and I've been in this chamber since 1955 – against all the arguments on the other side. I say this is necessary for Singapore. I say face up to the facts, get a good generation in, get the best of this generation. When it works, the World Bank will cite us again. You don't get cited because you are conventional, you follow other people. You become a model because you went against conventional wisdom and proved that they were wrong and you were right. And if we can keep honest, competent government, never mind about its being brilliant – that is a tremendous achievement.

Look at all the countries around us. They started off self-sacrificing revolutionaries – Vietnam, China. They went on long marches. Their friends died. Their families perished. Their systems are now corrupt. Their children are corrupt. We have not gone that way because we are realistic and we know adjustments have to be made. There is a price to be paid for hypocrisy. Ministers deal with billions of dollars in contracts. It is so easy. But when discovered, like Teh Cheang Wan [National Development Minister, suspected of corruption], he preferred death because he lost everything. In this society, you lose the respect of your friends and probably also of your relatives.

The fate of a country, when it's a matter of life and death, you throw up people who put personal considerations of safety and security and wealth aside. But that's when you have a revolutionary situation, when a whole people depend on the actions of a few. Now I believe if such a situation recurred again, some Singaporeans will again emerge and rise to the occasion.

So it is crucial when you have tranquil Singapore that you recognise that politics demands that extra of a person, a commitment to people and to ideals. You are not just doing a job. This is a vocation; not unlike the priesthood. You must feel for people, you must want to change society and make lives better. And if I had done that and got no satisfaction out of it, then I would be a fool doing it because I could have gone back to Lee & Lee umpteen years ago and ridden the boom and sat back, probably at least as rich as my brother or my two brothers – one is a doctor, another a lawyer. But why not? But somebody has to do this in order that they can prosper. And I am saying those who do this deserve not to be penalised or you will get nobody doing this.

## Will it change the name of the game?

Now, one journalist told me that there is some public concern that these higher salaries would change, and I quote him, "the name of the game and attract a different type of person with different motivations." It is possible that politically and socially uncommitted people from the higher management and professional brackets will be attracted to the idea of public office for this higher pay. I doubt it. But if it is so, and they can do better than the present ministers, they should come out and offer themselves as the alternative. That will be good for Singapore. Far better to have a credible alternative to the PAP than

One journalist told me that there is some public concern that these higher salaries would change, and I quote him, "the name of the game and attract a different type of person with different motivations."

the motley collection of lacklustre candidates put up by the Workers' Party, the Singapore Democratic Party, the National Solidarity Party, the Singapore People's Party and so on and so on and so on.

None of them has ever assembled a team remotely credible as an alternative government. Yes, they have got Mr Low Thia Khiang. He is a good MP. He looks after his constituency. But you need more than a good MP. To be a movement, to be a government, you must produce 15 men with the capability to run the government. I am not sure that a good MP can run a ministry. I am not passing derogatory remarks because being a teacher and being a public speaker, especially in Teochew, is a useful attribute. The PAP had plenty of that and they were very useful for campaigning. But at the end of the day you've got to sit down, look at the file, masses of figures, and zero in on the critical issues and say, "no, don't do that, do this".

If this salary formula can draw out higher quality men into politics, whatever their motivations, I say, let's have them. It's better than the opposition we now have. If we can get in opposition people of the calibre of the Nominated MPs, I say Singapore is better off. At least I respect them. I can join in the argument. The only one that I find worth listening to is Mr Low Thia Khiang. The others, I switch off. And I have asked the press. They say, yes, they also switch off, it's very difficult to put your earphones on. It is a sad commentary on the standard of Singapore opposition politics.

## What makes a good government

At the heart of the question is, what makes a good government? That is the core of the question. Can you have a good government without good men in charge of government? American liberals believe you can, that you can have a good system of government with proper separation of powers between the Executive, the Legislature and the Judiciary, plus checks and balances between them, regular tussles between Congress and the White House, and between the House of Representatives and the Senate in the US, and there will be good government even if weak or not so good men win elections and take charge. That's their belief.

My experience in Asia has led me to a different conclusion. To get good government, you must have good men in charge of government. I have observed in the last 40 years that even with a poor system of government, but with good strong men in charge, people get passable government with decent progress.

On the other hand, I have seen many ideal systems of government fail. Britain and France between them wrote over 80 constitutions for their different colonies. Nothing wrong with the constitution, with the institutions and the checks and the balances. But the societies did not have the leaders who could work those institutions, nor the men who respected those institutions. Furthermore, the esteem, the habits of obedience to a person because of his office, not because of his person, is something that takes generations to build into a people. But the leaders who inherited these constitutions were not equal to the job and their countries failed and their system collapsed in riots, in coups

*At the heart of the question is, what makes a good government? That is the core of the question.*

and in revolution. So every time I hear people criticising us. When we are successful, they say we are sterile. When you are not successful, they say look at the slums, look at the degradation, look at the filth. These are the wiseacres. We have got to live with the consequences of our actions and we are responsible for our own people and we take the right decisions for them.

You look at the old Philippines. The old Ceylon. The old East Pakistan and several others. I have been to these countries and places. When I went to Colombo for the first time in 1956 it was a better city than Singapore because Singapore had three and a half years of Japanese Occupation and Colombo was the centre or HQ of Mountbatten's Southeast Asia command. And they had large sterling reserves. They had two universities. Before the war, a thick layer of educated talent. So if you believe what American liberals or British liberals used to say, then it ought to have flourished. But it didn't. One-man-one-vote led to the domination of the majority Sinhalese over the minority Tamils who were the active and intelligent fellows who worked hard and got themselves penalised. And English was out. They were educated in English. Sinhalese was in. They got quotas in two universities and now they have become fanatical Tigers. And the country will never be put together again. Somebody should have told them – change the system, loosen up, or break off. And looking back, I think the Tunku was wise. I offered a loosening up of the system. He said, "Clean cut, go your way." Had we stayed in, and I look at Colombo and Ceylon, or Sri Lanka, I mean changing names, sometimes maybe you deceive the gods, but I don't think you are deceiving the people who live in them. It makes no great difference to the tragedy that is being enacted. They failed because they had weak or wrong leaders, like the Philippines.

Singapore must get some of its best in each year's crop of graduates into government. When I say best, I don't mean just academic results. His 'O' levels, 'A' levels, university degree will only tell you his powers of analysis. That is only one-third of the helicopter quality. You've then got to assess him for his sense of reality, his imagination, his quality of leadership, his dynamism. But most of all, his character and his motivation, because the smarter a man is, the more harm he will do society.

But I also believe from my experience that Muller and Van Lennep are right, that at 21 the man is fully developed and you can discover what he is if you can test him assiduously enough. But by 30, 25 to 30, it's obvious what he is. You want men with good character, good mind, strong convictions. Without that Singapore won't make it. My problem is how do you do that when the booming economy is drawing them away?

## Forget conventional attitudes

I don't think we can afford to be inhibited by conventional attitudes. Now editors of our newspapers, when they were given copies of the White Paper, were surprised at the high earnings of the top men in the professions. My answer is, let's have these figures every year independently verified. IRAS is not cooking them up. We know how much people are earning. Let's have them. Under oath of secrecy, a group of men independent of the government and the IRAS can testify and verify.

*You want men with good character, good mind, strong convictions. Without that Singapore won't make it. My problem is how do you do that when the booming economy is drawing them away?*

In any team, like a football team, there are strikers who score the goals. But he needs his fullback, his wings, to feed the ball in to him. And he has to decide how to deploy them.

But what is it we are arguing about? The government today – ministers, cabinet ministers, parliamentary secretaries, political secretaries, everybody – cost $17 million a year. That's the cost, working a GDP of nearly $90 billion growing at 8 per cent, which is $6 billion a year. You have wrong men here, it's a disaster. There's no way a prime minister can argue that any minister can walk out of his cabinet and get this kind of salary. Just as there was no way when I was a partner of a legal firm and we shared profits in a certain ratio that any partner could walk out and get that share.

In any team, like a football team, there are strikers who score the goals. But he needs his fullback, his wings, to feed the ball in to him. And he has to decide how to deploy them. And really we are arguing at the end of the day whether by this formula which over three, four years will pay them $5 million more, the whole lot … What on earth are we arguing about? Except people get envious and they say, "Oh well, they should really be sacrificing."

If it were possible to carry on with the system, I would be in favour of carrying on with what I've been familiar with. But I know it is not possible. I have explained to you on my recent journey how I met three persons and immediately the changed circumstances became obvious to me. And I came back reinforced in my belief that the Prime Minister has to move and move quickly.

Let me take Members now to a different angle to this problem. He is like the conductor of an orchestra. He's got to make great music. I think the best metaphor or simile for a prime minister is really a conductor; in other words, he's got to know something about each instrument; what sounds they make, where they come in. When I started my job I didn't, but I had to learn it quickly – home affairs, finance. You have to have stability. You have to have an economy going. You've got to have labour relations, education, national development, housing, the whole lot. You must know how to deploy your resources, not just money, but manpower. So at any one time a certain sector is the important one and I send my best minister and my best permanent secretary to support him to make sure that that sector succeeds.

And he's got to decide how he rewards them. Now he needs people in his team who are goal-scorers. Any team, to win, must have sharpshooters. In other words, in government, you must have ideas, you must create new concepts, build new institutions and be innovators and not simply followers of orthodoxy.

## Let's blow a few trumpets

I'll give you a few examples from the past. It's like blowing the trumpet of the old guards, but maybe they deserve to have a few trumpets blown on their behalf.

We had massive unemployment in 1959, more than 14 per cent. Every year 55,000 to 60,000 children were born, 4 per cent of our population growth. Quite frightening, beyond the capability of Singapore to solve it. We knew industrialisation was the only way. Commerce could not solve it. United Nations sent a team; Dr Albert Winsemius [the late Dutch economist who was Singapore's economic adviser for nearly 25 years until 1984] was their leader. He recommended, yes, proceed. Dr Goh discussed it with him and I discussed it with Dr Goh and met him and said, "Right, let's try EDB [Economic Development Board] and sell Singapore to America, to Europe, to Japan as a manufacturing centre." Nobody had an EDB in the world. We formed one.

And we put in our brightest and our best. You want to know why you've got good jobs, why you are doing well? Because every year I allowed Dr Goh to have his pick. Of course you make mistakes. Some are bright, but they are not much use, lacking judgement. But within a couple of years you know who's got judgement, sense of reality, imagination, leadership, dynamism, plus the powers of analysis. They served Singapore well. We innovated.

He created that organisation and he also built up Jurong, invested hundreds of millions of dollars, built roads, canals, filled up the earth, put in power, put in water. And for five years it was empty, capital lying fallow. We watched it, wringing our hands because two years in Malaysia, the finance minister of Malaysia squeezed us and didn't give us pioneer certificates. We nearly failed.

But we did not fail. I gave Dr Goh the best permanent secretary we had – Hon Sui Sen – to help him. He became chairman of EDB and he was a very good judge of people and persons, a very quiet man, didn't make great speeches, but understood people and knew who could do what. He built up a good team and from EDB sprang TDB (Trade Development Board), sprang DBS, because we had to build up the finances to help people start their industries. This is not administration, doing a job. This is entrepreneurship on the political stage, on a national scale. We changed the complexion of Singapore. You can bring him back to life and reward him?

In 1968, we were looking for ways to fill up our economy. Hon Sui Sen came to see me. He said, "Let's take a chance. Change our foreign exchange regulations. Release it." We were part of the sterling era. We had foreign exchange controls. He said, "Cancel it. Let's start the Asian Currency Unit. Collect all the dollars in the region, lend it to the world. We will be the link between New York closing and London opening."

I listened intently. I said, "Proceed." Took the Bills through. Today, Singapore is the third largest foreign exchange trading centre in the world, next to New York and London. We have also got a budding futures trading exchange in Simex. We have a great potential for growth and very high value-added. Can you thank Hon Sui Sen?

True, it wasn't all his idea. But he had the good sense to listen to people with ideas. So a Dutch banker called Van Oenen, who worked for Bank of America, who was a friend of Winsemius, said, "Try." But we made it work. Now, everybody wants to be a financial centre. We have overseas HQ. Kuala Lumpur immediately followed. We have no patent on it. They studied our laws. They upped the stakes. So we have to keep on innovating, moving ahead. You do that with a bunch of mediocrities?

I make no apologies for collecting the most talented team I could find. Without them, none of you would be enjoying life today in Singapore, including the reporters up there. I say this without any compunction. Who pays for all this? A Singapore economy which has been so finely tuned that it is able to take advantage of every opportunity that comes our way.

> I make no apologies for collecting the most talented team I could find. Without them, none of you would be enjoying life today in Singapore, including the reporters up there.

## This is political entrepreneurship

You want to know entrepreneurship? Without Dr Goh Keng Swee, there is no Singapore Armed Forces. He is the SAF. 1965 – we were suddenly independent. I said, "You are a corporal in the Singapore Volunteers. You know something about this. Better learn something more. Start it." He came back one day in February 1966 and he told me, "You know, we've got two battalions." And, you know, they were in Malaysia for two years. He said, "So, more than half the battalions are now Malaysian Malays."

So when one battalion came back from Sabah and the Malaysian Regiment refused to move out of their camp, they had to be put up at Farrer Park and they might have gone on riot or mutiny. So he came to see me. He said, "You have made me as if I am a British general in charge of troops, half of whom are Italians." So we worked day and night to sort that out so that we would have troops who are Singaporeans. Had we failed, I wouldn't be here to tell you this story. We got the Israelis, we studied the Swiss, we got an SAF that nobody believes is just for show.

But the most important entrepreneurship is really the structuring of Singapore. I was determined that before the soldier fights for Singapore he must have something to fight for. Each family must own their home. So I set out right from the word go against any opposition from any quarter to build up the Central Provident Fund. At each salary increase I pushed something into CPF and built up the home ownership programme that today gives 91 to 92 per cent who own their homes, which are going up in value year by year because the infrastructure is getting better, the economy is getting better and they are rising with it. So you can sell one five-room flat in Singapore and buy two bungalows in Perth. But before you do that, remember, your five-room will go up in price; your two bungalows there will be empty and will go down in price.

*It was Robin Hood but I succeeded in giving everybody their own home.*

I take this as a matter of fact. Things have to be done which are unpleasant. I changed the acquisition laws and cleared off compensation for sea frontages so that we could reclaim the land, then we've got East Coast Parkway. Fire sites – I reclaimed and acquired the right to acquire as of occupied status. It was Robin Hood but I succeeded in giving everybody their own home. Of course, not me alone, but the concepts, the planning, I make no bones, I took responsibility, and it has succeeded. I put in Medisave in place. I faced opposition in the Cabinet. Ministers came back from China and said, "Wonderful place. Everybody has got the same medical services and for free." I listened to this and I said, "Why do you believe this fairy tale?" I put 4, 5 per cent aside. I changed the minister and I put Mr Goh Chok Tong as Minister for Health. I said, "Implement this." And today we have our viable national health service which avoids waste, no buffet syndrome, but guarantees adequate support for everybody, adequate health.

The CPF [Central Provident Fund] also. Low interest rates, yes, but it has paid for all the infrastructure of our roads, bridges, airports, container ports, telecommunications, MRT, land reclamation. An ordinary group of people would think that up? If we didn't have the entrepreneurs, we would not be here. And look at all the housing estates. Public housing in Singapore is not an apology for slums. You go to Britain, you go to America

and vandalism and crime. Have you ever asked why it is different? Because from my own experience, as I went around on constituency tours in '62 and '63, I discovered there were grassroots organisations, *kompang* groups, Muslim mutual fund groups, clan associations, retailers' associations. I organised them and I made them community centres' management committees and they ran the place for themselves, for their community. From them I formed Citizens Consultative Committees, altered the face of Singapore. Then as we moved into the housing estates, the same experience. I said, "Start zone committees, residents' committees every five, ten blocks." So there is a nervous system of human beings transmitting messages, getting people together so that they know they are a community and not just anonymous individuals who shut their flat doors and live their own private lives …

Finally, let me put the issue very simply. I have been through this life and had I lived a different life in Lee & Lee, I would never have had this experience. Because I have gone through this, I say "do it". I am in a position to judge. I say I'm prepared to put my experience and my judgement against all the arguments the doubters can muster. In five to ten years, when it works and Singapore has got a good government, this formula will be accepted as conventional wisdom.

In five to ten years, when it works and Singapore has got a good government, this formula will be accepted as conventional wisdom.

What were the economic objectives of the PAP when it formed the government in 1959? Lee explained in this speech to the Rotary Club on February 24, 1960 that although the PAP was a revolutionary party determined to change the existing social order of the day, it would work with industry and business to increase prosperity for all, but with one important difference: at the end of the day, it would strive for a more just and equal distribution of opportunities for education and advancement.

# What I mean by a more just and equal society

A socialist believes that society as a whole will benefit, and there will be more happiness for more people, if all are given equal opportunities for education and advancement regardless of class or property.

I must confess to some hesitation in accepting your invitation to address the Rotary Club. I had, when the PAP was in the opposition, declined your invitation. You will forgive me if I explain why I declined in the past, and what considerations prompted me to accept on this occasion.

The political beliefs of the PAP would not normally commend themselves to a group of people who are successful in a given order of society. By the very nature of your constitution, your members are those who have succeeded in life. According to Article 3, Section 2 of your constitution, which lists out the qualifications for active membership, it is clear that only those who have already made good, or who are most likely to succeed, are admitted into your fellowship. It was not unnatural to infer that your membership consists of people who, having done well under an existing social order, are satisfied with that social order and therefore extremely anxious that nobody should alter things in case they may not do so well under a new order. Not wanting to arouse more animosity from those who are not likely to be politically sympathetic to the PAP, I did not take advantage of the opportunity you offered me in the past to inflict my political views on your members. However, now that the PAP is the governing party, although you probably still do not agree with its political objectives, you may be interested to know what these objectives are.

A whole set of political principles and socialist beliefs have often been summed up in the PAP phrase, "a more just and equal society". By this, the PAP does not mean that all men are equal and will be rewarded equally. Men are not born equal in either physical or mental capacity. But a socialist believes that society as a whole will benefit, and there will be more happiness for more people if all are given equal opportunities for education and advancement regardless of class or property. It therefore follows that even under the new social order there will be some men who are more successful than others, but with this fundamental distinction, that they have become more successful after free and equal competition and effort.

It is by now generally accepted that a revolution has taken place and is still taking place throughout Asia, and that Malaya and Singapore are a part of this revolution. The revolution began before the PAP was ever thought of, but the PAP hopes to endure to see this revolution through to its fulfilment. Last year, before we assumed power, we expounded the theme of the social revolution. It is useful briefly to summarise what is meant by the social revolution in the context of Singapore in the immediate future.

The term "revolution" connotes a sudden and far-reaching change, a major break in the continuity of development, and the qualifying adjective "social" denotes the emphasis we give to this aspect of the revolution. A recasting of the social order is a far more important characteristic of a revolution than a change in the political situation by the use of violence. A revolution occurs when the ruling class cannot, and the ruled class will not, continue the old system. And so in the proper sense of the word, the former colonial empires in Asia have all undergone a revolution. The upper class of the colonial society could not, and the lower class would not, continue the old colonial system, and so a sudden and far-reaching change has overtaken the social orders of these countries. But this is only the first stage of a revolution, a continuous and continuing process of change, the end result of which is very far from settled, and only brief glimpses are possible of the shape of things to come.

The PAP is basically a revolutionary and not a reformist movement, and the social and economic forces which threw the PAP into power have not altered. Although it is not practical or possible to have a profound change of social organisation by a major shift in the relations between social classes because of the entrepôt island economy of Singapore, it is nevertheless important to remember that the have-nots, who form the mass of the workers – the underprivileged, the underemployed and the unemployed, are seeking a change in their position in society. A government of Singapore which represents these urges cannot modify its social programme or political principles without forfeiting the trust and confidence that have been placed upon it by the underprivileged. Such a government can trim its economic programme to fit into the limitations of an entrepôt island economy only if a strenuous effort is made to redress the economic balance by a redistribution of social and economic benefits.

For some time before a revolution, the ruling class finds itself in a position of a minority, isolated from the rest of society. If the British colonial government had persisted in maintaining its domination, then the machinery of the state would have given way and there might well have been a complete breakdown by a concerted attack of revolutionary forces from the ground. We have been saved this inconvenience by Britain's policy of withdrawal from positions of open colonial rule in Asia.

> The revolution began before the PAP was ever thought of, but the PAP hopes to endure to see this revolution through to its fulfilment.

344

After the last elections, the political system was changed, and power passed from the last legitimate colonial government to the first representative government of the people, and thus the gulf between the rulers and ruled is for the time being bridged. It is important that, if the gulf is not to reappear, the government's social and political policies must reflect the sentiments and attitudes of the revolutionary mass from whence it draws its strength. But at the same time a revolutionary government which attempts in Singapore to upset the structure of the island entrepôt economy will only bring deprivations upon the people and disaster upon itself. So the art of government in Singapore, through this phase of its history, can be summed up in two guiding principles: first, to work to the best advantage the present entrepôt economy whilst slowly encouraging industrial expansion, partly through government capital but largely through private investment; and second, to satisfy the revolutionary urge of the mass of the people for a fundamental change in the relationship between social classes, and this in spite of the fact that there can be no fundamental change in the immediate future in the economic base of the society. An orthodox Marxist will say that is an impossible task. The business of the PAP, as a democratic socialist party, is to show that, difficult and delicate a task though it may be, it can be done. However, in the long run, it is inevitable that the economic base itself will be transformed.

Those who feared disastrous changes in the economic system with the advent of a PAP government, but who are now agreeably surprised that the world has not collapsed, should remember that our political opponents were frequently not truthful. Never at any time did we consider, or pretend, that drastic changes in economic relationships were possible in our given set of political circumstances. It is not for lack of revolutionary purpose that we have not made more drastic changes in the relationships of the social classes. It is more the appreciation of the limitations of the Singapore situation which has predetermined our line of policy and action. Basically we are not reformists. We do not believe that changes in the social order can be accomplished through the alteration of some particular institution, activity or condition.

But, revolution aside, the first business of a government is to govern firmly and wisely in the interests of the whole community. And the interests of the whole community in our entrepôt situation require the active participation and cooperation of the managerial and professional elite. We understand how you came to be leaders of trade and commerce, or captains of industry, or distinguished yourselves in the professions. We also understand that the incentives were material ones. And since it is our desire to see that the system continues to operate effectively and efficiently, it must necessarily follow that we are prepared to allow the old incentives to continue.

The problem of the government is how best to utilise the existing social order to produce the maximum results, and the only intervention envisaged in the next four years is a redistribution of the results of the fruits of the economy. At the end of our tenure of office, it is our intention that there should be more equality of opportunity for education and advancement. To fulfil this intention will require a tremendous expenditure of the

> Those who feared disastrous changes in the economic system with the advent of a PAP government, but who are now agreeably surprised that the world has not collapsed, should remember that our political opponents were frequently not truthful.

national revenue on education, expenditure which cannot be made unless there is an expansion of the whole economy. And if there is one overriding problem which we must resolve, it is that of creating sufficient expansion in the economy: (1) to provide the jobs for a growing population, and (2) to provide the revenue to educate the younger half of that growing population.

The curious position now is that a socialist government is entrusted with the responsibility for industrial expansion and development in what is still essentially a free enterprise and capitalist system. To the extent that you help the expansion of that system, you will have the support of the government. And the message that I would like to leave with you this evening is this: regardless of our differing political beliefs, we have enough common ground, albeit for different reasons, in desiring a rapid economic and industrial development in the immediate future. For this phase of our social revolution, the better business you do, the more things you buy and sell to and from Singapore, the more shops and factories that you open, the happier we are. Where we might not be in agreement is the way in which we hope to spread the benefits of prosperity. But so long as your activity not only assures your own prosperity but the prosperity of the whole community, you will find the apparatus of the government willing and ready to assist you in your enterprise.

Being competitive, equipping the population with the right skills, identifying niche industries for the economy: these are questions Lee thought about early on in Singapore's progress up the industrialisation ladder. In this speech to Singapore Polytechnic students on January 5, 1972, he dwelt on the skill level required in a modern economy.

# Endless arguments over how many engineers to produce

They did not produce engineers, technicians who could have run the Volta High Dam for them.

I think the lesson for us has already been learned dramatically in the last few years: over 30,000 redundancies in the British bases and those who found jobs were people who were skilled technicians or otherwise useful production digits. Those who did not get jobs were the clerks, the storekeepers and the unskilled. Recently, the Singapore Traction Company had a traumatic ending and the lesson was again learned. Those who were skilled, those who drove the buses, could get jobs. But right up till now, there are nearly a thousand people who were clerks, timekeepers, storekeepers still waiting for suitable appointments.

But I do not want to leave you with the impression that development means that you become a skilled technician or an industrial worker. It depends upon your country's level of development and the planning and programme with which a government, given that kind of society, can take its people forward to the next phase.

I think what is universally true of most new countries is that they inherited a system of education, which very often was carried on unthinkingly by indigenous independent governments for five, ten years with very serious repercussions for their own development and resulting in unemployment.

You find countries like Ghana, for instance, which in West Africa has been exposed to contacts with the West for several centuries. Before the British, there were the Danes and the early slave traders. They are people who have acquired quite a degree of sophistication, the ones on the coast as distinct from the ones in the hinterland. And the British have produced among them Greek scholars, Latin scholars. The Vice-Chancellor of the University of Ghana was a Greek and Latin scholar. But they did not produce engineers, technicians who could have run the Volta High Dam for them. Or perhaps more relevant, they did not produce good scientists in agriculture, in fertilisers, in how to make their economy move from a relatively simple agricultural pastoral base into something more productive.

At the other end of the scale are India and Pakistan – highly developed educational sectors, universities well-endowed and prepared. They got into a position where they were producing unemployed engineers because the economic development was not keeping pace with the engineers they were producing – the net result being, their doctors migrated. As British doctors migrated to America for better jobs, Indians and Pakistanis filled British hospitals.

And the lesson is that everybody has got to take a hardheaded look at his own position, decide in the context of his own base, the potential that it has, what is the next step forward. And for us the most important single thing is, of course, the development of our human resources, exploiting our strategic location which makes possible certain industries.

I often read in the newspapers – "leading sectors". And you ask an economist or an adviser to a bank, "Tell me what is going to be the leading sector. The sectors which are going to be the ones which will provide you with the most advanced progress in the next few years." He says, "Well, that is the whole secret. If you can identify the leading sectors then you are a success." And the Japanese did exactly that. Every few years, they decide which are the sectors they are going to concentrate on. And they threw all their resources into capturing a commanding position in that sector. Probably in the early '60s, they decided that transistors, cameras were leading sectors – great growth potential for export. And they had a group of men in their Ministry for Economic Development and Trade who explored the world markets, did their sums properly and decided that these were the areas of great potential growth for exports and these were the specific fields in which they would allocate their zaibatsus (their big combines), and they spread out the attacks – you will do radios, you will do cameras, you will do communications equipment, and so on. And by the early, middle '60s, they must have decided that small cars was going to be a leading sector, together with colour television. And they poured in a great deal of money, resources. Net result – they captured the small car market not only in America but in countries like Switzerland and the whole of Southeast Asia. So too with colour television.

It is no use, if you are a less developed country, to decide that you are going to compete in the leading sectors which the Japanese decided are leading sectors. Because that is not your level of economic growth and you have not got those skills. You have not reached that point where you can compete against them.

If you ask me what are our leading sectors I would be hard put to tell you, because apart from a few obvious ones – ship-repairing, oil exploration, rigging equipment, servicing of aircraft – there are few other areas which we think we should make a break in. And therefore, if it were possible, we should be training our boys and girls in school, in either secondary technical schools or vocational institutes, and preparing them for the kinds of jobs that will be available in industry, either in the polytechnic or in the university. But often it is wiser not to say what you think are the leading sectors until they have arrived, until you have succeeded.

It is no use, if you are a less developed country, to decide that you are going to compete in the leading sectors which the Japanese decided are leading sectors.

I would say, broadly, all those items of manufacture which contain a very high added skill value which, for instance, would be the case in a small country like Switzerland. But with this one differential – that the Swiss have to reach the sea through long and difficult rail and road journeys, whereas we have got the sea right on our doorstep. But with that variation, that differential, all the things which they can do and which their high labour cost now makes them less competitive. They will either have to farm out – export – their factories to countries like Singapore where our population can be trained to acquire the skills to produce the same finished products of quality in a minimum of time, to retain their markets whilst they move on to a higher stage, or they will lose out. So you can go through the whole of the export market of the Swiss. Or if you like, take the Swiss and the West Germans together and see which items would be suitable for us. But even after we are fairly confident that certain areas are likely to develop, like lenses, cameras, geodetic instruments for survey, photo-grammatic instruments – a great deal of skilled labour, which means from very low value raw material you introduce machines and labour and skills, to produce something of high added quality, you then work backwards and say, "What do you train our students to do?" But even when you have done that, you are still not in a position to say, "Well, we shall train these students, say, 50 per cent or 30 per cent of our students, in the working of quartz and crystals." Because there are open market forces, international trade factors which decide whether or not we will be able to expand in those sectors. Therefore, it means that you have got to give your students a broad base – basic disciplines – and leave the specialisation really at a very much later stage and possibly even on the factory floor. This means added cost in education.

By way of illustration, I asked for some figures from the Education Ministry, and they said to train an ordinary academic secondary school student costs us $300 per year, per student. If you send that student into a secondary technical stream, that means he goes twice a week to some vocational centre where he learns to do technical drawing and metalwork, woodwork and so on, the cost goes up to about $420. You send that student to a vocational institute, his cost is $800 a year, which is more than twice that of the ordinary secondary academic school student because of the benches he requires, the space he occupies, the equipment that he must be supplied with. And you can, of course, take this on to tertiary institutions and, broadly speaking, we are subsidising the cost of an engineering student, the subsidy per year is between $4,000 and $5,000, and the subsidy on the polytechnic student is anywhere between $2,000 and $3,000 a year.

Therefore, we are presented with a very difficult problem of priorities. How many engineers do you produce for a certain number of skilled workers and technicians? We have had endless arguments on the matter. If you follow the American system then you produce probably one engineer for every two technicians, which is what they do in America. And the engineers do the jobs of the technicians. They are more highly paid. Or you take the British system where there is a clear demarcation between the pragmatic trained technician and the engineer who is the theorist-cum-pragmatist, and the ratio works out to about 8 to 1.

*How many engineers do you produce for a certain number of skilled workers and technicians? We have had endless arguments on the matter.*

**349**

Well, for the time being, we have decided, not because we are convinced that the British system is right but because of the economics of it, that it is probably more sensible for us to produce more technicians than engineers. And as we progress, we will have to review this. In five years, we make a review and another ten years, we make a second review. And the guiding factors will be what is the best possible way, given our peculiar, almost unique circumstances, to mobilise our manpower and train them.

And for the time being, as far as we can project figures and the investment rates and export opportunities into the next five years, we simply cannot produce either enough engineers or enough technicians. Because we are unable not only to expand rapidly enough the training facilities that we have, also because there is a limit to how fast you can upgrade the skills of your population. And there is a final limit, however good your educational system, just to what levels you can go by training, teaching, jacking up standards, which means a large input of foreign management personnel, engineers and probably experienced technicians to make up, and also probably immigrant skilled workers.

By 1975, Singapore had already been classified as an intermediate country, no longer developing but not quite developed yet. It had been a decade of the highest economic growth for the country, but Lee was also concerned about whether it could make that qualitative leap into the First World. In this National Day Rally speech on August 17, 1975 at the National Theatre, he shared these concerns with the people: whether they had gone soft, whether they would always retain that drive and that capacity for hard work that had made the country do so well, so far.

# What's wrong with the Singapore worker

Unconsciously, we have entered into the free-spending consumer society of the West. Parents spoil their children. There are better clothes, better food, better housing. All the time their expectation goes up and up, believing that it is always going to be up the escalator.

The past decade was probably the most spectacular of all the ten years of Singapore's history. There had never been such rapid transformation in any ten years. The physical landscape changed with new buildings, new roads, flyovers, traffic jams, homes, new factories. Our GDP went up, at factor cost, nearly three times between 1965 and 1975. When we borrow from the World Bank or from the Asian Development Bank, there are no more soft loans. We are classified now as an intermediate country – not developed, not developing, but intermediate – and we pay the going market interest rate.

We seized every opportunity to develop as fast as we could because ten years ago, you will remember, there was massive unemployment – at least over 12 per cent. Ten years after, with the new standards of incomes, we have got ourselves into a different mood, the younger generation especially – people who were not old enough in 1965 to understand what hardship and unemployment meant. And they are truly a different generation. Expectations have gone up. Unconsciously, we have entered into the free-spending consumer society of the West. Parents spoil their children. There are better clothes, better food, better housing. All the time their expectation goes up and up, believing that it is always going to be up the escalator.

If there were no oil crisis, the 1973 prices did not quadruple, the developed world did not take a nosedive and GNPs weren't down by 12 per cent, 13 per cent, 14 per cent in America and Japan, perhaps we could put up with this. But let me, by way of illustration, show you the changed attitudes which we cannot afford because the next five years will not be like the last five years. With oil prices five times what they were in 1974 and likely to go up this September by anywhere between 10 per cent, perhaps more – some papers talk about 30 per cent – we are not going to get the 10 per cent to 14 per cent real growth which we made in the years 1968 to 1973.

Recently, we mounted an exercise to recruit drivers for the Singapore Bus Service. You know that we have got to have more buses to have a good bus service, and you need good drivers. So we thought that the National Serviceman who had learned how to drive a three-ton truck should be offered the opportunity. So we mounted three recruitment exercises this year.

Ten years ago, if you had introduced a man into the Singapore Traction Company or into a Chinese bus company as a driver, he would have been happy to have given you his one month's salary as commission. We circularised the posts. About 800 National Servicemen went on ROD [Run Out Date, the date their full-time National Service ends] between January and July. About 500 turned up to listen to the opportunities we were offering them. SBS produced a colour brochure, "The Bus Way to a Secure Future" – with diagrams and pictures. And on the face of the brochure it said, "This is not a sales brochure which you receive every day. This is a career prospectus which took us months to prepare just for you." You know how many applied? Seven the first batch, 34 the second batch, 20 the third. You know how many are working now? One driver and three temporary conductors training to be drivers. Remarkable! Whilst training you are paid $11.60 per day, one year, as recruits. Then $12.80. This bewildered me. I chased up the Central Manpower Base. I said, "What are they doing? What marvellous jobs are they holding?" Because I got the monthly returns as to how many workers are retrenched, how many work permits issued. And I know that in the last 18 months since the retrenchment started, 30,000 workers have been retrenched, 70 per cent women and girls. But I just took this year, January to July; of the 7,500 retrenched, 4,800 – nearly 4,900 – were women. In those same seven months, we issued 11,500 work permits of which 4,400 were for women. It does not square up.

What happened to these National Servicemen? They had primary six and secondary two – the highest levels. Many of them were just sitting at home! Some had gone out into the reserves in January. Forty or 50 are still unemployed. They go in at 18; they finish at 20. They only have a class 3 for driving a three-ton truck. You have got to be 21 before you take a class 4 to drive a bus. Originally, in the second batch, eight went in. They were asked – whilst practising to drive a bus and waiting to reach the age of 21 to get a class 4 licence – to sell tickets. They said pai-sei (shy). They liked their passengers behind them and did not want to face each chap to sell a ticket. This is the new generation Singaporean.

If there had been no oil crisis, no problems in the West, we could perhaps put up with this. I ask parents whose instinctive response to their own hardship when they meet good times is to pamper their children, to remember that we are in for a less good time. It is always comfortable and easy to move into a higher standard of living. But I believe we are lucky if we make in the next five years – nobody can look beyond three to five years – somewhere from 3 per cent to 5 per cent, maybe with luck 6 per cent, growth in real terms.

I will give you another illustration. We had some workers doing training in Japan in miniature ball-bearings. After one month they said, "What's this? I am still doing the

Ten years ago, if you had introduced a man into the Singapore Traction Company or into a Chinese bus company as a driver, he would have been happy to have given you his one month's salary as commission.

same job." So the EDB went out to investigate why they were being held back. The answer was simple. This is a precision job and it had to be done to perfection. And they just did not know how important it is that even if you have only one, out of a group of 30 or 40 ball-bearings, which is not the right size, the wear and tear will be uneven and there will be not only damages to be paid; worse, the brand will lose its reputation and sales will go down.

It reminded me of an incident some 11 years ago when I was touring some Third World group of countries. There was this Chinese restaurant thousands of miles away from Singapore. A Singapore Chinese had opened a restaurant there and he invited the whole chartered aircraft to his restaurant for dinner. I said to him, "The food wasn't bad. Who is the cook?" He said, "Oh, it is a Singapore Chinese cook." I said, "What about the locals, can't they cook?" He laughed and said, "Well, you know, it is very difficult. You take the simple dish, *foo yong hai*. It is an omelette. You add some vegetables, you add some prawns, crab. But you show it to him three times and he says, 'I know.' But he doesn't know. I tell him, 'Watch again. You have got to add this amount of water to the egg so that it won't be too hard. Then you've got to have the vegetables sufficiently cooked but still crisp. Then you must add the right salt and pepper and sugar and other condiments.' He says, 'I know.' But it is not edible. You lose business."

We are like that: "Yes, I know," when in fact you don't know.

We are like that: "Yes, I know," when in fact you don't know.

The growth that we have made has carried us up to a pretty high level compared to what was, not compared to what the Japanese and the Europeans or the Americans have. And to make the next jump is a qualitative change. We made this first run-up by just starting from a low baseline – mopping up the unemployment, doing mostly assembly-line operations. Then we moved on to polishing lenses, making theodolites and balancing instruments and so on. This year, we are getting only about a third of the investments committed or promised compared to the number we had last year. But they are good investments – in precision engineering, aircraft spare parts, petrochemicals, pharmaceuticals. And it means training, skills. It means that if you want to do your children good, make sure they don't lose the work ethic. Whether it is the Confucian work ethic, whether it is the Hindu work ethic, whether it is the Muslim work ethic, whether it is the Protestant work ethic, if you don't work, you are not going to make the grade and no amount of wizardry on the part of the EDB or the Ministry of Finance is going to pull this one off.

In the last ten years we hitched a ride as the world bounced away at about 10 per cent a year growth in world trade up till 1973. It took a nosedive in 1974. It is not quite recovered in 1975. But we managed, with the momentum of eight years behind us, to ride through 1973 and 1974.

Now it is going to be different. The oil crisis, with prices quintupling, plus a further problem of getting a new regional balance established with the new governments in Vietnam, Laos and Cambodia, which in turn will depend on the balance of forces between America, the Soviet Union and China. It is going to take two years to know how the interaction of these world powers will be and, in particular, the contest for influence over the Indo-Chinese states. It means that cooperation in Asean in the economic and the political fields must become a sincere effort to try and accommodate each other, in order that by being a more cohesive group, we can deal with a group of countries with different political and economic systems on more or less equal terms.

It is the need to be realistic that is paramount. It is better for the government to take the 10th anniversary celebrations to cap the successes of the last ten years in undiluted self-congratulation. It is the easier way out but it is not the best way forward. We have done as well as we could possibly have done in the past ten years. To do as well as we can in the next five years, let us have no scales on our eyes. Let us face the world as we find it – as we find the other countries, as we will find ourselves. And if we are to overcome these problems, many of them will depend on our own internal thrust, the drive that we have got, the capacity to face up to our problems before they become too big and too unmanageable …

And I hope that we shall together make the next five years at least not less successfully than the last one and three-quarter years since we ran into the oil crisis. If it is no worse than what it has been and better than what it has actually been up till now, at the end of another five years we will be all right. But it requires that constant drive and that willingness to learn, to achieve and to be proud of what you are doing; not just minimum of effort, maximum of monetary rewards. That attitude will never take us into the industrial society.

Lee has spent a lifetime watching how other societies progress, what they have done which might work in Singapore, and what mistakes they have committed which should be avoided here. In this speech in 1981, made at the National Day Rally held at the National Theatre on August 16, 1981, he zeroed in on the concept of productivity which he believed held the key to understanding why some economies were more competitive than others.

# Who does Singapore Airlines belong to?

They don't like to go to the factory floor and soil their hands. They don't know what happens on the factory floor. So how can they order more efficient work?

It's a simple word, "productivity". But I have had to spend several years grappling with this problem, to seize hold of the meaning, the simple word, "productivity". It means you get more out of a workforce with the same working hours. How do you get more? By more capital investment per worker. That's how the Japanese have done it.

And in the Japanese factory, a motor factory – I read the comparison recently – 9,000 recommendations from the workers on how to improve the assembly line. And all they get is recognition – their photographs and acknowledgement. General Motors pays a few thousand dollars for each suggestion proposed, and they get 900 suggestions a year, of which half are adopted.

So you see the difference in the motivation of the worker. He is always thinking how he is going to do his job better. He is always making suggestions. It's not the manager who can think up these ideas because the managers are not manipulating the machines, they are not on the assembly line; it is the highly motivated and intelligent workers who then sit down with a group of three or four, either called QC [Quality Control] circles or zero-defect circles, and they work it out. And, of course, the management is also efficient.

Our graduates – and I have got quite a lot of feedback from the employers' associations which I met recently – have paper qualifications. They are good engineers, they are good economists. They don't like to go to the factory floor and soil their hands. They don't know what happens on the factory floor. So how can they order more efficient work? Our economics graduates have no idea of personnel management, human industrial relations – social science graduates, whole lot. And so the Singapore National Employers Federation and the German business group in their submissions to the National Productivity Board suggested that part of the training during vacation is to send them to the offices and the factories. And more important, to send their teachers – the assistant professors and the

355

professors – so that they will understand what is the product that they are expected to produce in the students, what is he supposed to perform. There is no dovetailing at the moment. And of course, all this should start from the schools – team spirit, teamwork – and this should start with the teachers.

My meeting with the American, German, Japanese, Singapore National Employers Federation (which I am told is a group of British, Japanese, Germans and others, including Singaporeans) was most instructive. The most disturbing facet of my discussion, reading their submission (this was a carefully considered, written submission), was that if we had to depend on Singapore entrepreneurs we would not have today's Singapore. It's a damning admission for me as prime minister to tell you this. But I think you should know that.

Rollei may have failed, but no Singapore firm could have run Rollei [the German camera company that set up shop in Singapore in 1971 and ran into trouble in the late 1970s], would have failed long time ago. We may have been traders, but we do not understand management. Our managers do not understand productivity. Otherwise how can I get a submission from the Chinese Chamber of Commerce telling me, "Yes, why should we confine CPF being managed by employers, to only big employers of 300 or more employees? We, small shopkeepers, can also handle it." I don't think they have the slightest clue what this is all about.

I want to read to you extracts of four of the submissions, good ones. They educated me, they instructed me. I chose them in alphabetical order: Americans, Germans, Japanese and the Singapore National Employers Federation – A, G, J, S – because otherwise they may be invidious.

## The American and German View

There is a certain candour about the Americans which makes them likeable, and they put this out in their press conference. I didn't see it in the newspapers. Newspapers should have printed this in bold type. Fifth point: "The Singapore government in its desire to provide for its citizens have developed wage policies and social programmes such as CPF, which causes a worker to feel his future and security is dependent on the government rather than the employer."

That's a very profound remark – "that the Singapore worker believes his future and his security is dependent on the government than the employer". Then says the American Business Council, which should have been in bolder type: "Employers do not invest in Singapore to provide jobs and welfare programmes for the Singaporeans. Enterprises must strive for reasonable profit and control costs to ensure a competitive position in the market place. If this is not achieved, bankruptcy or receivership will surely happen."

You see, common sense. They go right to the heart of the problem. Then they add, just by the way, they find the Singapore workers hardworking, positive, highly motivated but individualistic, like the Americans. So the Americans are not as critical as the Japanese are of our workers. But then the Americans are losing to the Japanese. But they point out, as the Germans point out, "Productivity Councils should also review conditions where

> The most disturbing facet of my discussion, reading their submission (this was a carefully considered, written submission), was that if we had to depend on Singapore entrepreneurs we would not have today's Singapore.

many salesgirls are non-productive – department stores, hotels, restaurants and similar establishments." The Germans made this point. He is a very shrewd man, Mr Puorroy. He says, "The Singapore paradox … it is well known throughout the world that the workers of Singapore are busy and industrious. One can easily see this when looking around the Kallang area – small marine wharves build ships with the highest skill. One finds this in any area where demand for performance matches the ability to perform and the worker concerned can identify with the fate of the enterprise involved."

Then he says, "Touring the shopping centres, factories, office buildings, one often observes that operators or clerks are not in the least interested in the fate of the enterprise; just chatting and being non-productive." He is a German, you know. He is writing to me in English. He says, "To be successful you must instil a certain high-fidelity, feeling in something. That means a sense of loyalty, a sense of trustworthiness – high-fidelity." And he puts it in an attractive and vivid way. He says, "Management's problem is that they should not forget that not only the brains and the hands but also the hearts of people should be working for the company." That's well put – not only brains and hands but get the workers' hearts.

## What the Japanese say

> On the anniversary of the company, they invited the workers to bring all their families to come and celebrate. Nobody came! The family is not interested in the future of the company.

That's exactly what the Japanese have been doing. So when I met them here in Singapore – this is the managing director, you know, of the company, employing some 3,500 workers. On the anniversary of the company, they invited the workers to bring all their families to come and celebrate. Nobody came! The family is not interested in the future of the company. So he said, "Why is this? Maybe it's the wrong format. So all right, Chinese New Year, we invited them. They all came. Well, that's progress." His worker gets married, he turns up for the worker's wedding. He is interested in the future of his worker. I will be hard put if you tell me to attend my workers' wedding because I see quite a number of them are young and I don't think I should be attending weddings, but this man did because this is what he does in Japan. And he says, "It's very strange, you know, I was not introduced to the father-in-law, the mother-in-law and so on. We just sat around." I said, "Well, you know, we inherited the British tradition and British bosses never attend the weddings of their workers. They were probably honoured but embarrassed and at a loss what to do."

But the heart of the worker, that's what productivity is about.

Let me go back to the American Business Council. It says, "We favour the Productivity Council. We favour a portion of the fund now with the CPF to be managed by the employer as an employee's pension and other benefit programmes." But they point out that what's lacking is practical work exposure for young people both secondary and university. And this applies to the educators as well. And that's what's wrong. We are turning out students, graduates, VITB, polytechnic students, who think that their moment of achievement has arrived when they get a diploma or their degree. And they all take pictures with their caps and gowns, and that's the summit of their career. But any American will tell you that's the foothill and you then begin the long climb up the mountain.

And the Americans made a valid point when they said that if a company can show that the majority of its workers do not want a union, must we have a union? And I say, no, I agree with you. If the union serves no function, out with it.

Now, let me go back to the German. He is a practical man. He says, "Never mind all these talks about campaigns and movements. What you want are special action, training, more training." What do you mean by "productivity"? And you must train people on techniques – how to achieve a job with less effort, less time, less defects. That means training. And why is he having so much difficulty getting money out of the Skills Development Fund? One committee dealing with hundreds of applications. And if we want to be a technological society, why is our transport system not geared for shift work? Because you don't install expensive equipment to run one shift. If you are going to install automated computerised equipment you want to run it 24 hours a day and get as much return as you can. In other words, your transport system should be geared to make it convenient for the workers to go into the second and third shifts. So he says, "Let's sit down, coordinate working hours, recommend training priorities, tool-making, for instance, statistics on national productivity." And he also points out the lack of realism amongst postgraduates and he thinks it can be avoided by holiday work.

But the most impressive to me is the Japanese Chamber of Commerce. Their philosophy is one that will ensure that they will always be there out in the forefront. It permeates every sentence. I just read you extracts. It says, "Firstly, enterprises should be continuously rejuvenated by ceaseless investments, as we are of the belief that in order to compete worldwide, industries must always keep up with advanced technology. If not, senility symptoms will occur and the vitality of the enterprise will vanish."

Second point: "An enterprise cannot exist only with machinery." It's Japanese English. But, never mind, you understand what it means – it's not the machines. "The fundamental structures of an enterprise are human beings. Therefore, the ultimate results of the progress of the enterprises will be the progress of the human being. And therefore the loyalty towards the company reflects the happiness in the employees, and it's only rational." So he is investing not only in the machines but in the human being and he wants lifelong investment because having invested in him, he sees no point this chap hopping off to another competitor. It's a different philosophy. I don't think we can achieve that because we are more like the Americans. We are immigrants and who pays us better … well, that's the market rate and you can't … it's not just the company. The Singapore government, too. Chairman, PSC, tells me that this year he lost 16 top scholars, all bonded. Mind you, the inflation has gone on, so the company says, how much is the bond, $150,000, here you are, pay and out he goes. We have invested in him. I think we must index the bond for inflation and make it more expensive for the companies. What we favour is the prospect of long service where an employee will have the opportunity to innovate on his job, improve his skills and knowhow, creating an interest in his work.

"Japanese enterprises are still on the lookout for advanced technologies and are willing to invest enormous sums of money in improving technology and manufacturing new products in order to compete in world markets." They spent a lot of time thinking out

> If we want to be a technological society, why is our transport system not geared for shift work?

these problems and they give me a little table to show how different employers pay differently. In Japan, basic wage, if they put down 100 as index, fringe benefit is 80 to 100. And by "fringe benefits" they mean allowances, overtime, bonuses, compulsory welfare, voluntary welfare, 80 to 100. So the total index is 180 to 200.

In Europe and America, basic wage is 100, fringe benefit is 20; total 120. Of course, the 100 will be more because it will be a bigger wage but less fringe benefits.

So the Japanese concept is low wage, fringe benefits equal to wages. They have worked out our fringe benefits, which the Singapore Chinese Chamber of Commerce complains bitterly about. And it works out to Singapore's basic wage 100, fringe benefits 50 to 60; total 150 to 160 compared to the Japanese 180 to 200. If you ask me, I say I move towards the Japanese system. It's a safer method. It binds the link between the worker and his company.

Let me tell you the problem. The Singapore voter has voted for the PAP since 1959; '59, '63, '68, '72, '76, '80 – six times. We have delivered. One day there will be a worldwide recession. I hope not in the next four years. I think we are all right. So we will win '84, '85. But the link is: I vote for you, PAP, now you deliver. But how does the PAP deliver? The PAP has delivered by creating conditions which allow entrepreneurs to invest and get a good return on capital, create conditions of stability, certainty, good water supply, constant power, good communications, telex, telephone, aircraft, ships, containers, the lot – high returns, trainable workers. But the linkage is wrong, you know. The Japanese linkage is better.

No Japanese prime minister says, you vote for me, the LDP will give you all these things. No. Let me read you what a Japanese company does for his worker. In return for loyalty and identification with the company, he gets company welfare – medical and dental care, housing, which means hostels, housing loans, other types of loans at highly subsidised rates, family recreational facilities, education of employees' children paid for by the company, farewell and welcoming parties. When you retire, they say farewell. When you come, they welcome you. Long service gifts, employees' stocks, congratulatory and condolence allowances – your father dies, they give you something. Your wife has a child, they give you something. Discount on company products. What is all this about – heart, isn't it? They get the workers' hearts. The worker knows that if the company goes down, he is down, and so he is thinking up new ideas, and that's why Toyotas, Datsuns, Hondas are outselling now all the small-range cars in Europe and America and throughout the Third World. That's why the linkage.

## Getting out of the British system

So we have proposed that we get out of this British system. We are not magicians and I worry for the next generation leadership. I think we transfer welfare to the company. We can't do it overnight. And anyway, basic welfare, whether it's health, housing, will have to be – the bare minimum must be met by the government. But I think the extras, we shift on to the company. So when the company does well, you see, just like the Japanese

*No Japanese prime minister says, you vote for me, the LDP will give you all these things.*

– whole aeroplane load of company workers follow the flag on a holiday. That means the company prospered. If the company doesn't prosper, everybody stays at home. So there is a direct nexus. This is the problem.

We have inherited the British system and you see how grievously they have harmed themselves. They say, just nationalise, oh well, just redistribute wealth, squeeze the rich until the pips squeak. It sounds wonderful at election time. When they actually squeeze the pips they find the pips have run off and settled in Majorca or some tax-free haven and removed all their capital, and the country has gone down. And when the Germans begin to face that trouble I get very worried.

I want to end by telling you what Devan Nair [Member of Parliament and later President of Singapore] discovered when I sent him to SIA. And it's human relations gone wrong. I am not reciting this to castigate the management, or the pilots, or the workers of SATS, but to try and get everybody in Singapore to understand how even a successful company can begin to go sour when human relations go wrong, and how they can improve in spite of their good performance if they get the human relations right. First, Devan Nair asked: Who does SIA belong to? SATS said, many workers said: "The Singapore government." Some said it belongs to Joe Pillay. No worker said that SIA belongs to him. I have seen the Japanese – I think about 12 of them. And every one of them is proud that he is a Hitachi, or he is a Mitsubishi, or a Marubeni, or whatever man he is. And if you ask who does the company belong to: "The chairman and me – all of us." There is no identification with the company because the management do not identify themselves with the workers, and human relations are poor. Pilots: "This is a second-class hotel; since I am flying a 747, equal to Pan Am, BA, Qantas, I want a first-class, five-star hotel," and they got it. So the cabin crew, you know the girl that appears in the advertisements – millions of dollars – she goes into a three-star hotel, the captain and pilots – cockpit crew – go into a five-star hotel. That has been put right. Captain is the captain, he is in charge, including cabin crew. And Devan discovered that when the executives meet with the unions, everybody on the executive side wears a necktie, to the lowest clerk, to show that they are executives, you see. Everybody on the union side, open-neck shirt. There is something wrong with their psychology.

The first thing we did in 1955 was to campaign with open necks to make it possible for the worker to identify himself with me. If I am with a necktie and a coat and he doesn't own one, it's difficult, isn't it? If you cast your mind back to 1959, we changed the rules of Parliament to allow members to go without neckties. It was in the rules that we had to wear necktie and a coat. The British wanted everybody with a tie and a coat.

And Devan said he went to Hitachi Zosen Shipyard, and he saw a man in overalls with a helmet talking to him, and he said, "Who are you?" and he said, "I am the personnel manager." And he looked just like the other workers. And so did six other divisional directors. And one of the rules of the Japanese management system is, everybody wears the same. We are all in the same boat. Of course, some are up on the captain's bridge, and others are in the engine room. And if the ship sinks, all will sink and the captain must go down with the ship. But at least, the heart, as the German company puts it, you know,

Devan Nair asked: Who does SIA belong to? SATS said, many workers said: "The Singapore government." Some said it belongs to Joe Pillay. No worker said that SIA belongs to him.

the heart of the Japanese workers … and if you go to Korea or Taiwan where the Japanese had governed, for 40 years in the case of Korea and 50 years in the case of Taiwan, you go to their enterprises, they have learnt. They all wear the same. They all eat in the same canteen. But not in SIA; executives eat in a different canteen. All this makes for trouble, isn't it? So the union says, "Look, you can't deal with my workers, my members, any grievance, you deal with me." So the union leader becomes a power broker. No manager can settle a dispute. He must see the union leader and it becomes a big issue. Well, that's being changed. But once things go wrong, of course, then you get the "them-and-us" approach, "them" meaning the bosses.

We will stay on top of our problems provided we understand that there is no god-given law which says that Singapore will have 5 per cent to 10 per cent growth a year. You may end up with a minus. Then you will vote another government in, madder than the last one. Then you will end up with a bigger minus. Then all the bright people will flee and leave the country.

I've seen it. I was in Jamaica in 1975, in April – marvellous country, 2,000 square miles. They nationalise bauxite, they nationalise many things. They promise all things to all men. They are bankrupt. The World Bank has come to their rescue. But can they? All the good men have left. So the economy took a nosedive. Do you think you can get them to come back? It is not easy.

It's the same problem with Sri Lanka. When Air Lanka – and you might as well know this, because when you go down, to come up again may never be possible. The President wanted to restart Air Lanka. We had several Air Lanka nationals working for SIA. So he says, "Will you release my nationals?" I said, "Of course." Well, let me tell you that the Sri Lankans wanted to stay as SIA workers. They said, "We are seconded to Air Lanka." So they are Sri Lankans working for SIA running Air Lanka. And if there is a change of government in Sri Lanka, they are coming back to Singapore to work in SIA.

So, friends and fellow citizens, we have got one little island – 600 square kilometres. You unwind this, you will not drop down on soft padi fields, it is hard, hard concrete, your bones are broken and it's *kaput*.

And if you want to know why I am tough, it's because I know what happens. I travel and I am not looking at the tourist sites. As they show me those things I am carrying on quiet conversation. I say, "Look, by the way, how much are you paid?" And you get behind the wrappings, down to the skeleton. And you know that Singapore has only one chance and that is to go up – tighter, more discipline, up the ladder. You unwind this, it's curtains for everybody.

> You unwind this, you will not drop down on soft padi fields, it is hard, hard concrete, your bones are broken and it's *kaput*.

Politics, to Lee, was about leadership, asserting authority and helping to take the people forward and improve their lives. He spelt out his view of politics and leadership in a speech to civil servants at the Political Study Centre on June 14, 1962. He identified three factors for the successful transformation of developing states: a determined leadership, which was durable enough to remain in office to exercise its authority and get the country moving, an efficient administration and social discipline among the people. His speech, culled from experience gained from visiting and studying countries such as India, Egypt and Yugoslavia, was broadcast over the radio in Singapore.

# Leadership makes the difference

One of the most important lessons I think we have to learn, and learn very quickly, is that when people emerge to independence they don't necessarily emerge from decadence to progress. It often happens that things get worse and there is no doubt about it, that if you allow your social organisations to sag, it will take an awfully long time to hold the thing together again to make sense. And it is easy for it to sag.

The tragedy about the one-man-one-vote system is that it is often easier to raise the bid, not knowing or, even worse, knowing full well that you will never be able to fulfil your promises. And the highest bidder usually wins. In all new countries, the electorate is inexperienced, unsophisticated. It'll vote for the chap who says, "Well I give it to you. I will open up this street for hawkers and I will let you have the run of the place; I promise you the moon, the sun, stars and if there are some reserves left behind from before, well, you can exhaust it." They are invisible. People don't see it. And you can run through these things very quickly …

Authority has got to be exercised. And when authority is not backed by position, prestige or usage, then it has to defend actively against challenge. But let me explain this. I went to India, that is a different composition. Authority there is not challenged. Mr Nehru is there. He is there and has been there almost as long as the Himalayas. Nobody doubts that he is going to be there as long as he lives. And that immediately produces a stiffening effect on the population, on the civil service, on the administration, the people. There is the old boy, he is going to be there, never mind all that shouting going on, everybody knows he is the man to trust.

And you know the trade union chaps who met Devan Nair. They said, yes, that's right. We are communists but when it comes to voting, we vote for the Congress Party. And it is true. He was talking to one of what they call serving boys – Punkawallah – gentlemen with red cap and so on, who bring you a glass of syrup water. We asked him

The tragedy about the one-man-one-vote system is that it is often easier to raise the bid, not knowing or, even worse, knowing full well that you will never be able to fulfil your promises.

When they don't have this certainty, one day Tweedledum, the next day Tweedledee, everybody has a go at power – then pandemonium. And that is what we must never allow.

what union he belonged to; he said, his union is communist but, of course, when it comes to election, he votes Congress: they are not to be trusted, these communists, they will do something foolish. And that is because the leadership is traditional. They have got used to him [Nehru]. He, Gandhi, were big names in India. For 50 years they fought, and authority is exercised without challenge.

He who exercises authority has got to exercise it with firmness, competence and fairness, and what is most important, with a degree of continuity. The expectation of continuance of policy. And that is where the Federation of Malaya has succeeded. It is not the Tunku's great quality of charm, which he has in abundance, but the fact that he has left an impression that he is there to stay, and the fact that he has left that impression helps the whole position.

People expect the state of affairs to develop, change gradually, progress, then they make their calculations accordingly. So that is what is happening in India. But when they don't have this certainty, one day Tweedledum, the next day Tweedledee, everybody has a go at power – then pandemonium. And that is what we must never allow.

I have enumerated in several of my talks what I consider to be the three basic essentials for successful transformation of any society. First, a determined leadership, an effective, determined leadership; two, an administration which is efficient; and three, social discipline. If you don't have those three, nothing will be achieved. And that is one of the fatal effects of the democratic system. This business of seasonal change and your civil servants get rattled. They say, "My God! I'll be in trouble, I'd better succumb. Why not look for something for myself, then whatever happens, I am all right." It's all these creeping doubts, this wavering, this wishing to cushion oneself from trouble, that brings a complete sagging of the whole machinery and helps to bring about chaos and collapse.

But in these three countries which are making progress, India, Egypt, Yugoslavia (backward countries, no doubt about it), there was in every one, dedicated leadership and determination. Whatever there may be of petty corruption in the provincial governments, even the opposition in the Lok Sabha, the Lower House in Delhi – I had a chat with them – they admit the government is honest. That is important. You must be able to command respect. You may agree with Mr Nehru and his colleagues. You may agree with Mr Menon, you may like him, you may not like him, but you admit these are honest men who are out to do a decent job. If they command authority, that makes things easier. Their civil servants are self-respecting, the minister acts with reasonable decorum, the permanent secretary acts with reasonable confidence, the *tamby* feels he's got to behave himself; if he doesn't, he gets a rap on the knuckles. Everything ticks.

In every one of them, there was an effective administration. In the case of Egypt they had none, but they filled up. They changed the top hierarchy which was corrupt and everywhere they filled it with trusted army officers, young army revolutionary types. They knew nothing about administration. They have since learned, but the idea was to infuse a certain amount of backbone and stop the petty thieving that was going on. And in Yugoslavia the whole of the Partisan movement, the officer corps, went in and took over the administration.

The third quality: in every one of them, there was this social discipline. And what is strange is this. Where the social discipline is less, the progress is slower. And the social discipline was slightest in India. And tightest in Yugoslavia. You see, that is something which no politician, no political leader, no revolutionary band, can create overnight. It takes years to change a people in their habits, in their attitudes. If you don't get social discipline, everybody does what he likes to do, or will not bustle about what he is told to do. And that becalms the whole momentum.

When I was in Italy in 1957, everybody – that was the age of the scooter – everybody had a scooter. Five years ago, all Vespas running around. This time I went there and the first thing I noted was all the scooters had been replaced by little Fiats, 600, 500, and chaps who've got Fiats don't go and embark on revolution. They are thinking of the next instalment, how to make sure that they've got the next instalment to pay the Fiat dealer. Yes, it's a fact. We went out to the country one Sunday and I think there must have been 100,000 families with the same idea. They also went out, everybody with a little Fiat or an Alfa Romeo, depending upon your prosperity. And everybody brought a little tent or a fishing rod. They went round to the country; if they were young they made love, if they were old they just sat down under the sun and sipped mineral water. But no revolution.

Ah yes, the democratic system is erratic. Whilst I was there, the House or their Parliament was meeting day and night trying to elect a new president. And they couldn't elect the president because nobody had a majority. But they are kept down because their economy is bouncing. Men's minds turn to revolution when things are getting worse, not when things are getting better. That is fundamental. What we want to do here is to make things get better. And the reason why Barisan is not successful is because things are getting better. Supposing you have got no houses – you know the number of school children who are being registered, the number of chaps who are moving into flats in Singapore? These are the basic factors on our side, telling factors. Watch the Barisan branches, they opened like mushrooms. Now they are closing down one by one.

Why? Basically, because there is progress. Houses are going up, chaps are earning money, there are lots of scooters around. Yes. Last year, they registered nearly 8,000 scooters, that's what they told me, ROV. It's no laughing matter. It's a small state; 8,000 scooters, you just imagine that. Three in the family using it, you've got 24,000 people kept happy. With 24,000 girlfriends you've got 48,000 chaps happy. …

No government has yet gone down to communist subversion which has an effective administration. They only went down when the administration collapsed. And here you have got a determined leadership.

I say, compared to the rest of Southeast Asia, the administration is wholesome, but it needs to be shaken up, chaps get flat. Chaps get lazy, you shake them up, flap them up, sometimes rap them on the knuckles. Reward them when they do outstanding work.

And the social discipline? Well, it's not what's strictly desired, but it can be improved. In my prognosis for the future, I say, if I had to choose any place in Southeast Asia as the one most likely to survive for the longest possible time, in the best of possible circumstances, I say that is Malaysia.

Chaps who've got Fiats don't go and embark on revolution. They are thinking of the next instalment, how to make sure that they've got the next instalment to pay the Fiat dealer.

As early as the 1960s, Lee had expressed doubts about the applicability of the democratic ideal to developing countries. In a question-and-answer session following his address to the Royal Society of International Affairs in London in May 1962, he spelt out some of the difficulties of doing so. He also said that he believed he could govern Singapore more effectively if he did not have to face elections every five years. Below are excerpts of the question-and-answer session.

# What price democracy?

**QUESTION:** May I ask the Prime Minister if he will enlarge on his observations about one-man-one-vote?

**LEE KUAN YEW:** Yes! There are vagaries about the system of one-man-one-vote which make it an extremely hazardous system to run anywhere in the underdeveloped and the under-educated world. It is a hazardous system to run anywhere, as people who are in charge of the electoral machinery of major political parties here may well agree.

I would say that but for the enormous prestige of Mr Nehru and the quality of the leadership at the very top around him, I do not think it would have worked in India either.

We are not exceptional, we are neither more intelligent nor better-educated than many of our neighbours. We have been more fortunately endowed and enjoy a better standard of living, but I do not think the basic factors are materially different. Where the majority of your population is semi-literate, it responds more to the carrot than to the stick, and politicians at election time cannot use the stick. So this leads to a situation where he who bids the highest wins.

At a time when you want harder work with less return and more capital investment, one-man-one-vote produces just the opposite. The offer of more return with less work ends up in bankruptcy. I would say that but for the enormous prestige of Mr Nehru and the quality of the leadership at the very top around him, I do not think it would have worked in India either. It is not for me to say what is likely to happen in India in the next decade – Mr Nehru cannot go on forever.

But I do not think it is a coincidence that it has flopped in Pakistan, did not succeed in Burma, nearly came to grief and is already in severe difficulties in Ceylon which was the model of peaceful transfer of power from a governed to a governing nation. It has been abandoned, decried and condemned in Indonesia, and it is not held in esteem anywhere in Asia.

It is not a tradition with the Malays nor with the Chinese to count heads; it has always been [the tradition] to listen to the dicta of the elder. Mind you, I think it will endure in Malaya for some time, but for how long, I don't know. I should imagine that with every passing year there will be mutations made to the system in order to make it still work. We all know that barely five months ago the Tunku brought in several basic amendments to the constitution, a constitution drafted by five eminent jurists from the five Commonwealth countries. They settled in Rome and drafted what was jurisprudentially a sensible and an elegant constitution – but it was not going to work. Very wisely, the Tunku decided that he would change bits and pieces.

It was my unfortunate burden to attend a Law Society dinner shortly after that in the university, and hear a somewhat idealistic president of that society decry the fact that the Tunku had already moved 137 amendments, namely more amendments than there are articles in his constitution! Gratuitously I defended the need for making something work, even if it meant departing from my norms; and I should be surprised if in the course of the next five years there are not as many amendments as there were in the last five years.

**QUESTION:** May I follow up that question with a supplementary? One-man-one-vote has broken down already in various ex-territories of the Commonwealth – of the Empire. It has been succeeded in those cases by military dictatorships. You will not, I imagine from what I know, in Malaysia face the danger of a military government, but how are you going to secure a smooth transition from a system which will not work (I would agree there) in an illiterate – large illiterate – country? How are you going to secure a smooth transition to something else which will not involve autocratic government?

> How are you going to secure a smooth transition to something else which will not involve autocratic government?

**LEE:** I do not think it is quite true to say that the system of one-man-one-vote has been abandoned. Parliamentary government has been abandoned, but it has not necessarily been followed by a military dictatorship. President Nkrumah is not a military dictatorship. He was no general of any army.

**QUESTION:** Pakistan, Sudan …

**LEE:** Yes, true – Pakistan, Sudan, Burma; but Indonesia is not a military dictatorship; the President just decided one morning, with the support and concurrence of the executive powers of the State, that the Legislative Chamber should be dissolved and that power should be vested among those who were competent to exercise that power. But I do not think the proposition that it must be followed or superseded by a military dictatorship is valid, because I do not think it is.

What I think is valid as a general proposition is that the system of cutting up the country in accordance with the number of adult citizens of given proportions, to elect representatives who then elect among like-minded people a Cabinet which then elects a *primus inter pares* among the Cabinet, is one which presupposes so many basic conditions which are often nonexistent, that I do not think it will ever work. They have all been

*If I were in authority in Singapore indefinitely, without having to ask those who are governed whether they like what is being done, then I have not the slightest doubt that I could govern much more effectively in their own interests.*

superseded by systems which give power effectively to one man, or a group of men, for an indefinite period.

Government, to be effective, must at least give the impression of enduring, and a government which is open to the vagaries of the ballot box – when the people who put their crosses in the ballot boxes are not illiterate but semi-literate, which is worse – is a government which is already weakened before it starts to govern.

I say this with no desire to explain away my problem: if I were in authority in Singapore indefinitely, without having to ask those who are governed whether they like what is being done, then I have not the slightest doubt that I could govern much more effectively in their own interests. That is a fact which the educated understand, but we are all caught in this system which the British – I do not know what the French do in their colonies in Africa – export all over the place, hoping that somewhere it will take root.

India is still working it, but I think that but for the enormous prestige of Mr Nehru and the momentum of the independence movement – the Congress movement – it would not have endured. It would not have carried on for so long, and certainly would not have produced the results which in fact it has. But, in every country where it has been supplanted, the tendency is towards more – I would not say autocratic – centralised power; and power which is not open to question in the way the system of one-man-one-vote opens it at frequent periodic intervals.

I do not know what the answer is, and I would hate to commit myself on what I think the answer is for Malaya, but I am pretty sure that there must be amendments to the system in order to continue to provide effective government in Malaysia. When it happens, as I am sure it will within the next ten years – I think it is necessary, it has got to be done – there will be changes in Malaysia, otherwise it will lead to perdition, or, what is worse, the taking over of the organs of the State by soldiers who are not necessarily the best-equipped people to look after the administration of a country.

When it does happen you will perhaps remember that it is not the first time – nor will it be the last time – that the British parliamentary system, when planted on ground that is not suitable, does not take root.

QUESTION: I should like to follow up on that and ask the Prime Minister to be a little more specific. I am not quite sure whether the misgivings he expressed about democracy are based upon his belief if the wrong people get elected, or on his conviction that after they are elected, they are not able to carry on with their jobs. If it is the former, this would appear to be a contradiction, because he himself achieved power through democratic election. If it is the second, it would be very interesting to hear his exposition; in what way has his work been impeded by parliamentary democracy?

LEE: I would say without the slightest hesitation that it is not the first, and I would not put the second point quite in the way that Mr Sington has done.

Effective government, as I envisage it, in an underdeveloped situation means a government that must improve investment rate, that must demand more effort for less return over a sustained period – certainly more than five years. If you can make the demand for a period of two years, produce the results after the fourth, have the results enjoyed by the fifth, then all is well.

But unfortunately the process of economic growth is much slower and painful, and neither five nor ten years is an adequate enough period for the demands that you make on a population to be felt and enjoyed by the population. Therefore, the result would be – unless you had exceptional leadership and exceptional circumstances as in the case of India, where there is no doubt as to the dedication and the ability of the leadership at the top, where the momentum of the independence movement, plus the inherently stable character of the Hindu society, has prevented a sudden upset of the whole social structure of society.

But in many cases political leaders have got to yield to forces around and beneath them, and the answer always, unless you have a superhuman group of leaders is to take the solution which is least painful. Therefore the least painful solution is not to make undue demands on your population, to slide over the fact that not to do so is not to increase investment rate and not to jack up your society, or there is never any chance of taking office.

Then you are competing against people who not only promise not to maintain the investment rate, but positively promise to spend what there is [already saved] in the kitty, and you have three or four terms, and if an electorate is sufficiently naive to believe that these things can be done, you break the bank, as the Indonesians have done. They had very little in the bank to begin with; everybody promised that if he came in, whatever there was in the bank would be for the people, and they came in; the bank was broken anyway, and that was the end of it.

There is an inherent defect in working that system when one has to engage in a protracted period of economic growth; and if you had worked this one-man-one-vote in England in the 18th century, you would never have got your industrial revolution. You cannot get your coal miner to say he is going to put in more effort for less in order to build the industrial sinews of the state.

As many of my former colleagues (those who have gone over to the communists) told me last year, "If Mao Zedong had to stand for election today he would lose his deposit." There is no doubt about it, and nobody makes any pretence about it. You can govern as long as the organs of the state are effective and obedient and as long as the intelligentsia is with you. The intelligentsia is with Mao and he will continue to govern, but if he asked for a popular mandate, that is not possible. Who can do it apart from Mr Nehru, I do not know.

> "If Mao Zedong had to stand for election today he would lose his deposit."

# They would want the stars

"If we had British-style trade unions we would be bankrupt."

**KENNEDY:** Prime Minister, you had some quite harsh things to say about Britain recently. At the opening of your Parliament the other day, you said of us, "A great people have been temporarily reduced to straitened circumstances by excessive cushioning of life by state subsidies." Do you think that was quite fair?

**LEE KUAN YEW:** It is only one of the reasons for the economic and the social problems in Britain. It's a vast subject, which you know more about than I do. But the part that I am concerned with is that one-man-one-vote means that at every election time, it's an auction of, really, wealth that has not yet been created. So if I do not effectively debunk the theory that the government will provide – there is always more and more for less and less, there is no need really to try because we are doing all right now – we will be a broken-back state like so many of the others in the Third World. We've just got off the ground. We nearly fell flat on our faces with the problems of Confrontation during Dr Sukarno's Indonesia, British withdrawal, and with it the bases were closed and so on. And now just the first touch of comfort – we are above the rice-line, there are a number of aspiring Wedgewood Benns who think we ought to be giving things for free, that we should not have prescription charges; it is wicked to make people pay for their medicine; it is wicked to make them pay for the extras the children have in school, like going out on outings and so on. It is a very attractive election programme.

Look, what has happened? Vast government expenditure, which fortunately in Britain's case will all be paid for by North Sea oil. But we haven't got North Sea oil, and I think we will be bankrupt.

**KENNEDY:** You also said, Prime Minister, that "If we had British-style trade unions we would be bankrupt." Now, what did you mean by that?

LEE: Now, please! Some of the union leaders are good old friends of mine and I hope they will remain good old friends. In fact, they taught me a lot about labour and the labour movement and so on. But the way things have gone in Britain over the last ten years – well, really from 1964 onwards, 13 years – it's not the kind of labour movement that I knew in Britain when I was a student there watching it, watching socialism, the democratic way, that the will of the majority is expressed periodically, within a period of five years, and once expressed, that will must be respected. Well, it's a different Britain. That was old-fashioned constitutional theory. The new theory now which I am seeing evolved is: never mind what the majority will is. We, the union leaders who have been elected by a small group of very important people – the shop stewards and the people who stayed late into the early hours of the morning to make the crucial decisions when the others have got tired and gone home – have decided that this will be so. And quite rightly, Mr Denis Healey, as Chancellor of the Exchequer, tells the House of Commons what he hopes the budget should be, and then says, I will discuss it with the trade unions.

Well, if my colleague, who is Minister of Finance, is caught or trapped in that position, I think we are bankrupt. Yes, because they would want the moon, the stars and beyond, and why not? We have got some reserves, our credit is good, we could go on for five, maybe, seven years. Then what? Without North Sea oil.

KENNEDY: How can we put our house in order?

LEE: Why do you want to put your house in order? You've got North Sea oil that lubricates and will smooth out every friction. You will be as happy and as relaxed as the Arabs.

KENNEDY: I thought you were going to say, the same as you are.

LEE: No, I have got to work. Every grain of rice that we consume is paid for in foreign exchange. Nature did not intend that Singapore be an agricultural country. That's why it was uninhabited. It was intended to be discovered or re-discovered (if you want to be sensitive to the feelings of people who believe in myths and mythology of the region) in 1819 by someone called Stamford Raffles, later made a knight, turned into an emporium, a base, a manufacturing centre, a financial centre, an independent republic. And it's a fine mechanism, which, if we tamper around with the kind of screwdrivers and spanners that we have along the picket lines, when they squatted in front of the gate and didn't allow lorries carrying coal or oil to pass into the power stations, well, the clock stops ticking.

KENNEDY: Would it be fair to try and sum up what you have been saying about these – on this loss of civil liberties, such as they are – that some small liberties have to be sacrificed in order to make sure that you have the greater liberty? Would that be a fair assessment?

LEE: One way of putting it. If you ask me to put it, I would say simply: Never before have the people of Singapore had a government which they can kick out of office freely, without

Never before have the people of Singapore had a government which they can kick out of office freely, without hindrance, by just crossing them off the ballot.

hindrance, by just crossing them off the ballot. And never have they had a government which had to tend to their needs – every grumble, every bellyache – to make sure that the vote is on the side of the angels every five years.

**KENNEDY:** But did you ever feel, Prime Minister, it's often been said in the West that a good democracy, a good democratic society is one in which you not only have a good government but you have a good opposition to match that government. Do you not ever feel the lack of that?

*I often wonder whether the foreign journalists or the casual visitor like you has fathomed or can fathom the mind of an Oriental.*

**LEE:** As a Western-educated Singaporean, I understand what you are saying. And perhaps if I could get a nice sparring partner, it will provide me with a backdrop that contrasts. But I often wonder whether the foreign journalists, or the casual visitor like you, has fathomed or can fathom the mind of an Oriental. And I am having to look after Orientals whether they are of Chinese descent or Malay or Indian or Eurasian or Ceylonese and so on. What's inside is completely different: Is this a good government that I can trust to look after me and my family, and will see that my children are educated and will have a job better than mine, and have a home better than mine? Is it fair or is it unfair, unjust, favouring its relatives, its friends; looting the public purse for its relatives, for itself so that ministers live in luxury while the masses live in squalor?

Those are the crucial issues because those are the issues that have toppled governments in the Third World. You can ask any taxi driver – he is the most uninhibited Singaporean you can think of. You can ask any bartender in any hotel. He'll let off a bellyache. But at the end of the day, when he puts his cross, when election comes, he has given me and my colleagues over seventeen and a half years – come June, eighteen years in office. In five successive elections, the percentage of votes has gone up from a first-time high of 53 per cent to an all-time low of about $47^1/_2$, to an all-time high, last December, of $72^1/_2$ per cent, which I think is cause for some satisfaction.

# Universality of democracy?

The West, led by America, puts the credo simply as democracy is universally good for all peoples, and that to progress, modernise and become industrial societies, they should become democracies. Now that the Cold War has ended, I hope it is possible for Western political scientists to write in more objective terms. Why has democracy not worked in most of these newly independent countries? In particular, why has an American-based constitution failed to work in America's only former colony, the Philippines? The Philippines experiment in democracy started with independence and elections in 1946. That experiment in democracy failed in 1972 with martial law, long before Marcos was ousted in 1986. A second American-based constitution was promulgated by President Aquino in February 1987. While a constitutional commission was sitting to frame this constitution, four coups were attempted. In May 1987, elections were held for a Senate and a House of Representatives. This still did not settle the loyalty of the armed forces because three more coup attempts followed.

For many centuries democratic governments were found only in a few nations, where the character of the people and their circumstances were favourable: first in Britain, then exported to her former white colonies or dominions like America, Canada, Australia and New Zealand.

## When Westerners speak candidly

From time to time a Western leader speaks out from the heart. Mrs Thatcher did this in March this year. She was in the United States to receive the Medal of Freedom from President Bush. In a TV interview, talking about Europeans who want political union, she said, "We the UK are 700 years old. Germany's Parliament is only 40, Spain a dozen years old, Portugal even less." (*Sunday Times*, London, March 10, 1991.) She could have added that America's is over 200 years, Canada's 123, Australia's 90, New Zealand's 83. The French on the other hand have had 7 constitutions and governing charters in the 200 years since their revolution in 1789, and two of these were monarchical aristocracies, not democracies. And their present constitution is only 33 years old from 1958 when General de Gaulle took over after the collapse of the 4th French Republic.

Mrs Thatcher's view was that in spite of sharing a common European history and culture for over 2,000 years since the Roman Empire, only the British can claim 700 years of parliamentary democracy since Magna Carta. She also reminded the Germans that they have been democratic for only 40 years.

## Pessimistic British view of democracy for the Soviet Union

When Western commentators are not writing to convert a Third World country to democracy, they are more objective. For example, when they discuss the Soviet Union, they say openly that democracy will not work. Jonathan Eyal, Director of Studies, Royal United Services Institute in London, in *The Independent* newspaper (March 22, 1991) said, "The middle-class ethos, responsible in the West for enshrining compromise and moderation as supreme values, is still lacking in the USSR. … They are, therefore, advising Mr Gorbachev to create domestic institutions, in order to provide his country with the instruments for a social dialogue.

"Yet democracy is not simply a matter of ballot boxes, elections or political parties. Indeed, democracy may not be a political system at all but, rather, a way of life which depends on an accepted social contract, mutual respect, moderation and the explicit acceptance that no one is the possessor of a universal truth."

He concluded that "The Soviet empire will collapse sooner rather than later."

European historians ascribe Russia's lack of a liberal civic society to the fact that she missed the Renaissance (middle 15th to end 16th century) and also the Enlightenment (18th century). These were the two leavening experiences that lifted Western Europe to a more humane culture. Now if democracy will not work for the Russians, a white Christian people, can we assume that it will naturally work with Asians?

> Now if democracy will not work for the Russians, a white Christian people, can we assume that it will naturally work with Asians?

## Asia's top priority – political stability

The basic problem facing all Asian countries other than Japan is how to maintain political stability. Their old communities were in small territories ruled by tribal chiefs or sultans. European colonial governments later amalgamated these small territories into larger administrative units. Now these larger units embracing diverse peoples have become new nations. Rupert Emerson, Professor of Government in Harvard, defines a nation thus: "A single people, traditionally fixed on a well-defined territory, speaking the same language and preferably a language all its own, possessing a distinctive culture, and shaped to a common mould by many generations of shared historical experience."

Professor Robert Tilman, University of North Carolina, in his book *Southeast Asia and the Enemy Beyond* (Westview Press, 1987), pointed out that by this definition, Thailand is the only country in Southeast Asia which is a nation, and that only if Muslims in the south are excluded. He sums up the situation thus: "For every Asean member there are tigers at the door, tigers in the jungles, and tigers in the kitchen. The future is fraught with risks for every state in the region. The association is a fragile organisation, and every state belonging to it is also fragile. Outside forces over which each has no control could loose centrifugal forces tugging at Asean unity. Outside forces might also set off internal chain reactions that could topple any of the current regimes and wipe out the gains of the last few decades."

Political stability during a period of transition to a modern state is under great stress. But stability is the basic precondition for success. Whole people must acquire new knowledge and new skills so that they can work, repair and maintain machines, both for industry and agriculture. To do this there must be the firm framework of law and order within which learning, working and excelling are encouraged and rewarded. Several countries like South Korea and Taiwan have succeeded in industrialising.

## Need for democratic participation in NIEs

After they have achieved a certain level of modernisation, new pressures threaten their political stability. Their people's thinking and attitudes change as a result of education plus knowledge of the outside world, especially America, Europe and Japan. Educated Koreans and Taiwanese then question the basis of the legitimacy of their governments. The governments of South Korea and Taiwan have adopted more representative forms of governments. Both are in the process of adjusting to and absorbing these changes. South Korea has had more difficulties, especially with their trade unions. Korean culture has always extolled the fighter who fights to the bitter end. The spirit of give and take, to live and let live, is not part of traditional Korean culture.

## Traditional culture and democracy

Progress towards democracy amongst Asian countries has been uneven because often the losing side has been unwilling to accept the results of an election, and instead continued to agitate and oppose both inside and outside their legislative assemblies. This has led to instability, and as instability threatens progress, governments curtail democratic rights.

Many Asian countries which have worked democratic constitutions have from time to time had to invoke emergency rule or martial law. Even the British have had to do this in Northern Ireland. For democracy to work without being suspended from time to time, a people must acquire, if they have not inherited, cultural habits that make contending groups adjust differences or conflicts not by violence but by give and take. People must accept a view or policy as valid because that was the way the votes fell, whilst they work peacefully for a change in the next elections. But before this can happen, a people must have reached a certain high level of education and economic development which has produced a sizeable middle-class so that life is not such a fight for basic survival.

Japan reached that level long before World War Two. South Korea and Taiwan reached that level in the late 1970s. They are now moving towards more representative

*Many Asian countries which have worked democratic constitutions have from time to time had to invoke emergency rule or martial law.*

No Singaporean leader can afford to put political theory above the practical need of stability and orderly progress.

government. People in South Korea and Taiwan are at a stage where the active participation of knowledgeable managers, engineers, supervisors and workers in decision-making on the factory floor has become a way of life. Such people naturally have the urge to extend this habit of participation to matters of government.

In China, a country with a large rural mass, some 80 per cent of her 1,100 million people, political change has to be differently geared for the rural and the urban areas. Peasants in the countryside are often content to live quiet lives and let the government be run by their betters, be they emperors or communist mandarins. This is why the communists in Albania were able to garner support from the rural areas. The problem for China is how to accommodate the desire of their educated and knowledgeable people in the cities to decide how they are to be governed. These are people who are well-informed about other societies, including Taiwan and Hongkong. But the 900 million peasants have different priorities and concerns. One-man-one-vote for 1,100 million Chinese to choose a president, a congress or a senate will lead to chaotic results. But then neither can a self-perpetuating communist party claim to represent the people. They have to win the support and cooperation of their educated in the cities because, without their participation, modernisation will be slow and difficult.

## Political change – a Darwinian process

Each country in Asia will chart its own way forward. Every country wants to be developed and wealthy. They will adopt and adapt those features or attributes of successful countries which they think will help them succeed. If these features work and improve their rate of progress, they will be permanently incorporated. If they do not work or cause difficulties, they will be abandoned. It is akin to social Darwinism, a process of trial and error in which survival is the test of what works.

Simply modelling a system on the American, British or West European constitution is not how Asian countries will or can go about it. The peoples of Asia want higher standards of living in an orderly society. They want to have as much individual choice in lifestyle, political liberties and freedoms as is compatible with the interests of the community. After a certain stage of advance in education and industrialisation, a people may need representative government, however chosen, in order to reconcile conflicting group interests in society and maintain social order and stability. Representative government is also one way for a people to forge a new consensus, a social compact, on how a society settles the trade-off between further rapid economic growth and individual freedoms.

In Singapore, the British gave us their form of parliamentary government. Our problem has been how to maintain stability in spite of the destabilising tendencies of one-man-one-vote in a new society divided by race, language and religion. We have had to put political stability as the first priority. As we progressed to higher educational and economic levels, we have widened participation in decision making. But no Singaporean leader can afford to put political theory above the practical need of stability and orderly progress. On this, I believe I speak for most, if not all of Asia, at present.

In a keynote address at the Create 21 Asahi Forum on November 20, 1992, in Tokyo, Lee took on those advocates who argued that human rights and democracy were universal phenomena to be applied to all societies. They added that governments should be pressured into adopting Western standards, which they said Asian authoritarians, such as Lee, were obstructing. He countered these views in this speech, which spelt out his alternative view that what people wanted was good government, not democracy per se.

# What people want is good government

## UK and US: Established modern democracies

In modern times two nations have long and unbroken records for democratic government. First, the United Kingdom, next the United States.

The British trace their democracy to the signing of Magna Carta in 1215, which led to the development of their Parliament. Indeed, up to 1911, the hereditary noblemen in the House of Lords had as much power as the people's representatives in the House of Commons. Women got the vote only in 1928. And extra votes for Oxbridge University graduates and businessmen were abolished only in 1948.

The United States declared independence in 1776. In 1788 the constitution gave the vote only to those who paid property tax or poll tax, which meant the well-to-do. There were barriers of age, colour and sex. In 1860 income and property qualifications were abolished, but other barriers like literacy tests and poll taxes discriminated against blacks and other disadvantaged groups. In 1920 women got the vote. Only in 1965 did the Voting Rights Act suspend literacy tests and other voter qualification devices which kept the blacks out.

So full democracy was established in the UK in 1948 and in the US in 1965.

## France

The French Revolution was in 1789 when they stormed the Bastille. Since then France has had five republics and two monarchs. *Equalite*, *fraternite* and *egalite* in 1789 did not succeed as a democracy until the 20th century.

Is it any wonder then that so many Third World countries, former colonies that have received democratic institutions fashioned after US, British, French, Belgian, Dutch, Portuguese constitutions were not able to make these constitutions work without radically

*When Anand Panyarachun was appointed prime minister, there was widespread support and no protest. But he was not elected.*

altering their nature, like converting themselves into one-party systems? What the UK, US and France took 200 years to evolve, these new countries, without the economic, educational and social preconditions, were expected to work upon independence, when during all the years of colonial tutelage there were no elections and no democratic government.

## Western democracy universality presumed but unproven

The existence of a civic society is a precondition for success in democratic government. What is a civic society? It is a society with the whole series of institutions between family and state to which citizens belong, independent voluntary associations, religious institutions, trade unions, professional organisations, movements to promote specific common interests, whether the Green movement, or the gun lobby, or anti-smoking, and so on.

Professor Seymore Lipset of George Mason University (BBC World Service broadcast April 19, 1991) states the conditions for democracy in a different way: "A large middle class, economically secure, many people having skills, knowledge and security to take part in politics."

Dr Barbara Goodwin of Brunnel University (BBC World Service broadcast April 29, 1991) said that liberal democracy needs economic development, literacy, a growing middle-class, political institutions supporting free speech and human rights. It needs a civic culture resting on shared values making people with different and conflicting views willing to cooperate. She adds that democracy does not require everybody to be thinking the same but thrives on division or cleavages.

The crucial point is that they must be able to live with their differences, as Professor Werber of Harvard University (BBC World Service broadcast April 29, 1991) says, cultural preconditions where the majority want to live in this community with relatively low conflict, relatively low violence and agree to a set of rule procedures governing collective life, where a set of deep beliefs and values to their culture is fundamental for democratic government.

If we apply these preconditions to countries in Asia, we will understand why Asian democracy has had such a chequered history.

Take Thailand. In May this year we saw Bangkok's population of about seven to eight million willing to demonstrate its anger against a military regime whose coup it had a year earlier approved of. But it disapproved of General Suchinda becoming the prime minister when he was not elected, or at least that was the ostensible reason. The trouble was that the opposition or outrage of seven to eight million people of Bangkok was not shared by the 50 million other Thais in the countryside. Bangkok opposed Suchinda not because he was not elected, but because they felt that the military were not honest themselves, and that honest government was what they wanted. They wanted to remove the military and get an honest government. When Anand Panyarachun was appointed prime minister, there was widespread support and no protest. But he was not elected.

Indeed he had not participated in elections and said publicly that he did not want to. What the people wanted was to get rid not only of the military but also of the corrupt drug traffickers. They have now got rid of the military, but they still have drug traffickers. Narong Wongwan, the man who was named as prime minister after the March elections before General Suchinda became prime minister, was denied a visa to the United States in July 1991 because he was suspected of being involved in drug trafficking. He has won again in the September elections. In due course he will again become a minister. Overall, in the September elections, the four pro-democracy parties only marginally improved their positions, winning 185 seats, an increase of only 23 seats or six per cent. The traditional big-spending parties maintained their grip in the rural areas of the north and centre. What is needed for democracy to produce good governments are fundamental social and educational changes so that good men like Anand will contest and win elections without vote-buying or intimidation.

Next the Philippines. Six years ago, Mrs Imelda Marcos fled the country (with her husband); so did Eduardo Cojuangco. Yet they were able to return and contest in elections for president. They were among the top four candidates. The president, Fidel Ramos, got 5.3 million votes, Cojuangco got 4.1, and Mrs Marcos 2.3. In other words, had Cojuangco and Mrs Marcos combined, their votes could have beaten Fidel Ramos.

A society where such remarkable events are possible needs a special kind of democracy. In other societies, when a dictator is overthrown, the wife and close collaborators would probably have been mobbed and lynched before they got away, and if they got away would never return.

Take Pakistan. In 1988, after General Zia Ul Haq, the president, was killed in an aircraft explosion, elections were set for October 1988. On August 21, 1988 in *Sunday Telegraph*, London, the late Professor Elie Kedourie, Professor of Politics at the London School of Economics, who has studied Pakistan, explained that to expect the coming elections to re-establish democracy was a triumph of hope over experience. He wrote: "Civilian, constitutional government was proved to be inept, corrupt, and quite unable to arrange a Third World economy, or deal with the ills and conflicts of a divided society suffering from deep rivalries, mutual fears and antagonisms … For such a style of government to be practicable and tolerable, it has to be rooted in attitudes to, and traditions of, governance which are common ground between the rulers and the ruled: the supremacy of law, the accountability of those in power and continuous intercourse with the public from whom they derive their authority; the sturdiness of civil society, and the practical impossibility for any government to ride roughshod for long over its innumerable and multifarious interests and associations. None of this, of course, obtains in Pakistan, or in the Indian subcontinent from which it was carved. Here the ruling tradition was of Oriental despotism where the will of the ruler was law … May it not be that a regime of elections, parliaments and responsible government is unworkable in countries like Pakistan, and that to persist in attempts to set up or restore such a regime must lead to continual tumults in the body politic, and successive interventions by the armed forces?"

In other societies, when a dictator is overthrown, the wife and close collaborators would probably have been mobbed and lynched before they got away, and if they got away would never return.

Pakistan held its elections in December 1988. Mrs Benazir Bhutto won and became prime minister. In less than two years, her government was dismissed on allegations of massive corruption. Nawaz Sharif's Islamic Alliance won the elections in October 1990 and he became prime minister. In less than two years, his coalition was under stress. The army was sent in in May 1992 to put down violence and lawlessness in the province of Sind. I know both Prime Ministers Benazir Bhutto and Nawaz Sharif personally. They are capable leaders and the equals of other leaders in the Third World. But the essential preconditions for democracy in Pakistani society are missing.

Let me mention one simple but fundamental problem. The majority of the voters, both in the Philippines and in Pakistan, are peasants or farmers. The landlords control their lives and their votes. The majority of members elected into the legislatures of both countries are landlords. They have blocked legislation for land reforms without which there can be no fundamental change in the economy. They have also blocked moves to have the children of their peasants educated. They prefer to have them uneducated but loyal, and beholden to them.

Neither country has a background for democratic government. There are no habits in the people for dissension or disagreement within a restrained and peaceful context. Murders and violence are part of every Filipino election. The lawlessness that is in Sind province, the shootings with heavy weapons and automatics between warring Sindhis, Muhajirs, Pashtuns, Baluchis in Karachi bear witness to the absence of a civic society.

## Adverse economy breaks down democracy

There is one phenomenon which poses the question of whether democracy is secure even in the developed countries. Democracies broke down and gave way to dictatorships in Europe during the world depression of the 1930s. The two earliest democracies, UK and US, withstood the Great Depression pressures. They were severely tested. There were general strikes in Britain. But constitutional democracy weathered the storm. A Labour coalition government was formed in which the Labour Party was a minority supported by Conservatives, to accommodate the demands of the workers. But the Labour Party was soon discredited for having taken office in this opportunistic way and produced no results.

In the US, a charismatic leader in Franklin D. Roosevelt brought in the New Deal. He laid the foundations for the social security programmes that were to be carried to excess in the 1960s.

But in Italy in the 1920s the Depression led to the rise of Mussolini and the Fascist Party. In Germany Hitler and the Nazi Party came to power in 1932. In Japan the military took charge and led Japan first into Manchuria, in 1931, and next into China, in 1937. In 1941 General Tojo took charge openly as prime minister and led Japan into Southeast Asia in December 1941. In Spain, there was the dictatorship of General Franco, in Portugal that of Salazar.

There is no guarantee that the present democracies will survive if there is a prolonged world depression.

There is no guarantee that the present democracies will survive if there is a prolonged world depression.

## People want good government

All peoples of all countries need good government. A country must first have economic development, then democracy may follow. With a few exceptions, democracy has not brought good government to new developing countries. Democracy has not led to development because the governments did not establish the stability and discipline necessary for development. What is good government? This depends on the values of a people. What Asians value may not necessarily be what Americans or Europeans value. Westerners value the freedoms and liberties of the individual.

As an Asian of Chinese cultural background, my values are for a government which is honest, effective and efficient in protecting its people, and allowing opportunities for all to advance themselves in a stable and orderly society, where they can live a good life and raise their children to do better than themselves. In other words:

(a) People are well cared for, their food, housing, employment, health.

(b) There is order and justice under the rule of law, and not the capricious, arbitrariness of individual rulers. There is no discrimination between peoples, regardless of race, language, religion. No great extremes of wealth.

(c) As much personal freedom as possible but without infringing on the freedom of others.

(d) Growth in the economy and progress in society.

(e) Good and ever improving education.

(f) High moral standards of rulers and of the people.

(g) Good physical infrastructure, facilities for recreation, music, culture and the arts; spiritual and religious freedoms, and a full intellectual life.

Very few democratically elected governments in the Third World uphold these values. But it is what their people want.

When Asians visit the US many are puzzled and disturbed by conditions there:

(a) Law and order out of control, with riots, drugs, guns, muggings, rape and crimes.

(b) Poverty in the midst of great wealth.

(c) Excessive rights of the individual at the expense of the community as a whole; criminals regularly escape punishment because the law which presumes innocence over-protects their human rights.

The United States cannot tackle its drug problem by solving the problem within its country. So it has to try to solve the problem by attacking the drug problem in the drug-producing countries. It has invaded Panama to capture Noriega. It has secretly kidnapped the Mexican doctor for having tortured and killed a US drug enforcement agent. The United States courts have held these actions as legal. But if put to the International Court at the Hague there can be little doubt that they are clear violations of international law, whether or not they were in accordance with US law.

It is Asian values that have enabled Singapore to contain its drug problem. To protect the community we have passed laws which entitle police, drug enforcement or immigration officers to have the urine of any person who behaves in a suspicious way tested for drugs. If the result is positive, treatment is compulsory.

My values are for a government which is honest, effective and efficient in protecting its people, and allowing opportunities for all to advance themselves in a stable and orderly society, where they can live a good life and raise their children to do better than themselves.

Such a law in the United States will be unconstitutional, because it will be an invasion of privacy of the individual. Any urine test would lead to a suit for damages for battery and assault and an invasion of privacy. Only members of the US armed forces can be required to have urine tests. That is because they are presumed to have consented when they enlisted. So in the US the community's interests have been sacrificed because of the human rights of drug traffickers and drug consumers. Drug-related crimes flourish. Schools are infected. There is high delinquency and violence amongst students, a high dropout rate, poor discipline and teaching, producing students who make poor workers. So a vicious cycle has set in.

## Democracy and human rights presumed to lead to good government

Whilst democracy and human rights are worthwhile ideas, we should be clear that the real objective is good government. That should be the test for ODA. Is this a good government that deserves ODA [Overseas Development Assistance]? Is it honest and effective? Does it look after its people? Is there an orderly, stable society where people are being educated and trained to lead a productive life?

You may well ask: How do people get a good government in a developing country? I believe we can learn a valuable lesson from the property and educational qualifications the UK and the US had in their early stages of democracy. This can work well in the towns where most people are educated. Moreover it will encourage people to get educated. In the rural areas, the educated are fewer. So more traditional methods of representation, like the village headman or chief, can be the basis of representation. Such an approach can be criticised as elitist, but the chances of getting a good government will be better.

## Human rights: Progress likely if approach is more realistic

On the whole, I think it is more difficult to achieve a working democracy than to make some progress in human rights. Greater respect for human rights is a worthwhile objective. The only practical way forward is the step-by-step incremental approach. Standards of what is civilised behaviour vary with the history and culture of a people, and with the level of deterrence or punishment people in a society are accustomed to.

Our common humanity requires us to persuade all peoples and their governments to move towards more humane, open, responsible and accountable government. Governments should treat their own people, including prisoners, in a humane way. Helmut Schmidt wrote in *Die Zeit* on May 29, 1992, after a visit to China, on the Yellow Emperor: "It seems that the formative force of the Confucian cultural heritage with its tendencies towards vertical meritocracy and hierarchy according to age, with its willingness to learn and to be thrifty, and with the tendency to family and group cohesiveness, does not need Europe's and North America's religious ethics, which are based on a totally different spiritual concept, in order to achieve equal economic performance. Perhaps the West must admit to itself that people living in other continents and other cultural groups with firmly rooted traditions can be thoroughly happy even without the democratic structures

> "Perhaps the West must admit to itself that people living in other continents and other cultural groups with firmly rooted traditions can be thoroughly happy even without the democratic structures which Euro-Americans consider indispensable."

**381**

which Euro-Americans consider indispensable. Therefore we should not ask China to profess democracy, but we should insist on respect of the person, personal dignity and rights."

And one cannot ignore the history, culture and background of a society. Societies have developed separately for thousands of years at different speeds and in different ways. Their ideals and their norms are different. American or European standards of the late 20th century cannot be universal.

Attitudes are changing. Worldwide satellite television makes it increasingly difficult for any government to hide its cruelties to its own people. By international convention, what a government does with its own people is an internal matter and does not concern foreign governments. This convention is difficult to uphold when people worldwide see and condemn the cruelties and want something done to stop them. On the other hand, Western governments often use public opinion as an excuse to interfere with another government's actions. But are Western governments prepared to help financially to ease the severe economic difficulties which are often the cause of upheavals and their suppression by force? Only if they are do they have a moral right to interfere and to be listened to. Eventually the international community will find a balance between non-interference in a country's internal affairs and the moral right to press for more civilised standards of behaviour by all governments. However, I doubt if there will ever be a common universal standard of what is acceptable behaviour.

In the next 20 to 30 years, few societies will be isolated. All will be ever more open to outside contacts, through trade, tourism, investments, TV and radio. These contacts will influence their behaviour, because their values, perceptions and attitudes will change. There will be no convergence to a common world standard. But we can expect more acceptable standards where bizarre, cruel, oppressive practices will become shameful and unacceptable.

We cannot force faster change, unless the advanced countries are prepared to intervene actively. If a target delinquent government collapses and the country breaks down, are the donor countries prepared to move in and put the country together again? In other words, re-colonise and create the preconditions for democracy?

Take the case of Burma. Tough sanctions can break the grip of the military regime. It is better to do it with UN Security Council authority. When the regime breaks down and disorder breaks out in Burma, the UN must be prepared to move in and restore order. Do they move in as peacekeepers or peacemakers? As peacekeepers, they will not be able to control the minorities who are armed and have been fighting the Burmese government since independence in 1947. The Karens, Kachins and others, all want independence. Should they get their independence? Or should they be put down and incorporated into one Burmese union or made into more autonomous states in a loose federation? Will advanced countries undertake the responsibilities for their fate?

If Japan presses for democracy in return for ODA, is she prepared to undertake the responsibility for the integrity of the state and the people's welfare if a government loses its capability to govern, or otherwise disintegrates?

> If a target delinquent government collapses and the country breaks down, are the donor countries prepared to move in and put the country together again?

An analogous dilemma faced the United States in Iraq. Iraqi Republican guards and forces were on the run. President Bush decided not to break the Republican guards. If he brought down the Iraqi government, he would run the risk of the Shi'ites in the south and the Kurds in the north rising up in rebellion against the Sunni Muslims. If President Bush had decided on an imposed democracy, the result would have been difficult. One-man-one-vote means that the Shi'ites who outnumber the Sunnis will become the majority group to the Iraqi government. Then Iraq would get closer to Iran which would be unacceptable to the United States and to Saudi Arabia. Worse and more likely, Iraq would have been broken up into three states, with Kurds in the north, Sunnis in the centre and Shi'ites in the south.

Therefore, for geopolitical reasons, the American mission to convert the world to democracy and human rights had to be put aside. The US allowed Saddam Hussein's dictatorship to carry on. The likelihood of an unsatisfactory geopolitical balance in the Gulf was the reason.

## Some questionable assumptions

If we had a world government for this small interdependent world, will one-man-one-vote lead to progress or regression?

There are some flaws in the assumptions made for democracy. It is assumed that all men and women are equal or should be equal. Hence one-man-one-vote. But is equality realistic? If it is not, to insist on equality must lead to regression. Let me put it to the test in some theoretical situations. If we had a world government for this small interdependent world, will one-man-one-vote lead to progress or regression? All can immediately see that the developed and educated peoples of the world will be swamped by the undeveloped and uneducated, and that no progress will be possible. Indeed if the UK and US had given universal suffrage to their peoples in the 19th century, then economic and social progress might well have been less rapid.

The weakness of democracy is that the assumption that all men are equal and capable of equal contribution to the common good is flawed. This is a dilemma. Do we insist on ideals when they do not fit into practical realities of the world as we know it? Or do we compromise and adjust to realities?

Lee proposed modifying Singapore's voting system to give those aged 35 to 60 years, married and with children, two votes each to reflect their heavier responsibilities and bigger contributions to society. He made these comments in an interview with Warren Fernandez and other Singapore reporters in Perth at the end of his visit to New Zealand and Australia, on May 8, 1994.

# Some men, two votes?

**FERNANDEZ:** May I take up a point that was made in the citation in your honour at the University of Melbourne, which referred to your contribution to the post-colonial debate on the nature of representative government? In that regard, could I refer to your comments to the American journal, *Foreign Affairs*, about the possibility of a "some-men-two-votes system" for Singapore? Is this on the cards? Have there, for example, been Cabinet discussions about it?

**LEE:** No, this is purely my point of view. I have told my younger colleagues a long time ago that we should not make unnecessary changes to the constitution, but that they have to look ahead and keep in mind that no constitution can stay unchanged for all time. The nature of society will change, the external environment that Singapore faces will change, and we have to change. If you want one-man-one-vote or representative government to succeed, from time to time, you will have to adjust your system to make it more viable, and less volatile.

The New Zealanders have run their one-man-one-vote system for 170 to 180 years. But because they have had some 12 years of hardship as their economy ran into trouble, they first voted for a Labour government. That Labour government inflicted pain on them, so they voted for the opposition, National Party. The National government also inflicted pain on them. So they decided to change the system.

It nearly happened in Britain. In the '70s and '80s, they were discussing proportional representation because the old system was not producing results.

The Japanese have had to change their multiple-members constituency system. In America, in the old days, one-man-one-vote excluded blacks. Then the mood changed, and they decided that it would look very bad for them with the world, especially black

Constitutional amendments— Since 1965, more than 25 amendments have been made to the constitution. Major ones include the 1972 provision which sets a two-thirds majority vote in a national referendum to vote on the sovereignty of Singapore, the implementation of the Group Representation Constituency in 1988 and the creation of an Elected Presidency office in 1991.

It is not going to satisfy the purists, who believe that big or small, all contributors to society should have one vote.

Africa. So after the black civil rights movement in the 1960s, they included blacks in one-man-one-vote.

It is not necessary to change our system at present. But, later, we may have to give more weighting to the people whose views should carry more weight because their contributions are greater, and their responsibilities are greater; in which case, we should consider giving those between the ages of 35 and 60, married and with families, one extra vote. Their contribution to the economy and to society is greatest at this stage of life. Also, they need to vote for themselves and also for their children. Their children have an interest that needs to be protected. Once past 60, their children would have grown up, and would vote for themselves. Then the parents should drop back to one vote. But during those critical years, 35–60, people who carry twice as much responsibility should have two votes. This will make for a more viable system and a more stable society.

It is not going to satisfy the purists, who believe that big or small, all contributors to society should have one vote. But at the end of the day, we need a system that works, that enables representative government to function in an effective way.

FERNANDEZ: You have said Singapore may need to consider such a change in the future. When do you think this is likely to happen?

LEE: Maybe in 15 to 20 years. It is a sound way of moving forward. Don't go into proportional representation and these other complicated formulas, hoping that out of coalitions, you will get stability and therefore right decisions.

LIANHE ZAOBAO: But under what circumstances should such a change in the system be made?

LEE: When the system no longer begins to work as efficiently. Because the population has changed in its complexion.

If by 2020 our population policies have not increased our birth rates so that there are enough young workers to make up for those over 60 who have retired from the work force, and we are also unable to get new immigrants to replace Singaporeans who have emigrated, then we will have a lot of old people – about 30 per cent of the population.

Then the interests of the old will be disproportionate in influencing policies, as has happened in some countries of Europe and in America. Then the system will malfunction.

FERNANDEZ: So, in a way, this proposal is tied to the ageing of the population in Singapore?

LEE: Yes. I believe this is one problem we are bound to face. It is already a problem in America. President Reagan tried in 1982 to cut back on social security because it was going to bankrupt the country. But the old people just solidly voted against him and so Reagan backed off.

There are not enough old people in Singapore yet. But I think in 20 years there will be. They would have run through their CPF. We tell them today, keep your CPF in reserve because you will need it, you will live till 75. But they don't believe us. Or if they do, they push it to the back of their minds. But in 20 years' time, when they are over 70 years old and they have run out of their CPF, they are going to vote for a government that promises them more.

**FERNANDEZ:** In which case, would it not be even more difficult to change the system in 20 years' time?

**LEE:** Therefore the need for good timing by the government, before the situation gets out of hand, to shift the centre of gravity to the people who are at their most productive and carrying the responsibilities for the next generation. They have to bring up the next generation and protect their children's future interests. So it's logical to give one vote for themselves and one vote for their children.

**FERNANDEZ:** How do you think such a change to the system will be received by Singaporeans?

**LEE:** We have to do what is fair and practical to avoid the system malfunctioning.

**LIANHE ZAOBAO:** But you are not so worried about the youngsters?

**LEE:** No, not so much. The youngsters will become more productive as they gain experience. That's not the problem. The fickleness or volatility of the young has not been a serious problem. Once they get married and have children, they sober up. But the problem of old people without enough savings will not be easy to handle. We have to keep family ties and obligations strong to solve this problem.

I see more and more of my generation as I wander through the HDB blocks, in senior citizens' corners.

> I see more and more of my generation as I wander through the HDB blocks, in senior citizens' corners.

While declaring himself an "unrepentant socialist", Lee argued that social democrats would have to find ways to keep workers motivated to put in their maximum effort. Only then could socialist countries develop and be in a position to improve workers' lives, he said at the opening session of the Asian Socialist Conference in Bombay on May 6, 1965. For the time being, the socialist credo of giving each according to his need might have to be put on hold. Lee suggested a less utopian but more practical stand: "From each his economic best, To each his economic worth."

# An unrepentant socialist

It is 12 years since the first Asian Socialist Conference in Rangoon in 1953. They have been 12 years of many disappointments and few successes for democratic socialists. Many of the leaders who foregathered on that occasion are now no longer able to lead their countries towards socialism.

Quite a number are in gaols, put there by governments that assert themselves as equally if not more socialist and nationalist than the people they have displaced. Why have these things happened? Why have the hopes of inevitable progress towards a socialist world so lamentably failed to materialise in Asia? How is it that some manifestly non-socialist governments in the region have made more economic progress and increased their Gross National Product more rapidly than countries in Southeast Asia that have had socialist governments?

True, the capitalists, and in particular the Americans, have poured in aid and investments, and perhaps a part of this massive economic transfusion has to some degree benefited the workers. And for a long while Americans preferred to support only anti-communist governments. Indeed they used to find it difficult to distinguish socialists from communists.

Why then did not the advanced countries in Europe with socialist governments give corresponding assistance to their counterparts in Asia? We knew that the communists would never help the democratic socialists. But what of the democratic socialist governments in Europe? Perhaps they did not have the abundance of resources to have helped the enormous populations of South Asia to any appreciable degree. But the fault was nearer home.

The democratic socialists who were in charge of some of these governments in South Asia lacked the managerial and technical expertise in administration, management and the technological and industrial skills to be able to realise their plans for economic transformation. The lack of these instruments of policy implementation could have been made up by borrowing expertise from abroad. This could have helped these countries tide over the period of transition when local men were acquiring the training and skills. Indeed some of this was done on an appreciable scale as in India, with technical assistance from both United Nations agencies and direct from government to government.

But the most grievous indictment against the democratic socialists for their failure to put up a better showing is that in preaching individual human liberties and human freedoms, they forgot to insist, as the communists and the capitalists did, on the individual human duty to work hard and give his utmost. For in the last analysis the better life is produced only by sustained and intense effort.

As democratic socialists we should uphold all individual human liberties. Perhaps we have underestimated the human problems of finding the techniques of organising men for production, and of persuading men to accept the disciplines of modernised agricultural and industrial production, if we are to fulfil their dreams. If we want to mobilise human resources, to pitchfork our countries and backward economies into the industrial and technological era, then no person has the right to slack.

The capitalists make people work through monetary incentives which we call sweated and exploited labour. The communists do it by regimentation and exhortation and a systematically induced state of semi-hysteria for work, using both the stick and the carrot. The democratic socialist is less ruthless and consequently less efficient, torn between his loathing for regimentation and mass coercion and his inhibition to making more effective use of the carrot by his desire to distribute the rewards more fairly and equally too soon.

I am an unrepentant socialist. But in my own state, I have to concede that because it takes a long time to inculcate the high values of public duty and sense of service to the community, performance has been best only when workers are offered high incentives for high performance.

Our building programmes have progressed rapidly because we allowed the individual worker to earn as much as he can over his other workers by working as hard as he likes. Our lowest productivity level is in many sections of our own government services such as our publicly owned dockyards where managers are on salary scales instead of the profit-sharing and bonus schemes of private industry, and where our workers are on wage rates which apply equally between the proficient hardworking man and the mediocre and not so hardworking man.

We have had to recognise these faults. It has not changed our belief in the basic tenet that no man should exploit his fellowman. We believe it is immoral that the ownership of property should allow some to exploit others. But in order to get economic growth we have had to base our policies on the principle, "From each his economic best, To each his economic worth." The ultimate ideal, "From each his best, To each his need", can only be relevant after we have moved away from ignorance, illiteracy, poverty, and economic backwardness.

In order to get economic growth we have had to base our policies on the principle, "From each his economic best, To each his economic worth."

Reflecting on the past decade of few achievements and many omissions is a sobering exercise. But the fact that we are today gathered in Bombay to discuss these problems is in a small way a tribute to the tenacity of the democratic socialist. If we re-evaluate and re-formulate our thinking and policy to make a more effective contribution in the next decade we can still make a contribution to Asia's and Africa's advance.

Lee had a deep aversion to welfarism, having seen how it had sapped the
people of their will to work and given rise to a culture of dependency in
welfare states in the West. He rose to hammer home this point during the
1991 Budget debate in Parliament on March 19, 1991, his first major
speech in the House since stepping down as prime minister in November
1990. He took his longtime political adversary Lee Siew Choh to task for
advocating that Singapore emulate the welfare systems found abroad.

# Why the welfare states failed

Mr Deputy Speaker, Sir, the divide between Dr Lee Siew Choh and me is an unbridgeable
one, although we originally had him as part of the PAP. And it stems from a fundamental
difference in approach to life and to society. We were both idealistic enough to believe
that in a more compassionate world with equal opportunities, there would be less poverty,
less misery, more opportunities, more prosperity. That is why he joined the PAP. He then
went in for utopian politics. He believed in the communist (socialist) credo that all men
should be made equal and be equally treated and equally rewarded.

Once upon a time, in the 1950s, many Singaporeans, especially the Chinese-educated,
believed that China was a stupendous success in instant revolution and industrialisation,
arising from glossy magazines and brilliant broadcasts to production figures and spick and
span showpieces for distinguished visitors to be taken to, children's palaces, model factories,
model villages. I believe the majority of young Singaporeans or young Chinese in Singapore
in the 1950s would have voted for that system. That is the danger of one-man-one-vote.
It was a mirage, it was a con job. We knew it only in the 1970s and it became obvious to
everyone in the 1980s.

After all these years, let me pose one simple question to the Member: 70 years in
the Soviet Union of the egalitarian society, have they banished begging, prostitution,
misery, hunger? Is that the way? To suppress the individual instinct to perform, to excel,
to be better than the other, to get better rewards, bigger prizes, to increase his family's
chances in life, so that they can have a better kickoff? All that was stifled with the objective
of an equal egalitarian society.

God did not make the Russians equal. Lenin and Stalin tried to. You are too long,
they chop you down. The end result is total misery. They tried it in China, it has failed.
They tried it in Vietnam, boat people. In North Korea, total devastation.

God did not make
the Russians
equal. Lenin and
Stalin tried to.

Let me take a few instances. Even in the capitalist West where they have tried throwing money at problems, what is the end result? You go down New York, Broadway. You will see the beggars, people on the streets. Worse than in the '50s and in the early '60s, before the Great Society programmes. Why? Why did it get worse after compassion moved a president, motivated with a great vision of a society which was wealthy and cared for, could look after everybody – the blacks, the minorities, the dispossessed, the disadvantaged. There is more unhappiness and more hardship today and more beggars, more muggers. Why is that? Have we not learnt?

Where are the beggars in Singapore? Show me. I take pride in that. Has anybody died of starvation? Anybody without a home left to die in the streets, to be collected as corpses?

Because we came to the realistic conclusion that the human being is motivated by instincts that go down to the basic genes in life. And the first basic instinct is to protect yourself, and stronger than that, to protect your offspring so that there is the next generation. You kill that link, you have killed off mankind. They half killed that link in China by removing the children from parental control to the communes, and disaster followed. We went with the instinct of the individual.

Not all can perform in a free and equal society. Free chances, there will always be the losers. There is the altruistic streak in society. Individuals who have done well, who want to do something for their fellowmen, and we should use that. Not everybody has it in the same measure, and we have used it. You ignore that and substitute for the altruistic individual with that drive to do something for his fellowmen, a bureaucracy, and you have got corruption, inefficiency, and failure.

It has happened over and over again. Do we need to learn all over again when we can see what happened to the British and the Australians? They went in for compassionate welfare programmes. They paid their unemployed almost as much as the employed when they lost their jobs. They had the right to refuse three or four jobs until the right one came along, commensurate with what they were getting the last time, to their liking. The result was layabouts. So finally the Australians gave up, and a Labour government in Australia has struck down unemployment benefits. If we do not learn from other people's errors, costly errors, we would be ruined, wouldn't we? We have got very little margin to spare.

I take this advantage, not because I believe Dr Lee will influence a younger generation of Singaporeans, but just in case there are the few errant minds, to remind them where we would have been if we had pursued the policies he advocated. I am proud of the ethos with which we have infused a younger generation of Singaporeans. We have given them the chance to stand up, be self-reliant, and be enough of a team, of a nation, so that all can perform at their best, and the whole group, including the losers, will not perish. And that is achieved by going with human instincts, going with basic culture, and making adjustments along the way for those who would otherwise lose.

Watch any tennis tournament. There are vast differences in ability. There are vast differences in the prizes they award and the royalties that go with the first prize, as you

> Where are the beggars in Singapore? Show me. I take pride in that.

sponsor shirts, rackets, tennis shoes, tennis bands, wrist bands. But what we do not see are the preliminary eliminations. They get prizes too. Otherwise, for every competition you may not get more than eight turning up, and you may find the same players competing to be the final eight.

I therefore ask him, even at this late stage: Does he really want to mock our urging the younger generation to respect their elders and look after them? Watch out. There may come a day when he will be grateful that his grandchildren had listened to us and respect him and have affection for him and visit him in his old age. Otherwise he may be left to Mr Wong Kan Seng's old folks' home, and that will be a tragedy which I would not like to visit on my worst enemy.

Education was always one of Lee's key concerns. But not for him the egalitarian idea that all students are equally able, if given equal attention in schools, or extra tuition to make up for what they lack at home. To him, some children are obviously more gifted than others. Rather than holding these bright ones back in the name of equality, he argued in a meeting with school principals at the Victoria Theatre on August 29, 1966, that they should be drawn out and helped to excel. These children would form the elite in Singapore, from which would be drawn the country's future leaders. On their shoulders would be the task of raising the lot of all in society.

# Schools must have character

**The ideal product is the student, the university graduate who is strong, robust, rugged, with tremendous qualities of stamina, endurance, great intellectual discipline and, most important of all, humility and love for his community; a readiness to serve whether God or king or country or, if you like, just his community.**

Supposing now, I am given superhuman powers. I say, "Look, here is Singapore with this limitation: 2 million people. What kind of schools, education would I have?" I will tell you what I think I would want to do if I were endowed with superhuman powers.

I would like first, at the very top of your society, to rear a generation that has all the qualities needed to lead and give the people the inspiration, the drive to make it succeed. This would be your elite. If you go to any country, even young ones like Australia, they have special schools.

What is the ideal product? The ideal product is the student, the university graduate who is strong, robust, rugged, with tremendous qualities of stamina, endurance and, at the same time, with great intellectual discipline and, most important of all, humility and love for his community; a readiness to serve whether God or king or country or, if you like, just his community.

Every society produces this type or they try to. The British have special schools for them. They send them to Eton and Harrow and a few very exclusive private schools which they call "public schools", then they send them on to Oxford and Cambridge. They have legends that the Battle of Waterloo was won on the playing fields of Eton.

The Australians are trying to do it. Recently, Prince Charles went to this school at Geelong. This is their equivalent where they try to build the complete Australian with great vitality, outdoor life, resourcefulness. Even caught in the bush, he will learn how to survive, and he will have great qualities of discipline and heart. That is your ideal.

And, from time to time, such people are produced. The Americans produce them, the Russians produce them, the Chinese produce them. The Germans produce them; the Indians produce them, but with this slight difference: that the Indians have never placed the emphasis on the physical side. They have always placed it on the spiritual side.

We should try to do that. Not every boy is equal in his endowments in either physical stamina or mental capacity or character. But you want to try and get all those with the potential to blossom forth. That is your spearhead in your society. On them depends the pace of progress.

This government at the moment – the whole of this administration – is running on I would say the ability and drive and dedication – not on the basis of what they get in salaries – of about 150 people. You remove these 150 people, if you can identify the 150; whoever wants to destroy this society, identifies these 150 people and kills them, the push will be gone. This is a very thin crust of leadership. This has to be spread quickly, more and more.

Then you have your middle strata of good executives. Not everybody can be a leader, can be a general, can be a prime minister, can be a top scientist or a physicist. And you can be the best general in the world or the best prime minister in the world, but if you do not have high-quality executives to help you carry out your ideas, thinking and planning, you cannot succeed. So you need the middle strata of good executives. And then, finally you have your broad base.

In any army, in one battalion, you have 60 to 70 officers, one to two hundred sergeants and corporals, and the others, about 500, are privates. It must be. This is life. And the quality of your privates determines the quality of your army as much as the quality of the generals does.

I am as much interested in the bottom as I am in the top of this pyramid. But we must accept the fact that this is life.

If I were given superhuman powers, I would say, "Right, then I form these schools." Not just one. I will probably form three or four; and boys and girls, all who have potential, near-geniuses, people who can read your poetry in three languages if you give them the training, give them the character that goes with it. Then you have this middle strata.

Then – which is what Singapore has not reconciled itself to – there are people who are just average. But even that average, we must nurture. That average person must be one who has a sense of discipline in himself, and social discipline. He respects his community and does not spit all over the place.

There are societies in the world where things have dropped so low that your social discipline has collapsed. Recently, I went through a capital where the army had taken over and they decided to smack down a whole row of shanty-huts built on pavements and roads. The structure had collapsed. The state was no longer able to control; the politicians were in a hopeless mess. So, people built all these huts all over the place. The army came with the gun and cleaned it up. They were ashamed of it. But they did not solve the social problems. Because the people still had nowhere to go. They probably slept on the pavements and they excreted on the pavements. The society had collapsed. And this has happened in a number of places in Asia. Because that bottom layer of average boys and girls was never given the care, the attention and the inculcation of good responses, good habits, good attitudes.

> You remove these 150 people, if you can identify the 150; whoever wants to destroy this society, identifies these 150 people and kills them, the push will be gone.

How do you produce this sort of structure: top leaders, good executives, well-disciplined and highly civic-conscious broad mass? I say it goes back to the school and the teacher. And the school or the teacher is a very personal thing. We have expanded all these schools so fast, you might as well now call these schools by numbers – School No. 75 or School No. 85. We are taking names of roads and streets for schools. They have no special character.

To me, just reading the Cabinet paper from the Ministry of Education of our requirements for secondary schools and about there being no need for more primary schools, my mind goes back to the day I went to school. And to me, the school was the beginning and end of life, with the teachers who were in charge of me.

You know, the school must have character; it must belong. You cannot have anonymous schools and anonymous teachers – which was what we tended to do because we were expanding so rapidly. You take Raffles Institution, change it and call it Beach Road School. You have lost something. That is why the schools that did not expand too rapidly, Chinese High School, Chung Cheng, Nanyang, Catholic High School, St Joseph's, ACS: they maintained an *esprit de corps*. The boys were proud for it. And, because we expanded so much, the government schools went down so low that we abolished the inter-school sports because there were no sports masters.

I say we reverse that. There must be enough talent in the population. Build it up; reverse the process. Identify the school; make it mean something. A teacher cannot really perform his duty unless he feels he is doing something worthwhile. I want every school teacher in the classroom to feel for and with his flock of 35 or 32 children. If you do not feel that, you cannot give the pupil something.

You cannot have anonymous schools and anonymous teachers.

# Being a hard nation

I think you must have something in you to be a "have" nation. You must want. That is the crucial thing. Before you have, you must want to have. And to want to have means to be able first, to perceive what it is you want; secondly, to discipline and organise yourself in order to possess the things you want – the industrial sinews of our modern economic base; and thirdly, the grit and the stamina, which means cultural mutations in the way of life in large parts of the tropical areas of the world where the human being has never found it necessary to work in the summer, harvest before the autumn, and save it up for the winter.

You must want. That is the crucial thing.

In large areas of the world, a cultural pattern is determined by many things, including climatic conditions. As long as that persists, nothing will ever emerge. And for it to emerge, there must be this desire between contending factions of the "have" nations to try and mould the "have-not" nations after their own selves. If they want that strongly enough, competition must act as an accelerator, and no more than an accelerator to the creation of modern, industrial, technological societies in the primitive agricultural regions of the world.

I think Asia can be very clearly demarcated into several distinct parts – East Asia is one: it has got a different tempo of its own. So have South Asia and Southeast Asia. I think this is crucial to an understanding of the possibilities of either development for the good or development which is not in the interest of peace and human happiness in the region.

I like to demarcate – I mean not in political terms – demarcate them half in jest, but I think half with some reality on the basis of difference in the tempo according to the people who know what these things are. I mean East Asia: Korea, Japan and mainland China and including the Republic of China in Taiwan and Vietnam. They are supposed

I have Mahayanas and Hinayanas all mixed up in Singapore.

to be Mahayana Buddhists. And then there is Cambodia, Thailand, Burma, Ceylon, which are supposed to be Hinayana Buddhists. According to the Hinayana Buddhists, if the bedbug disturbs you then you take your mattress and shake it off; there is that compassion not only for the human being but for the bedbug, and you give it another chance and you let it off. Either it finds its way on to some other creature or it finds its way back to your bed. But watching the Japanese over the years, I have not the slightest doubt that is not what they do. And I think this makes some difference. I am not talking now – isms or ideologies. It is something deeper. It is part of the tempo, the way of life.

My interest now in this thing is that I have Mahayanas and Hinayanas all mixed up in Singapore. So at any one particular time, I have to find out which is the dominant consensus. There is always a consensus either on one side or the other, but I have to find out which is the dominant one. And I would like to believe that, in the long run, besides Hinayana and Mahayana Buddhists, there are lots of other people interested in maintaining peace, stability and some semblance of man's inevitable progress – or, at least, supposedly inevitable progress – towards the better life for everybody to make it possible for all those in South and Southeast Asia who want – this is crucial – who want and are prepared to pay the price of what they want, to join the world community of "haves".

As leader of a multiracial society, Lee was acutely aware of the political problems that would arise if the different races progressed at different rates. Lee sought a deep understanding of the problem, turning to anthropology and sociology for answers to difficult questions, such as why the Malays in Singapore were less predisposed to the pursuit of material wealth than the other races here. He believed that the problem of the Malays falling behind economically could only be addressed if such thorny issues were faced head on, as he did in a speech to the Southeast Asia Business Committee Meeting Dinner, at Hotel Singapura on May 12, 1968.

# The difference between the Malays and the Chinese

This is Southeast Asia. It is tropical and equatorial, and before the air-conditioner, it was only a half-working day. This has had its effect upon the habits of successive generations. One of the habits is not to put something by. People do not save for the winter, because there is no winter. So capital accumulation is slow.

When the Portuguese, Spanish, Dutch, British, French and Americans moved into this region they later brought in people who knew how to save for the winter. So the Indians went with the British into Burma. The Indians came with the British into Singapore and Malaya. The Dutch made use of the Chinese as tax collectors. And the Chinese were encouraged to come to Singapore and Malaya. The Spaniards, after two successive massacres of the Chinese, still brought them back to the Philippines.

Is it coincidence that throughout East Africa, small shopkeepers and merchants are nearly all Indians? And throughout West Africa they are Lebanese. They ran the little banking and retail businesses. They knew who was a good risk and was sure to bring in the harvest. They knew who was not a good risk because the chances were his harvests would never come to fruition, or he would not bring them in to discharge the immediate credits he sought.

We have in Singapore a fair sample of the various types in Northeast, South and Southeast Asia, and of the wider world beyond. To the untutored eye we were just so many Chinese, Indians and Malays. But not to a Singaporean. The Chinese could be classified distinctly in the past, though less so now – Hokkiens, who were the majority of the labourers and the small shopkeepers; the rice merchants are Teochews because they have organised the rice wholesale trade in Bangkok, and Teochews also do the textile

*Is it coincidence that throughout East Africa, small shopkeepers and merchants are nearly all Indians?*

Singapore's 3 million people (1997) is 77.7 per cent Chinese, 14.1 per cent Malay, 7.1 per cent Indian and 1.1 per cent other races.

wholesale and retail trade. The Cantonese are goldsmiths; and the Hakkas the jewellers, [and own] pawnshops and Chinese medicine shops. The Hainanese originally ran coffee shops but now are in charge of the whole of the catering business. So with the Indians. The Tamils are small shopkeepers and labourers. The Malayalees, with a high level of education and inadequate opportunities, voted in the communist state government in Kerala. They are clerks and artisans in Singapore. The Punjabis, the Sikhs are a remarkable people. There are only about 10,000 in Singapore. But if you watch a passing out parade of our officer cadets, you might think that Singapore comprised about 15 to 20 per cent of Sikhs, because the people with turbans are distinctive. Anthropologists say it is a myth that created warrior and non-warrior castes in India. But whatever it is, they seem to jump, run and charge better. They were brought in as burly watchmen. They turned to money-lending and lent at keen rates of interest. They educated their children to be high court judges, surgeons and to fill the other professions.

We have Singapore Malays. To those not from this part of the world, they are all Malays. But Singaporeans know that there is a big difference between a Rhio or a Johor Malay, or a Sumatran, and between a Menangkabau and an Achinese or a Batak, all from Sumatra, a Boyanese or Javanese. We know that the Boyanese are the most thrifty of the Malay groups.

However, there has been a great deal of intermarriages within the ethnic groups. Hokkiens marry Hakkas, Teochews, Cantonese, Hainanese; the Tamils marry Malayalees, Bengalis or Punjabis. There is much less of those who marry across ethnic groups. But all groups have in common that desire to make good. They are migrants who have left their past behind them. They are determined to make good, and have a passion for education and learning. There is a zealous striving which did not exist in the original societies from whence they sprang.

One of the problems which has worried me is the uneven rate of development within the community, because the Chinese, Indians, Ceylonese and Eurasians progress at a faster rate than our Malays. If we do not correct this imbalance, then, in another 10 to 20 years, we will have a Harlem, something not to be proud of.

So from politics I have had to go to anthropology and sociology to seek the reasons for this. I am not sure whether this is the final explanation. This is my tentative reading on the subject: that cultural-ethnic factors have a decisive influence on performance. Let me quote a paragraph from a treatise by Mr Bryan Parkinson, a Fellow attached to the Centre for Southeast Asian Studies in the University of Hull, in the January 1967 issue of *Modern Asian Studies*, page 30, published by Cambridge University Press.

"The degree and pace of economic development experienced by any society are the consequences of two influences: the influence of man's environment on man and of man on his environment. Even though man's ultimate economic potential may be determined by his environment, the present stage of his economic development depends not insignificantly upon his ability and willingness to transform his environment and perhaps more important, upon the strides made in that direction by his forebears. In some instances, an unfavourable economic environment can be converted into one which produces continuing economic development; in other circumstances, a rather more favourable environment may sustain very little economic development."

On page 33:

"Drawing upon some of the observations made, the evidence suggests, first, that there is a tendency among the rural Malays to resist change, and secondly, that there are some understandable reasons for it.

"… For instance, there is still considerable opposition to the government's appeal for the planting of more than one rice crop per year, even though rice-fields lie fallow for about six months per year under the present system. A reason sometimes given by the farmers for their reluctance to plant a three-month variety of rice in an off season is that its yield is very much lower than the yield of the six-month variety, but the work entailed in growing the six-month variety remains roughly similar to the work entailed in growing the three-month variety …"

Further on the same page:

"However, it is the women who seem to be most opposed to changing the location of the seed-bed, and the ones that I spoke to said that, in any event, the old way was more agreeable since planting seedlings on an up-country dry land had become a social occasion which was enjoyed by the entire village."

In a footnote he explained, *"Buat kerja chara dulu."* That means, work in the old way. The footnote adds that planting rice in seed-beds in up-country land is an occasion for a picnic.

In case this was a bias of one particular sociologist I turned to several others. Let me quote Judith Djamour, a sociologist and wife of a professor of anthropology, University of London, who did research on the Malays in Singapore in the late 1940s and in the early 1950s. In *Malay kinship and marriage in Singapore*, London School of Economics, Monographs on Social Anthropology, page 10:

"Singapore Malays and Chinese certainly appear to have different cultural values. Singapore Chinese on the whole considered the acquisition of wealth to be one of the most important aims in life, and almost an end in itself; they were indefatigable workers and keen businessmen. Singapore Malays, on the other hand, attached great importance to easy and graceful living."

And by way of example, on page 11 she recited this anecdote:

"I had a neighbour whose husband was a lorry driver earning $120/– a month. One day she told me cheerfully that she was very happy because her husband had found another job, driving a small van for $80/– a month. It was a better job because it meant shorter hours than driving the lorry and was less tiring. It also meant that her husband came home earlier in the evenings and could have more leisure; this was much better than working until 9 or 10 p.m. on most evenings and earning $120/– per month. What was the use of earning a larger salary if one could not rest and have some leisure? she asked. Moreover, driving the van dirtied his clothes less than driving the lorry and she would not have as much washing to do."

In case we tend to think this unreasonable or irrational, Bryan Parkinson goes on to explain on page 43 of the first article I cited:

"Neither one is necessarily superior to the other, it is simply that the maximising postulates of the Chinese are more likely to lead to economic development in the Western sense than are the maximising postulates of the Malays."

And in case "maximising postulates" is too complicated a phrase, may I just go back to a short sentence on page 42:

"This desire to succeed is no more absent from rural Malay society than it is from any other, but to the Malay success means something different from what it does, for example, to the Malaysian Chinese. The Chinese seem to regard success as being the improvement of their economic position even if this requires some fundamental change or innovation. The Malays seem to regard success as doing what their forebears have approved and practised, but doing it as well as they can. Wealth and economic advancement are desired by the Malays, but not at the expense of renouncing utterly the traditions and traditional occupations of their forebears to which they have grown accustomed. …"

And he ends by saying this:

"There is nothing irrational about Malay values, and to criticise them in terms of other values is reprehensible."

"That is not to say that all Chinese succeed. But succeed or fail, the main point is that they are not content to accept, or to follow unquestioningly, a financially unrewarding occupation if it is in their power to change that occupation. It is the fact that so many of them are trying to improve their economic lot, trying to master their economic environment, and are willing to take risks and to innovate, that enables many of them to succeed. And it is upon this type of creative individual that economic growth under capitalism, rightly or wrongly, depends.

"… There is nothing irrational about Malay values, and to criticise them in terms of other values is reprehensible. But if the values of the Malays remain basically unaltered, and there is no reason in Malay terms to explain why they should alter, then it is likely that economic advance for them will remain relatively slow."

This poses an extremely delicate problem. We tried over the last nine years systematically to provide free education from primary school right up to university for any Singapore citizen who is a Malay. This is something we don't give to the majority ethnic group – the Chinese. They pay fees from secondary school onwards. We don't find it necessary to do it for the other ethnic minorities, because broadly speaking, they are making similar progress as the Chinese. All are achievement-orientated, striving, acquisitive communities.

The reluctant conclusion that we have come to after a decade of the free education policy is that learning does not begin in school. It starts in the home with the parents and the other members of the family. Certainly the adoption of values comes more from the home, the mother, than the teacher. This means change will be a slow process. It can be accelerated in some cases by our judicious intermingling of the communities so that, thrown into the more multiracial milieu we have in our new housing estates, Malay children are becoming more competitive and more striving.

Culture to Lee was a vital factor in a society's success. It embodied the society's values and shared memories and was reflected in its religion and language. But rapid socioeconomic change had blunted the ability of an older generation to transmit these values to the young. Lee raised the alarm about this in a speech at a Chinese New Year reception at the Istana on February 15, 1984.

# It's not just about firing crackers and New Year food

Language is related to, but not synonymous with, culture. Culture has been defined (by Webster's) as the ideas, customs, skills, arts, etc. of a given people in a given period. In anthropology it means all knowledge that is acquired by man by virtue of his membership of society. A culture incorporates all the shared knowledge, expectations and beliefs of a group. Language gives access to the literature which expresses a culture, but language is not culture. English is the language of Britain, America, Canada, Australia, New Zealand, South Africa, Jamaica, Barbados, and the English-speaking Caribbean countries. Their cultures are all different from the British, especially those of the Caribbean. …

Nor have the English language and British culture stayed immutable. Their culture is not as dynamic as before the war. The people are less achievement-orientated because they have become dependent in the welfare state. This loss of dynamism is also reflected in their language. British English has not developed as vigorously as American English. It is American television features, not British, which dominate world markets.

Language and culture must both change to enable a people to solve new problems. Indeed the strength of the language and culture of a people depends on their suppleness to help the people adjust to changed conditions. For example, Japanese language and culture of a century ago since the Meiji Restoration of 1868 have been considerably developed and adjusted to meet new needs. The Japanese people successfully adopted Western science and technology because they were supple and pragmatic about their language and culture. They borrowed new Western institutions and ideas. They introduced universal education, created a two-chamber Parliament, introduced legal codes, and revamped their army and navy on German and British models. They freely adopted

The Japanese people successfully adopted Western science and technology because they were supple and pragmatic about their language and culture.

Western words, adding vigour to the Japanese language. Similarly, after defeat in World War II, during and after the American occupation of Japan, American words, ideas, and social organisations were adapted and adopted by the Japanese. They learned of productivity and quality control from the Americans and improved on them, just as they had copied and improved on many Chinese innovations like the abacus.

The strongest and most durable of value systems or culture is religion. Christians, through translations of the Bible into hundreds of languages, from Hebrew and Greek to Latin, English, French, German, Spanish, Chinese, etc., have spread their faith through all continents. And it is the same faith, whatever the language they pray in. It proves how the content, the ideas that the language carries endure despite changing the medium or language which carries the ideas.

I do not expect Singapore to become a purely English-speaking society. The majority of the older generation cannot speak English. They still use dialects, although they now understand Mandarin, through TV. Next, the majority of the younger generation speak Mandarin and will continue to use it if we succeed in creating a supportive Mandarin-speaking environment. Further, a small proportion of the young Chinese, perhaps as much as 10 per cent, may not be able to master English. They will master Mandarin because it is closer to the dialect their parents speak at home. So others have to speak Mandarin to them. And there will also be some Malays who cannot master English and will have to be addressed in Malay. …

The threat to our culture comes from the fundamental social and economic changes that have taken place. Our women are all educated and have equal job opportunities. This has increased family incomes. This has also given financial independence to wives. Fortunately, the older generation had successfully transmitted their values to the present generation, or there would have been a large increase in the number of divorces. That divorces have not shot up is a tribute to the way traditional marriage values have survived.

Working mothers who do not spend enough time with their children, plus the break-up of the extended families – these two changes are the real dangers to the transmission of our traditional values, or culture. Unless both mother and father make time to inculcate the values and to shape the attitudes of their children, or enlist the help of grandparents, the children will acquire more of their values from outside the home, their peers. And these values may not be what they should be.

Another powerful factor in shaping values is the pervasive influence of our television. Most of our TV features are imported from America or Hongkong.

With nuclear families and working mothers increasing, our teachers will inevitably play a more important role as the imparter of values. Unfortunately, the quality of our teachers recruited in the 1960s and early 1970s is not as high as that of the 1950s. Rapid economic growth drew the able students to banking and industry, away from teaching. This was made worse because there was no comparable increase in teachers' salaries. We have to reverse this trend and recruit better qualified teachers, which means paying them what they can get in industry, commerce or banking.

That divorces have not shot up is a tribute to the way traditional marriage values have survived.

Speaking to my three friends over lunch, I was reinforced in my view that the future of our children cannot depend on happy recollections of crackers and special Chinese New Year cakes or food.

Even after we have improved moral teaching in schools by teachers of high moral standing, parents must still make time for their children in the evenings and at weekends. And those who can should maintain the extended family so that the grandparents can help bring up and influence their children. We have educated our women and want them to work. We intend to provide their children with well-run creches, nursery schools, and allow them to employ foreign domestic workers. But do our women need to value their careers more than, and at the expense of, their families?

Speaking to my three friends over lunch, I was reinforced in my view that the future of our children cannot depend on happy recollections of crackers and special Chinese New Year cakes or food. There are more fundamental attributes in our way of life than the sound of crackers, and special flowers and fruits, and new clothes connected with Chinese New Year, however much joy these memories may bring. The relationships between children and parents, between brothers and sisters, between husband and wife, and the rights and duties of parents and of children – these are crucial to the continuity of any civilisation. The day we divorce each other freely, as they already do in the West, and toss the children about like football between father and mother, although we may speak Chinese and may be able to quote the classics, we would already have changed, and for the worse.

Although Singapore, Hongkong, Taipei and Guangzhou are different societies with different lifestyles, nevertheless, for the present, there are common features in all of them: the close-knit ties of family, where the respect for and care of parents is the mirror image of love and responsibility for the upbringing and training of children. Chinese in these societies still place the interests of family and society above those of the individual. These are profoundly Chinese traditional values. These are worth preserving.

Preserving a society's culture and ethos involved more than keeping up with traditions and outward forms. More important were the underlying values and world view held by the masses. In a speech, titled "Changes in Singapore: The Obvious and the Imperceptible", to undergraduates at the National University of Singapore and Nanyang Technological Institute, on August 22, 1988, Lee spelt out his concerns about the changes he observed in the society.

# We are too Westernised

… the people who work in the lower echelons, they were hardworking, thrifty, had tremendous stamina, grit, and they put society above self, particularly the Chinese who formed the majority.

If we had a British-type workforce, we would not have made it. We had a Singapore-type workforce that produced the results. So it was the bi-cultural leadership that understood them and at the same time understood the modern world, and therefore meshed in the desires, the urges of the people at large and the mechanisms, investments, manufacturing processes, services that we were able to export to the world, primarily the West. …

I met a group of Hongkong professionals who were extremely uneasy, and we discussed a scheme that would make it possible for them to consider using Singapore as a perch in case of need, and continuing to work in Hongkong. At the end of their stay, when I met them, they said, "You are a very Western society, we are very Chinese." I said, what's the difference? They said, "Your people, right down to ordinary workers, they look so Westernised, their behaviour is extremely Western. We are very Oriental."

I then started to probe this. As I met friends, looked up their data, I discovered that this casual remark had profound significance. This was '84. It's the software in the younger generation which will determine whether Singapore continues to thrive, to prosper, to be a dynamo as it used to be, as it has been, or whether it will plateau like so many Western societies, like Europe or Britain, where they've just lost steam. They don't see the point of striving and achieving any more. They're just comfortable and they're happy. And the Europeans in particular, more than the Americans, they feel comfortable with an enlarged community in 1992. They can afford some protectionism. It does not matter if world trade becomes too fierce and too competitive for them. Life could go on, for at least some time.

"You are a very Western society, we are very Chinese. Your people, right down to ordinary workers, they look so Westernised, their behaviour is extremely Western. We are very Oriental."

I don't think how you dress, whether you wear shorts or ties or open-neck shirts, or wear your hair short or long, makes the slightest difference.

One problem therefore is a difficult, almost an intractable one. We can't reverse track. In fact there was no option. We couldn't have used Chinese. It would have caused tremendous conflict, would have not got us here. If we continued with Malay as the national language, our economy would not have made it and the people would have rejected the government. Tamil was out of the question. So there was no choice. The consequence is to ask ourselves, is it possible to maintain our core values in spite of this barrage of books, television, magazines, travel, people?

First, to succeed, we must decide, yes, this is a problem, we are under assault, what is it we want to keep?

I am not familiar with basic Malay and Indian values as much as I am with Chinese values. But I do not believe there's all that much disparity between the Asian cultures. The Malays are least under assault because they have religion – Islam. The strongest single factor in any culture is your religion. It is the book by which you live, your behaviour, your rituals, your prayers, the things you say and do, your day of remembrances. And theirs is strong and resurgent. The Indians, more than the Chinese, attend their temples, keep to custom. And I agree with this writer in the *Sunday Times*, I think it was yesterday, Miss Tan Sai Siong, that Indians have changed less than Chinese. Malays, least of all. Indians still observe their customs, still have arranged marriages.

What is it that we should consider core values? I don't think how you dress, whether you wear shorts or ties or open-neck shirts, or wear your hair short or long, makes the slightest difference. Unless it's a manifestation of an inner urge. But these core values, I believe, are basic. Do you consider your basic relationships to be fundamental? The human relationships. What Confucius described as the five critical relationships. Mencius epigrammatised it in this way. I read it to you in translation – "Mo Tze taught the people how to cultivate land. He appointed Xie as the Minister of Education, whose duty was to teach the people human relationships. Love between father and son, one; two, duty between ruler and subject; three, distinction between husband and wife; four, precedence of the old over the young; and five, faith between friends." Father and son, ruler and subject, husband and wife, old over young, faith between friends. In other words, the family is absolutely the fundamental unit in society. From family, to extended family, to clan, to nation.

In the West, with the tendency of modern government taking over more and more the functions of caring for the young and caring for the old, and in fact, caring for everybody – the unemployed, the disabled and so on, the family is becoming irrelevant. So much so that half the children born in some American societies are born out of wedlock. They are living together but they don't feel that there is any need yet to make a commitment to each other. But they have committed the next generation. …

Have we changed? Let's go through some of the basic core values.

Strong family ties? Yes, but only the immediate family, the nuclear family, father, mother, children. It does not include grandfather, uncles, cousins. They're remote. They live somewhere else, in some other flat, perhaps near by and they can leave the baby with them. But the links are not as close as when I grew up.

I grew up in a big extended family home. A rambling house in Siglap, Katong. I grew up with a wealth of cousins. … There were five households – grandparents and four married sons and daughters and their children. So the relationship was a close one until, just before the war, we set up home on our own. But because the years of childhood were years of living in an extended family, the bonds are close.

Marriage pattern? Altered beyond recognition. The arranged marriages are gone. Children are better educated than their parents. They decide the parents' ways and tastes and choices are not acceptable. The result, you all know.

Relationship with authority? Ruler and subject by and large still abiding. But the older generation is more deferential, respectful of ministers, of officials, than the younger generation. I'm not saying it's good or bad. It's just an observation. The younger generation feels more equal with the official they deal with, the less educated or better educated than the counter clerk. And because it's one-man-one-vote, the ministers go out of their way to be approachable, friendly, and a sense of equality, of talking on level terms, has become the norm. Not necessarily bad provided that doesn't lead to what it has led to in the West, in Britain and America, where they are contemptuous of politicians. Politicians make them promises with no intention, with no capability of ever fulfilling them. And they carry out polls to discover who are the people least respected or honoured or thought well of – politicians and journalists way down at the bottom. Why? Multiple reasons. If you keep on making ingratiating statements, put out in response to secret polls you have taken, it must lead to cynicism and eventually to scorn, contempt.

Thrift, hard work, faith between friends? Hard work, yes; thrift, with CPF, less so. Faith between friends – I have not noticed deterioration, but with time, with mobility, we may get what Alvin Toffler once described as "the disposable society". As you move up, you dispose of your furniture, your old wives, your old clothes and you acquire new ones and you dispose of your friends too. I do not think we've come to that but we are becoming a rapidly mobile population. If you are good, you've got a personable character, you've got the right drive, you get into the right career path, it's the express way to the top. And rapid change in lifestyles as you get up to the top. Now, all that we can get in our stride, provided the core values remain. The ones who are 30 and above probably are already secured because they grew up at one time when their parents had large families and plenty of time to spend on them. It's the ones now in primary school perhaps, even in lower secondary school. Both parents working, huge classes – one teacher to 40 students, no individual attention. And the nature of the teacher also has changed. She used or he used to be a very respected member of society because there were very few educated people in the 1940s, in the 1950s. Teachers were educated and they were well paid. They had good moral standards, were well-behaved and imparted, by example, those values.

Then came rapid growth – the late '60s and into the '70s and on to the '80s. Good teachers left. By the droves. I see it because I get the CVs [curriculum vitae], they are in the foreign office, they are going abroad, they are in the Economic Development division. They have left the schools. Enterprising, the able, the ones with the drive.

> As you move up, you dispose of your furniture, your old wives, your old clothes and you acquire new ones and you dispose of your friends too.

The hotel manager looked at me and said, ah, Chiang Kai Shek. I said, no, no, I come from Singapore. He says, yes, Chiang Kai Shek, good man.

The result? If you become a teacher, you are less successful, morale goes down, the less successful stay behind and are recruited, they are less of a model for students. We've spent the last 10 years reversing that trend, trying not only to pay them more, but also to give them a status in our very achievement-conscious society.

By and large, it's a problem still at the top. Only the highly educated have that degree of bi-culturism where they are more Western than Eastern. At the middle and in the lower ranges, it's still very much an Asian society. The Western habits, songs, dances, whether it's a disco or Swing Singapore, their dress styles or their fast foods, that's just a veneer. But if it seeps down, if we are not conscious of what is happening and we allow this process to go on unchecked, and it seeps down, then I believe we have a bigger problem to deal with, where the middle ranges will also be more Western than Asian.

The problem is going to be acute over the next 10, 15 years. If we can hold out in these next 10, 15, at the most 20 years, I believe the pendulum will swing the other way. It is based on my observation, it's human nature. Race is an obvious part of your being. I once turned up after the war in a hotel in Switzerland. I was not a wealthy student, but I had some savings and decided I'd have a holiday in 1947, '48. And the hotel manager looked at me and said, ah, Chiang Kai Shek. I said, no, no, I come from Singapore. He says, yes, Chiang Kai Shek, good man.

So, whether you like it or not, your identification is settled by how people perceive you to be. And if you're not a Caucasian or an African, you just are not, that's all. You can think like one, you can behave like one, but you are not accepted as one. That creates very big problems for those who have emigrated and for their children too, a sense of frustration, of non-fulfilment, because you're not functioning as a full member of that society. So every vacation, you will notice, we have Nobel prize winners and other very distinguished scholars happy to come to Singapore. Asians, to give of themselves. Most of them are from China, not from Singapore, but they feel a certain ethnic affinity, they feel at ease, they are accepted as what they are, Chinese, or Indians, whatever.

In 10, 15 years, Taiwan, Korea, Hongkong are going to be successful beyond doubt, industrial modernised societies. By that time, Japan will be even further ahead, and China would have got going. I remember this distinctly as part of my vivid experience, travelling on a bullet train in the early '60s in Japan, when the Japanese were still unsure of themselves and the Americans were the models. And I saw them earnestly in conversation with the Americans, almost obsequious. And I shook my head. Almost fawning to please the Americans. I've seen less and less of that as they've discovered that they've learnt almost everything they needed to learn from the Americans. Now they are on par, except for the armed forces. And they are ahead in several fields of research. And with it has come pride in being Japanese, and of course admiration from other Asians and the rest of the world. …

I would hate to believe that the poor, ragged, undernourished Chinese coolie and the equally ragged Malay peon and driver and Indian labourer had the inner strength to build today's Singapore, and their children with all the nice mod clothes, well-fed, all the vitamins, all the calories, protein, careful dental care, careful medical checks, PT, well-ventilated homes, they lost that inner drive. It's not something which we can treat as fantasy and unlikely to happen. If you search within yourself and see how different am I from my father and my mother and from my older cousins and brothers, you will begin to know what I mean.

If we are unconscious of these stimuli that are working on us that make us automatically accept certain norms of behaviour as desirable because the people who behave like that are successful or apparently successful, then we run a risk of losing that set of core values and unconsciously absorbing one which is not suitable to us as a people and to our environment.

While acknowledging the virtues of the British legal system Lee argued often that it could not be applied wholesale to Singapore, where Anglo-Saxon cultural conditions did not apply. Instead the system would have to be adapted to suit the new society's circumstances, he argued in a speech to the University of Singapore Law Society on January 18, 1962.

# Justice and fair play

Our architects learn of classical forms of Grecian colonnades and the Roman forum, of the grace and beauty of Christopher Wren's St Paul's, buildings of beauty and grace built out of marble and sandstone, of ancient Greece and ancient Rome and not so ancient London, to fit the style and climates of their time and their people. But then architects have to come back to Malaya and mould from granite and cement the buildings to fit our people and our climate.

> The acid test of any legal system is not the greatness or the grandeur of its ideal concepts, but whether in fact it is able to produce order and justice.

There is a gulf between the principles of the rule of law, distilled to its quintessence in the background of peaceful 19th century England, and its actual practice in contemporary Britain. The gulf is even wider between the principle and its practical application in the hard realities of the social and economic conditions of Malaya. You will have to bridge the gulf between the ideal principle and its practice in our given sociological and economic milieu. For if the forms are not adapted and principles not adjusted to meet our own circumstances but blindly applied, it may be to our undoing. You must bridge this gulf quickly if you are not to spend the first few years of your practice after graduation floundering in confusion.

The rule of law talks of habeas corpus, freedom, the right of association and expression, of assembly, of peaceful demonstration, concepts which first stemmed from the French Revolution and were later refined in Victorian England. But nowhere in the world today are these rights allowed to practise without limitations, for, blindly applied, these ideals can work towards the undoing of organised society. For the acid test of any legal system is not the greatness or the grandeur of its ideal concepts, but whether in fact it is able to produce order and justice in the relationships between man and man and between man and the state. To maintain this order with the best degree of tolerance and humanity is a problem which has faced us acutely in the last few years as our own Malayans took over the key positions of the legislature, the executive and the judiciary.

The British colonial system was a pragmatic one. Its legal system used the trappings and some of the forms of Westminster, but its content was adapted to meet local circumstances. The skill of the colonial legal and judicial system rested not in the straightforward application of the forms and rules spelt out in the Courts of Justice at Westminster and in the Inns of Court, but in ensuring that these rules were adapted to maintain good government with the largest practical measure of individual freedom. For accompanying the written rules was a set of unwritten ones which was handed down within the service.

Let me give you an example of how a blind application of the forms and rules of law and the rules of evidence led to a complete and utter miscarriage of justice in Singapore. Some three years ago a storekeeper of a bus company took a can of petrol, burst into the directors' room when a meeting was in progress, spilt the can and set the whole room and building in flames. Several persons were literally burnt alive. The jury convicted without hesitation. But after the fumbling and bungling of the rules of procedure and evidence and the summing up, the court of appeal, according to the rules of precedent, allowed the appeal. Another charge on a second murder committed in the same *actus reus* followed. A plea was made to the Attorney-General to observe the best traditions of his high office and the practice of the law in never asking a man to stand trial on a capital charge twice for the same act. In response to such an appeal a *nolle prosequis* was entered. Five bereaved families swore vengeance in their rage at the utter miscarriage of justice which resulted from a blind application of the forms and rules. For if the state cannot maintain the balance between the subjects and if the public wrath cannot be settled by the courts, then private vengeance becomes inevitable and lawlessness must increase.

Those of you who are just embarking on the study of the law will learn the phrase "law and order". In a settled and established society, law appears to be a precursor of order. Good laws lead to good order, that is the form that you will learn. But the hard realities of keeping the peace between man and man and between authority and the individual can be more accurately described if the phrase were inverted to "order and law", for without order the operation of law is impossible. Order having been established and the rules having become enforceable in a settled society, only then is it possible to work out human relationships between subject and subject, and subject and the state in accordance with predetermined rules of law.

And when a state of increasing disorder and defiance of authority cannot be checked by the rules then existing, new and sometimes drastic rules have to be forged to maintain order so that the law can continue to govern human relations. The alternative is to surrender order for chaos and anarchy. So it is that we have to allow the use of extraordinary powers of detention, first in the case of political offenders under the PPSO [Preservation of Public Security Order], and next in the case of secret society gangsters under the Criminal Law (Temporary Provisions) Ordinance.

It must be realised that if you abolish the powers of arrest and detention and insist on trial in open court in accordance with the strict laws of evidence of a criminal trial, then

> Five bereaved families swore vengeance in their rage at the utter miscarriage of justice which resulted from a blind application of the forms and rules.

law and order becomes without the slightest exaggeration utterly impossible, because whilst you may still nominally have law and order, the wherewithal to enforce it would have disappeared. The choice in many of these cases is either to go through the motions of a trial and let a guilty man off to continue his damage to society or to keep him confined without trial.

These extraordinary powers do not measure well against the ideals of habeas corpus and the precedents of individual liberty embroidered in two centuries of peaceful non-revolutionary England. But the sociological and political conditions in which we find ourselves make it vital that there should be radical departures from the British patterns.

A curious position that has arisen in Malaya is the temporary alliance of the pure academic who talks in terms of the absolute qualities of freedom, liberty and the rights of man and a strange fellow traveller … the communist revolutionary whose whole philosophy is a complete denial of these liberal concepts. The academic liberal may or may not believe in the practicability of his enunciations of absolute ideals. But the communist revolutionary certainly does not. He is utterly contemptuous of this philosophy of what he believes to be a decadent free society. But the communist is sufficiently cynical to calculate that if he joins forces with the liberal in the name of human rights and human liberty, he is more likely to be able to work up more hostility and dissatisfaction. For "liberty" and "freedom against the authority of state" are better rallying slogans than "communism" and "the dictatorship of the proletariat".

> If the state disintegrates then the rules of all laws must vanish.

The realities of the sociological and political milieu of Malaya and of the world of 1962, are that if you allow these shibboleths of "law and order" to be uttered out of context and without regard to the actual social and political conditions we are in, you may unwittingly make these words be your own undoing. For in the last analysis if the state disintegrates then the rules of all laws must vanish. …

Justice and fair play according to predetermined rules of law can be achieved within our situation if there is integrity of purpose and an intelligent search for forms which will work and which will meet the needs of our society. Reality is relatively more fixed than form. So if we allow form to become fixed because reality cannot be so easily varied, then calamity must befall us.

# Don't be afraid to innovate the law

The fact that today the rule of law is reasonably established – no one believes that anyone will be executed at the whim and fancy of somebody else – is cause for quiet congratulations. For it might so very easily have been otherwise in so many ways. There were moments in 1964 and in 1965 when we felt that perhaps we were going the way of so many other places in the world. But we did not.

In 1964, I visited in the course of my duties as a representative of the prime minister of what is now a foreign neighbouring government, a country where the Chief Justice has only recently been detained. And why? Because he acquitted on appeal, or in a trial, a former minister of some charge that he was out to kill the president of the newly independent nation. And the whole judiciary was changed. It was not just the Chief Justice who was detained. A new Chief Justice was appointed and all the judges were left in no doubt as to who was the most important *ratio decidendi* in any case.

In other parts of the world where there are more refined, polite and courteous ways of doing things, one does not put the Chief Justice in jail. One merely appoints a relative to the post. You do not have to hang your relative. You just make sure that he understands how he got there!

Newly independent countries share one thing in common. They all have a tremendous addiction to pomp and panoply of office. Protocol is most important. If you just get a person shot in a dark corner, it is not so satisfying as to have him go through the ritual of a trial, and he is cross-examined and all his wicked deeds – unconnected with the charge – exposed.

I read of somebody who was in charge of some banking institution of a country of great natural wealth. And we heard all about the beautiful women who were supplied to presidents and the guests of presidents. But I often wondered what that had to do with the

A new Chief Justice was appointed and all the judges were left in no doubt as to who was the most important *ratio decidendi* in any case.

charge that was brought against him. It was irrelevant! The man was going to be summarily executed. But it would be such a shame just to take him round the corner and finish him off so quickly. So one does it with some ceremonial splendour and thereby establishes the ascendancy of the new regime!

We have, fortunately, escaped some of these excesses. And I would like, apart from congratulations, to hope that we are sufficiently perceptive and determined that it will never happen to us.

It might be good fortune, perhaps, that not just I alone but some of my colleagues were brought up in fairly liberal traditions. We don't have to be lawyers to understand right, wrong, good, evil. This is basic and fundamental in the values of a people. And I think even if the Minister for Law and myself were to go wrong, you will have some consolation, Mr President, in the knowledge that quite a number of my colleagues are men imbued with some of the values, some of the traditions of an open, of an equal, of a tolerant society.

You cannot maintain that kind of a society unless you are prepared to practise it yourself. In other words, your style must be open. You must yourself be tolerant. And, most important of all, you must be able to ensure, insofar as you can, that your successors – even though they may not be of the same political colour as you are – are imbued with this value.

> Let us not deceive ourselves that we can do all these things because we just believe in democracy, the rule of law and the certainty of the law.

Let us not deceive ourselves that we can do all these things because we just believe in democracy, the rule of law and the certainty of the law.

You know, we have paid a very heavy price. We have departed in quite a number of material aspects – in very material fields from the principles of justice and the liberty of the individual, in particular – in order to maintain these standards, in order that there shall be a Bar; that there will be judges who will sit in judgement over right and wrong; that police will produce witnesses and that witnesses for certain crimes shall require corroboration and evidence shall be in accordance with the Evidence Ordinance.

But let me tell you the price today, right at this moment: 620 criminal detainees under the Criminal Law Temporary Provisions Ordinance, 100 of whom are murderers, kidnappers and armed robbers. And quite a number of these cases, though self-confessed, were acquitted at trial. You are landed with a murderer who has confessed to a murder and you know it is true by all the circumstantial evidence, and that to let him out is to run the very grave risk of undermining your whole social fabric. But you played it according to the rules of the game and it did not work.

There are 720 criminal law supervisees – men on whom the due processes of law were unable to place even an iota of evidence. But for the fact that they are required to stay at home by night, I think life would be less what it is in Singapore, for their nocturnal activities can make your motorcar outside a less useful vehicle of transportation, among other things.

This is true. We have had to adjust, to deviate temporarily from ideals and norms. This is a heavy price. We have over a hundred political detainees, men against whom we are unable to prove anything in a court of law. Nearly 50 of them are men who gave us a great deal of anxiety during the years of Confrontation because they were Malay extremists. Your life and this dinner would not be what it is if my colleagues and I had decided to play it according to the rules of the game.

So let us always remember the price that we have had to pay in order to maintain the general standards – relationship between man and man; man and authority; citizen and citizen; citizen and authority – except in the cost of these 620 detainees under the Criminal Law Temporary Provisions Ordinance. But it is an expression of an ideal when we say "Temporary Provisions".

You know, it has gone on for the last 8 years. I remember being a party to it, saying "Aye" when the previous government moved it some 11 years ago. And we have had to change the law itself. For instance, the Vehicles Theft Ordinance – too many cars were being stolen. Heavy penalties were sought – 7 or 8 years ago we did that and we said, "10 years punishment". And yet young magistrates sometimes say, "Poor man. He is just trying the first time. Let him off for a year!"

And there is the new law in regard to poster pasting. If you do it in an indelible form, you get a whacking. I and the Minister of Law, who is a lawyer, had to fight a tremendous duel with the Attorney-General's Office to formulate this law. We knew there was a plan for the whole city to be plastered with paint – red paint, black paint. But the magistrate doesn't understand. He doesn't read Chinese. He doesn't know what these things exhort. It is just so much messy paint on the walls. He doesn't know how difficult it is to catch one man out of the hundreds that did it; how difficult it is to be on the spot at 3 or 4 o'clock in the morning and to apprehend one of them. It is quite an effort.

And when you get one, to the utter and absolute disgust of the police, he is just cautioned and discharged. And so we said, "Second conviction – compulsory caning." And you know, we have a lot of liberal lawyers in the Attorney-General's Chambers. They would not put up a draft. They literally refused. They wrote long screeds why this was against the best traditions of penology.

I was happy, Mr President, that you used the phrase "a conscientious Bar". But I don't think, Mr President, you understand why I was happy. I knew what you intended. I learnt as a student that a word has three meanings: what the speaker intends it to mean; what the mass of people understand it to mean; what I understand it to mean.

And I think I knew what you intended it to mean, and I think I knew what the mass of people here knew what a conscientious Bar to mean – people who assiduously, in pursuit of their profession, turn up the law books, take every technical point in favour of their client and, thereby, have discharged their obligations, and justice is done.

That wasn't the meaning that I suddenly felt when you said, "a conscientious Bar". I thought of a bar with a conscience, a social conscience towards your own society. Do you feel for them? Every time a criminal law detainee is taken in, it is an admission of failure – failure in providing that man with sufficient opportunity to develop his talent in a meaningful way.

Your life and this dinner would not be what it is if my colleagues and I had decided to play it according to the rules of the game.

416

> Every time I go to a Works Brigade Camp where these detainees are being rehabilitated, I am reminded what tremendous glands they must have had. But they went wrong somewhere. In other words, we failed.

And every time I go to a Works Brigade Camp where these detainees are being rehabilitated and I see the productivity in it compared with the other Works Brigade Camps, I am reminded what tremendous glands they must have had. They rear chickens and plant vegetables better than any other Works Brigade Camp. But they went wrong somewhere. In other words, we failed.

I would like, therefore, to appeal to your conscience this evening since it is, as your President has said, "a conscientious Bar". I appeal to your conscience to try and help us find the answers to some of these problems.

First of all, the Bar: the courts, the administration of justice. If we continue as in the past, it will fail. I will tell you how the British maintained it in Singapore.

They recruited the younger sons of wealthy families – or not so wealthy families – who could not afford to have the young man dawdling and earning very little at the Bar in the first five years of his career. They offered him stability, security, early retirement, handsome pensions, a good life whilst he performed his duties. He was not attracted by what was happening in private practice – not until Malayanisation came in. And then the picture got distorted.

Now you are recruiting from within the system. And the man who is going to make your potential Attorney-General is not going to stay in government service when he sees his contemporaries earn more in private practice. It is an insult to a man's self-esteem to watch what a really good advocate with a good legal mind can earn outside. In government service the most he can hope for is $2,000-odd, plus certain perks of office. So how are you going to get the right people to man your High Court Bench?

Then there is the other problem – of a weak magistrate or a judge buffeted between two powerful counsels. And I have, from time to time, seen these proceedings, particularly in the lower courts. The magistrate's or judge's main concern is not with the man or the woman or the case – the rights or the wrongs of the law – but with the counsel who is going to upset his judgement on appeal. For too many appeals upset must mean some blot on the copybook when it comes to promotion. There is a Legal Service Commission with a Chief Justice, two senior judges and the chairman of the Public Service Commission, who do not know all these problems that the poor young man was fearful of, all the tremendous barrage of arguments put forward. All he wanted to do was the right thing and the right thing was to convict the chap. But how? He did not know how and he said, "Well, who is likely to hold me up on appeal?"

And I remember on one occasion – it was already beginning to happen even whilst I was in practice – one of the advocates had to assure the judge that he would be there on the appeal. He would be doing the appeal. And the judgement went his way.

I can tell you all the other things that could go wrong. You know, income tax cases. Mediocrity on the government side, talent in private practice, and you will lose millions of dollars. And the number of kidnappers, murderers, armed robbers who get off and had to be detained – contrary to our ideals of a free democratic society.

So many other things could go wrong, you know. But we could safeguard ourselves against these if we remember that there are certain ideals, certain standards, certain norms which are desirable and should be striven for; then relate those to your existing society, your existing circumstances: what is achievable in this given situation. The crucial thing is: do not be afraid to innovate.

I will give you an illustration of where I am at the moment thinking of real innovations. This is in regard to the problem of bribery and corruption.

We live in an area where to be corrupt is a way of life. And there are scales starting from 20 cents for this and 40 cents for that, to two dollars for this. There are rates for the job. You know it, I know it. What is most important really for us is that because it is a way of life for others around us, it has to be understood.

What is your answer? I say unless you are able to give our civil servants that pride in their standards and reward them for being able to maintain those standards, the standards in the end will be undermined.

I am seriously contemplating an innovation in the law because corruption is one of our key problems. Singapore's progress, its verve, its vitality is assured because the administrative machine works. There is no grit. You don't have to grease somebody to crank up the machine. We must keep it that way. To ensure this I am thinking of an amendment to the law. The innovation is: if any official is found with wealth which cannot be explained and there is uncorroborative evidence of corruption, his whole property can be sequestered. There must be some punishment or they get away. And I have not the slightest doubt that there will be an uproar from a lot of people, not least of all from members practising in the criminal law.

You have done me the great compliment, Mr President, of reminding those present how long we have been in office. But I think the deepest compliment we could pay to ourselves is to remember that there must come a time – and not so very long – when the torch must be passed on. And there is no greater compliment that a man can pay to himself and to his group than to pass the torch on to like-minded people, fired by the same ideals, but younger, more vigorous, more capable to meet a more contemporary situation.

I would like to believe that, as with me, so with you: as you pass the torch on to the next generation, you pass it on not only to capable hands but to good minds and good hearts.

> We live in an area where to be corrupt is a way of life. And there are scales starting from 20 cents for this and 40 cents for that, to two dollars for this.

Over the years, Lee often faced criticism for his tough stance on law and order, not least from foreign commentators. In a face-to-face encounter with the British Broadcasting Corporation's Ludovic Kennedy, on March 5, 1977, he defended his government's abolition of the jury system and its detention of communist agitators and journalists without trial. He also fielded Kennedy's allegations that he had changed his position on such detentions after taking office.

# The ballot and the bullet

**KENNEDY:** Prime Minister, when one talks about justice in Singapore – you have in fact abolished trial by jury.

**LEE:** Yes, since 1969, and we've had far better administration of the criminal law and justice. You see, the Anglo-Saxon tradition of trial by jury may be good for Anglo-Saxons or the descendants thereof. It never really worked for non-Anglo-Saxons.

**KENNEDY:** Why not?

**LEE:** I don't know – many reasons. The French don't have it. They are Latin. I think the idea of 12 random jurors sitting there and deciding whether you ought to go to jail or not or whether you ought to pay damages or not, it's completely alien.

I never forget my first case, when I was assigned to defend four murderers. Remember the famous jungle girl case in Singapore in 1950, '51?

A Dutch woman was running away from the Japanese, gave her daughter to a Malay woman to look after. She came back after the war, reclaimed the daughter. The Chief Justice, then an Englishman, pending hearing of the case, sent the girl who had been converted into Islam to a convent to be looked after, and hell broke loose. The police force mutinied. Malays and Muslims took out their knives and a lot of white men, just because they were white, nothing to do with the case, were killed. These four men were accused of killing a Royal Air Force officer and his wife and child. They were travelling on a bus from RAF Changi down to town.

I was assigned – I had no choice. My job was not to ask them whether they were guilty or not because I knew what the position was and so did they. All I did – and it was

> I think the idea of 12 random jurors sitting there and deciding whether you ought to go to jail or not or whether you ought to pay damages or not, it's completely alien.

my first case – was to work on the weaknesses of the jury – their biases, their prejudices, their reluctance really to find four Mussulmen [Muslims] guilty of killing in cold blood or in a heat of great passion, religious passion, an RAF officer, his wife and child. I did the simple tricks of advocacy – contradictions between one witness and another, contradiction between a witness and his previous statement to the police and the preliminary enquiry – and after a long submission by the judge, the four were acquitted.

The judge was thoroughly disgusted. I went home feeling quite sick because I knew I'd discharged my duty as required of me, but I knew I had done wrong. I decided when we became the government, we will not allow this foolish, completely incongruous system which will never take root here, because no juror will take upon himself the onus of saying, "Yes, he will go to jail."

**KENNEDY:** Prime Minister, what do you say to the fact that some people have been detained in prison here for something like 13 years without trial. Is that justice?

**LEE:** It is outside the laws of the courts. It's legislation which the British passed when they were faced with a communist insurgency – a revolt. Same laws, the same ones, I suspect, are now in operation in Ulster. There are three of them – you are right – 13 years since 1963, really coming to 14. Two of them are doctors. I defended them for sedition when we were fighting the British together. I brought out the most ferocious sedition trial QC then at the British Bar – Dennis Pritt. We became great friends. He was a communist or sympathiser – a Marxist; I wasn't. I learnt a lot of tricks of the trade, including how to lose in a controlled manner one's temper or pretend to. How to put up a specious argument – a sound, solid law, and we got them off, between him and us. And the two doctors know that all they have to do is to say, "I renounce the use of armed force to overthrow the government and therefore do not support the Malayan Communist Party in their attempt to do so", and they will be released. And they refused to do that.

**KENNEDY:** But are you saying, Prime Minister, in a strong and prosperous society that you have here now in Singapore – the last election you won the biggest victory ever, you got all the seats in Parliament – that if you release these three people, you couldn't contain them?

**LEE:** No, that's not the point. We can release these three people. We released one – Dr Poh Soo Kai – as a trial to see what would happen. We released him in 1972 after we won the last elections with nearly as good a majority – 69 per cent of the electorate. And what did he do? He gave medicine and treated a known, wanted, injured terrorist. There is now evidence by a lawyer, at present under interrogation, who has gone to a magistrate and made a confession, on his own. Now, we have to get him struck off the rolls. But that's not all. He also gave large quantities of antibiotics and other essential medical supplies to couriers, to send them to terrorist forces in the jungle, all in the course of the four years he was out – from 1972 to 1976.

> I went home feeling quite sick because I knew I'd discharged my duty as required of me, but I knew I had done wrong.

**KENNEDY:** So these other two will have to stay there, forever?

**LEE:** No.

**KENNEDY:** Until they sign your document?

**LEE:** No, they don't have to sign a document. All they say is: "I renounce the use of force. I do not support the Malayan Communist Party in their use of force to overthrow the government." But if they believe, as I think they do, that this is inevitable, that there will one day be a great victory parade and they will be on the rostrum where all the local Lenins and Maos will be – well, then they stand firm on principle and wait for tomorrow. I am offering them another alternative: go to any country that's willing to accept you. I am not trading. I am not doing a Chilean exchange with the Russians. You are free to go. They are good doctors, well-trained. You need them for your medical help. I would let them go and help you relieve your shortage of doctors with no conditions whatsoever. But if I allow them here to go out and feed medicine, treat injured terrorists, slip supplies into the jungle – apart from the trouble I am creating for myself, I think the Malaysian government will take a very dim view of my cooperation in joint security problems.

**KENNEDY:** I am also told, Prime Minister, that there are other people who have been put in prison because you personally brought charges against them for saying libellous things about you during the elections. Is that so?

**LEE:** No, no, no.

**KENNEDY:** I have got it wrong?

These men during an election campaign went around saying that I have made through my wife and my brother, who are practising law, $500 per conveyance per flat.

**LEE:** You have got it wrong. I can't bring a criminal charge against anybody. The Attorney-General does that. There are two forms of libel – criminal libel, civil libel. These men during an election campaign went around saying that I have made through my wife and my brother, who are practising law, $500 per conveyance per flat. And as we have already sold 150,000 flats – public housing, I am therefore worth somewhere between $50 to $70 million.

**KENNEDY:** He said all that?

**LEE:** Yes. Well, the Attorney-General – and I thank him for it – did not act during the election or that would have lost me votes. But after the election, with modern tape recorders, you can't deny what you have said. So they pleaded guilty.

**KENNEDY:** Did the Attorney-General ask you? Did he have your permission to do this?

**LEE:** No, he doesn't have to ask me.

**KENNEDY:** So you didn't know anything about it?

**LEE:** No, I knew that he must act. If he knows his job, he must act. I am a lawyer, he is a lawyer. In fact, I am more senior a lawyer than he is. I was called to the Bar earlier than he was. Then, you see, what's the point of suing them in civil libel because they are men of straw. But I have still got to sue them because some of them, whilst they may be men of straw, have the capacity to make a really rousing speech. And corruption in a developing country – sad to say – is very often a way of life for those in office.

**KENNEDY:** Wouldn't it be more generous of you, Prime Minister, to have said about these people, if they will withdraw what they said, if they will make an apology, then you will forget about it?

**LEE:** That's for the civil side. I have offered that. However, I will not forget about it because I think we must still enter judgement so that they cannot interfere in the next elections. If you get bankrupts turning up and uttering more and reckless falsehoods in the next round, I am in trouble, because some fool one day may light a prairie fire.

But when a man – and I've got one, unfortunately – who is a lawyer and therefore must be presumed by the public to be a person who knows the law, says words to the effect which he contests as defamatory, which my lawyers advised me is defamatory. Well, let the case be argued whether I am corrupt or whether I am not. Because if they can make this corruption stigma stick, then I have had it. Then all the good that you have done is wiped off because there is one thing which a Singaporean voter expects and has been made to expect: absolute integrity on the part of those in office. They may make mistakes. They will forgive me. But they know that they were honest mistakes, not one where there was a 5 per cent kickback.

**KENNEDY:** Can I go back to something that you were reported to have said in 1955 when you first entered Parliament? At that time, when your party, the People's Action Party, spoke out against arbitrary arrest, of detention without trial and you yourself are reported to have said, "We either believe in democracy or we do not. If you believe that men should be free then they should have the right of free association, of free publication. No law should permit those democratic processes to be set at naught". Prime Minister, do you believe that, today?

**LEE:** Yes. I believed that in the circumstances of that time. I mean, I could, you know, quote you Churchill, that "That was what I believed then."

**KENNEDY:** But that was a worse time than now, was it not?

> Wouldn't it be more generous of you, Prime Minister, to have said about these people, if they will withdraw what they said, if they will make an apology, then you will forget about it?

**LEE:** Yes, of course. That was against a British colonial government responsible to nobody other than Whitehall. This is 1977. I am 22 years older. I hope more mellow. I hope more charitable. I hope more magnanimous. But I am also a realist. The magnitude of what one terms "licence" or "civil liberties" or "personal freedom" has got to be adjusted to the circumstances. And as far as the communists are concerned, they wanted both ways – both the ballot and the bullet. You can't. They want the ballot and the processes that go before the ballot, to aid them both internally and internationally in the use of the bullet. They learnt it from the Vietnamese: the battle was not fought in Vietnam alone; it was fought in Washington, it was fought in the streets of Stockholm, it was fought in Sydney, in Melbourne, in Paris, in London. "Vietnam" became a dirty word. They are trying to do to me – which they must try and they are trying to do to all the other non-communist governments in the region – what they did to Thieu. If they can portray me as corrupt, fatuous, dictatorial, capricious, wicked, vicious, then half the battle is won because when the fight begins, I've got to get arms. I have got to buy them …

**KENNEDY:** Can I interrupt you here for a moment. It seems to me that you are saying that these things that I read out to you, you believed in at that time …

**LEE:** Yes, of course. And I still believe in them.

**KENNEDY:** But … qualify them today because of changed circumstances.

**LEE:** No, because you can't have the ballot and the bullet at the same time.

**KENNEDY:** Well, you say you believe in free publication? But isn't it true that newspapers here have to be licensed, that some have been closed, some journalists have been put in jail …?

**LEE:** No, just a moment. You are mixing them all up. It has always been the case that a newspaper in Singapore and in Malaya, where the British governed, must have a licence. And there has been only one newspaper that had its licence withdrawn, and that was when it could not prove where the money came from, besides a former chief minister of the state of Sabah.

**KENNEDY:** And have journalists been put in jail?

**LEE:** There is one at the moment, and he is, as a good journalist, writing this time a real true story of what he has been doing. And I hope by the end of this week, the composition would have gone before a proper magistrate with no police officers. At least that's what I hope they have the sense to do, because it really is a very interesting story of how a non-communist began associating with communists and slowly began to imbibe communist views and interpolated communist views in his interpretation of Singapore.

> Isn't it true that newspapers here have to be licensed, that some have been closed, some journalists have been put in jail?

**KENNEDY:** Would it be fair to try and sum up what you have been saying about these – on this loss of civil liberties, such as they are – that some small liberties have to be sacrificed in order to make sure that you have the greater liberty? Would that be a fair assessment?

**LEE:** One way of putting it. If you ask me to put it, I would say simply: Never have the people of Singapore had a government which they can kick out of office freely, without hindrance, by just crossing them off the ballot. And never have they had a government which had to tend to their needs – every grumble, every bellyache – to make sure that the vote is on the side of the angels every five years.

The media in developing societies had a role in helping to foster the societal values which would help them succeed. They were bulwarks against the foreign values and mores which these societies were exposed to in their quest to acquire foreign knowhow and technology. The media had a duty to galvanise the people behind the government and its policies so as to facilitate the country's efforts to make material progress, Lee argued in a speech at the general assembly of the International Press Institute in Helsinki on June 9, 1971.

# The mass media in new countries

The recent bitter rows over TV and newspaper coverage of the war in Vietnam was a sad admission that even in highly developed countries, objectivity was the subjective views of the owners and commentators of the mass media as against those of the Nixon administration.

In the midterm elections in America in November 1970, television, the most powerful of contemporary mass media, did not prove to be decisive in winning elections. The neat packaging and slick presentation of programmes and personalities, and frequent spot advertisements, could not sell a candidate as well as TV could sell soap and detergents. For it is not improbable that the way people vote depends on more complex factors than what they are told on the mass media. Their pay packet, their subsidised housing, schooling, health and social services, the way specific policies hurt or advance their interests, these are probably more decisive in how they vote.

The sustained repeated "sell" through all mass media – television, radio, newspapers and magazines – undoubtedly helps to shape attitudes to fashions in clothes, foods and consumer durables. Although this power of persuasion falls short of what John Kenneth Galbraith expounded in his Manchester Lectures in 1968, that the consumer bought what he was insidiously told to buy, not what he wanted, the huge and ever growing advertisement industry is evidence that sellers believe it helps sales. It is therefore not improbable that the sustained plugging of a line can also mould public opinion on political issues and policies. The recent bitter rows over TV and newspaper coverage of the war in Vietnam was a sad admission that even in highly developed countries, objectivity was the subjective views of the owners and commentators of the mass media as against those of the Nixon administration.

New countries can choose either this *laissez-faire* system of the West and allow complete free play and competition between TV stations, dailies and weeklies, or follow the closed and controlled system of communist countries, or some intermediate point between the two, depending on the level of education and sophistication of their peoples

**425**

and the political traditions and style of the governments. But in practice, new countries, particularly the smaller ones, cannot altogether insulate themselves from outside news and views.

Some governments, like China or the Soviet Union in pre-Khrushchev days, effectively sealed off their people from the outside world. Then the world is what the rulers say it is. And the rulers are unchanging for long years. But there is a heavy price to be paid for such isolation. The incessant exhortation to progress, the constant stress on conformity in ideology, ideas and action, they lead to drab uniformity.

But watching the chaos and confusion that have followed the election of temporarily popular governments in many new countries, many leaders, especially in Africa, have decided against free play and opted for the one-party state with all mass media supporting the one party. On the other hand, in several new countries in Asia, every election is an exercise in auctioning the country's nonexistent reserves and future production. With an electorate ignorant of the economic and administrative facts of life, it is no surprise that governments do get elected on programmes and promises the countries' resources and administrative capacity cannot fulfil.

In just about all new countries, radio and television are controlled by the state. When power was handed over from a colonial government to the first elected government, they remained in state control, with varying degrees of latitude for dissenting views. But the problem, despite ownership and control of TV and radio stations, is that the economies of operation makes it necessary to buy foreign programmes. At best, these programmes entertain without offending good taste. At worst, they can undo all that is being inculcated in the schools and universities. This is particularly so in the new countries where the English language is widely used. Francophone states have only France (and perhaps Quebec) to worry about. English-speaking ones find their mass media carrying large chunks of canned programmes and syndicated features from the developed English-speaking world.

Their newspapers, even if nationalised, carry reports from the well-organised worldwide news agencies of the West. There is also a whole range of American and British language magazines and journals to cater for all tastes. And if people cannot afford them, USIS [United States Information Service] and the British Information Services provide ample library facilities.

At a time when new nations require their peoples to work hard and be disciplined to make progress, their peoples are confused by watching and reading the happenings in the West. They read in newspapers and see on TV violent demonstrations in support of peace, urban guerillas, drugs, free love and "hippie-ism".

Many people are uncritically imitative. A report of an airplane hijacking leads to a rash of hijackings in other unexpected places. A report of a foreign diplomat kidnapped for ransom by dissident groups is quickly followed by similar kidnapping in other countries. Some monks burned themselves to death in South Vietnam in acts of gruesome protest. Others in Ceylon and elsewhere followed suit.

> At a time when new nations require their peoples to work hard and be disciplined to make progress, their peoples are confused by watching and reading the happenings in the West.

Is it not possible to take in only the best of the West? Why does TV in new countries not cut out the sensational and the crude, and screen only the educational and aesthetic, the scientific and technological triumphs of the West? We have tried this in Singapore. However, the costs of acquiring good programmes become higher, the less popular they are with other potential buyers in the region. Thus we are caught in the lowest common denominator of viewers in the region.

As for the newspapers, the vernacular press, before independence, had usually joined in the anti-colonial crusade. After independence they often seek an uncritical reversion to a mythical, romantic past. In the second phase, the more intelligent of these papers try to find some balance in retaining the best of the old, whilst absorbing the best of the new in the West. But in any case foreign news and features are still extensively translated and published.

The English-language press in new countries, however, were, by and large, unenthusiastic about independence in colonial times. They were often owned by Western investors. Most change ownership after the colonial governments have relinquished power. In countries like India and Ceylon there has been a plethora of anti-establishment newspapers. Twice the left-inclined Ceylonese government has threatened to nationalise the English-language newspapers. At this moment all editorials are censored. And foreign correspondents had to be restrained or be expelled for what the Ceylonese consider over-imaginative reports of the Che Guevarist uprising. How much of the confusion and dissensions in these new countries are compounded by the daily outpourings of hundreds of anti-establishment newspapers, no one will know.

What role would men and governments in new countries like the mass media to play? I can answer only for Singapore. The mass media can help to present Singapore's problems simply and clearly and then explain how, if they support certain programmes and policies, these problems can be solved.

More important, we want the mass media to reinforce, not to undermine, the cultural values and social attitudes being inculcated in our schools and universities. The mass media can create a mood in which people become keen to acquire the knowledge, skills and disciplines of advanced countries. Without these, we can never hope to raise the standards of living of our people.

If they are to develop, people in new countries cannot afford to imitate the fads and fetishes of the contemporary West. The strange behaviour of demonstration and violence-prone young men and women in wealthy America, seen on TV and the newspapers, are not relevant to the social and economic circumstances of new underdeveloped countries. The importance of education, the need for stability and work discipline, the acquisition of skills and expertise, sufficient men trained in the sciences and technology, and their ability to adapt this knowledge and techniques to fit the conditions of their country – these are vital factors for progress.

But when the puritan ethics of hard work, thrift and discipline are at a discount in America, and generally in the West, the mass media reflecting this malaise can, and does, confuse the young in new countries.

We want the mass media to reinforce, not to undermine, the cultural values and social attitudes being inculcated in our schools and universities.

We have this problem in a particularly acute form in Singapore. We are an international junction for ships, aircraft and telecommunications by cable and satellite. People from the richer countries of the West, their magazines, newspapers, television and films, all come in. We are very exposed. It is impossible to insulate Singaporeans from the outside world. One consoling thought is Arnold Toynbee's thesis that crossroads like the Lebanon benefit from the stimulation of ideas and inventions from abroad.

Western investments in industries in Singapore mean importing Western machinery. With the machinery come Western engineers and managers, and their families. They live in Singapore, reinforcing by personal contact the impact of Western mass media. To take in Western science, technology and industry, we find that we cannot completely exclude the undesirable ethos of the contemporary West. This ethos flakes off on Singaporeans. So we must educate Singaporeans not to imitate the more erratic behaviour of the West.

Few viewers and readers of the mass media in new countries know of the torment amongst Western intellectuals. Some Americans question where their bureaucratised science and technology, their military-industrial complex, are leading them. Even fewer read of the torment of American intellectuals who question the wisdom of exporting this science and technology to the impoverished people of the underdeveloped world, when it has wrought such havoc on America, dehumanising an opulent society.

But the underdeveloped have no choice. Whatever the side effects of importing Western science and technology, not to do so will be worse.

With parts of our population it has been wiser to inoculate them from these maladies. Those who have been brought up in their own traditional lifestyles and cultural values have greater resistance to Western ills. By all means have the pill to keep the birth rate down. But must it lead to promiscuity, venereal diseases, exhibitionism and a breakdown of the family unit? I do not have all the answers. I can only hope the pill, plus the traditional importance of the Asian family unit, where paternity is seldom in doubt, can prevent the excesses from imitating contemporary Western sexual mores.

To compound our problems, the population of Singapore is not homogenous. There are several racial, linguistic, cultural and religious groups. For the Singapore Chinese, about 76 per cent of the population, there is a wide range between Confucianism and Taoism to Maoist materialism. They can view or read the output of local talent, or that of freewheeling Hongkong, with its own brand of Westernised lifestyles, or the archaic values and political styles of Taiwan, by and large still those of Kuomintang Nanking, or films and publications of the People's Republic of China, every product dyed in Maoist red. Censorship can only partially cut off these influences. It is more crucial that local production of films and publication of newspapers should not be surreptitiously captured by their proxies.

The Malays of Singapore, some 14 per cent of the population, have the mass media from peninsular Malaya and Indonesia. These irredentist pulls are reinforced by visits of businessmen and tourists.

By all means have the pill to keep the birth rate down. But must it lead to promiscuity, venereal diseases, exhibitionism and a breakdown of the family unit?

For the Indians of Singapore, some 7 per cent, there are Indian publications and films, primarily from South India, carrying the pulls at the heartstrings of cultural and ethnic loyalties. But the second generation are nearly all English-educated, more interested in their future in Singapore, and less in India's destiny.

The rest of the population – 3 per cent – are Eurasians, Ceylonese, Pakistanis. They are nearly all English-educated and present no problems of irredentism.

But with nearly all sectors of the population the deleterious influence from the mass media of the West is an increasing problem. Fortunately, we have not got to the stage of mod styles, communal living, drugs and escapism.

An interesting question is whether the mass media can affect a people to an extent where, over a sustained period, they not only determine social behaviour but also spark off political action. I believe every now and again they do. People are affected by the suggestion of the printed word, or the voice on radio, particularly if reinforced by the television picture.

12,000 Sikhs from Punjab form one of the smallest communities in Singapore. They are split into contending factions, reflecting the contest between contending groups in the Punjab, of which they have heard on radio and have read in Punjabi language news-sheets. A recent fast to death by a Sikh leader in the Punjab to get Chandigarh given to the Sikhs generated tension among Sikhs in Singapore. True, nearly 60 per cent of the adult Sikhs were born and bred in the Punjab and emigrated to Singapore after their cultural values were settled. I believe, and hope, the second generation Sikh will be different.

In 1950, the publication of a photograph in a Malay newspaper of a Muslim girl in a convent, with the Virgin Mary in the background, caused riots. It was known as the jungle girl case. A Dutch girl, given to a Muslim Malay woman to look after, as the Japanese overran Southeast Asia, was rediscovered by her Dutch mother. She claimed her return. The girl had become a Muslim convert. The court, presided by an English judge, ordered the girl to be sent to a convent pending the outcome of the trial. There were four days of rioting. Some 50 Europeans were slaughtered and many more maimed by Malay and Indian Muslims. Their sin was to be European Christians, like the judge. The police, then mainly Muslims, just looked on.

In 1950, the publication of a photograph in a Malay newspaper of a Muslim girl in a convent, with the Virgin Mary in the background, caused riots.

And again, on July 21, 1964, a sustained campaign in a Malay language newspaper, falsely alleging the suppression of the rights of the Malay and Muslim minority by the Chinese majority, led to riots in which 36 people were killed and many more injured, during a Prophet Mohammed's birthday procession.

There have been several outbursts of violence by young Chinese workers and students. They were communist-inspired though few were themselves communists. These riots and arson were invariably preceded by calculated campaigns in which the newspapers and broadsheets played an important role. The printed word reinforced the staged mass rallies to stoke up enough emotional steam for the explosions the communists required for their "people's uprising".

I used to believe that when Singaporeans become more sophisticated, with higher standards of education, these problems will diminish. But watching Belfast, Brussels and Montreal, rioting over religion and language, I wonder whether such phenomena can ever disappear.

Finally, making for more pressures is the interest in Singapore of our smaller neighbours and that of several great powers. The smaller countries do not have the resources or the stamina to be a threat. But in the growing contest for maritime supremacy of the Indian Ocean and the South China Sea, the great powers are prepared to spend time and money to influence Singaporeans towards policies more to their advantage. They play it long and cool. Radio reception on handy transistors gives Singaporeans a whole variety of programmes, from the Voice of America to Radio Peking, and also the Voice of the Malayan National Liberation League clandestine radio station. The Malayan Communist Party want to liberate not only West Malaysia, but also Singapore. On top of this, foreign agencies from time to time use local proxies to set up or buy into newspapers, not to make money but to make political gains by shaping opinions and attitudes.

My colleagues and I have the responsibility to neutralise their intentions. In such a situation, freedom of the press, freedom of the news media, must be subordinated to the overriding needs of the integrity of Singapore, and to the primary purposes of an elected government. The government has taken, and will from time to time have to take, firm measures to ensure that, despite divisive forces of different cultural values and lifestyles, there is enough unity of purpose to carry the people of Singapore forward to higher standards of life, without which the mass media cannot thrive.

I used to believe that when Singaporeans become more sophisticated, with higher standards of education, these problems will diminish. But watching Belfast, Brussels and Montreal, rioting over religion and language, I wonder whether such phenomena can ever disappear.

In a fledgling society such as Singapore, with all its internal divisions of race, language and religion, the media would have to play a role in helping to keep the society together as well as upholding its values, Lee told Singapore pressmen at a talk to the Singapore Press Club on November 15, 1972.

# Why everything and anything cannot go

The power of the mass media is a factor of present-day life. It started off with the printing press and the billboards. Then came the radio and the cinema. Now it has found its most comprehensive and powerful weapon in television, and via satellite.

The efficacy of the mass media in shaping attitudes and influencing behaviour is beyond doubt. Over a sustained period it can influence people's attitudes towards ideas and beliefs, policies and programmes. What amazes me is that this powerful instrument does not require of its practitioners special professional training nor codes of conduct to govern them. You can be a journalist without understanding the impact on the minds of millions when you write smut and circulate it through millions of copies to literate and semi-literate people.

You can be a powerful influence for good or for bad by just having a good television personality. But special qualifications and acceptance of a code of ethics are not demanded. To be a doctor, a surgeon, a lawyer, an engineer, you have to pass stringent professional examinations. The governing body of experienced practitioners decides whether or not you are qualified to join their ranks. If they pass you, you have to abide by certain rules of conduct, which experience over the decades has made necessary. Those who breach these rules are punished by disciplinary committees for improper conduct. Hence doctors abusing their position of trust can be struck off the register. Perhaps the mass media, especially TV, is a relatively recent innovation. Perhaps governing bodies and rules will grow out of the problems TV is creating.

In this respect, the communist countries are thoroughly consistent. They have decided that the mass media is a very powerful instrument. They do not let anyone use it, other than those who will advance the cause of the communist state, and to advance its current policies. The Russians have even objected to anybody beaming any television programme

> You can be a powerful influence for good or for bad by just having a good television personality.

**431**

on them without their consent. This is in anticipation of the next stage through satellite dissemination, when simple television sets can receive programmes via satellite.

For developing countries the mass media, developed in the West, presents a specially sensitive problem. Its impact is bad enough in developed countries. Most Western democracies have problems in getting majority governments. Most governments are returned on a minority vote, whether it is in Canada or Britain. If you have *laissez-faire* in dissemination of views, regardless of whether they are truthful, sound or relevant, but because they sound smart or witty, the end result tends to be very erratic.

However, when it comes to garnering votes, provided you are allowed to get your point of view across, however hostile the press or the TV commentators, a determined and effective political leadership can beat them.

This is because the more hostile the media are, the more people make a mental discount of criticism and attacks. Those of you who lived through the Japanese occupation know how we interpreted the newspapers and the news broadcasts. When the Japanese said they had a famous victory in the Coral Sea, we looked for the small print to see how many ships they claimed to have sunk. Then we waited a few weeks to see how many hospital ships came back to harbour.

But the mass media, particularly the TV, has an insidious and dangerous way of influencing values and changing behaviour patterns.

You have to fill television time. You open your station at 5.30 pm. It has got to be kept going till midnight and on two channels. It costs thousands of dollars, creative minds and good supporting technicians to make a good feature. So it is easier to fill up by buying programmes, usually American or British. I have seen Perry Mason in Cairo, speaking Arabic. I watched in astonishment. Here was a country absolutely against the American system and establishment. But they faced the problem of filling time. There are many such popular series. But these programmes convey the whole ethos of the producer society.

> I have seen Perry Mason in Cairo, speaking Arabic.

Similarly with newspapers. They have got to fill the pages. What is easier than to buy features? Some features are good. I enjoy reading James Reston, even though from time to time I disagree with his views. But many features are of indifferent quality, and some are positively bad.

The most dangerous part of the mass media is its power of suggestion. People are imitative. If nobody had reported hijacking, or how easy and successful hijacking can be, there would not have been so many hijackings. I believe the Pilots' Association was right that if you want to cut down hijackings, then report all the hijacking failures, and block out all the hijacking successes, particularly how they were successfully executed. The craze spread by imitation, until the impossible happened – they hijacked a Soviet aircraft. That took some doing. Obviously, despite the Iron Curtain, the ideas leaked through.

This brings me to Singapore. I read a recent series in the *New Nation*. It was imitating what the Western journalists are doing. It was ostensibly respectable. First, a serious study of homosexuality. Then a protracted series on lesbianism. Then unwanted babies.

The Lord Chief Justice of Britain said, in a recent case on pornography, that if anybody showed the muck in a case before him to his daughters, he would take the man and wring

Twisting the necks of language and culture chauvinists would not have best served our purposes. They deserve special treatment.

his neck with his own hands. How did it come to such a pass? By a gradual, insidious process of suggesting that this is all right, that there is nothing wrong with it. It has led to "anything and everything goes".

Fortunately for us, the *New Nation*, *The Straits Times*, or for that matter the *Herald* and the *Eastern Sun*, they did not, and do not, have the same impact on our population. The Chinese or the Malay press and, in a more limited way, the Indian press, in the mother language, makes much more emotive and powerful appeals. They pull at the heartstrings. That is why in the case of the *Nanyang Siang Pau*, though I did not twist their necks, we took firm measures. And the business is not over yet. Twisting the necks of language and culture chauvinists would not have best served our purposes. They deserve special treatment.

Although the *Straits Times* prides itself on a very large circulation, of 120,000 on weekdays and 150,000 on Sundays, the total Chinese press circulation, *Nanyang, Sin Chew, Shin Min, Min Pao*, is double that. Every copy of a Chinese newspaper has at least two and a half to three times the readers of an English newspaper. Not only are the families who buy them larger, Chinese papers are found in all coffee shops, clan associations, clubs, eating places. The Bertha Hertogh riots took place not because of *The Straits Times*, but because of *Utusan Melayu*, though both printed pictures of the Dutch Eurasian Muslim convert in a convent. The Malay paper tugged at Muslim emotions in a way the English paper could not.

We are a very exposed society. We cannot adopt either the Russian or Chinese method. We cannot shut off the outside world, jamming broadcasts and banning imports of publications. Even jamming is a difficult and expensive game.

Whether it is on permissiveness of pornography, or on any subject, your duty, as indeed it is that of RTS [Radio and Television Singapore], is to inform, educate and entertain. Inform people of what is happening in Singapore and in all parts of the world, of events relevant to us. Educate them, not just in the three Rs, but continue the process which we are doing in the schools, inculcate values which will make Singapore a more cohesive society, and a viable nation. Entertain to sell your papers, but this can be done without unnecessary salacious or blue jokes.

Even in business, news must be factual and correct. Let me read you the chairman's statement of a British investment company called Hume's Holdings Ltd, from their 46th annual report, September 1972. A sound, balanced chairman of an investment trust said this of his financial press. Whoever is responsible for our business pages should take this to heart. "Takeovers. A major factor affecting activity in the stock and share markets during the past year was the continuing and growing turnover in the 'takeover' market. Genuine mergers arising from quiet and objective negotiations between company boards with a view to commercial and industrial efficiency seem to be outdated. The spotlight of publicity given to the emotive and sometimes intemperate arguments employed by offering companies with a view to promoting vast industrial conglomerates, followed by greater commercial and industrial power in fewer hands, seems to be a fashion which some people may regard as being extremely inimical to the public interest."

The important part is: "The investor and the consumer, under these conditions (meaning emotive reporting), must find it increasingly difficult to judge the efficiency of and the fair price for the component parts of the various industrial and commercial processes which produce the end product or service. Whether the public is presented with an entirely objective view on these matters by spokesmen in the city and by the financial press, must be open to question."

He does not want to invite a libel suit, hence his phrase "an open question". You should not be overawed just by the technical competence of the production. Because people in advanced countries write well, in polished rounded phrases, it does not mean the content is right. We should not follow them, imitating them stupidly and mindlessly. We should exercise our own moral judgement on whether that is good or bad for us.

We have many cultural, many linguistic groups. One of the dangers of bilingualism is that one day, sooner or later, large numbers of our population will be exposed to communist Chinese publications. I believe the risk is a calculated one, and minimal. Provided a person is also educated in the English language, he has a window open to another world. Then he can read communist literature and propaganda with some detachment, and exercise his own critical judgement.

But when we ban communist literature, the Western press applauds. Nobody questions the rightness of that policy. These are dual standards the West imposes on us. If freedom of the press is not affected by banning most communist Chinese publications, then why not ban Western publications? But imagine the howl of protest every time *Time* or *Newsweek* is banned in Saigon or Thailand.

The Western press had praised Manila as one of the great centres for freedom of expression, for giving full liberty to the human soul and spirit. I was amused to read that the gentleman who came to see me last year on behalf of the Press Foundation of Asia, Mr Roces, was recently arrested and detained. Now he is under house arrest.

Even as we block communist printed propaganda every day, *Nanyang, Sin Chew, Min Pao* and *Shin Min* bypass it [the block] in exactly the way the *Straits Times* does. *Straits Times* picks up foreign news services – *Observer, New York Times*, and so on. So the Chinese press picks up from *Ta Kung Pao* of Hongkong, a communist newspaper. They only reproduce what is published in Hongkong, and so pretend it is perfectly legitimate. After all, Hongkong is part of the free world.

Every morning, my task begins with reading five, four now, newspapers. It can be tiresome. I note the scurrilous, the scandalous. I can live with that. But when any newspaper pours a daily dose of language, cultural or religious poison, I put my knuckle-dusters on.

Do not believe you can beat the state. Mr Nixon, with Mr Agnew's help, demonstrated that. I watched a programme one night 4 years ago, when Mr Nixon introduced his Cabinet, after he had just won the elections. Mr Agnew quite rightly said he, at least, had been voted for by the people and speaks for the majority. But these wiseacres, the skilful commentators, who can convey so much just by the right twinkle of an eye as they read the news – who voted for them? What right have they to pass hasty value judgements and tear down a president's policies the instant they were announced?

> Every morning, my task begins with reading five, four now, newspapers. It can be tiresome. I note the scurrilous, the scandalous. I can live with that. But when any newspaper pours a daily dose of language, cultural or religious poison, I put my knuckle-dusters on.

As Mr Nixon presented his first Cabinet, CBS had a panel of very quick, agile and nimble minds, ready to go. The moment Nixon was over, this panel of demolishers came on. They included John Kenneth Galbraith of *The Affluent Society*. He has a very felicitous turn of phrase which, if turned against you, can be quite waspish.

He and most of the others began to shoot every one of Nixon's team down. It made quite an impact on me. The Governor of Massachusetts, a Mr Volpe, was appointed Secretary for Transport. The Governor had been voted for, and had won his election. Most probably he would have beaten Galbraith if ever Galbraith stood for election against him. Galbraith said, "As for Governor Volpe, Massachusetts can well do better without him when he goes to Washington." I am paraphrasing him. I cannot convey the derisive nuances.

This panel did not know who would be in Mr Nixon's team, or what job each member would be doing until it was announced that night. The panel had no time for considered judgements. The attitude was one of showbiz: "Right, let's have some fun." They shot the Nixon team down like clay pigeons – or so they thought.

But in the end Mr Nixon won in spite of a hostile press and TV. I was interested to see how *Time* magazine quickly switched over support from McGovern and hailed the victor.

Now, if in a developed society they can have such disorders aggravated, if not partly caused by the mass media, commentators and journalists in developing countries should not unthinkingly toss poison and pollution into the pool.

I know even RTS trips up. I watched a programme one night at 11.30 pm. There was one feature of a series. It must have cost very little to produce. All it had was a girl in a nightdress, a married man putting his clothes on and a telephone through which she was talking to all her other lovers. I wondered, "Is it Channel 5 or Channel 3?" I pressed again. It was Channel 5. First thing next morning, I shot off a note. RTS said it had been vetted. They put up a plausible explanation. A young university lady graduate thought the feature was good since it debunked the permissive society. This married man had got the 7-year itch. He needed to reassure himself of his virility. Telecasting it would show up the hollowness of the permissive society. When the middle-aged married man discovered that he was one among seven lovers, one for every day of the week, he collapsed, discomfited and demoralised. In the conversations over the phone, it turned out that none of the six minded his having his one day a week!

Filling time on television by buying feature serials allows this pervasive mood of promiscuity from the West to float in. We have got to fight it.

Twenty years ago, you would not see Singapore boys and girls walking about with arms around each other's waists. British boys and girls did that. Singaporeans did not. Their parents would frown upon it. Their friends would not admire them for having a boyfriend fondling them round the waist and parading them round the streets. But, gradually, through the daily exposure, they have come to accept this as normal decent behaviour.

Twenty years ago, you would not see Singapore boys and girls walking about with arms around each other's waists.

435

But there are certain norms of public conduct which, unless maintained, must affect the whole texture of that society. It is not possible to sustain the moral fibre of your society if "everything goes". Everything does not go in Singapore. There are incentives and disincentives which will be applied. Some have a special responsibility – people in the news media, the PR man who draws his posters, the producers of snippets for television or cinema advertisement.

Only one society is more exposed than us – Hongkong. There, everything goes. But nobody cares. Nobody is trying to build a nation in Hongkong. If they try, Beijing will come down on them. Nor does Hongkong have one-man-one-vote every five years. So everything goes, from the US 7th Fleet, to agents from Taiwan, to communist officials working in the Bank of China on top of which is the neon slogan "Long Live Chairman Mao"! The few Britons in charge read the *South China Morning Post* and the *Hongkong Standard*. The English press influences about 5 per cent of the population. When I am in Hongkong, I make a point of reading the Chinese press. If they tried representative government, one-man-one-vote, they would be ruined.

We can control the input of the pernicious and the vicious and prevent our people from overexposure to what is bad. I believe the safest way is cultural inoculation, steeped early in our own traditional values. We can watch the temporary aberrations of the West without harm to ourselves. Americans can afford to lose five to six years in riotous, drug-induced madness. They can continue to grow and not collapse, because 208 million people have that momentum to carry them through these lost years.

Nevertheless, I was astounded to learn how this madness had penetrated even their institutions of excellence. When I saw the decorations outside, I thought it was a bit early for Christmas. Then they told me it was for Thanksgiving! My mind went back to one Thanksgiving at Harvard not long ago. The whole college was closed for Thanksgiving. There was nothing to eat. So the Master of the College invited me to his home. And he had also invited several of his brightest students. The discussion turned to drugs. The brightest of them said he had tried LSD. This discussion was absolutely deadpan. There was no disapproval, no opprobrium expressed by anyone. The Master expressed surprise. He inquired what it was like. The student said, "That is exactly the point. Lots of people like to know about it. I think I might write about it in the next issue of the college magazine!"

This must be corrosive. In 1968, they told me 40 per cent smoked marijuana at weekends. In 1970, they told me 60 per cent smoked marijuana regularly. But they claimed it did no harm at all.

One night, in October 1970, somebody pressed the fire alarm at 12.30 am. Dogs, cats, boys, girls who should not have been there, all tumbled down into the quadrangle. But the young in America have reached a stage where if you were a girl, and you had no boy to go to for the weekend, you feel there must be something wrong with you. Maybe a new society will evolve in which roles are switched. All a male has to do is to spawn away. The female will look after herself and the children. The women are qualified to work. They can, if necessary, nurture any accidental or intended children. It does not matter

> One night, in October 1970, somebody pressed the fire alarm at 12.30 am. Dogs, cats, boys, girls who should not have been there, all tumbled down into the quadrangle.

Of course, man is adulterous. So is woman. And there is considerable hypocrisy about. But hypocrisy helps to maintain public decorum.

whose child it is. Maybe such children will grow up less inhibited and more creative. The idea of knowing your father and your mother may become old-fashioned.

But I would like to see this brave new world tried out elsewhere, for at least one generation. I am not in favour of experimentation until it has been proven. Until it is demonstrated that the change is for a better, stronger society, this experimentation is not for Singapore.

Many a once scandalous conduct has become acceptable. Traditional values are being gradually eroded. There is a reason for taboos in society.

For instance, in the old days, if you are a divorcee, you are not invited to Buckingham Palace. The reason was to discourage divorces and remarriages. Not that adultery did not take place. But then Cabinet ministers divorced their wives and remarried. Things become complicated. Eventually, their wives had to be accepted at the Palace. Because ministers have set an example, others followed. A principle once breached is easily demolished.

We must inoculate ourselves from this epidemic. When the children are young, make them understand that there are basic traditional values they should hold fast to – what is good, what is bad, what is to be admired, what is to be despised, who is a hero, who is a villain. This is what we are trying to do in the schools through bilingualism. Do not shoot this down. If you do, you have got to fight me. I feel strongly about certain things, and this is one of them.

Bilingualism must be thorough, the values inculcated when people are young and impressionable, for the inoculation to be successful. The unsuccessful bilingualist, the monolinguist, in our situation, is a dangerous person. A completely monolingual Chinese-educated type who reads only the Chinese script is as dangerous as a completely monolingual Malay-educated type who reads the Jawi script. Remember what happened? Communist-led riots and Muslim religious riots. The innocent were casually murdered.

We must hold on to the quintessence of 4,000 years of civilised living, although it was punctuated by intermittent periods of disorder, chaos, famine, pestilence. But continuance of civilisation was maintained and made possible only by certain precepts. They existed 4,000 years before Mao. I have a feeling they will survive 4,000 years after Mao. I do not know what the equivalent is in Tamil, but I am sure the Tamil language and culture which lasted 3,000 years must have been sustained by certain fundamental precepts. One of the fundamentals is the sanctity of the family unit.

Of course, man is adulterous. So is woman. And there is considerable hypocrisy about. But hypocrisy helps to maintain public decorum. Only when certain norms of public conduct obtain, is orderly, cultivated living possible.

Lee was never averse to putting his controversial views on the role of the press and limits of press freedom to the test. In an address to the American Society of Newspaper Editors on April 14, 1988, in Washington DC, he spelt out the Singapore government's policy, insisting on its right to reply to articles in the foreign press, as well as its readiness to restrict the circulation of publications which denied it this right or tried to interfere in Singapore's internal politics.

# Which role model for the Singapore press?

The media play a key role in the life of every country, but it is a role which differs from one country to another. When these differences are misunderstood or ignored, as frequently happens with Western media operating in developing countries, the result is friction.

## Experience of other countries

In the US, the press enjoys considerable influence in political and public affairs. This US model is a particularly important one. It represents the ultimate in terms of media freedoms and prerogatives.

*The US model is not a universal standard.*

In March 1987 the US State Department explained in an *aide-mémoire* to the Singapore Ministry of Foreign Affairs that it deplored the government's action to restrict the sale of the *Asian Wall Street Journal* despite the fact that the *Journal* had refused the Singapore government the right of reply to an inaccurate report. It was because Americans believed that "the press (should be) free to publish or not to publish what it chooses, however irresponsible or biased its actions may seem to be". (US State Department *aide-mémoire*, March 10, 1987) The logic is that "where the media are free, the marketplace of ideas sorts the irresponsible from the responsible and rewards the latter."

But the US model is not a universal standard. The media in other countries play different roles. These roles have grown out of their different historical experiences, political systems and national temperaments. They represent equally valid functions which the press fulfils in different environments.

A more appropriate model for the Singapore media would be the BBC World Service, which reports events impartially, but provides an interpretation from a definite perspective – in the BBC's case, the point of view of Western liberalism. The BBC broadcasts in Singapore on FM 24 hours daily. It was a service meant for the British community including

When the
marketplace
contest of ideas
has been practised
in newly
independent
nations, it has
ended in less than
happy results.

their troops stationed in Singapore. When they departed in 1971, I personally asked them to continue it as a service to Singaporeans.

Another model is the Japanese media, which also stay out of partisan politics, but go beyond plain reporting to shape public opinion to help build up a national consensus on important issues.

Singapore was a British colony. It has no history of a freewheeling rambunctious press. In fact if the British did not have press laws which they invoked to prevent the Chinese language press in Singapore from crusading for the Malayan Communist Party (MCP) in the 1950s and 1960s, the MCP might have succeeded in doing to Singapore and Malaya what the Chinese Communist Party has done to China. Singapore's experience has made Singaporeans chary, even suspicious, of any paper crusading for causes or policies which people feel should be left to those who are openly in the political arena.

When the marketplace contest of ideas has been practised in newly independent nations, it has ended in less than happy results. This has happened in Sri Lanka and India. Both are heterogeneous, multiracial societies. In both there are intense racial and regional disagreements on important, emotional issues, such as race, language and culture. In both a plethora of media propound divergent and incompatible policies, mobilising sectional constituencies and arousing emotions. In both the result has been confusion and dissension, rather than enlightenment and consensus.

Similarly, the Philippines, before martial law, was an Asian version of the US system. The Philippines press enjoyed all the freedoms but they failed the Filipino people. A wildly partisan press helped Filipino politicians to flood the marketplace of ideas with junk, and confused and befuddled the people so that they could not see what their vital interests were in a developing country. And because basic issues like economic growth and equitable distribution were seldom discussed and never tackled, the democratic system malfunctioned and President Marcos declared martial law. Fortunately a miraculous demonstration of people's power in February 1986 saved the country from impending disaster.

Thus while the US model of the role of the press is good for the US, as a universal standard, its applicability has not been proven.

### Singapore unique

Singapore's case is unique, even among countries with colonial backgrounds. We do not have one press, but four major ones, in four different languages, catering to four different segments of population – English, Chinese, Malay, and Tamil. Each has different key values and world views. In the past, the English press took the standpoint of the colonial government. The Chinese press promoted Chinese language, education and chauvinism, looking to China for inspiration. The Malay press agitated for Malay rights and privileges and promoted Malay nationalism, identifying itself with the Malay Muslim communities of Malaysia and Indonesia. The Tamil press maintained the ties of the local Tamil community with the mother country – Tamil Nadu in India.

Imagine an island one-fifth the size of Rhode Island, inhabited by 2.5 million, with over half of its adults first generation immigrants. Seventy-five per cent are Chinese from seven major clan and dialect groups, springing from south and southeastern China, 15 per cent Malays and Indonesians from the archipelago around Singapore, 10 per cent Indians, Pakistanis, Bangladeshis, Sri Lankans, Burmese and Eurasians. They have never been one community. For decades, they coexisted in separate segments of the island demarcated by the British for disparate immigrants.

From these unpromising beginnings we have had to try to build one Singapore nation. But the "melting pot" was not an option. We have been independent for less than 23 years. Parents are determined to remain the different kinds of Asians they are and keep their children that way. We cannot obliterate the cultural and religious distinctions between the racial groups. Yet we have to create enough shared values and a single national identity. It has taken the government many years to get the different races intermingled into new towns. Gradually we hope to reconcile these centrifugal trends and to bring the press in the different languages closer by approximating, however inadequately, one national view.

The process has been helped by the adoption of English as a common working language. A new generation of Singaporeans has been educated with English as its first language, a stepmother tongue. But this has created a new danger. If we lose too much of our original cultures and their value systems, we may lose our bearings altogether. Singaporeans have to be Asians because Singapore is forever a part of Asia. Parents know that if their children take in too much of America and the West daily on TV and in the newspapers, the result will be disorientation, for Singapore is not the West.

One value which does not fit Singapore is the theory of the press as the fourth estate. From British times, the Singapore press was never the fourth estate. And in Singapore's experience, because of our volatile racial and religious mix, the American concept of the "marketplace of ideas", instead of producing harmonious enlightenment, has time and again led to riots and bloodshed.

One example was the jungle girl or Maria Hertogh riots in the 1950s. An English woman in the *Singapore Standard* wrote up a human interest story about a Dutch woman who handed her baby daughter to a Malay woman as the Japanese swept through Southeast Asia. After the war, the Dutch mother traced her daughter. In the meantime, she had been brought up as a Muslim. The Singapore Chief Justice, an Englishman, sent the child to a convent pending his decision on the custody of the child. It was good colourful journalism in English. Unfortunately, the Malay language press took up the story, and hell broke loose. Bloody anti-white riots broke out, with the Singapore police force of Muslim Malays inert. In one week, 18 were killed and 173 injured, nearly all Europeans. If the events were repeated today, because of the resurgence of Islam, the results could be as disastrous, if not worse. Recently, in November 1986, Muslim Malaysians mounted demonstrations against the visit of Israel's President Herzog to Singapore, because they said the Singapore government showed a lack of sensitivity for the anti-Zionist feelings

It was good colourful journalism in English. Unfortunately, the Malay language press took up the story, and hell broke loose.

of their neighbours. Reports of these demonstrations in the press and TV set off similar protests from Muslim Singaporeans.

### The foreign press

Singapore welcomes a free flow of information from abroad. It keeps us up to date with developments overseas. Foreign correspondents can and do report us to their domestic readers in America or Europe in any way they choose. Of course, when foreign journals get important facts wrong, we write to correct them. But it does not matter to us what their ideological slants may be.

### The offshore press

Right up to the late 1970s, Singaporeans were mainly Chinese-educated. The foreign English-language newspapers had few readers and little impact. It was Hongkong-based communist Chinese newspapers which caused problems. We banned all of them.

The 1980s marked a turning point in the electorate of Singapore, from a Chinese-educated majority to an English-educated majority. In 1981 English displaced Chinese, Malay and Tamil to become the language of instruction in all schools and universities in Singapore. The English language carries with it the cultural values of the British and Americans whose civilisation they encompass. But Singapore cannot model itself on America. It does not have the cultural, historical or economic base for an American approach to life and politics. If you put 2.5 million Americans into Singapore, you will come to grief with your neighbours and the rest of Southeast Asia within six weeks.

At about the same time in the late 1970s and early 1980s new publications like the *Asian Wall Street Journal* based in Hongkong began to report Singapore daily not to readers in America or Europe but to Singaporeans themselves and to the rest of the region. In fact they are no longer the foreign press. They have become domestic Singapore press, based offshore. Their correspondents act like journalists do in America, taking sides to determine the outcome of issues under debate.

Americans tend to think of Singapore as one of the NICs. But it is very different from Korea, Taiwan and Hongkong. They are racially homogeneous, speaking their own language, and living their own culture. Unlike Singapore, English is not the language of their peoples, not even in British-governed Hongkong. English has to be translated into Korean for South Korea, Mandarin or Hokkien in Taiwan, and Cantonese in Hongkong, to reach the people.

None of the NICs nor our Asean neighbours can be penetrated by the offshore English-language press like Singapore. Singapore, a country with one of the smallest populations in Asia (2.6 million), was the largest single-country market for the *Far Eastern Economic Review*, and the second largest for the *Asian Wall Street Journal* (see table). Sales per million population in the NICs and Asean compared to Singapore were:

> If you put 2.5 million Americans into Singapore, you will come to grief with your neighbours and the rest of Southeast Asia within six weeks.

|  | *FEER* | *AWSJ* |  | *FEER* | *AWSJ* |
|---|---|---|---|---|---|
| **NICs** | | | **Asean** | | |
| Hongkong | 1/2 | 4/5 | Malaysia | 1/6 | 1/14 |
| Taiwan | 1/80 | 1/20 | Philippines | 1/80 | 1/40 |
| South Korea | 1/70 | 1/40 | Thailand | 1/80 | 1/50 |
| | | | Indonesia | 1/280 | 1/30 |

## No involvement in domestic politics

Singapore's domestic debate is a matter for Singaporeans. We allow American journalists in Singapore in order to report Singapore to their fellow countrymen. We allow their papers to sell in Singapore so that we can know what foreigners are reading about us. But we cannot allow them to assume a role in Singapore that the American media play in America, that of invigilator, adversary, and inquisitor of the administration. If allowed to do so, they will radically change the nature of Singapore society, and I doubt if our social glue is strong enough to withstand such treatment.

For example, few foreigners are aware that to lessen our inter-communal conflicts, Singapore and Malaysia have banned each other's newspapers for about 20 years. The last big Malay-Chinese riots in Malaysia in 1969 sparked off similar riots in Singapore. We are the closest of neighbours. Unfortunately, one country's newspaper reporting what its people are doing and saying can cause Malay-Chinese troubles in the other. The reason is simple, that the two countries have different solutions to their not dissimilar interracial problems.

## No right to circulate

No foreign television station claims the right to telecast its programmes in Singapore. Indeed America's Federal Communications Commission regulations bar foreigners from owning more than 25 per cent of a TV or radio station. In other words, only Americans can control a business which influences public opinion in America. Thus before Rupert Murdoch purchased the independent TV stations of the Metromedia group in 1985, he first took up US citizenship. If a mighty nation of 240 million finds such safeguards necessary, what about a plastic, unformed society like Singapore?

As for the US print media, in 1976 the South African Ministry of Information was negotiating covertly to buy the *Washington Star* to soft-sell apartheid. When the story broke, a storm broke out in Washington and the purchase fell through. Americans were outraged at this South African attempt to soft-sell apartheid in America's marketplace of ideas. But apartheid is patently abhorrent. If the marketplace of ideas automatically separates the good from the bad, and rewards the good, why this outrage at an attempt which is doomed to fail? When America reacts in this way, is it surprising that Singapore feels it cannot take chances with the offshore press taking sides on Singapore's domestic debate?

Americans were outraged at this South African attempt to soft-sell apartheid in America's marketplace of ideas.

Circulation in Singapore is a privilege granted by the Singapore government on our terms. The terms are that they should report as outsiders for outsiders, i.e., do not become a partisan in our domestic debate. If they do not want to accept these conditions, they do not have to sell in Singapore.

### The disputes with *Time*, etc.

In the last one and a half years, the Singapore government has restricted the circulations of a number of offshore publications in Singapore: *Time*, *AWSJ*, *Asiaweek* and *FEER*.

The disputes with *Time*, *AWSJ* and *Asiaweek* have been over the right of reply. All three published inaccurate reports. The government wrote to set the facts straight. *Time* and *AWSJ* refused to publish the government replies. *Asiaweek* published a government reply, but without our consent tampered with it and attributed the doctored version to the Singapore government spokesman.

*FEER* published a story which was not only false but defamatory. The government challenged it either to substantiate or to withdraw its allegations. Only when *FEER* repeatedly refused to do so did the government restrict its circulation. I also had to sue them for libel, for unless I demolish their damaging misrepresentations they will affect my standing with my own people.

### Restriction of circulation

The government could simply have banned these journals. But to ban them would have been an overreaction. Since sales is one of the principal motivations of these journals, it was sufficient to restrict their circulation.

Restricting the circulations does not deprive Singaporeans of access to information. Once a few hundred copies are available in Singapore, anyone who needs any information in them can make a photocopy for himself. Alternatively, he can buy an advertisement-free copy of the journal, since the law now allows individuals to reproduce and sell copies of restricted journals, provided all advertisements are removed, and the person doing so makes no profits from his public service.

By not allowing journals to increase their sales, the government has achieved some concessions. Both *Time* and *Asiaweek*, after they had been gazetted, published the disputed letters intact. So we restored *Time*'s circulation, and in due course, we would restore *Asiaweek*'s.

### Conclusion

I have not come to convert you to my point of view, for that would be impossible. All I aim to do is to persuade you that the Singapore government's position is not irrational, that we seek no quarrel with the foreign press when we require them to remember that they are observers, not participants, in Singapore's domestic politics.

I had to sue them for libel, for unless I demolish their damaging misrepresentations they will affect my standing with my own people.

Lee has always given short shrift to opinion polls. He made this point to New Zealand academics and journalists in Christchurch on April 15, 1975.

# You appear to some degree dictatorial

QUESTION: But Prime Minister, I think many people around the world admire very much what you have done for Singapore, you and your party. Yet there are some things in people's minds which appear to be to some degree dictatorial within your attitude. I'd like to know – how do you think the history books are going to see Lee Kuan Yew?

LEE KUAN YEW: I don't think I worry too much about what people think. And when you say people here, you mean the people in the news media, people in academia, the so-called liberals with a small *l*. I think I can put up with them. In fact, criticism or general debunking even stimulates me because I think it is foolish not to have your people read you being made fun of. And we have got books circulating in Singapore written specially for this purpose by foreigners. Fine! But I would like to believe – never mind what historians say, but whoever wants to do a Ph.D. thesis, and perhaps there will be quite a few who might want to dig up the archives – they might come to the conclusion that here was a group of men who went through quite an unusual set of experiences in a very momentous period of the world, beginning with the Second World War and decolonisation and the setting up of new countries, so many that the United Nations now has become quite unwieldy, and not many of which are likely to succeed. And perhaps if we don't fail, and we will not know that really for a very long time until we have stepped down from office, then obviously despite the criticisms, despite the doubts and queries of how Westerners would have done it, we had our feet on the ground, our heads fairly screwed to our shoulders and we did the right thing by those whose fate was temporarily entrusted in our hands and by our own convictions.

> Criticism or general debunking even stimulates me because I think it is foolish not to have your people read you being made fun of.

Lee's ability as a leader to get to the heart of a problem has been instrumental in helping Singapore achieve much success in many fields, including its national airline. In this speech, on July 16, 1972, on the eve of the break-up of Malaysia-Singapore Airlines, out of which Singapore Airlines emerged, he pinpointed what was needed to make SIA succeed. The speech was delivered to the Singapore Air Transport Workers' Union.

# How to make SIA a great way to fly

A traveller, before boarding an aeroplane, asks himself three questions in this order of importance:

Will I get there?

Will I get there on time?

How comfortable will I be on board?

Singapore Airlines will inherit 25 years of experience. Malayan Airways started off in Singapore 25 years ago with three "Air Speed Consul" aircraft.

There is little to choose between aircraft. All major airlines now use standard proven aircraft. Between established major airlines, there is also little difference in standards of maintenance, or the professionalism of engineers and technicians or pilots. The differences there are lie in the efficiency of the organisation, management, which takes years to build up, and labour and wage costs.

The major airlines of the industrialised countries have established reputations for getting people more or less punctually to their destinations. But there is scepticism whether airlines run by countries not yet industrialised can provide such services.

Fortunately, we are establishing ourselves as one of the few countries which, though still in the process of being industrialised, have already developed the habit for tiptop maintenance and a zeal for efficiency. It is reflected in a people's philosophy of life – either easy-going and tolerant of substandard work, or active and insistent on nothing less than the best achievable.

I know little of the mysteries of advertising and the soft sell. But I believe no magic set of initials, no logo, can sell, to more than the first few, something which is not good. By skilful publicity, the PR man can attract attention and get across an idea. But if the idea got across does not tally with the reality, then the value of the advertisement, however attractive, is soon dissipated.

> I know little of the mysteries of advertising and the soft sell. But I believe no magic set of initials, no logo, can sell, to more than the first few, something which is not good.

Our best asset is in the reputation of Singapore itself. To most people abroad – in governments, in finance, in business, and to many ordinary newspaper readers in the main cities of the world – "Singapore" means a hardworking and hardheaded people, a thrusting new nation rapidly climbing up the technological ladder. This is a reputation forged out of our struggle for survival. A reputation earned this hard way is a durable one, and very different from the "image" created by skilful image-makers. The future of Singapore Airlines depends more on the reality SIA leaves behind on their passengers than on any advertisement. To improve efficiency of organisation, promptness and friendliness of service, these must be our constant aims.

Reputations are continually made and lost. Within a matter of months, we can either enhance the reputation we inherit from MSA or fritter it away. What passengers actually experience and pass on to their friends is far more effective than any glossy advertisement, however useful in selling an airline.

Singapore runs an airline not for reasons of prestige, but for plain economic benefit. We are at the centre of the main North-South and Northwest-Southwest jet routes. Other countries will give us landing rights because they want to land in Singapore. But if we cannot make profitable use of any of these landing rights, we should have no compunction in closing a service down. This is our approach to life.

We are not flying in a restricted and protected home market. We are flying the international jet routes in competition with major world airlines. Our standards must always go up, never slide down. We have to get new aircraft as soon as they are proven after profitable operations by major airlines. You must match our faith in you by never letting Singapore be apologetic for your slovenly or slack work.

One great advantage we have over the major airlines of the wealthy world is in our service. As Americans and Europeans become more and more affluent, their people are less eager to please customers whether in shops or in aircraft. But the never-tiring courtesy and efficiency of our cabin crew have won recognition from all seasoned travellers, who have sampled all the major airlines. This will help make our airline.

> Singapore runs an airline not for reasons of prestige, but for plain economic benefit.

Over the years, Lee has kept his private life mostly private. He has not, for example, been one to celebrate his birthdays in public. Among those which he did was his 60th birthday, on September 16, 1983. On that occasion, celebrated at the Mandarin Hotel, he made this speech.

# My birthday wish

I have had only one birthday publicly celebrated. It was in September 1973, 10 years ago. Devan Nair, then Secretary-General of the NTUC, wanted to organise one to mark the occasion. After reflection, I agreed because I hoped it would serve a wider purpose of bringing the different segments of our society together rather than simply be an occasion for luxuriating in felicitations and congratulations. In the same way, I hope this dinner will serve more significant needs than those of my personal joy and satisfaction.

A momentous event took place on my 40th birthday 20 years ago. On September 16, 1963, Malaysia was proclaimed and Singapore became part of it. I celebrated my 40th birthday by going to Kuala Lumpur to attend the formal declaration of Malaysia at the Stadium Negara and returned the same evening to continue a crucial general election in Singapore.

The original date fixed for Malaysia Day had been August 31, 1963. Sukarno had raised objections and the United Nations observers were sent to Borneo to ascertain the wishes of the people of North Borneo and Sarawak. Hence the date was postponed. When the date September 16, 1963 was fixed, the Tunku did not know it was my birthday, nor did he intend it as recognition for the work that I had done to help bring about the Federation of Malaysia.

Eight was his lucky number. Since the United Nations report was not expected to be ready by the 8th he fixed it for the 16th: 2 times 8. It is as well that I am not a believer in lucky numbers, or other charms. Otherwise, when Singapore parted from Malaysia, I would have suffered an immense psychological blow, believing my birthday date is inauspicious.

Well, what have I done in the 10 years since 1973? I hope I have helped to consolidate Singapore's advance in economic growth and social development. More important, I

> It is as well that I am not a believer in lucky numbers, or other charms. Otherwise, when Singapore parted from Malaysia, I would have suffered an immense psychological blow, believing my birthday date is inauspicious.

have got together a core group of younger ministers who can make for continuity of honest, effective, and responsive government.

What have I learned since 1973? Some more basic unchangeables about human beings and human societies, the ways in which they can be made to do better, and the ever present danger of regression and even collapse, as in Cambodia.

I realise how very fragile a civilised society is, especially in Southeast Asia, in this historic period of rapid change and revolutions. I have also come to understand the insignificance of personal achievements. For at 60, more than at 50, comes the realisation of the transient nature of all earthly glories and successes, and the ephemeral quality of sensory joys and pleasures, when compared to intellectual, moral or spiritual satisfactions.

I consider the last 10 years in office as less eventful and significant compared to my first 10 years: 1959–69. Then it was a matter of life and death, not only for my colleagues and me but for most people in Singapore.

First, we battled against the communists, a battle we did not look like winning, until the referendum to join Malaysia on September 1, 1962, and September 21, 1963, when we won a second term at the general elections. Then followed our troubles with the communalists. In the two years we were in Malaysia, until separation on August 9, 1965, we went through the agonies of intimidation, and the fear of irrational or mindless communal killings.

Next, in November 1967 came the devaluation of the British pound, followed, in January 1968, by the British government announcement of their decision to withdraw from their bases in Singapore. 1959–69 were 10 tumultuous, exciting and exhausting years. They were also years during which we laid the foundations for national stability, unity and development. Had I been older, say 55 instead of 35, when I started in 1959, I would not have had the sheer physical stamina and vigour nor the emotional zest and enthusiasm needed to meet the daunting difficulties and threats.

I have wondered how much of what I am is nature and how much was nurture. Would I have been a different person if I had not been tempered through the crucible of struggle? In moments of whimsy, I have asked myself: what would have happened to my identical twin, if I had one and he had been brought up, say, in Hongkong? He would have become totally different in his values, attitudes, and motivations. After reading the studies on identical twins, I have to concede that in his physical, mental and emotional makeup, my twin must be like me.

However, I think it impossible that he could have my attitude to life without my experiences. Placed in Hongkong, where the only outlet for his energies would be the pursuit of wealth, he must have acquired a different set of values and have set himself different goals in life. For these studies showed that identical twins sometimes do have different habits. Some smoke, some do not. If being a smoker is out of conscious choice, an act of will, then there are many areas where human beings are not totally pre-programmed.

My Hongkong twin might have wanted to rebel against the British, but he would have found himself frustrated. He would then set out to make money, a useful activity,

> In moments of whimsy, I have asked myself: what would have happened to my identical twin, if I had one and he had been brought up, say, in Hongkong?

Having taken
life-and-death
decisions and gone
through one acute
crisis after
another, my
perspectives,
ambitions and
priorities have
undergone a
fundamental,
and I believe, a
permanent
transformation.

and exciting for the successful. But after the trials and tribulations I went through in the '50s and '60s I would find this an arid life. Having taken life-and-death decisions and gone through one acute crisis after another, my perspectives, ambitions and priorities have undergone a fundamental, and I believe, a permanent transformation. I may not have changed in my physical, mental and emotional makeup, the hardware side. But the software side, my responses to God, glory or gold, have been conditioned by my experiences. In other words, however capacious the hardware (nature) without the software (nurture), not much can be made of the hardware.

Would I like to know the future, to know what Singapore will be like ten, twenty years from now? Yes, of course. So would all of us. But we do not have this privilege. Perhaps as well, for that makes us strive all the more to secure the future. My experiences have left me with some indelible lessons, and a set of ingrained habits. Both the experiences and the habits force me to ensure that the precious gains we have made will not be lost because the base on which our security and prosperity rest is so narrow. Hence my ceaseless search for younger men of ability and dedication.

Most Singaporeans below 25 take for granted what were only dreams when they were born two decades ago: the well-paid jobs available, the strength of the Singapore dollar which buys the homes they own, or soon will, the furniture and furnishings, TV, home appliances, the smart clothes and shoes, motorcycles and cars. They do not remember a Singapore which was not an orderly society, where the environment was not clean and green, and when life for most was a hard struggle for bare existence. Those who have travelled abroad know that full employment, annual increase in purchasing power, and a healthy environment – these are not the natural order of things. They require social discipline and the will to work and to achieve.

There are times when I get glimpses of the challenges facing the next generation. We are on our own, responsible for our own defence and survival. There are no safety nets like the British-Australian-New Zealand forces. We have to weave our regional net of relationships to help maintain stability and security. Otherwise economic development is impossible. There are many imponderables. The present leaders of Asean are in accord and harmony because they share common objectives. They all have strong memories of the last war and of the insurrections that followed when communist insurgents attempted to seize power. By the 1990s, Asean leaders will come from a generation that did not have this common experience. Therefore, we must make these personal experiences into a part of Asean's institutional memories so that not too much will have to be learned all over again, and at too high a cost.

I would like to conclude by recounting one unforgettable social encounter. On May 8, 1973, I was in Nagasaki. My wife launched a 240,000 ton oil tanker, the *Neptune World*, at the Mitsubishi Shipyards that morning. After lunch, my Japanese host took me out to the golf course. After 9 holes he asked if I wanted to go on. It was wet and windy. He was a slim, wiry man, some 6–8 cm shorter than me. He looked some ten years older than me. I told him I would play the second nine. He went on to play a lively game on a hilly course.

That night he gave us dinner. As he relaxed on the *tatami* with food and *sake*, he turned to me on his right and said, "Today, I am a grand senior." I asked him what it meant. He said "Today is my 70th birthday. In Japan you are a grand senior at 70." I gasped. He was actually 20 years older than me. And he had played 18 holes on a hard course to please me. Then he recounted how he was born, been schooled, and had married in Nagasaki. He had several children. And on August 9, 1945, as he was coming home from a journey outstation, he saw an intensely brilliant flash and a mushroom cloud over Nagasaki. He was on the other side of the mountain. Later that day, when he got on to the ridge, he saw Nagasaki devastated. His home, his wife and his children had been obliterated.

He spoke without bitterness, only deep sorrow. Then he regained his bounce to reassure me that he had remarried and started another family. That 70th birthday was a day of fulfilment for him, a life rebuilt, a new ship launched, and 18 holes of golf to celebrate his vigour. He was satisfied with his 70 years. How much of that was in his nature, how much was due to his nurture, the culture of the Japanese and their tradition of fatalism and unremitting effort to rebuild after each earthquake, each typhoon, each tidal wave, I shall never know.

I have been spared such a devastating experience. Ten years hence, barring the unexpected, I hope I shall have cause for a celebration dinner. For it will be satisfying to know that what my colleagues and I are trying to do in the next few years will not have been in vain. I would like to be able to sit back, if only for the day I become a grand senior, to survey a thriving Singapore, with a younger prime minister and his Cabinet well established, in a relationship of trust and confidence with the people of Singapore, and on top of the many problems that come with high growth and rapid change.

The past 24 years were not preordained. Nor is the future. There will be unexpected problems ahead, as there were in the past. They have to be met, grappled with, and resolved. For only a people who are willing to face up to their problems and are prepared to work with their leaders to meet unexpected hardships with courage and resolution deserve to thrive and to prosper. In responding to the toast, may I express the hope that Singaporeans will be such a people.

> I would like to be able to sit back, if only for the day I become a grand senior, to survey a thriving Singapore, with a younger prime minister and his Cabinet well established, in a relationship of trust and confidence with the people of Singapore, and on top of the many problems that come with high growth and rapid change.

# Bibliography

Bloodworth, Dennis. *The Tiger and the Trojan Horse*. Singapore: Times Books International, 1986.

Drysdale, John. *Singapore: Struggle for Success*. Singapore: Times Books International, 1984.

Josey, Alex. *Lee Kuan Yew, The Crucial Years*. Singapore: Times Books International, 1980.

Turnbull, C.M. *A History of Singapore: 1819–1975*. Singapore: Oxford University Press, 1977.

You Poh Seng and Lim Chong Yah (editors). *Singapore: Twenty-five Years of Development*. Singapore: Lianhe Zaobao, 1984.

# Photographs

Photographs reproduced in this book other than those listed below come from Mrs Lee Kuan Yew's family album, the Straits Times archives and the National Archives of Singapore. We are grateful to the following suppliers of the remaining photographs.

Agence France Presse: page 206

Associated Press: page 214

Bangkok Post: page 58

Camera Press: page 20

First Photo: page 118

George Gascon: jacket and pages 2, 6, 8, 17, 130, 226 and 228

Paul Popper Photo: page 96 (Bloodhound)

Reuter: pages 124, 160

# Index